THE
B I B L E
Summarized
HANDBOOK

THE
BIBLE
Summarized
HANDBOOK

BY
KEITH L. BROOKS

WORLD PUBLISHING
Grand Rapids, Michigan 49418 U.S.A.

Reprinted 1999 by
World Bible Publishers, Inc.
by special arrangement with
Baker Book House Company

ISBN: 0-529-06935-0

PREFACE

THIS work is compiled with the hope that it will be the means of stimulating Christians to pursue a daily course for reading in the Bible. It will act as an aid to the ordinary reader, in gathering into brief statements the definite spiritual lessons for the daily life contained in every chapter of the Bible. It will also show how clearly the image of Christ appears on every page of the Word of God.

The **calendar for Bible reading** found in the front, if followed, will take the reader through the entire Bible in one year's time. There are many long and many short chapters in the Bible, and this calendar is designed to properly proportion the daily studies.

The **Index to the Bible,** found in the back of the book, will enable the reader to turn to any important Bible event, without the use of a concordance. It is suggested that the Bible student, by studying this index may memorize the location of many of the more vital portions of Scripture, greatly to his profit.

The **index of Bible promises,** also found in the back, is designed as a ready devotional help to Christians, enabling them to find the strongest promises of God's Word, to fit any need that may arise in the life.

This work is also suitable for use as a text book in teaching the "chapter summary" method of Bible study.

The author does not claim originality for all of the statements in this work. The work was compiled largely from notes in the margin of the author's Bible, kept, for the most part, without regard to the sources. If the work may be used of God to bring some to apply themselves wholly to the Scriptures and the Scriptures wholly to themselves, we shall feel abundantly repaid for the effort.

KEITH L. BROOKS.

DAILY CALENDAR

January

Date	Morning	Evening
1	Gen. 1, 2, 3	Matt. 1
2	Gen. 4, 5, 6	Matt. 2
3	Gen. 7, 8, 9	Matt. 3
4	Gen. 10, 11, 12	Matt. 4
5	Gen. 13, 14, 15	Matt. 5: 1-26
6	Gen. 16, 17	Matt. 5:27-48
7	Gen. 18, 19	Matt. 6: 1-18
8	Gen. 20, 21, 22	Matt. 6:19-34
9	Gen. 23, 24	Matt. 7
10	Gen. 25, 26	Matt. 8: 1-17
11	Gen. 27, 28	Matt. 8:18-34
12	Gen. 29, 30	Matt. 9: 1-27
13	Gen. 31, 32	Matt. 9:18-38
14	Gen. 33, 34, 35	Matt. 10: 1-20
15	Gen. 36, 37, 38	Matt. 10:21-42
16	Gen. 39,40	Matt. 11
17	Gen. 41, 42	Matt. 12: 1-23
18	Gen. 43, 44, 45	Matt. 12:24-50
19	Gen. 46, 47, 48	Matt. 13: 1-30
20	Gen. 49, 50	Matt. 13:31-58
21	Ex. 1, 2, 3	Matt. 14: 1-21
22	Ex. 4, 5, 6	Matt. 14:22-36
23	Ex. 7, 8	Matt. 15: 1-20
24	Ex. 9, 10,11	Matt. 15:21-39
25	Ex. 12, 13	Matt. 16
26	Ex. 14, 15	Matt. 17
27	Ex. 16, 17, 18	Matt. 18: 1-20
28	Ex. 19, 20	Matt. 18:21-35
29	Ex. 21, 22	Matt. 19
30	Ex. 23, 24	Matt. 20: 1-16
31	Ex. 25, 26	Matt. 20:17-34

February

Date	Morning	Evening
1	Ex. 27, 28	Matt. 21: 1-22
2	Ex. 29, 30	Matt. 21:23-46
3	Ex. 31, 32, 33	Matt. 22: 1-22
4	Ex. 34, 35	Matt. 22:23-46
5	Ex. 36, 37, 38	Matt. 23: 1-22
6	Ex. 39, 40	Matt. 23:23-39
7	Lev. 1, 2, 3	Matt. 24: 1-28
8	Lev. 4, 5	Matt. 24:29-51
9	Lev. 6, 7	Matt. 25: 1-30
10	Lev. 8, 9, 10	Matt. 25:31-46
11	Lev. 11, 12	Matt. 26: 1-25
12	Lev. 13	Matt. 26:26-50
13	Lev. 14	Matt. 26:51-75
14	Lev. 15, 16	Matt. 27: 1-26
15	Lev. 17, 18	Matt. 27:27-50
16	Lev. 19, 20	Matt. 27:51-66
17	Lev. 21, 22	Matt. 28
18	Lev. 23, 24	Mark 1: 1-22
19	Lev. 25	Mark 1:23-45
20	Lev. 26, 27	Mark 2
21	Num. 1, 2	Mark 3: 1-19
22	Num. 3, 4	Mark 3:20-35
23	Num. 5, 6	Mark 4: 1-20
24	Num. 7, 8	Mark 4:21-41
25	Num. 9, 10, 11	Mark 5: 1-20
26	Num. 12, 13, 14	Mark 5:21-43
27	Num. 15, 16	Mark 6: 1-29
28	Num. 17, 18, 19	Mark 6:30-56
29	Num. 20, 21, 22	Mark 7: 1-13

Note:—When February has but twenty-eight days, read the portion for the 29th with that for the 28th.

March

Date	Morning	Evening
1	Num. 23, 24, 25	Mark 7:14-37
2	Num. 26, 27	Mark 8: 1-21
3	Num. 28, 29, 30	Mark 8:22-38
4	Num. 31, 32, 33	Mark 9: 1-29
5	Num. 34, 35, 36	Mark 9:30-50
6	Deut. 1, 2	Mark 10: 1-31
7	Deut. 3, 4	Mark 10:32-52
8	Deut. 5, 6, 7	Mark 11: 1-18
9	Deut. 8, 9, 10	Mark 11:19-33
10	Deut. 11, 12, 13	Mark 12: 1-27
11	Deut. 14, 15, 16	Mark 12:28-44
12	Deut. 17, 18, 19	Mark 13: 1-20
13	Deut. 20, 21, 22	Mark 13:21
14	Deut. 23, 24, 25	Mark 14: 1-26
15	Deut. 26, 27	Mark 14:27-53
16	Deut. 28, 29	Mark 14:54-72
17	Deut. 30, 31	Mark 15: 1-25
18	Deut. 32, 33, 34	Mark 15:26-47
19	Josh. 1, 2, 3	Mark 16
20	Josh. 4, 5, 6	Luke 1: 1-20
21	Josh. 7, 8, 9	Luke 1:21-38
22	Josh. 10, 11, 12	Luke 1:39-56
23	Josh. 13, 14, 15	Luke 1:57-80
24	Josh. 16, 17, 18	Luke 2: 1-24
25	Josh. 19, 20, 21	Luke 2:25-52
26	Josh. 22, 23, 24	Luke 3
27	Judg. 1, 2, 3	Luke 4: 1-30
28	Judg. 4, 5, 6	Luke 4:31-44
29	Judg. 7, 8	Luke 5: 1-16
30	Judg. 9, 10	Luke 5:17-39
31	Judg. 11, 12	Luke 6: 1-26

April

Date	Morning	Evening
1	Judg. 13, 14, 15	Luke 6:27-49
2	Judg. 16, 17, 18	Luke 7: 1-30
3	Judg. 19, 20, 21	Luke 7:31-50
4	Ruth 1, 2, 3, 4	Luke 8: 1-25
5	I. Sa. 1, 2, 3	Luke 8:26-56
6	I. Sa. 4, 5, 6	Luke 9: 1-17
7	I. Sa. 7, 8, 9	Luke 9:18-36
8	I. Sa. 10, 11, 12	Luke 9:37-62
9	I. Sa. 13, 14	Luke 10: 1-24
10	I. Sa. 15, 16	Luke 10:25-42
11	I. Sa. 17, 18	Luke 11: 1-28
12	I. Sa. 19, 20, 21	Luke 11:29-54
13	I. Sa. 22, 23, 24	Luke 12: 1-31
14	I. Sa. 25, 26	Luke 12:32-59
15	I. Sa. 27, 28, 29	Luke 13: 1-22
16	I. Sa. 30, 31	Luke 13:23-35
17	II. Sa. 1, 2	Luke 14: 1-24
18	II. Sa. 3, 4, 5	Luke 14:25-35
19	II. Sa. 6, 7, 8	Luke 15: 1-10
20	II. Sa. 9, 10, 11	Luke 15:11-32
21	II. Sa. 12, 13	Luke 16
22	II. Sa. 14, 15	Luke 17: 1-19
23	II. Sa. 16, 17, 18	Luke 17:20-37
24	II. Sa. 19, 20	Luke 18: 1-23
25	II. Sa. 21, 22	Luke 18:24-43
26	II. Sa. 23, 24	Luke 19: 1-27
27	I. Ki. 1, 2	Luke 19:28-48
28	I. Ki. 3, 4, 5	Luke 20: 1-26
29	I. Ki. 6, 7	Luke 20:27-47
30	I. Ki. 8, 9	Luke 21: 1-19

May

Date	Morning	Evening
1	I. Ki. 10, 11	Luke 21:20-38
2	I. Ki. 12, 13	Luke 22: 1-20
3	I. Ki. 14, 15	Luke 22:21-46
4	I. Ki. 16, 17, 18	Luke 22:47-71
5	I. Ki. 19, 20	Luke 23: 1-25
6	I. Ki. 21, 22	Luke 23:26-56
7	II. Ki. 1, 2, 3	Luke 24: 1-35
8	II. Ki. 4, 5, 6	Luke 24:36-53
9	II. Ki. 7, 8, 9	John 1: 1-28
10	II. Ki. 10, 11, 12	John 1:29-51
11	II. Ki. 13, 14	John 2
12	II. Ki. 15, 16	John 3: 1-18
13	II. Ki. 17, 18	John 3:19-36
14	II. Ki. 19, 20, 21	John 4: 1-30
15	II. Ki. 22, 23	John 4:31-54
16	II. Ki. 24, 25	John 5: 1-24
17	I. Ch. 1, 2, 3	John 5:25-47
18	I. Ch. 4, 5, 6	John 6: 1-21
19	I. Ch. 7, 8, 9	John 6:22-44
20	I. Ch. 10, 11, 12	John 6:45-71
21	I. Ch. 13, 14, 15	John 7: 1-27
22	I. Ch. 16, 17, 18	John 7:28-53
23	I. Ch. 19, 20, 21	John 8: 1-27
24	I. Ch. 22, 23, 24	John 8:28-59
25	I. Ch. 25, 26, 27	John 9: 1-23
26	I. Ch. 28, 29	John 9:24-41
27	II. Ch. 1, 2, 3	John 10: 1-23
28	II. Ch. 4, 5, 6	John 10:24-42
29	II. Ch. 7, 8, 9	John 11: 1-29
30	II. Ch. 10, 11, 12	John 11:30-57
31	II. Ch. 13, 14	John 12: 1-26

June

Date	Morning	Evening
1	II. Ch. 15, 16	John 12:27-50
2	II. Ch. 17, 18	John 13: 1-20
3	II. Ch. 19, 20	John 13:21-38
4	II. Ch. 21, 22	John 14
5	II. Ch. 23, 24	John 15
6	II. Ch. 25, 26, 27	John 16
7	II. Ch. 28, 29	John 17
8	II. Ch. 30, 31	John 18: 1-18
9	II. Ch. 32, 33	John 18:19-40
10	II. Ch. 34, 35, 36	John 19: 1-22
11	Ezra 1, 2	John 19:23-42
12	Ezra 3, 4, 5	John 20
13	Ezra 6, 7, 8	John 21
14	Ezra 9, 10	Acts 1
15	Neh. 1, 2, 3	Acts 2: 1-21
16	Neh. 4, 5, 6	Acts 2:22-47
17	Neh. 7, 8, 9	Acts 3
18	Neh. 10, 11	Acts 4: 1-22
19	Neh. 12, 13	Acts 4:23-37
20	Esth. 1, 2	Acts 5: 1-21
21	Esth. 3, 4, 5	Acts 5:22-42
22	Esth. 6, 7, 8	Acts 6
23	Esth. 9, 10	Acts 7: 1-21
24	Job 1, 2	Acts 7:22-43
25	Job 3, 4	Acts 7:44-60
26	Job 5, 6, 7	Acts 8: 1-25
27	Job 8, 9,10	Acts 8:26-40
28	Job 11, 12, 13	Acts 9: 1-21
29	Job 14, 15, 16	Acts 9:22-43
30	Job 17, 18, 19	Acts 10: 1-23

July

Date	Morning	Evening
1	Job 20, 21	Acts 10:24-48
2	Job 22, 23, 24	Acts 11
3	Job 25, 26, 27	Acts 12
4	Job 28, 29	Acts 13: 1-25
5	Job 30, 31	Acts 13:26-52
6	Job 32, 33	Acts 14
7	Job 34, 35	Acts 15: 1-21
8	Job 36, 37	Acts 15:22-41
9	Job 38, 39, 40	Acts 16: 1-21
10	Job 41, 42	Acts 16:22-40
11	Ps. 1, 2, 3	Acts 17: 1-15
12	Ps. 4, 5, 6	Acts 17:16-34
13	Ps. 7, 8, 9	Acts 18
14	Ps. 10, 11, 12	Acts 19: 1-20
15	Ps. 13, 14, 15	Acts 19:21-41
16	Ps. 16, 17	Acts 20: 1-16
17	Ps. 18, 19	Acts 20:17-38
18	Ps. 20, 21, 22	Acts 21: 1-17
19	Ps. 23, 24, 25	Acts 21:18-40
20	Ps. 26, 27, 28	Acts 22
21	Ps. 29, 30	Acts 23: 1-15
22	Ps. 31, 32	Acts 23:-16-35
23	Ps. 33, 34	Acts 24
24	Ps. 35, 36	Acts 25
25	Ps. 37, 38, 39	Acts 26
26	Ps. 40, 41, 42	Acts 27: 1-26
27	Ps. 43, 44, 45	Acts 27:27-44
28	Ps. 46, 47, 48	Acts 28
29	Ps. 49, 50	Rom. 1
30	Ps. 51, 52, 53	Rom. 2
31	Ps. 54, 55, 56	Rom. 3

August

Date	Morning	Evening
1	Ps. 57, 58, 59	Rom. 4
2	Ps. 60, 61, 62	Rom. 5
3	Ps. 63, 64, 65	Rom. 6
4	Ps. 66, 67	Rom. 7
5	Ps. 68, 69	Rom. 8: 1-21
6	Ps. 70, 71	Rom. 8:22-39
7	Ps. 72, 73	Rom. 9: 1-15
8	Ps. 74, 75, 76	Rom. 9:16-33
9	Ps. 77, 78	Rom. 10
10	Ps. 79, 80	Rom. 11: 1-18
11	Ps. 81, 82, 83	Rom. 11:19-36
12	Ps. 84, 85, 86	Rom. 12
13	Ps. 87, 88	Rom. 13
14	Ps. 89, 90	Rom. 14
15	Ps. 91, 92, 93	Rom. 15: 1-13
16	Ps. 94, 95, 96	Rom. 15:14-33
17	Ps. 97, 98, 99	Rom. 16
18	Ps. 100, 101, 102	I. Co. 1
19	Ps. 103, 104	I. Co. 2
20	Ps. 105, 106	I. Co. 3
21	Ps. 107, 108, 109	I. Co. 4
22	Ps. 110, 111, 112	I. Co. 5
23	Ps. 113, 114, 115	I. Co. 6
24	Ps. 116, 117, 118	I. Co. 7: 1-19
25	Ps. 119:1-88	I. Co. 7:20-40
26	Ps. 119:89-176	I. Co. 8
27	Ps. 120, 121, 122	I. Co. 9
28	Ps. 123, 124, 125	I. Co. 10: 1-18
29	Ps. 126, 127, 128	I. Co. 10:19-33
30	Ps. 129, 130, 131	I. Co. 11: 1-16
31	Ps. 132, 133, 134	I. Co. 11:17-34

September

Date	Morning	Evening
1	Ps. 135, 136	I. Co. 12
2	Ps. 137, 138, 139	I. Co. 13
3	Ps. 140, 141, 142	I. Co. 14: 1-20
4	Ps. 143, 144, 145	I. Co. 14:21-40
5	Ps. 146, 147	I. Co. 15: 1-28
6	Ps. 148, 149, 150	I. Co. 15:29-58
7	Prov. 1, 2	I. Co. 16
8	Prov. 3, 4, 5	II. Co. 1
9	Prov. 6, 7	II. Co. 2
10	Prov. 8, 9	II. Co. 3
11	Prov. 10, 11, 12	II. Co. 4
12	Prov. 13, 14, 15	II. Co. 5
13	Prov. 16, 17, 18	II. Co. 6
14	Prov. 19, 20, 21	II. Co. 7
15	Prov. 22, 23, 24	II. Co. 8
16	Prov. 25, 26	II. Co. 9
17	Prov. 27, 28, 29	II. Co. 10
18	Prov. 30, 31	II. Co. 11: 1-15
19	Eccl. 1, 2, 3	II. Co. 11:16-33
20	Eccl. 4, 5, 6	II. Co. 12
21	Eccl. 7, 8, 9	II. Co. 13
22	Eccl. 10, 11, 12	Gal. 1
23	Song 1, 2, 3	Gal. 2
24	Song 4, 5	Gal. 3
25	Song 6, 7, 8	Gal. 4
26	Isa. 1, 2	Gal. 5
27	Isa. 3, 4	Gal. 6
28	Isa. 5, 6	Eph. 1
29	Isa. 7, 8	Eph. 2
30	Isa. 9, 10	Eph. 3

October

Date	Morning	Evening
1	Isa. 11, 12, 13	Eph. 4
2	Isa. 14, 15, 16	Eph. 5: 1-16
3	Isa. 17, 18, 19	Eph. 5:17-33
4	Isa. 20, 21, 22	Eph. 6
5	Isa. 23, 24, 25	Phil. 1
6	Isa. 26, 27	Phil. 2
7	Isa. 28, 29	Phil. 3
8	Isa. 30, 31	Phil. 4
9	Isa. 32, 33	Col. 1
10	Isa. 34, 35, 36	Col. 2
11	Isa. 37, 38	Col. 3
12	Isa. 39, 40	Col. 4
13	Isa. 41, 42	I. Thes. 1
14	Isa. 43, 44	I. Thes. 2
15	Isa. 45, 46	I. Thes. 3
16	Isa. 47, 48, 49	I. Thes. 4
17	Isa. 50, 51, 52	I. Thes. 5
18	Isa. 53, 54, 55	II. Thes. 1
19	Isa. 56, 57, 58	II. Thes. 2
20	Isa. 59, 60, 61	II. Thes. 3
21	Isa. 62, 63, 64	I. Tim. 1
22	Isa. 65, 66	I. Tim. 2
23	Jer. 1, 2	I. Tim. 3
24	Jer. 3, 4, 5	I. Tim. 4
25	Jer. 6, 7, 8	I. Tim. 5
26	Jer. 9, 10, 11	I. Tim. 6
27	Jer. 12, 13, 14	II. Tim. 1
28	Jer. 15, 16, 17	II. Tim. 2
29	Jer. 18, 19	II. Tim. 3
30	Jer. 20, 21	II. Tim. 4
31	Jer. 22, 23	Titus 1

November

Date	Morning	Evening
1	Jer. 24, 25, 26	Titus 2
2	Jer. 27, 28, 29	Titus 3
3	Jer. 30, 31	Philemon
4	Jer. 32,33	Heb. 1
5	Jer. 34, 35, 36	Heb. 2
6	Jer. 37, 38, 39	Heb. 3
7	Jer. 40, 41, 42	Heb. 4
8	Jer. 43, 44, 45	Heb. 5
9	Jer. 46, 47	Heb. 6
10	Jer. 48, 49	Heb. 7
11	Jer. 50	Heb. 8
12	Jer. 51, 52	Heb. 9
13	Lam. 1, 2	Heb. 10: 1-18
14	Lam. 3, 4, 5	Heb. 10:19-39
15	Ezek. 1, 2	Heb. 11: 1-19
16	Ezek. 3, 4	Heb. 11:20-40
17	Ezek. 5, 6, 7	Heb. 12
18	Ezek. 8, 9, 10	Heb. 13
19	Ezek. 11, 12, 13	Jas. 1
20	Ezek. 14, 15	Jas. 2
21	Ezek. 16, 17	Jas. 3
22	Ezek. 18, 19	Jas. 4
23	Ezek. 20, 21	Jas. 5
24	Ezek. 22, 23	I. Pet. 1
25	Ezek. 24, 25, 26	I. Pet. 2
26	Ezek. 27, 28,29	I. Pet. 3
27	Ezek. 30, 31, 32	I. Pet. 1
28	Ezek. 33, 34	I. Pet. 5
29	Ezek. 35, 36	II. Pet. 1
30	Ezek. 37, 38, 39	II. Pet. 2

December

Date	Morning	Evening
1	Ezek. 40, 41	II. Pet. 3
2	Ezek. 42, 43, 44	I. John 1
3	Ezek. 45, 46	I. John 2
4	Ezek. 47, 48	I. John 3
5	Dan. 1, 2	I. John 4
6	Dan. 3, 4	I. John 5
7	Dan. 5, 6, 7	II. John
8	Dan. 8, 9,10	III. John
9	Dan. 11, 12	Jude
10	Hos. 1, 2, 3, 4	Rev. 1
11	Hos. 5, 6, 7, 8	Rev. 2
12	Hos. 9, 10, 11	Rev. 3
13	Hos. 12, 13, 14	Rev. 4
14	Joel 1, 2, 3	Rev. 5
15	Amos 1, 2, 3	Rev. 6
16	Amos 4, 5, 6	Rev. 7
17	Amos 7, 8, 9	Rev. 8
18	Obadiah	Rev. 9
19	Jon. 1, 2, 3, 4	Rev. 10
20	Mic. 1, 2, 3	Rev. 11
21	Mic. 4, 5	Rev. 12
22	Mic. 6, 7	Rev. 13
23	Nah. 1, 2, 3	Rev. 14
24	Hab. 1, 2, 3	Rev. 15
25	Zeph. 1, 2, 3	Rev. 16
26	Hag. 1, 2	Rev. 17
27	Zec. 1, 2 ,3, 4	Rev. 18
28	Zec. 5, 6, 7, 8	Rev. 19
29	Zec. 9, 10, 11, 12	Rev. 20
30	Zec. 13, 14	Rev. 21
31	Mal. 1, 2, 3, 4	Rev. 22

OLD TESTAMENT
GENESIS

Key Thought:	Number of Chapters:	Key Verse:	Christ seen as:
Beginnings	50	1:1	Seed of Abraham

Writer of the Book:	Date:	Conclusion of the Book:
Moses	About 1500 B. C.	The failure of man under every condition is met by the salvation of God.

SUMMARY

CHAPTER ONE

Contents: Original creation and the renovating of earth for habitation of man. Creation of animal and human life.

Conclusion: An all-wise, all-powerful, loving God formed all things perfect in the beginning. He made man, the crown of His creation, perfect and capable of fellowship with Himself and able to enjoy and govern Eden.

Key Word: Beginnings, v. 1.

Strong Verses: 1, 27.

Christ Seen: v. 1. Be sure to compare John 1:1, 2, 3, 14. Not only was Jesus Christ present in creation, but creation was bound up with Him as its secret. Col. 1:15-17. See Heb. 1:3.

Gen. 1 is not a history of the original creation, but of a reconstruction following a cataclysmic judgment which had befallen the original creation. v. 1 Original creation. v. 2 Its destruction. v. 3 and on, Reconstruction.

CHAPTER TWO

Contents: God's Sabbath rest. The creative act of Gen. 1:27 explained. The Edenic covenant.

Conclusion: Man is a threefold being, body, soul and spirit. The real man is soul and spirit, conferred directly from God. The body, the outward casing, is dust and to dust it returns.

Key Word: Man, v. 7.

Strong Verses: 3, 7, 18, 24.

Christ Seen: Eve, a type of the Church, the Bride of Christ, was not formed of dust, but came from an opened side. The Church is a heavenly Body, born from the opened side of the Second Adam, God's Son.

CHAPTER THREE

Contents: Temptation of Eve and entrance of sin into the race. God's covenant with fallen man and the expulsion from Eden.

Conclusion: Doubt lies at the root of all sin. Altering the Word, v. 1; adding to the Word, v. 3, or taking from the Word, v. 5, are dangerous acts.

Key Word: Serpent, v. 1.

Strong Verses: 9, 19, 22, 23. Promise: 15.

Christ Seen: Conscience, the realization of what man is, must be met by salvation, the revelation of what God is in Grace, before peace can be restored to man. Through woman sin entered and by her seed alone was salvation promised. Isa. 7:14, 9:6, 7.

CHAPTER FOUR

Contents: First sons of Adam, Cain and Abel. Murder of Abel. First civilization. Birth of Seth.

Conclusion: Attainment can never take the place of Atonement. Without the recognition of Christ as our substitute and sacrifice there can be no approach to God.

Key Word: Offering, v. 4.

Strong Verses: 4, 26.

Christ Seen: Abel, acknowledging his sinfulness, placed the death of an appointed victim between himself and the consequence of sin. Christ, the Lamb of God, is the spotless Victim who stands between us and our sins if we willingly accept His finished work.

CHAPTER FIVE

Contents: Generations from Adam to Noah.
Conclusion: By man came death. In Adam all die. In Christ shall all who believe be made alive.
Key Word: Generations, v. 1.
Strong Verses: 24.
Christ Seen: Enoch, the seventh from Adam, was translated and made the trophy of God's power over death. As such he is a type of Christ who was translated bodily into heaven, a victor over the grave.

CHAPTER SIX

Contents: Flood announced. Compromise of sons of God with daughters of men.
Conclusion: The true believer can float in peace on the very waters by which the wicked world is judged.
Key Word: Flood, v. 17.
Strong Verses: 8, 9, 18, 22.
Christ Seen: The plan whereby Noah was saved was no invention of his own but one revealed by God, v. 13. Faith is governed by the pure Word of God. Heb. 11:7. The ark is a type of Christ as the refuge of His people from the judgment.

CHAPTER SEVEN

Contents: The flood comes. Noah and family preserved.
Conclusion: God has prepared a refuge from divine judgment and will give us perfect security in Him if we will but heed His call to "come into the ark."
Key Word: Ark, v. 7.
Strong Verses: 16.
Christ Seen: It is the blood of Christ that keeps out the waters of judgment and makes the believer's position in Christ (our ark of safety) a secure one. (v. 16; Jn. 17:9).
There was a window in the top of the ark whereby they could look up in communion with God, knowing that no judgment remained for them. (Heb. 12:1, 2).

CHAPTER EIGHT

Contents: Waters receding, exit from the ark. Noah's altar.
Conclusion: When judgment days are past, the believer will find himself safely landed in a better world.
Key Word: Rest, v. 4.
Strong Verses: 1, 20.
Christ Seen: The dove by bringing in the olive leaf (emblem of the renewed mind in Christ) furnished proof that judgment was past and a new condition coming into view. So the believer finds his rest and portion in Christ and proves that judgment days are over for him.

CHAPTER NINE

Contents: Noahic covenant. Noah's shame and Ham's sin.
Conclusion: The believer is as secure as God's promises are true. No promise of God can fail.
Key Word: Covenant, v. 9.
Strong Verses: 9. Promise: 13.
Christ Seen: The bow seen upon the storm clouds of judgment speaks of the cross where judgment never to be repeated has been visited upon the believer's sins.

CHAPTER TEN

Contents: Establishing of the nations.
Conclusion: God made all nations of one blood and determined the bounds of their habitations.
Key Word: Nations, v. 31.
Strong Verses: 32.
Striking Fact: From the seven sons of Japheth, the Gentile nations are descended.

CHAPTER ELEVEN

Contents: Failure under Noahic covenant. Tower of Babel. Scattering of the people. Ancestry of Abram.
Conclusion: Man ever builds under the heavens, seeking a name and a portion in the earth. The believer builds on an imperishable foundation laid in heaven by God. Man's devices all fail.
Key Word: Confusion (Babel), v. 9.
Strong Verses: 5, 9.
Christ Seen: The only safe way for man to be exalted is in Christ, in whom he may "sit in heavenly places." To be elevated outside of Christ is to reach a dizzy height from which he is sure to fall.

CHAPTER TWELVE

Contents: Call of Abram. His worship and testing. The error in Egypt.
Conclusion: The path into which God calls the believer may often be trying to the flesh, but this does not necessarily indicate that he is out of God'ʟ will.
Key Word: Sojourners, v. 10.
Strong Verses: 8. Promise: 3.
Christ Seen: Abraham's altar marks him as a worshipper. His tent marks him as a pilgrim in a strange land. These are distinguishing marks of all believers. Those who are Christ's are separated from the world and are seen to find their portion only in Him.

CHAPTER THIRTEEN

Contents: Abram's return to the land and the altar. Separation from Lot. Lot's backsliding and choice of the land.
Conclusion: Material blessings are often accompanied by moral blight. Let nature range where it will, it can never take faith's treasure. It never pays to try to make the best of both worlds.
Key Word: Separation, v. 9.
Strong Verses: 4, 17, 18.
Christ Seen: We are truly safe only as we remember that our portion is in Christ, not in the world. If through His grace we pursue the path of simple faith, we will be thrown completely outside the range of the world's circumstances. If we are after a name and place in the world, we may expect to be caught in its convulsions.

CHAPTER FOURTEEN

Contents: Abram delivers Lot. Abram's refusal to compromise with the King of Sodom.
Conclusion: Genuine faith never wraps itself in fleece while a brother shivers in the cold. The farther a believer lives from the world, the greater power he will have over it.
Key Word: Deliverance, v. 20.
Strong Verses: 22, 23.
Christ Seen: (v. 14). Abram here may be taken as a type of Christ, the Christian's Deliverer. He it is, in His intercessory work, who comes to our rescue when we are taken captive by Satan. (1 Cor. 10:13).

CHAPTER FIFTEEN

Contents: Abrahamic covenant confirmed and spiritual seed promised.
Conclusion: The promises to faith are more certain than the conclusions of logic (v. 25). Faith is the key that unlocks the cabinet of promises.
Key Word: Seed, v. 5.
Strong Verses: 6. Promise: 1.
Christ Seen: (v. 2). The believer's relationships to Christ are suggested in Abram's manner of addressing God. "Lord"—is literally "Master," and the word is used both in relation to God and to man. As applied to man it is sometimes translated "husband." Both of these relationships exist between Christ and the believer. (Jn. 13:13; 2 Cor. 12:2, 3).

CHAPTER SIXTEEN

Contents: Birth of Ishmael.

Conclusion: The moment the believer takes his eyes away from God's promises he is ready for mean devices of unbelief which bring him untold suffering.
Key Word: Despised, v. 4.
Strong Verse: 13.
Christ Seen: Hagar is used as a type of the law "which gendereth to bondage." (Gal. 4:24, 25). Like Sarah, the Galatians tried to add something of nature to what Christ had already accomplished for them on the cross. If we will not trust solely in Christ, we will become a debtor to nature or the world and will be robbed of His peace.

CHAPTER SEVENTEEN

Contents: The revelation of God. Abram's name changed. Covenant confirmed. Circumcision established. Promise of Isaac.
Conclusion: When man is in the dust God can talk to him in grace. In spite of the believer's mistakes, God is faithful.
Key Word: Covenant, v. 2.
Strong Verses: 19. Promise: 1, 2.
Christ Seen: Abram means "father of altitude." Abraham means "father of breadth." The perpendicular of justice is transversed by the horizontal beam of embracing love. In the two names we see a picture of the cross.

CHAPTER EIGHTEEN

Contents: Abraham, the friend of God. Promise of the seed renewed. The plea of Sodom.
Conclusion: The closer the believer walks with God, the more he will know of God's mind about everything. The secrets of the Lord are with those who fear Him.
Key Word: Communion, v. 33.
Strong Verses: 17, 18.
Christ Seen: The way to know the divine purpose about the world is not to be mixed up with its schemes and speculations but walking in communion with Christ.

CHAPTER NINETEEN

Contents: Destruction of Sodom and Gomorrah. Lot's backsliding and escape.
Conclusion: No Christian can find his pleasure and profit in the world and at the same time bear effectual testimony against the world. No heart can mature two crops—choose between the Word and the world.
Key Word: Destruction, v. 13.
Strong Verses: 27, 29.
Christ Seen: It was Jesus who said, "He that is not with me is against me." To follow Him faithfully means to participate in His rejection with the world. To profess to be His, while at the same time seeking great worldly influence, will mean the loss of all influence and spiritual power, even over the members of one's own family.

CHAPTER TWENTY

Contents: Abraham's lapse at Gerar. Lying to Abimelech about his wife.
Conclusion: Sin has many tools but a lie is a handle that fits them all. If the truth is stretched, expect it eventually to fly back and sting you.
Key Word: Sin, v. 9.
Strong Verses: 6, 17.
Christ Seen: One is often struck with the amazing difference between what God's people are in His view and what they are in the world's view. God sees His own through Christ, although in themselves, they are often feeble and inconsistent.

CHAPTER TWENTY-ONE

Contents: Birth of Isaac. Bondwoman and her son cast out. Abraham at Beersheba.
Conclusion: Behind every promise of God is the purpose and power of God, therefore faith should know that God's bonds are as good as ready money "at the set time."
Key Word: Isaac, v. 3.
Strong Verse: 1.

Christ Seen: (v. 10). Christ will have the first place or no place at all. "The crooked cannot be made straight." That which is crooked must be gotten rid of altogether before one can fellowship with Him. (Col. 3:9). Human religion would keep the bondwoman and her son in the house. God would have them put away (Gal. 5:1).

CHAPTER TWENTY-TWO

Contents: Offering of Isaac. Abrahamic covenant again confirmed.
Conclusion: The man of faith must keep his eye on God, looking not at circumstances, nor pondering the results of what God asks of him. The trial of faith is precious.
Key Word: Worship, v. 5.
Strong Verses: 15, 16, 17. Promise: 18.
Christ Seen: Isaac is a type of Christ "obedient unto death." Abraham illustrates the Father who "spared not His own Son." The resurrection is illustrated in the deliverance of Isaac.

CHAPTER TWENTY-THREE

Contents: Death of Sarah. Burial in cave of Machpelah.
Conclusion: Although the man of faith knows that in the resurrection glory he shall be heir to the land, until that time he will be no debtor to those in temporary possession. (vv. 15, 16).
Key Word: Burial, v. 4.
Strong Verse: 19.
Christ Seen: Abraham knew by faith that the land in which he would bury Sarah, was his in prospect and that in resurrection glory his seed should possess it. Until then he would be no debtor to those to be dispossessed. So the Christian is joint heir with Christ who is heir of all things, yet in passing through this world he must needs be in subjection to those who for the present dispossess him.

CHAPTER TWENTY-FOUR

Contents: Bride of Isaac secured by Abraham's servant.
Conclusion: God leads in every detail of our lives. The marriage which is not according to His will as shown by His Word, and the leading of His Servant, the Holy Spirit, will not be blessed of Him.
Key Word: Wife, v. 4.
Strong Verses: 27, 40.
Christ Seen: Abraham stands for the Father (Matt. 22:2). The servant stands for the Holy Spirit (John 16:13, 14; 1 Cor. 12:7-11). Rebekah stands for the Bride of Christ (Eph. 5:25-32). Isaac stands for the Bridegroom who is coming to receive His Bride (1 Thess. 4:14-16).

CHAPTER TWENTY-FIVE

Contents: Abraham weds Keturah. Isaac becomes Abraham's heir. Death of Abraham. Generations of Ishmael and Isaac. Birth of Esau and Jacob and the sale of the birthright.
Conclusion: The natural man values only what he can see and puts no value on the things of God. Many despise their birthright as sons of God because it is a spiritual thing, of value only as there is faith to apprehend it.
Key Word: Birthright, v. 31.
Strong Verse: 23.
Christ Seen: Esau is a type of the man of the earth, Heb. 12:16, 17. In many respects a nobler man than Jacob, yet the fact that he was destitute of faith caused him to despise his birthright. God's choice of His children does not depend on their character but upon Christ's character, with whom they may be identified by faith.

CHAPTER TWENTY-SIX

Contents: Covenant confirmed to Isaac. Isaac's lapse at Gerar. Isaac as a well digger.
Conclusion: It is peculiarly comforting to see that God has ever been dealing with men of like passions as we are and patiently bearing with the same failures. When the believer falls, God is still with him.

Key Word: Blessed, v. 12.
Strong Verses: 2, 24, 25, 28.
Christ Seen: (v. 4). Christ is seen here as the seed through whom all the nations should be blessed. Some see a distinction between the promised seed of Abraham compared to the "sand of the sea" (22:17) and the seed compared to the "stars of heaven"—one referring to his earthly seed— Israel to be blessed in the kingdom, the other referring to his spiritual seed, those who through faith are seated in heavenly places in him.

CHAPTER TWENTY-SEVEN

Contents: Fraudulent methods of Jacob in getting Isaac's blessing. Remorse of Esau.
Conclusion: Human nature is prone to scheme to bring about what God would do without any scheming. He does not need our cunning or deceit to accomplish His purpose. Seek spiritual blessings in the right way or get with them years of sorrow afterward. One only needs to read the history of Jacob to learn that it does not pay to take things into one's own hands.
Key Word: Supplanter, v. 36.
Strong Verses: 28, 29, 33.
Christ Seen: (v. 22). This is the only recorded case where one is said to have gone by his feelings—and he went wrong. Faith in Christ is the only sure way of guidance in spiritual matters.

CHAPTER TWENTY-EIGHT

Contents: Jacob at Bethel and the Abrahamic covenant confirmed to him in a dream.
Conclusion: The believer should realize that he is ever in God's presence. However, no heart can feel at home in His presence until emptied of self and broken.
Key Word: Bethel (house of God), v. 19.
Strong Verses: 12, 15, 22.
Christ Seen: Bethel to the Christian stands for a realization although imperfect, of the abiding presence of Christ and the spiritual contents of faith.

CHAPTER TWENTY-NINE

Contents: Jacob and Laban, two bargain makers, meet.
Conclusion: The believer who has erred may not be forsaken of God, but he is permitted to reap the shame and sorrow of his self-chosen way. Matt. 7:2.
Key Word: Beguiled, v. 25.
Strong Verse: 20.
Christ Seen: To learn the riches of God in Christ, go to Bethel. To learn the utter misery of man, go to Haran. If we fail to take in the revelation God has given us in Christ, we will have to go to Haran to learn our weakness.

CHAPTER THIRTY

Contents: Jacob's posterity in Padan-aram. Another bargain between Jacob and Laban.
Conclusion: The toiling and scheming of men is the result of ignorance of God's grace, and inability to put implicit confidence in God's promises. (The success of Jacob's policy was not sufficient to justify it, had it been unjust toward the shrewd Laban, but evidently it was not unjust, for see 31:12).
Key Word: Blessed, v. 27.
Strong Verse: 27.
Christ Seen: (v. 33). It is the birth of Christ that resulted in the reproach of sin being removed (Col. 2:13-15).

CHAPTER THIRTY-ONE

Contents: Jacob's resolution to return. Laban's hot pursuit; their quarrel and final agreement.
Conclusion: The safety of believers under trying circumstances is much due to the hold God has on the consciences of bad men. In the path of obedience, we may count on God's care.
Key Word: Flight, v. 21.
Strong Verse: 49.

Christ Seen: (v. 49). Though some Christians may not be able to be of one mind in some matters, they may live in habitual recognition of Christ and the eternal sanction of His presence (Matt. 28:20).

CHAPTER THIRTY-TWO

Contents: Jacob becomes Israel. Preparation for meeting Esau. Wrestling against the angel.
Conclusion: Either we lean on God or on our own plans. The arrangements of unbelief and impatience prevent God acting for us and He must bring us to the end of our own strength.
Key Word: Afraid, v. 7.
Strong Verses: 24, 30.
Christ Seen: To be alone with Christ is the only way to arrive at a knowledge of ourselves and our ways. Jacob was a wrestled-with man, and until the seat of his own strength was touched, he did not reach the place of blessing.

CHAPTER THIRTY-THREE

Contents: Jacob meets Esau. Settles in Canaan.
Conclusion: How groundless are all the Christian's fears and how useless all his self-devised plans. "When a man's ways please the Lord, He maketh even his enemies to be at peace with him."
Key Word: Meeting, v. 4.
Strong Verse: 11.
Christ Seen: (v. 1). Failure to take God at His word causes one on every fresh occasion to doubt and hesitate, anticipating destruction. If we are walking in communion with Christ, we will be at peace notwithstanding outward circumstances, knowing that in Him we are safe.

CHAPTER THIRTY-FOUR

Contents: Harvest of evil years comes on Jacob and family. Dinah defiled and the bloody revenge.
Conclusion: Untaught maidens who go out to "gad" with the daughters of the land fall into a snare and involve their relatives in great trouble.
Key Word: Defiled, v. 2.
Strong Verse: 19.
Christ Seen: God had directed Jacob to Bethel. He settled at Shechem. If Christ is to be our leader, He demands whole obedience. Partial obedience to Him is responsible for much trouble that befalls Christian families.

CHAPTER THIRTY-FIVE

Contents: Jacob's return to Bethel and renewed communion. Birth of Benjamin. Death of Rachel. Death of Isaac.
Conclusion: There is no perfect communion with God until all idols are put away and we come into His presence as He directs.
Key Word: Altar, v. 1.
Strong Verses: 3, 7.
Christ Seen: "Arise and go to Bethel." God is ever calling the soul back to Himself. It is Christ who says to the Church, "Remember from whence thou art fallen and repent and do thy first works."

CHAPTER THIRTY-SIX

Contents: Generations of Esau and their settlements.
Conclusion: Though one have not a spiritual right by promise, they may still have, in the mercy of God, temporary rights to rich estates in this world. "But what is a man profited if he gain the whole world and lose his own soul?"
Key Word: Generations, v. 1.
Strong Verses: 6, 7.
Christ Seen: Edom, a name by which the foolish bargain was perpetuated, means "red pottage." If men sell their birthright in Christ for a mess of pottage, they must thank themselves when afterwards, it is remembered against them to their reproach.

CHAPTER THIRTY-SEVEN

Contents: Generations of Joseph. Joseph hated and rejected by his brothers. Cast into pit. Carried away by Gentiles.

Conclusion: Envy is a canker to the soul and hates those excellencies it cannot reach. "Hatred stirreth up strife" and left to itself, only stops at murder.

Key Word: Envied, v. 11.

Strong Verse: 4.

Christ Seen: Joseph, a marvelous type of Christ. Rejected because of his testimony to his brethren, sent by the Father on a mission of love, cast into a pit, sold to Gentiles, the Gentiles blessed through him.

CHAPTER THIRTY-EIGHT

Contents: Shame of Judah and his sons.

Conclusion: The sins which dishonor God and defile the body are evidences of vile affection and are very displeasing to God, often visited with quick punishment.

Key Word: Shamed, v. 23.

Strong Verses: 10, 26.

Christ Seen: It is evident that our Lord sprang out of Judah. Heb. 7:14. Divine grace is seen rising above man's sin to bring about His purpose. The Spirit is conducting us by this chapter, along the line through which, on the flesh side, our Lord came. Man would never have devised such a genealogy.

CHAPTER THIRTY-NINE

Contents: Joseph tested in Egypt in the house of Potiphar.

Conclusion: Loyalty to God may bring a believer into serious testings but the almighty grace of God will enable him to overcome the enemy's assaults. Though stripped of possessions, we need not be stripped of virtue.

Key Word: Goodly, v. 6.

Strong Verses: 2, 3, 21.

Christ Seen: The one taken from the pit, into which he came through rejection, is coming to the place of ruler, the channel of blessing to the Gentiles, sustainer of life to the brethren. (Christ).

CHAPTER FORTY

Contents: Joseph in prison in Egypt. Interprets dreams.

Conclusion: Whatever our lot in God's providence, we may ever be a blessing to companions in tribulation by showing a concern in their troubles and doing our best, by God's help, to lift their burdens.

Key Word: Interpretation, v. 8.

Strong Verse: 8.

Christ Seen: (v. 8). It is Jesus who is the great interpreter of all the circumstances of our lives (Matt. 13:34, 35). If we would know God's purposes in our difficulties, we must hear Jesus (Matt. 17:5).

CHAPTER FORTY-ONE

Contents: Pharaoh's dream. Joseph's exaltation in Egypt and his Gentile bride.

Conclusion: The faithful believer will be abundantly recompensed for the disgrace he has patiently suffered and his righteousness will shine forth so all will know that God is with him.

Key Word: Exalted (set over), v. 41.

Strong Verses: 38, 39.

Christ Seen: As Joseph solved Pharaoh's vexing problems, so Jesus relieves the heart of its burdens. Rejected, exalted, Jesus is now taking a Gentile Bride to be with Him when the "Time of Jacob's trouble" comes upon the earth.

CHAPTER FORTY-TWO

Contents: Joseph preserves his brethren from the famine.

Conclusion: Times of testing await those who are guilty and often prove the effectual means of awakening conscience and bringing sin to remembrance.

Key Word: Proved (tested), v. 15.

Strong Verses: 8, 23, 24.

Christ Seen: While Jesus is unrecognized by His brethren, the Jews, they are passing through deep troubles, but a tribulation awaits them which will bring them to the feet of Him Whom they crucified.

CHAPTER FORTY-THREE

Contents: Second visit of Joseph's brethren to Egypt in their necessity.
Conclusion: The way to find mercy with men is to seek it of God Who has all hearts in His hand and Who works in strange ways for His children, when they know it not.
Key Word: Mercy, v. 14.
Strong Verses: 14, 23, 29.
Christ Seen: Before Him, who in their blindness they do not know, the Jews will plead for their Benjamin who has been lost to them, and in the agony of the hour, the opened heavens will reveal the Christ they crucified, as their Deliverer. The sufferer and the conqueror are one.

CHAPTER FORTY-FOUR

Contents: Joseph's brethren further tested. Arrest on charge of taking a cup.
Conclusion: Even in afflictions wherein the believer thinks himself wronged by men, he must own that God has a righteous purpose and possibly it is to make him confess his sin and develop his better nature.
Key Word: Sorrow, v. 31.
Strong Verses: 16, 33.
Christ Seen: As Joseph laid a plan to bring about full confession from his brethren that they might come into fellowship with him, so Christ will deal with the Jews, culminating in a great day of confession and mourning.

CHAPTER FORTY-FIVE

Contents: Joseph reveals himself to his brethren whom he blesses and sends back to Egypt.
Conclusion: "He worketh all things together for good to them that love God and are called according to His purpose." He can work wonders for His own, when He has surrendered men through whom to work.
Key Word: Revealed (made known), v. 1.
Strong Verses: 5, 7, 8.
Christ Seen: A sacred scene is coming for Israel (Ezek. 22:19) when Christ shall be revealed. As they stand self-condemned before Him, He will pour balm into their hearts (Zech. 13:1; 12:9) and will show all to have been decreed for their blessing (Rom. 11:11, 12).

CHAPTER FORTY-SIX

Contents: Jacob's journey to Egypt and meeting with Joseph.
Conclusion: A glorious meeting day is coming after the trials and mistakes of earth. Jesus prepares a place for the believer and comes again to receive him unto Himself, that where He is, there they may be also.
Key Word: Meeting, v. 29.
Strong Verses: 1, 3, 4.
Christ Seen: The absolute will of God for Israel was in Canaan, not Egypt (26:1-5). His permissive will allows them to settle in Goshen and as far as possible He blesses them there. The Jews sidestepped God's absolute will by rejecting the Messiah, but a day of mingled joy and mourning awaits those living at His second advent.

CHAPTER FORTY-SEVEN

Contents: Jacob and descendants exalted in Goshen.
Conclusion: Notwithstanding former unkindnesses received, the believer who is prospered in this world, must not overlook nor despise his poor relatives in their need. The measure of a truly great man is the way he treats men who in themselves have been small.
Key Word: Nourished, v. 12.
Strong Verses: 12, 29, 30.
Christ Seen: Christ will, at His second advent, present His brethren, the Jews, in the court of heaven, restoring them to the place of blessing in the earth. As Jacob here blesses King Pharaoh, so Israel's portion in the Millennium will be that of blessing the kings of the earth.

CHAPTER FORTY-EIGHT

Contents: Jacob on his death bed blesses Joseph's sons.
Conclusion: God in His grace, does not always observe the order of nature in bestowing His blessings, nor prefer those whom we think fittest to be preferred, but as it pleases Him, He chooses the weak to confound the mighty, thus His grace becomes more illustrious.
Key Word: Blessed, v. 15.
Strong Verses: 21.
Christ Seen: (v. 11). To nature's view Joseph was dead, yet in God's sight he was seated in the place of authority. So to the natural man, the Lord Jesus is but a dead saint, while to the saint God has revealed Him seated in the place of power (1 Cor. 2:9).

CHAPTER FORTY-NINE

Contents: Jacob's dying blessing, prophetic of the tribes of Israel.
Conclusion: It is a great blessing to attend upon Godly parents in their last hours that we might learn how to die as well as live, and profit by their reproofs, counsels, and comforts. Though they cannot prophecy, they can tell us from God's Word what will befall us in the last day if we do not do the will of the Father.
Key Word: Prophecy (shall befall), v. 1.
Promise: v. 10.
Christ Seen: (v. 10). Shiloh means "peace river"—a fragrant name for our Lord. To His cross and to His throne shall the gathering of the people be.

CHAPTER FIFTY

Contents: Jacob's burial. Joseph's death.
Conclusion: As it is an honor to die lamented, so it is a duty to honor the dead who have been useful in the Lord. Sincere and humble lament over Godly men is proper, for their death is a great loss to any place.
Key Word: Mourning, v. 10.
Strong Verses: 17, 19, 20, 21.
Christ Seen: (v. 15-21). Fears might legitimately arise in our hearts had not our forgiveness been based on the finished work of Christ. He is the Mediator between God and man (v. 19) and His mediatorial work is sufficient.

EXODUS

Key Thought:	Number of Chapters:	Key Verse:	Christ seen as:
Covenants	40	12:23	Lamb of God.

Writer of the Book:	Date:	Conclusion of the Book: Redemption is by the
Moses	About 1500 B. C.	blood and that alone.

SUMMARY

CHAPTER ONE

Contents: Israel in Egypt and their bondage.
Conclusion: God's providences may at times seem to thwart His promises that His peoples' faith may be tried and His power the more magnified. In their persecutions, He will sustain all who trust Him.
Key Word: Bondage, v. 14.
Strong Verse: 21.
Christ Seen: Christ is the true Deliverer from bondage (Heb. 2:14, 15). Those who have vital union with Him are completely saved from the fear of death, knowing that He has made complete reconciliation to God for them.

CHAPTER TWO

Contents: Deliverer prepared for Israel. Moses' birth. boyhood and marriage.
Conclusion: When men are plotting the ruin of God's people, God is planning His peoples' salvation. One apparently marked for obscurity and poverty may be destined to rise before the world to show God's power. Even enemies may be used to carry out God's purposes.
Key Word: Moses, v. 10.
Strong Verses: 24, 25.
Christ Seen: Moses is a striking type of Christ. Rejected by Israel, He turns to the Gentiles. In His rejection, He takes a Gentile bride, then later appears as Israel's deliverer and is accepted.

CHAPTER THREE

Contents: Moses called as deliverer. The burning bush.
Conclusion: Those qualified for great service may expect for a time to be confined to obscurity for special preparation and the vision of God's purpose. If God gives opportunity and heart to serve Him, it is an ernest of His power to accomplish the work.
Key Word: Deliverance, vv. 8, 10.
Strong Verses: 7. Promises: 12, 14.
Christ Seen: (v. 14). The name "I am" here applied to Jehovah, is taken by Christ in John 8:57, 58, proving His pre-existence and identification with Deity. Because Jesus laid claim to Deity in this way, He was stoned and finally killed by the Jews.

CHAPTER FOUR

Contents: Moses' objections. Unbelief of the people and Moses' lack of eloquence. Return to Egypt. Message delivered to elders.
Conclusion: Unbelief refuses to believe God because it does not find in self a reason for believing. With God, the merest stammerer may prove an efficient minister, neither need he be uneasy as to the reception of the message.
Key Word: Spokesman, v. 16.
Strong Verses: 11, 31. Promise: 12.
Christ Seen: The rod, symbol of power in Christ's hand, was not wrenched away from Moses, but cast down by Moses. It remained a serpent only while out of his hand. The rod, temporarily out of Christ's hand, will soon be taken up again and Satan's power will be over.

CHAPTER FIVE

Conclusion: God, in coming toward His people in mercy may sometimes employ strange methods so that people will think themselves ill-treated. God suffers it to be so that we may learn to cease from man and cease depending on second causes.

Key Word: Burdens, v. 4.

Strong Verse: 3.

Christ Seen: Those called to public service for Christ may expect to be tried as Christ Himself was, not only by the proud threats of enemies, but the unjust, unkind censures of friends who judge by outward appearances.

CHAPTER SIX

Contents: Jehovah's answer to Moses' first prayer. Covenant renewed. Families of Israel. Moses' commission renewed.

Conclusion: Man's extremity is God's opportunity of helping and saving. God's covenants are as firm as the power and truth of God can make them and we may venture upon all His promises.

Key Word: Covenant, v. 4.

Strong Verses: 3. Promises: 6, 7, 8.

Christ Seen: (v. 12). Disconsolate spirits often cause us to put from us the comforts we are entitled to in Christ and we stand in our own light. If we indulge in fretfulness, we lose the comfort of His word and must thank ourselves if we go comfortless. Christ's calls are His enablings.

CHAPTER SEVEN

Contents: Contest with Pharaoh. First plague. Water turned to blood.

Conclusion: We see God's almighty power, the unstability of all things under the sun and the changes we may meet with in them. What is water today may be blood tomorrow. Sin turns man's comforts into crosses.

Key Word: Smitten (waters), vv. 1, 17.

Strong Verses: 5, 17.

Christ Seen: Satanic resistance to God's testimony of His Son is often offered by those who have a "form of godliness without the power thereof." The magician finally failed, proving (8:7) their tricks, "lying wonders." (Rev. 13:15). So will all imitators fail in their efforts to counterfeit Christ's Gospel.

CHAPTER EIGHT

Contents: Plagues of frogs, lice, flies. Pharaoh's compromising offer.

Conclusion: If God be against us, all creatures can be made to be at war with us. God can, as He pleases, arm the smallest parts of creation against men. He may choose contemptible instruments to defeat one, that He might magnify His own power.

Key Word: Smitten, v. 2.

Strong Verses: 1, 2, 19.

Christ Seen: Pharaoh's compromises are types of those Satan makes with the Christian. "Be a Christian, but stay in Egypt or at least don't be so narrow as to come out entirely from the world." The salvation that leaves one in or near Egypt is not Christ's salvation.

CHAPTER NINE

Contents: Plagues of murraine, boils and hail.

Conclusion: The creature is made subject to vanity by reason of man's sins, liable to serve man's wickedness or share his punishment. When judgments are abroad, they may fall both on righteous and wicked but they are not the same to one as the other in the final reckoning.

Key Word:....Smitten, vv. 15, 27.

Strong Verse: 5.

Christ Seen: v. 12. The Lord hardened his heart. Before this, Pharaoh hardened his own heart resisting God's grace. There is a time when God gives one up to his own reprobate mind. Wilful hardness to the calls of Christ is sooner or later punished with judicial hardness so that one has no desire to accept Him. If men persist in shutting their eyes to Christ's Gospel, God will close them.

CHAPTER TEN

Contents: Plagues of locusts and darkness.
Conclusion: God's terms of reconciliation are fixed and cannot be disputed or lowered.   Men must meet the demand of God's will or God will permit their delusions and answer them according to their sin.
Key Word: Smitten, v. 21.
Strong Verses: 12, 17, 25.
Christ Seen: v. 11.   Christ would have no silent partners.   Godly men make a subtle compromise if they desire for their children a position in the world, or (v. 24) if they fail to consecrate their possessions along with themselves to Christ.

CHAPTER ELEVEN

Contents: Last plague.   Death of firstborn prophesied.
Conclusion: Persistent enemies of God' and His people will be made to fall under at last and those who have approved themselves, will look great in the eyes of those who have viewed them with contempt.
Key Word: Death, vv. 1, 5.
Strong Verses: 3, 7.
Christ Seen: In some way, God will always redress the injured, who in humble silence, commit their cause to Christ and in the end, they will not be losers by their adherence to Him (Mk. 10:30).

CHAPTER TWELVE

Contents: Deliverance for Israel through the Passover.
Conclusion: Deliverance for the believer is based entirely upon the shedding of the blood of a divinely appointed substitute and its application to the heart once for all.   If death has taken place for us, it cannot come to us.
Key Word: Passover, v. 13.
Strong Verses: 2, 14, 27.   Promise: 13.
Christ Seen: v. 8.   Secured by the blood, the believer feeds on the Person of the Lamb of God, roast with fire, not raw.   If Christ is not seen as the One subjected to the fires of God's wrath against sin, one cannot feed upon Him.   He cannot be an example if He is not first an atoning sacrifice.

CHAPTER THIRTEEN

Contents: Firstborn set apart for Jehovah.   Directions for feast of unleavened bread and consecration of males.
Conclusion: The believer should retain remembrance of God's great deliverance and to impress it on the heart, should use the appointed means for preserving remembrance.   (So, under the Gospel, Christ said, "This do in remembrance of me").
Key Word: Remember, v. 3.
Strong Verses: 9, 16, 21, 22.
Christ Seen: v. 13.   The redemption of the firstlings was a memorial sign to Israel of their own redemption.   Man by nature is represented by an ass with a broken neck.   By grace we are represented by a risen glorified Christ in heaven.

CHAPTER FOURTEEN

Contents: God's power exerted to redeem Israel.   Passing the Red Sea.
Conclusion: The believer cannot go ahead in the strength of Christ until he has learned to stand still in his own helplessness.   God can then place Himself between us and our circumstances and wonderfully deliver.
Key Word: Saved, v. 30.
Strong Verses: 19, 30, 31.   Promises: 13, 14.
Christ Seen: By the blood, God comes beween us and our sins.   By His presence, if we will permit, He will come between us and every overcoming circumstance.   The cross separates from sin; the cloud from circumstances.

CHAPTER FIFTEEN

Contents: The song of the redeemed.
Conclusion: Those who love God triumph in His triumphs and what is His honor is their joy.   Our first thought should be to give glory to God.

Key Word: Triumph, v. 1.
Strong Verses: 2, 6, 7, 18.
Christ Seen: Bitter water (v. 23) in the path of God's leading, remind us of the trials that come to God's people for their edification, not punishment. The tree (cross, Gal. 3:13) cast into the bitter waters, will make them all sweet.

CHAPTER SIXTEEN

Contents: Murmuring of the people. Manna and quails given by God.
Conclusion: The believer is apt to forget a thousand mercies in the presence of one trifling privation. God is longsuffering. Better to be in a desert with God than in the brick kilns of Egypt with Pharaoh.
Key Word: Murmuring, v. 2.
Strong Verses: 4, 7, 12.
Christ Seen: Jesus, the Bread of Life (John 6) is the true wilderness bread for believers, ministered by the Spirit through the Word. Christ may be partaken of unreservedly but we have no more of Him than faith appropriates. v. 16.

CHAPTER SEVENTEEN

Contents: Smitten rock at Meribah.
Conclusion: Fed by the Bread of Life; refreshed by the Water of Life (John 7:37) means victory for the believer in every conflict with the world, the flesh and the devil.
Key Word: Jehovah-nissi (The Lord our banner), v. 15.
Strong Verses: 7, 15.
Christ Seen: Christ is the Rock (1 Cor. 10:4) He was smitten, and resulting from His finished work was the outpouring of the Holy Spirit giving power to all those who believe.

CHAPTER EIGHTEEN

Contents: Moses joined by his wife and children. Judges selected to solve the problems of the people.
Conclusion: Telling of God's wondrous works is good to the use of edifying What we have the joy of, let God have the praise of, thereby confirming others to faith and encouraging them to real worship.
Key Word: Told, v. 8 (testimony).
Strong Verses: 8, 9, 10.
Christ Seen: It will be noticed (Num. 11:14-17) that God ignored Jethro's counsel and his man-made organization, putting in its place, His own order (v. 18). We are not called to service on the ground of our ability, but Christ's ability (Phil. 4:13), in whom we trust.

CHAPTER NINETEEN

Contents: Israel at Sinai and the preparation for receiving the law.
Conclusion: Humble reverence should possess the minds of those who draw near to God for we are sinners in the presence of a holy and righteous Judge; mean creatures before the Mighty Creator.
Key Word: Ready, vv. 11, 15.
Promise: v. 5, 6.
Christ Seen: (Cp. 1 Pet. 2:9; Rev. 1:6; 5:10 with Ex. 19:5). Note that what under law, was conditional, under grace is freely given in Christ to every believer. Note also that God did not impose law until it was proposed and accepted by man.

CHAPTER TWENTY

Contents: Ten commandments delivered to Moses at Sinai.
Conclusion: A holy and righteous God has holy and righteous standards. Those who love God will constantly endeavor to live as He requires, enabled by the Holy Spirit.
Key Word: Commands, v. 6.
Strong Verses: 3-17.
Christ Seen: Law proposes life and righteousness as the end to be attained by keeping it, but proves at the outset that man is in a state of death

(Rom. 5:20; 7:7, 13; 3:20). Life and righteousness cannot come by that which only curses, but only through the grace of God in Christ.

CHAPTER TWENTY-ONE
Contents: Laws concerning servants. Injuries to the person.
Conclusion: The great God of heaven stoops to take interest in the detail affairs between man and man and makes regulations even as to the loss of a tooth.
Key Word: Judgments, v. 1.
Strong Verse: 12.
Christ Seen: v. 5. Here we have an illustration of Christ's devotedness to the Father. (Ps. 40:7, 8). The servant here voluntarily bound himself to perpetual service although free to do as he liked. He was willing to bear the marks of servitude. So Jesus could have eternally occupied heaven, but for our sakes "humbled Himself."

CHAPTER TWENTY-TWO
Contents: Judgments on rights of property; crimes against humanity.
Conclusion: Man's attitude to his fellow man will be based on his attitude to God and His law.
Key Word: Judgments, 21:1.
Strong Verses: 29, 30, 31.
Christ Seen: One is struck by the number of things we are told NOT to do. These negative commands reveal human nature to itself. All is changed in the New Testament through Christ's sacrifice.

CHAPTER TWENTY-THREE
Contents: Judgments on the national feasts. Instructions concerning the conquest of Canaan.
Conclusion: God's angels will keep the believer in the way, though it lie through the enemy's country and will bring him into the place God has prepared. A precept of obedience goes with every promise.
Key Word: Judgments, 21:1.
Strong Verses: 7, 12. Promises: 20, 22, 25.
Christ Seen: Familiarity with idolators is forbidden (32, 33). The believer by familiar converse with false worshippers, is often drawn into worship with them and his detestation of sin wears off. Those who walk closely with Christ will have a great sensitiveness to sin (Lk. 5:8).

CHAPTER TWENTY-FOUR
Contents: Order of worship prescribed, pending the building of the tabernacle.
Conclusion: The unapproachable glory of God tells a sinner to keep off, but the altar shows him how he can feast and worship in God's presence.
Key Word: Worship, v. 1.
Strong Verses: 8, 17.
Christ Seen: We never hear "draw near" (Heb. 10:22) from the shadows of the law, for Christ's work was not then done which entitled the sinner to draw near. Law says "worship afar off."

CHAPTER TWENTY-FIVE
Contents: Moses in the mount; first directions concerning the tabernacle.
Conclusion: The only way for God and man to meet is in the precise way and place which He has appointed (v. 22). When a righteous God and a ruined sinner meet on a bloodsprinkled platform, all is well. (1 Pet. 1:18, 19).
Key Word: Pattern, v. 9.
Promise: v. 22.
Christ Seen: The tabernacle in every detail foreshadows Christ. Gold is a type of deity, silver of redemption, brass of judgment, blue the heavenly color, purple for royalty, scarlet for atonement, etc.

CHAPTER TWENTY-SIX
Contents: Further directions regarding the tabernacle.
Conclusion: The wonders of God's presence are known only to those, who by the proper ceremonies, have come inside the curtains of His grace. The natural man is screened out from the things of the Spirit.

Key Word: Fashion (pattern), v. 30.
Strong Verse: 30.
Christ Seen: We as Christ's followers have here no continuing city, being strangers and pilgrims through this world to a better land, having a moveable tabernacle. The presence of Christ is not tied to any place (Matt. 28:20).

CHAPTER TWENTY-SEVEN

Contents: Directions about the brazen altar and the court.
Conclusion: Sinful man dare not approach God (at the ark) Heb. 9:8; but God approaches man as a sinner through Christ (brazen altar). There were blood prints all the way from the ark to the altar. Redeemed on that path, the sinner is safe in the courts of God.
Key Word: Pattern, 25:9.
Strong Verse: 20.
Christ Seen: In Jesus, God comes down in grace to the sinner. In Jesus the sinner is brought up in righteousness to God. These are our only grounds of standing before God.

CHAPTER TWENTY-EIGHT

Contents: Directions about the priesthood.
Conclusion: The believer need never fear God has forgotten him for the Great High Priest bears the names of His own on His breast before God, presenting them as "those accepted in the beloved."
Key Word: Ministry, v. 1.
Strong Verses: 29, 41.
Christ Seen: Every true believer, through identification with Christ, is an earthly priest of God's family (Rev. 1:8) properly clothed for the work, (Rev. 19:7, 8), and should be duly consecrated and sanctified for his work of testimony.

CHAPTER TWENTY-NINE

Contents: Consecration of the priests and the offerings.
Conclusion: Those representing God should be set apart in solemn consecration. All their service must be based on the ground of the burnt offering.
Key Word: Consecration, v. 26.
Strong Verses: 18. Promises: 45, 46.
Christ Seen: Consecration means "to fill the hand." It is not the believer filling God's hand. In the arms of Aaron's sons were put the parts of the sacrifice which speak of the inherent richness and power of Christ. This was their acknowledgment that the power for service was not in themselves, but in another. This is consecration.

CHAPTER THIRTY

Contents: The altar of incense and the brazen laver.
Conclusion: (See Psa. 141:2). The prayer of a contrite believer ascends as a fragrant cloud to God. (Prov. 15:8).
Key Word: Incense (worship), v. 7.
Strong Verse: 30.
Christ Seen: Fire under the incense altar brought out the fragrance (Rom. 8: 26, 27). The fire was from the blood-sprinkled altar (Heb. 10: 19, 20). Their prayers were based on the intercession of a priest (Rom. 8:34).

CHAPTER THIRTY-ONE

Contents: The tabernacle and its workmen. Sabbath made a sign between God and Israel.
Conclusion: When God gives a commission, He will, in some measure give the qualifications according as the service is. When God has work to be done, He will not be without instruments.
Key Word: Workmanship, v. 3.
Strong Verses: 3, 17.
Christ Seen: When Christ sent His apostles to rear the Gospel tabernacle He poured out His Holy Spirit upon them to enable them to speak with power the wonderful works of God.

CHAPTER THIRTY-TWO

Contents: The broken law; Israel worships a golden calf. Intercession of Moses.

Conclusion: It is a great sin to make gold, or anything else, a god, as those do who let it become a supreme object of their affections, taking the place of God in any degree.

Key Word: Great Sin, v. 30.

Strong Verses: 26, 29, 32.

Christ Seen: Moses typified Christ, who went above (Acts 1:9) telling the people to tarry. In His absence, some forget his promised return (John. 14:3; Acts 1:11) and make themselves gods (2 Tim. 3:1-4; 4:3-4; Matt. 24:12) denying His return (2 Pet. 3:3-4; Matt. 24:48, 49). Jesus will come unexpectedly (Matt. 25:13) punishing evil doers (2 Thess. 2:7, 8) who are naked (Rev. 6·16, 17) and gathering the true to Himself (1 Thess. 4:13-18).

CHAPTER THIRTY-THREE

Contents: The journey to be resumed. God's presence assured.

Conclusion: God's special presence with us in the wilderness by His Spirit and grace to direct, defend and comfort, is the surest pledge of His acceptance of us. The bitter fruit of sin in the believer is the lost sense of His presence, which will cause any true believer to lament.

Key Word: Presence, v. 14.

Strong Verses: 11, 20. Promise: 14.

Christ Seen: Moses, as a prince who had power with God, was a type of Christ the great Intercessor whom the Father heareth always. Through His intercession, we obtain constant assurance of the blessings of salvation.

CHAPTER THIRTY-FOUR

Contents: Second tables of the law. The new vision and commission.

Conclusion: (12-17). We cannot expect the benefit of God's promises unless we make conscience of His precepts. God's name is "Jealous" and we cannot worship Him aright if we do not worship Him alone.

Key Word: Tables of testimony, v. 29.

Strong Verses: 12, 29. Promises: 6, 7.

Christ Seen: The shining of Moses' face was a great honor to him but nothing compared to the glory which excelled. We read of Jesus, that not only His face shone, but His whole body and His raiment was glistening (Luke 9:29).

CHAPTER THIRTY-FIVE

Contents: People instructed as to the tabernacle. The gifts of the people for the work.

Conclusion: God loves a cheerful giver and is best pleased with a free-will offering. Our gifts are our acknowledgment that we receive all from Him and dedicate all to Him.

Key Word: Gifts, v. 5.

Strong Verses: 21, 29.

Christ Seen: If we cannot do what others do for God, we are not to sit still and no nothing. Though our offering gains us no reputation with men, if given according to ability, it does not fail of acceptance with Him. (2 Cor. 8:12). Christ's rewards are based on the "will to do," not on ability to do.

CHAPTER THIRTY-SIX

Contents: The tabernacle work begun. The curtains, coverings, sockets, bars, vail.

Conclusion: The talents with which God has entrusted the believer are not to be laid up but laid out. Have your tools ready and God will find you work.

Key Word: Work, v. 1.

Strong Verses: 1, 5, 6.

Christ Seen: Precious souls redeemed by Christ are the material of the Gospel tabernacle. (1 Pet. 2:5). Those called to the building of this house are those whom God has in some measure made fit for the work. Ability and willingness are the two things to be regarded in the call of the Christian worker.

CHAPTER THIRTY-SEVEN

Contents: Making of the ark, mercy seat, table, candlestick, altar.

Conclusion: As the workmen were to take great care to make all according to God's pattern, so the believer should have respect to all the light God gives, even to every iota and tittle of His commandments. God delights in sincere obedience and keeps exact account of it.

Key Word: Work, 36:1.

Strong Verses: 6, 9.

Christ Seen: Jesus Christ, the great propitiation, has made reconciliation for the believer, restoring communion with God. From the mercy seat, He accepts us and teaches us, and under the shadow of the Spirit we are safe.

CHAPTER THIRTY-EIGHT

Contents: Altar of burnt offering, laver, court, gate.

Conclusion: God wants of us explicit obedience to His revealed plans. His plans may not be accompanied with reasons, but they always have blessings attached.

Key Word: Work, v. 1. 36:1.

Strong Verse: 21.

Christ Seen: On the altar of burnt offering all the sacrifices were made. The altar is a type of Calvary's cross on which Christ, our whole burnt offering, offered Himself without spot to God (Heb. 9:14).

CHAPTER THIRTY-NINE

Contents: Garments for Aaron.

Conclusion: All believers are spiritual priests and their service-clothes are provided (Rev. 19:8). All who converse with them should be able to see that they are properly clothed as God's representatives.

Key Word: Garments, v. 1.

Strong Verses: 42, 43.

Christ Seen: Christ, our High Priest, in undertaking the work of man's restoration, wore the clothes of service—the gifts and graces of the Holy Spirit, which He had without measure.

CHAPTER FORTY

Contents: Tabernacle set up. God's glory manifested.

Conclusion: God will dwell with those who prepare Him a habitation. Where God has a throne and an altar in the heart, there is a living temple in which the Spirit will be manifested.

Key Word: Finished, v. 33.

Strong Verses: 17, 34, 38.

Christ Seen: What the glory cloud was to the tabernacle, the Holy Spirit, Christ's representative in the believer, (Jn. 16:7) is to the Church and the temple, which is the believer's body. (1 Cor. 6:19).

LEVITICUS

Key Thought: Atonement	Number of Chapters: 27	Key Verse: 16:34	Christ seen as: High Priest

Writer of the Book:	Date:	Conclusion of the Book: Access of the redeemed to God is only through
Moses	About 1500 B. C.	the blood. Holiness of the redeemed is impera- tive.

SUMMARY

CHAPTER ONE

Contents: The burnt offering laws.
Conclusion: Utter dependence upon the sacrifices, typifying the great sac-
rifice of Christ on which the iniquity of us all was laid is God's require-
ment. (The laying on of the offerer's hands signified identification of the
believer with his offering).
Key Word: Burnt sacrifice, v. 3.
Strong Verse: 4.
Christ Seen: The burnt offering stands for Christ who offered Himself
without spot to God in delight to do the Father's will even unto death.
Fire, symbol of God's holiness, consumes the offering.

CHAPTER TWO

Contents: Meat offering and first-fruits laws.
Conclusion: Leaven, typifying malice, wickedness and human pride is not
accepted in spiritual sacrifices. Take heed of those sins which will certainly spoil the acceptableness of worship.
Key Word: Fine flour offering, v. 1. First-fruits, v. 12.
Strong Verse: 11.
Christ Seen: Fine flour speaks of the balance of the character of Christ;
fire of His testing by suffering; frankincense of the fragrance of His life
to God; absence of leaven, His character as "The Truth;" absence of
honey—His life was not mere natural sweetness which may exist apart
from God; oil mingled, Christ as born of the Spirit; oil upon, Christ
baptized with the Spirit.

CHAPTER THREE

Contents: Peace offering laws.
Conclusion: In Christ, God and the sinner meet in peace. God is propitiated
and the sinner reconciled; both alike satisfied with Christ's work. "He
is our peace."
Key Word: Peace offering, v. 1.
Strong Verse: 2.
Christ Seen: Details of the peace offering, typifying Christ's propitiatory work,
bring out the thought of fellowship, hence the peace offering is set forth
as affording food for the priests, (7:31-34).

CHAPTER FOUR

Contents: Sin offering laws.
Conclusion: Even sins done in ignorance need to be atoned for by sacrifice.
To plead ignorance when charged with sin will not deliver. Our only
hope is in acceptance of Him who "became sin for us."
Key Word: Sin offering, v. 3.
Strong Verse: 3.
Christ Seen: The sin offering is Christ seen laden with the believer's sins,
absolutely in the sinner's place and stead, and not as in the sweet savor
offerings, in His own perfections. Read Isa. 53.

CHAPTER FIVE

Contents: Trespass offering laws.
Conclusion: Even when a man unwittingly breaks the laws of God, full restitution must be made, which is possible only through the presentation of the sacrifice.
Key Word: Trespass offering, v. 6.
Strong Verses: 17, 18.
Christ Seen: The chapter teaches us that we all have need to pray with David, "Cleanse thou me from secret faults." Ps. 19:12. Christ is the searcher of hearts and the only One who can cleanse us. 1 Jn. 1:7, 9.

CHAPTER SIX

Contents: Further directions about offerings.
Conclusion: Since Christ has "made His soul an offering for sin" we should seek to make restitution to any person we have injured or defrauded, and until we do, we will not enjoy the comfort of His forgiveness of our sins.
Key Word: Offerings.
Strong Verses: 6, 7.
Christ Seen: Trespass against our neighbor is trespass against God, because it is an affront to our Saviour who has redeemed us and the injury reflects upon God who has commanded that we should love our neighbor as ourselves.

CHAPTER SEVEN

Contents: Further directions concerning offerings.
Conclusion: We are not left to our liberty in the solemn acts of religious worship, but are under obligation to perform them in the manner God directs in His Word.
Key Word: Offerings, v. 1.
Strong Verses: 37, 38.
Christ Seen: Use of leaven, v. 13, is significant. In v. 12, as the believer thanks God for his peace, he first of all presents Christ, Eph. 2:13, so leaven is excluded. In v. 13, he gives thanks for his participation in the peace, and the leaven signifies, that although having peace through Christ, the believer in himself is not perfect.

CHAPTER EIGHT

Contents: Consecration of Aaron and sons for the priesthood.
Conclusion: All who minister about holy things must have an eye to God's commands as their rule and warrant, for only in the observance of these may they expect to be owned of God in their service.
Key Word: Sanctification, v. 12.
Strong Verses: 13, 36.
Christ Seen: Priests did not consecrate themselves. Moses was the appointed instrument of God to do this work as it is Christ who is our consecrator. The sons of Aaron simply presented themselves for the work. See Rom. 12:1, where the believer presents himself unreservedly to Christ.

CHAPTER NINE

Contents: Priests begin their ministry before the Lord.
Conclusion: God draws nigh to those who draw nigh to Him in the appointed way—the offering of faith in His Son, the Great Sacrifice being acceptable to Him.
Key Word: Offering presented, v. 12.
Strong Verses: 6, 23, 24.
Christ Seen: God does not ordain priests to be idle. Without a day's respite after their consecration, Aaron and his sons were immediately employed. God's spiritual priests have work laid out for them by Christ, the great High Priest.

CHAPTER TEN

Contents: Strange fire of Nadab and Abihu.
Conclusion: It is fatal to act in the things of God without seeking the mind of God (will worship, Col. 2:23.)
Key Word: Strange fire, v. 1.

Strong Verses: 9.
Christ Seen: Strange fire typifies any use of carnal means to kindle the fires of devotion and praise, which, if true, come only from Christ and the Holy Spirit.

CHAPTER ELEVEN

Contents: The proper food for God's people defined.
Conclusion: The body is the Lord's and it is sin against God to prejudice health for the pleasing of appetite.
Key Word: Eating, v. 2.
Strong Verse: 45.
Christ Seen: God's covenant people, Israel, by having a diet peculiar to themselves, would be kept from familiar conversation with idolatrous neighbors. The laws, however, were probably primarily sanitary and necessary to the good of the people. Let us remember that Christ will concern Himself in our social as well as our religious life if we look to Him and will direct us to that which is best for us.

CHAPTER TWELVE

Contents: The law of motherhood.
Conclusion: All are conceived and born in sin (Psa. 51:5) for, if the root be impure, so is the branch. It is only by Christ, the great sin offering, that the corruption of the child nature is done away.
Key Word: Conceiving, v. 2.
Strong Verse: 8.
Christ Seen: Our Lord, though not conceived in sin—his mother accomplished the days of purification' (Luke 2:22-24) and so poor were His parents that they could not bring a lamb.

CHAPTER THIRTEEN

Contents: Laws concerning those afflicted with leprosy.
Conclusion: Man is beset with troops of diseases on every side and all entered by sin. If not afflicted with any of these terrible sores, we are bound to praise God and glorify Him the more with our bodies.
Key Word: Leprosy, v. 2.
Strong Verses: 45, 46.
Christ Seen: Leprosy is a figure of the moral pollution of men's minds by sin, which is the leprosy of the soul, curable only through Christ's atoning work.

CHAPTER FOURTEEN

Contents: Laws concerning cleansing of lepers.
Conclusion: As the leper was cleansed from his fearful malady through the water and the blood, so Christ comes into the soul for its cleansing "by water and blood" (1 John 5:6). See John 19:34.
Key Word: Cleansing, v. 2.
Strong Verse: 20.
Christ Seen: The leper did nothing toward his own cleansing. He was sought out by the priest and cleansed by him. Our cleansing is by Christ alone, not by anything we can do. Titus 3:5.

CHAPTER FIFTEEN

Contents: Imperative personal cleanliness.
Conclusion: Unclean diseases of the flesh are a wound and dishonor, the consumption of the body, and a sin which is often its own punishment more than any other.
Key Word: Unclean, v. 2.
Strong Verses: 30, 31.
Christ Seen: The chapter speaks to us of the contagion of sin and the danger of being polluted by conversing with those who are polluted. Christ alone can keep us in this epidemic of sin. (Heb. 12:1, 2; 7:25).

CHAPTER SIXTEEN

Contents: Day of atonement laws.
Conclusion: "Without the shedding of blood there is no remission for sin."
Key Word: Atonement, v. 6.
Strong Verses: 30, 34.
Christ Seen: As the priest entered the holiest with the blood, so Christ

entered heaven itself with His own blood for us (Heb. 9:11, 12). His blood makes the throne of God a mercy seat which otherwise must have been a throne of judgment.

CHAPTER SEVENTEEN

Contents: The place of sacrifice and the sanctity of the blood.

Conclusion: God's people all meet at one altar in His appointed way, thereby preserving unity and family love among themselves.

Key Word: Blood, v. 11.

Strong Verse: 11.

Christ Seen: The worship of Christians is not now confined to one place (John 4:21; 1 Tim. 2:8) yet Christ is our altar and through Him, God dwells among us by His Spirit. It is in Him that our sacrifices are acceptable to God. 1 Pet. 2:5.

CHAPTER EIGHTEEN

Contents: Relationship and walk of God's people.

Conclusion: Fleshly lusts war against the soul and will certainly be the ruin of it, if God's mercy and grace prevent not.

Key Word: Abominations, v. 26.

Strong Verses: 3, 4, 5, 24, 26, 30.

Christ Seen: There are many sins which level men with the beasts but these here mentioned sink men lower than beasts. Even in the Christian the flesh lusteth against the Spirit. Only as we are filled with the mind of Jesus may we live in victory. He is our Victory. Phil. 2:5.

CHAPTER NINETEEN

Contents: Further laws concerning proper relationships.

Conclusion: God's people being distinguished from all other people by a peculiar relationship with Him through Christ, should teach them real separation from the things of the world and flesh and entire devotedness to the will of God.

Key Word: Holy, v. 2.

Strong Verses: 2, 12, 18, 31.

Christ Seen: Notice the caution against having anything to do with spiritism. Seek not to them for discovery or advice and regard not their offers. It is an abomination to God. "One is our Master, even Christ." "In all thy ways acknowledge Him and He will direct thy paths."

CHAPTER TWENTY

Contents: Further laws on relationship and walk of God's people.

Conclusion: God has distinguished His people from all others by a holy covenant with them through Christ, therefore they should distinguish themselves by consistent and holy living.

Key Word: Separated, v. 24.

Strong Verses: 6, 8, 22, 23, 24.

Christ Seen: Observe again the plain warning against spiritism. What greater madness than to go to an enemy for advice. Spiritualism is spiritual adultery, giving honor to the devil which is due to Christ alone. What direction we need we are to seek from Christ.

CHAPTER TWENTY-ONE

Contents: Relationship and walk of the priests.

Conclusion: Those whose office it is to instruct in God's truth must do it by example as well as precept.

Key Word: Holy, v. 6.

Strong Verses: 6, 8.

Christ Seen: We must honor those whom Christ has called as His representatives, and every Christian should consider himself as concerned to be the guardians of their honor, who are ambassadors of Christ, lest His cause suffer.

CHAPTER TWENTY-TWO

Contents: Separation of the priests; perfection of the sacrifices.

Conclusion: Those contract great guilt who profane sacred things, doing in their own uncleanness, service which pretends to be hallowed to Him.

Key Word: Separate, v. 2.

Strong Verses: 3, 31, 32.
Christ Seen: v. 19 a law to make sacrifices fitter to be types of Christ, the great Sacrifice from which all these derive their virtue. He is called a "lamb without spot and without blemish" (1 Pet. 1:19).

CHAPTER TWENTY-THREE

Contents: The feasts of Jehovah.
Conclusion: The Sabbaths of the Lord in our dwellings will be their beauty, strength and safety (by rising on the first day of the week and meeting His disciples again and again on that day, Christ appointed that day a holy convocation).
Key Word: Feasts, v. 2.
Strong Verses: 3, 22.
Christ Seen: As given to Israel, there were seven great religious festivals. Passover, feast of unleavened bread, feast of first-fruits, feast of Pentecost, feast of Trumpets, Day of Atonement, feast of Tabernacles,—all typical of Christ.

CHAPTER TWENTY-FOUR

Contents: Penalty of blasphemy.
Conclusion: If those who profane the name of God escape punishment from men, yet the Lord our God will not suffer them to escape His righteous judgments.
Key Word: Blasphemy, v. 11.
Strong Verse: 15.
Christ Seen: v. 12. Those who sit in judgment should sincerely desire, and by prayer to Christ for wisdom, should endeavor to know, the mind of the Lord. Christ is "made unto us wisdom." (1 Cor. 1:30).

CHAPTER TWENTY-FIVE

Contents: Laws of the land. Sabbatic year and year of Jubilee.
Conclusion: The blessing of God upon our provision will make a little go a long way and satisfy even the poor with bread. We can lose nothing by faith in God's promises and self-denial in our obedience.
Key Word: Sabbatic year, v. 4.
Strong Verses: 18, 19, 35, 36, 37.
Christ Seen: v. 25, the kinsman redeemer is an illustration of Christ who assumed our nature that He might be our kinsman, redeeming our inheritance which we by sin had forfeited. He made a settlement for all who become allied with Him by faith.

CHAPTER TWENTY-SIX

Contents: Conditions of blessing and warnings of chastisement.
Conclusion: All adverse circumstances that come upon a people are God's servants, used often as a scourge wherewith He chastises a provoking people. If less judgments will not do their work, God will send greater, for when He judges a nation He will overcome.
Key Word: Punishment, v. 24.
Strong Verses: 40, 41, 42. Promises: *, 9.
Christ Seen: If God's people faithfully observe His statutes they are assured that His hand (vv. 7, 8) will so signally appear with them that no disproportion of numbers could make against them. If we put ourselves on Christ's side by obeying His precepts, He will champion our side.

CHAPTER TWENTY-SEVEN

Contents: Laws concerning dedicated persons and things.
Conclusion: We should be cautious in making vows and constant in keeping those we have made. What is once devoted to the Lord should be His forever by a perpetual covenant.
Key Word: Vows, v. 2.
Strong Verse: 30.
Christ Seen: Let us not think because we are not tied to ceremonial laws that we are free of religious obligations. "Having boldness to enter into the holiest by the blood of Jesus, let us draw near with a true heart in full assurance of faith" saying "Blessed be God for the gift of His Son."

NUMBERS

Key Thought:	Number of Chapters:	Key Verse:	Christ seen as:
Discipline	36	33:1	Star of Jacob

Writer of the Book:	Date:	Conclusion of the Book:
		The redeemed are saved
Moses	About 1500 B. C.	to serve and must be on
		their guard against un-
		belief.

SUMMARY

CHAPTER ONE

Contents: Moses commanded to take census.
Conclusion: The Lord knows all those that are His (2 Tim. 2:19) by name (Phil. 4:3) and even the hairs of their heads are numbered. To all others He will say "I never knew you."
Key Word: Numbered, v. 2.
Strong Verse: 54.
Christ Seen: For Christians, too, there is a census, for Christ numbers His jewels and "knoweth them that are His." "In thy book all my members are written."

CHAPTER TWO

Contents: Order of the host and arrangement of the camp.
Conclusion: God is a God of order and not confusion, thus the camp of the saints should be compact, everyone knowing and keeping his God appointed place.
Key Word: Camp, v. 3.
Strong Verse: 34.
Christ Seen: The chapter furnishes an illustration of the movable state of Christ's people in the world, "strangers and pilgrims." At the same time it is a military state—our life is a warfare, as "good soldiers of Jesus Christ."

CHAPTER THREE

Contents: Order of the host; placing of the Levites.
Conclusion: Having gifts differing according to the grace given us—if ministry, let us wait on our ministering (Rom. 12:7). God has a place of definite service for each of His children.
Key Word: Levites, v. 6.
Strong Verse: 13.
Christ Seen: The Church is called "the church of the firstborn" which is redeemed not as the firstborn of the Israelites, with silver and gold, but ransomed with the precious blood of Christ.

CHAPTER FOUR

Contents: The service of the Kohathites. Gershonites and Merarites.
Conclusion: There is a service appointed to each of God's people in connection with His Church, and no matter how obscure the place it is important in God's program.
Key Word: Service, v. 4.
Strong Verse: 49.
Christ Seen: v. 3. They were not employed until 30 years old. This is not obligatory on Christ's ministers, but gives us a suggestion that, His ambassadors should not be novices but should be men of steadiness, and ripeness of judgment, knowing Christ well.

CHAPTER FIVE

Contents: Defilement of the camp.
Conclusion: The purity of the church must be as carefully guarded as the order of it and it is for the edification of it that those who are openly

and incorrigibly vicious should be cut off from communion until they repent.

Key Word: Defilement, v. 2.

Strong Verse: 3.

Christ Seen: Christians need to be saved not only from sin but from the appearance of sin, and a walk in fellowship with Christ secures them from both. He also is sufficient to keep us from causeless or unjust suspicions of others.

CHAPTER SIX

Contents: The Nazarite laws.

Conclusion: The Christian should be a true Nazarite, fully consecrated to God and separated from the things of this world, thus securing the special blessing of God.

Key Word: Separation, v. 2.

Strong Verses: 24, 25, 26.

Christ Seen: The Nazarite type found a perfect fulfillment in Jesus who was "holy, harmless, undefiled and separate from sinners" (Heb. 7:26) and allowed no mere natural claims to divert Him.

CHAPTER SEVEN

Contents: The gifts of the princes.

Conclusion: The great men should with their wealth and power uphold the work of God and should make conscience of being devout because of their great influence.

Key Word: Offering, v. 3.

Strong Verse: 89.

Christ Seen: Observe that the offerings of the princes were identical yet each is separately recorded by the pen of inspiration, showing how God takes notice of every whole-hearted gift, made in Christ's name. Mark 12:41-44. Christ is God's Treasurer.

CHAPTER EIGHT

Contents: Cleansing of the Levites for the ministry of the tabernacle.

Conclusion: All Christians, and especially ministers, should cleanse themselves from all filthiness of the flesh and spirit, perfecting holiness in the fear of the Lord. Those who bear the vessels of the Lord must be clean.

Key Word: Cleanse, v. 6.

Strong Verses: 21, 22.

Christ Seen: It is a great kindness to the Church that God has appointed overseers to go before the people in the things of God and religious worship. When Christ ascended, He supplied the gifts for His work (Eph. 4:8-12).

CHAPTER NINE

Contents: Law of the Passover; the guiding cloud.

Conclusion: Those who by circumstances are compelled to absent themselves from God's ordinances, may expect the favor of God's grace under their afflictions, and those who of choice absent themselves may justly expect the tokens of God's displeasure.

Key Word: Passover, v. 2.

Strong Verses: 8, 18.

Christ Seen: As it was safe and pleasant going for Israel when led by the cloud, token of God's presence, so there is peace for the Christian who has set Christ, the Great Shepherd, before him.

CHAPTER TEN

Contents: The first march of the camp.

Conclusion: Those who have given themselves up to the leading of God's Word and Spirit, steer a safe course and so long as they walk in fellowship with their Guide, they need not fear losing the way.

Key Word: Journeying, v. 13.

Strong Verses: 33, 34.

Christ Seen: Those who through Christ, are bound for the heavenly Canaan should invite and encourage their friends to go along with them. (Jno. 1:46).

CHAPTER ELEVEN

Contents: Complaints about the manna and the consequences.

Conclusion: Though God graciously gives us leave to complain to Him when there is cause, yet He is justly provoked if we are fretful when there is no cause and especially when we have been surrounded with His special favors.

Key Word: Complaining, v. 1.

Christ Seen: Unconverted church members with no healthy appetite for the Bread of God, the things of Christ, will clamor for things pleasing to the flesh in the work and way of the church.

CHAPTER TWELVE

Contents: Murmuring of Miriam and Aaron and the consequences.

Conclusion: We have reason to be exceedingly cautious of saying or doing anything against the servants of God, for God will plead their cause if they are true servants and will reckon with the critic.

Key Word: Criticism, (speaking against), v. 1.

Strong Verses: 3, 8.

Christ Seen: When we hand our cause over to Christ, our Shepherd, He takes a hand for us (v. 5), rebuking the enemy and avenger. As Moses won the commendation of faithfulness so every Christian may hear Christ's "Well done."

CHAPTER THIRTEEN

Contents: Spies sent into Kadesh-barnea, and their report.

Conclusion: Faith looks at difficulties through God but unbelief looks through difficulties at God. All things are possible, if but promised, to him who believes.

Key Word: Searching, v. 25.

Strong Verses: 27, 30.

Christ Seen: Many Christians are forever getting frightened at these tremendous giants in the land who make them feel like grasshoppers. Giants cannot stand in the way of Christ's work if His people will be valiant in His strength. (Phil. 4:13).

CHAPTER FOURTEEN

Contents: Murmuring over the spies' reports and the consequences.

Conclusion: All the dangers that we are in are from our own distrust. We would succeed against all enemies if we did not make God our enemy. We are excluded from God's blessing only by excluding ourselves.

Key Word: Murmured, v. 2.

Strong Verses: 8, 9, 18.

Christ Seen: vv. 13-19. The best pleas in prayer are those taken from Christ's honor. The more danger there is of others reproaching Christ's power, the more desirous we should be to see it glorified.

CHAPTER FIFTEEN

Contents: Burnt and free will offerings.

Conclusion: Sins committed ignorantly must have atonement made for them, for although God is very merciful with the ignorant, their ignorance cannot justify them. The presumptuous sinner invites severe judgments.

Key Word: Offerings, v. 3.

Strong Verse: 30.

Christ Seen: v. 35. Sins of ignorance may be forgiven (vv. 22-29). Debts of shortcoming need pardon equally as do trespasses. Through Christ we may confidently count on forgiveness for evil things done unwittingly. (1 Tim. 1:12-14; Heb. 5:2).

CHAPTER SIXTEEN

Contents: The gainsaying of Korah.

Conclusion: Proud and ambitious men projecting their own advancement by thrusting themselves into a place to which God has not appointed them, hurry on to a shameful fall.

Key Word: Murmur, v. 11.

Strong Verses: 26, 48.

Christ Seen: Men who have been true to Christ need not fear being slurred by others. Men who are most serviceable to Christ are often abused most shamefully, as was Christ Himself, although He was without a flaw.

CHAPTER SEVENTEEN

Contents: Aaron's rod that budded.
Conclusion: Fruitfulness is the best evidence of a divine call. The plants of God's setting will flourish.
Key Word: Chosen, v. 5.
Strong Verse: 8.
Christ Seen: The budding rod is a type of Christ, who in His resurrection was owned of God as High Priest. All other authors of religion have died. Christ alone is exalted as High Priest.

CHAPTER EIGHTEEN

Contents: Regulations concerning maintenance of the priests.
Conclusion: We are to value as a great gift of divine bounty those called to be serviceable to us in the work of the church.
Key Word: Given, v. 6.
Strong Verses: 6, 12, 20.
Christ Seen: God orders that Christ's ministers should be well recompensed that they might be the more entirely addicted to their ministry and not be disturbed in it by worldly care. Christ alone must be their portion here on earth.

CHAPTER NINETEEN

Contents: The ordinance of the red heifer.
Conclusion: The believer needs constant cleansing from defilement contracted in his pilgrim walk through the world.
Key Word: Unclean, v. 7.
Strong Verse: 2.
Christ Seen: Water typifies the Spirit and the Word. The Spirit uses the Word to convict the believer of some sin allowed. Thus convicted, he remembers that the guilt of his sin has been met by the sacrifice of Christ, therefore instead of despairing, he judges and confesses the sin and is forgiven and cleansed. (1 John 1).

CHAPTER TWENTY

Contents: Water from the rock and Moses' sin.
Conclusion: God is able to supply His people with necessaries even in their greatest straits and in the utmost failure of second causes.
Key Word: Complaint, v. 3.
Strong Verse: 12.
Christ Seen: v. 8. The rock Christ (1 Cor. 10:4) once smitten, needs not to be smitten (crucified) again. Moses' act implied in type that the one sacrifice was ineffectual. The abundant water speaks of the streams of grace.

CHAPTER TWENTY-ONE

Contents: Victories of Israel; the serpent of brass.
Conclusion: Those who cry without cause will be given just cause to cry and they will be compelled to receive their course from God in God's way.
Key Word: Sinned, v. 7.
Strong Verse: 9.
Christ Seen: Serpent here, a symbol of sin judged; brass speaks of divine judgment. The brass serpent becomes a type of Christ "made sin for us" (2 Cor. 5:21; John 3:14-15) in bearing our judgment.

CHAPTER TWENTY-TWO

Contents: Balaam's visit to Balak and the strange warning on the way.
Conclusion: The enemies of God's people are restless and unwearied in their attempts, but He who sits in heaven laughs at them and often uses "foolish things to confound the wise."
Key Word: Balaam, v. 5.
Strong Verses: 12, 38.

Christ Seen: It is impossible to serve Christ and Satan at the same time—to speak as He bids us (Lk. 12:11) but to please the enemy and pocket his gold. (See 2 Pet. 2:15-16).

CHAPTER TWENTY-THREE

Contents: Balaam blesses instead of curses Israel.

Conclusion: Those who have the good will of heaven may expect the ill will of hell but God will not suffer real injury done to His people and what is done against them He takes as done against Himself and reckons accordingly.

Key Word: Blessed, v. 11.

Strong Verses: 8, 12, 21.

Christ Seen: In this chapter God testifies to the standing of Israel as a redeemed people, in spite of their bad moral state which awaited His discipline. So, in Christ the believer's standing is perfect though our state may require discipline (1 Cor. 11:30-32; Heb. 12).

CHAPTER TWENTY-FOUR

Contents: Balaam foretells prosperity for Israel.

Conclusion: Those who oppose God and His people will sooner or later be made to see themselves wretchedly deceived.

Key Word: Latter days, v. 14.

Strong Verses: 13, 17.

Christ Seen: v. 17 is an illustrious prophecy of Christ who is coming to reign in great glory, not only over Israel but over all men.

CHAPTER TWENTY-FIVE

Contents: Sin of Israel with daughters of Moab.

Conclusion: God's people are more endangered by the charms of a smiling world than by the terrors of a frowning world. The daughters of Moab have conquered many strong men who could not be conquered by the sword.

Key Word: Whoredom, v. 1.

Strong Verses: 12, 13.

Christ Seen: Pinehas, v. 11, is pronounced his country's patriot and best friend. To be zealous for Jesus Christ is the best service we can do for the people and service to Him is sure of abounding recognition, if not in this life, in the life hereafter (1 Cor. 15:58).

CHAPTER TWENTY-SIX

Contents: The new generation of Israel numbered.

Conclusion: God is faithful to His threatenings as well as to His promises. Millions may fall to the ground, but His Word cannot fail.

Key Word: Numbered, v. 64.

Strong Verses: 64, 65.

Christ Seen: God is always enumerating His people. Can we claim to be included in the divine enumeration and enrolled in the Lamb's Book of Life? (Rev. 3:5).

CHAPTER TWENTY-SEVEN

Contents: The law of inheritance. Joshua appointed Moses' successor.

Conclusion: The minister of Christ should concern himself in his prayers and endeavors for the rising generation, that work may flourish and the interest of the kingdom be maintained and advanced after he is gone.

Key Word: Appointment (set over), v. 16.

Strong Verses: 16, 17.

Christ Seen: The law-giver brings the people only to the borders of the land of rest. There he must give up. Law cannot bring the soul to rest. This is the prerogative of Joshua. (Jesus, Heb. 4:8).

CHAPTER TWENTY-EIGHT

Contents: The order of offerings.

Conclusion: God asks of all His children continual offerings, v. 3, which intimates that we are to "pray without ceasing" on the ground of Christ's sacrifice, and at least, every morning and evening, v. 4, we are to offer solemn prayer and praise through Christ.

Key Word: Offering, v. 2.
Strong Verse: 2.
Christ Seen: The enumeration of these offerings reminds us how much greater
is our privilege under the dispensation of grace when our offering has
been once for all made.   (Heb. 9:26).

CHAPTER TWENTY-NINE

Contents: Commands concerning the feast of Trumpets, Feast of Tabernacles,
and Day of Atonement.
Conclusion: We must not seek occasion to abate our zeal in God's service nor
be glad of excuses to omit religious duties, but rather rejoice in the many
privileges of worship.   (Not omitting private worship on days we go to
church.   Not omitting secret prayer because of family devotions, etc.).
Key Word: Convocations, v. 1.
Strong Verse: 39.
Christ Seen: We have in Christ, the Lamb of God, an offering that is sufficient
for every day, needing no repetition.   (Heb. 10:10).

CHAPTER THIRTY

Contents: The laws of vows.
Conclusion: Our promises before God are bonds upon the soul and by them
we must conscientiously consider ourselves bound out from all sin and
bound up to the whole will of God.
Key Word: Vows, v. 2.
Strong Verse: 2.

CHAPTER THIRTY-ONE

Contents: The judgment of Midian.
Conclusion: Our worst enemies are those that draw us to sin.   Over all such
enemies there is absolute victory for those who take sides with God
against them.
Key Word: Avenge, v. 3.
Strong Verse: 49.
Christ Seen: The highest law for dealing with personal enemies is found in
Jesus' teachings.   Jesus clearly distinguished between what "they of old"
had said, and His own teachings (Mt. 5:21, 27) which superceded.

CHAPTER THIRTY-TWO

Contents: The choice of the world-borderers.
Conclusion: · Would we choose our portion aright we must look above the
things which are seen—otherwise we will be guided by the lust of the eye
and the pride of life.
Key Word: Inheritance, v. 19.
Strong Verses: 11, 12, 23.
Christ Seen: Reuben and Gad are types of those whose "much cattle" hinder
the full realization of the heavenly inheritance in Christ.   Beware of living
on the world's side of the cross.

CHAPTER THIRTY-THREE

Contents: Summary of the journey from Egypt to Jordan.
Conclusion: It is good for believers to preserve in writing an account of the
providences of God concerning them, showing the series of mercies they
have experienced, that deceitful memories might be helped and ground
given for new faith.
Key Word: Journeys, v. 1.
Strong Verse: 53.
Christ Seen: God has given us in Christ the promise of rest and victory.   Let
us enter upon our inheritance without wandering in by-paths.

CHAPTER THIRTY-FOUR

Contents: Preparations to enter the land.
Conclusion: God sets bounds to our lot; let us therefore set bounds to our
desires and bring our minds to our condition.
Key Word: Borders, v. 4.
Strong Verse: 2.

Christ Seen: God gives to Christ's people but a small share of this world. Those who are seated in heavenly places in Christ have reason to be content with a small pittance of earth.

CHAPTER THIRTY-FIVE

Contents: The cities of refuge.

Conclusion: God would teach us to conceive a dread and horror of the guilt of blood and to be very careful of life, lest even by negligence we occasion the death of any. (This is taught by confinement to the city of refuge, of those who killed even by accident.)

Key Word: Refuge, v. 6.

Strong Verses: 12, 30.

Christ Seen: Christ is the believer's refuge. In Him we are protected from the wrath of God and the curse of the law. Heb. 6:18; Phil. 3:9.

Wilful murder is to be punished with death and no commutation of the punishment was to be accepted.

CHAPTER THIRTY-SIX

Contents: Regulations concerning inheritance.

Conclusion: It is the wisdom of those who have estates in this world to settle them and dispose of them so that strife and contention shall not arise about them among their posterity.

Key Word: Inheritances, v. 2.

Strong Verse: 7.

Christ Seen: Daughters can but marry well and to their satisfaction when they have looked to Christ to direct their choice of a husband. No one makes a safe choice who unites to one who is not united to Christ.

DEUTERONOMY

Key Thought:	Number of Chapters:	Key Verse:	Christ seen as:
Obedience	34	10:12, 13	Prophet like Moses

Writer of the Book:	Date:	Conclusion of the Book:
Moses	About 1500 B. C.	Obedience to God is imperative.

SUMMARY

CHAPTER ONE

Contents: Review of the failure at Kadesh-barnea.
Conclusion: A sad pass it has come to with us when the God of eternal truth cannot be believed. All disobedience to His laws and forgetfulness of His power and goodness flow from disbelief in His Word.
Key Word: Unbelief, v. 32.
Strong Verses: 17, 21, 30.
Christ Seen: "God has blessed us with all spiritual blessings in Christ," but we must appropriate and possess by faith. The faith that claims depends on obedience to Christ's requirements. (Eph. 1:3; 2 Pet. 1:3).

CHAPTER TWO

Contents: The wanderings and conflicts in the wilderness.
Conclusion: It is a work of time to make souls meet for the heavenly Canaan and it must be done by many a long train of experiences.
Key Word: Journeys, v. 1.
Strong Verse: 7.
Christ Seen: vv. 25, 36. Those who meddle with the people of Christ do it to their own eventual hurt, for He is their Captain with "all power in heaven and in earth," and can easily ruin the enemies of His people by their own resolves.

CHAPTER THREE

Contents: Further review of journeyings.
Conclusion: That cause cannot but be victorious for which the Lord of Hosts fights. "If God be for us who can be against us?"
Key Word: Conquest, v. 22.
Strong Verse: 24. Promise: 22.
Christ Seen: vv. 25, 27. If God does not by His providence give us what we desire, He can, by His grace in Jesus Christ, make us content with it. Be satisfied with this—Christ is all-sufficient. (Col. 2:10).

CHAPTER FOUR

Contents: The new generations taught the lessons of Sinai. Cities of refuge designated.
Conclusion: The review of God's providences concerning us should quicken us and engage us to duty and obedience.
Key Word: Keep (Obedience), v. 2.
Strong Verses: 2, 6, 9, 23, 24, 39.
Christ Seen: vv. 25, 31. Moses forsees the Jewish apostasy and consequent scattering. Those nations that refuse to recognize Christ in their prosperity cannot expect the comforts of His gospel when they come to be in distress.

CHAPTER FIVE

Contents: New generations taught the Mosaic covenant.
Conclusion: Many have their consciences startled by the Law, who are not purified (v. 29). Promises are made but the good principles are not rooted in them. Oh, to be sincere in our covenant with God.
Key Word: Covenant, v. 2.
Strong Verses: 6, 29. Promise: 33.

Christ Seen: v. 5. Moses stood between. Herein he is a type of Christ who stands between God and man, as the true mediator, so that we both hear from God and speak to Him without trembling.

CHAPTER SIX

Contents: Israel exhorted to observe all God's commandments.

Conclusion: The fear of God in the heart is the most powerful principle of obedience (vv. 2, 5, etc.).

Key Word: Observe, v. 3.

Strong Verses: 3, 5, 7.

Christ Seen: Those who love the Lord Jesus Christ themselves should do all they can to engage the affections of their children to Him, to prevent the religion of the family from being cut off. (Mk. 10:14').

CHAPTER SEVEN

Contents: Command to be separate people and to destroy opposing nations.

Conclusion: Those who are taken into communion with God must have no communication with the unfruitful works of darkness.

Key Word: Chosen, v. 6.

Strong Verse: 6. Promise: 9.

Christ Seen: The destruction of enemies furnishes an illustration of the Christian conflict. We are commanded not to let sin reign, nor to countenance it, but to hate it and take sides with Christ against it. God has promised it shall not have dominion over us. (Rom. 6:12, 14).

CHAPTER EIGHT

Contents: Israel reminded of God's gracious past dealings and warned to walk in His way.

Conclusion: It is good for us to remember all the ways both of God's providences and grace by which He has led us hitherto through this wilderness, that we may be prevailed upon cheerfully to serve Him and trust Him.

Key Word: Remember, v. 2.

Strong Verses: 2, 5, 11.

Christ Seen: v. 4. Those who follow the Lord Jesus have the promise of not only being safe, but easy (Matt. 11:30). If we walk "in His steps," our feet will not swell. It is the "way of the transgressor" that is "hard" (Prov. 13:15).

CHAPTER NINE

Contents: Israel reminded of their unworthiness to possess the land in themselves.

Conclusion: Our gaining of the heavenly Canaan must be attributed to God's power, not our might, and ascribed to His grace, not our merit. In Christ we have both righteousness and strength—in Him therefore we must glory, and not in ourselves. Gal. 6:14.

Key Word: Remember, v. 7 (stubbornness, v. 27).

Strong Verse: 4.

Christ Seen: It is good often to review the records conscience keeps of our past life of sin that we may see how much we are indebted to God's marvelous grace in Jesus Christ (Eph. 2:8-10), and may humbly own that we never merited anything at God's hand but wrath and the curse.

CHAPTER TEN

Contents: Further warnings and exhortation and reminders of God's dealings.

Conclusion: Since we have received so many mercies from God, it becomes us to enquire what returns we shall make to Him. It should certainly cause us to devote our lives to His honor and to lay ourselves out to advance the interest of His kingdom.

Key Word: Commandments, v. 13.

Strong Verses: 12, 17, 21.

Christ Seen. vv. 10, 11. Moses, Israel's intercessor, had the conduct and command of Israel. Herein he was a type of Christ, who ever lives to make intercession and who has all power in heaven and earth.

CHAPTER ELEVEN

Contents: Warnings and exhortations to obedience.
Conclusion: The closer dependence we have had on God, the more cheerful should be our obedience to Him. In absolute obedience to Him is strength and true success.
Key Word: Obey, v. 27.
Strong Verses: 8, 16, 26
Christ Seen: v. 12. The Bible magnifies the land of Canaan above all others. God's eyes are still upon it for it is the center of much unfulfilled prophecy, and the land where His Son will descend as King of Kings.

CHAPTER TWELVE

Contents: Statements of conditions of blessing in the land.
Conclusion: We must not think that our religion is only for our years of servitude or our entertainment in the place of solitude, or our consolation in affliction. We must keep up devout worship in our Canaan experiences as well as our wilderness experiences.
Key Word: Observe, vv. 1, 28, 32.
Strong Verse: 32.
Christ Seen: The one precept pressed harder than any other by Moses is in regard to the necessity of bringing the sacrifice to one altar at the court of the tabernacle and there to perform all rituals. We are to offer up all spiritual sacrifices to God in the name of Jesus Christ, hoping for acceptance only on the ground of His mediation. 1 Pet. 2:5.

CHAPTER THIRTEEN

Contents: The test of false prophets.
Conclusion: "Though we or an angel from heaven preach any other Gospel unto you than that which we have preached unto you, let him be accursed," Gal. 1:8. We are to be on our guard against imposition and lying wonders.
Key Word: Dreamers, v. 5.
Strong Verse: 4.
Christ Seen: Observe in v. 3, etc., that they were warned not even to patiently listen to false teachers and dreamers, but to instantly reject their teaching with disdain as unscriptural. The doctrine of Christ is the one test of all doctrines (2 Jn. 9:10). See Rom. 16:17, 18; 2 Tim. 3:5.

CHAPTER FOURTEEN

Contents: Dietary laws.
Conclusion: The precepts concerning food belonged only to the Jews and were not moral or of perpetual use because of not universal obligation. What they might not eat themselves they might give to a stranger or a proselyte who had renounced idolatry or they might sell to an alien. It was evidently intended to keep them from mingling with and conforming themselves to idolatrous neighbors.
Key Word: Eating, v. 3.
Strong Verse: 2.
Christ Seen: One quality of a good minister of Christ may be seen in 1 Tim. 4:3-6.

CHAPTER FIFTEEN

Contents: Laws concerning Sabbatic year and bondservants.
Conclusion: That we who have received in abundance from God should be rigorous and severe in our demands from poor brethren, is displeasing to God. His tender care of us obliges us to be kind to those who have a dependence upon us.
Key Word: Release, v. 1.
Strong Verses: 7, 8, 10. Promise: 6.
Christ Seen: The year of release typifies the grace of the Gospel in which is proclaimed the acceptable year of the Lord, by which we obtain the release of our debts, the pardon of our sins, teaching us to forgive others as we have been forgiven.

CHAPTER SIXTEEN

Contents: Laws concerning annual feasts.

Conclusion: By frequent and regular meeting to worship God at appointed places and by recognized rules, we are kept faithful and constant in that holy religion which Christ has established among us.

Key Word: Feasts, v. 10.

Strong Verse: 17.

Christ Seen: Christ is our Sacrifice (1 Cor. 5:7). We are to keep this feast in holy conversation, free from the leaven of malice and hypocrisy, and with the unleavened bread of sincerity and love.

CHAPTER SEVENTEEN

Contents: Laws concerning idolators and obedience to authority and kings.

Conclusion: God would possess men with a dread of that sin—worshipping false gods—which is a sin in itself exceedingly heinous and the highest affront that can be offered to Almighty God.

Key Word: Transgressing, v. 2.

Strong Verses: 18, 19, 20.

Christ Seen: v. 1. Old Testament sacrifices were required to be perfect because types of Christ, 1 Pet. 1:19, who was perfectly pure from all sin and all appearances of it.

CHAPTER EIGHTEEN

Contents: Laws concerning Levites, idolatrous practices and prophets.

Conclusion: vv. 9-14. Let those who give heed to fortune tellers or run to wizards for the discovery of things secret, that use spells for cures, are in league with familiar spirits or fellowship with those who are—know that they have no fellowship with God, but with demons.

Key Word: Prophet, v. 15.

Strong Verses: 15, 18.

Christ Seen: God has made Himself known to men through One above all prophets (Acts 3:22; 7:37; John 6:14). Hear ye Him.

CHAPTER NINETEEN

Contents: Cities of refuge; landmarks, witnesses.

Conclusion: God would possess men with a great horror and dread of the sin of killing another, even by chance. If by willful violence, see 1 John. 3:15.

Key Word: Refuge (cities), v. 2.

Strong Verses: 9, 10.

Christ Seen: Cities of refuge were located in the center of districts so every a distance (Rom. 10:8) but brings salvatino through the Gospel, to our door.

CHAPTER TWENTY

Contents: Laws of warfare.

Conclusion: Those enterprises which we undertake by a divine warrant and prosecute by divine direction, we may expect to succeed in. Those who have God with them have no reason to fear in the battles of life.

Key Word: Battle, v. 1.

Strong Verse: 1. Promise: 4.

Christ Seen: In contrast with these ancient laws of warfare, the Christian will find his warrants in Eph. 6.

CHAPTER TWENTY-ONE

Contents: Inquest for the slain. Domestic regulations.

Conclusion: We are to have a dread of the guilt of blood, which defiles not only the conscience of the murderer but the land in which it is shed. When we hear of the wickedness of the wicked, we have need to cry earnestly for mercy for our land which groans and trembles under it.

Key Word: Guilt, v. 9 (wife, 10-17), rebellious son, (18-23).

Strong Verse: 8.

Christ Seen: v. 23. Cf. Gal. 3:13; John 19:31. Christ underwent the curse of the law for us and was exposed to shame for us. In the evening, He was taken down, in token that now the law was satisfied.

CHAPTER TWENTY-TWO
Contents: Law of brotherhood, separation, unchaste wives and husbands.
Conclusion: Christianity teaches us to be neighborly and to be ready to do all good offices as we have opportunity, to all men.   Chastity should be as dear to us as our lives.
Key Word: Brotherly, v. 1, (whoredom, v. 21).
Strong Verse: 4.
Christ Seen: (v. 10).   Those who are Christ's are not to be yoked with those who belong to the devil.· See 2 Cor. 6:14-16.

CHAPTER TWENTY-THREE
Contents: Divers regulations.
Conclusion: We must take care to keep the camp of the saints pure from moral, ceremonial and natural pollution.
Key Word: Holy, v. 14.
Strong Verse: 9.   Promises: 14.
Christ Seen: Outward cleanliness is a reverence of the divine Majesty.   Filthiness is offensive to the senses God has endued us with, is a wrong to human life and an insult to the Holy One who lives within us.   We should give Christ clean temples (1 Cor. 6:19-20).

CHAPTER TWENTY-FOUR
Contents: Law concerning divorce; miscellaneous regulations.
Conclusion: It is of great consequence that love be kept up between husband and wife and that everything be carefully avoided which would estrange them.   The changes made by discontent often prove for the worst.
Key Word: Divorce, v. 1.
Strong Verse: 22.
Christ Seen: The creditor who cares not though his debtor and his family starve, nor is at all concerned what becomes of them so he gets his money, goes contrary to both the law of Moses and of Christ.   (Mt. 6:42).

CHAPTER TWENTY-FIVE
Contents: Divers regulations.
Conclusion: Justice and equity will bring down upon us the blessing of God.   Those who do unrighteously are an abomination to the Lord and miserable is the man who is distasteful to his God.
Key Word: Abominations, v. 16.
Strong Verse: 16.
Striking Facts: v. 3.   See 2 Cor. 11:24.   They always gave Paul as many stripes as ever they gave to any malefactor.

CHAPTER TWENTY-SIX
Contents: Law of the offering of the firstfruits.
Conclusion: We are to acknowledge God as giver of all good things which are the support and comfort of our natural lives and are therefore to give to God the first and best as those who believe Him to be the first and best.
Key Word: Firstfruits, v. 10.
Strong Verses: 10, 18.
Christ Seen: All we are, all we possess and all we earn are equally the gift of God in Christ.   How can we acknowledge the riches of His grace but by dedicating to His service a fixed portion of the results of our daily work?   (Phil. 4:19).

CHAPTER TWENTY-SEVEN
Contents: The blessing and cursing from Mt. Ebal and Gerizim.
Conclusion: We are all compelled to say Amen to the law of God, owning ourselves justly under its curse and that we must certainly have perished had not Christ redeemed us from the curse of the law, being made a curse for us.
Key Word: Law, v. 8.
Strong Verses: 9, 10.
Christ Seen: v. 5.   Christ, our altar, is a stone cut out without hands (Dan. 2:34, 35) refused by the builders but accepted of God and made the headstone of the corner.

CHAPTER TWENTY-EIGHT

Contents: Conditions of blessing in the land and causes of chastisement.

Conclusion: If we do not delight in God's will, we not only come short of the blessing promised but lay ourselves under chastisement, which is as comprehensive of all misery as His blessings are of all happiness.

Key Word: Obedience (keep commandments), v. 1.

Strong Verses: 2, 58.

Christ Seen: vv. 64, 65. Remarkably fulfilled in the present dispersion of the Jews. They have, through the centuries been continually on the move, either in hope of gain or in fear of persecution and so will continue until Christ, the King, comes and they are restored by Him to the promised land.

CHAPTER TWENTY-NINE

Contents: Introductory words to the Palestinian covenant.

Conclusion: We are bound in gratitude as well as duty and faithfulness to keep the words of the solemn covenant of God.

Key Word: Covenant, v. 1.

Strong Verses: 9, 29.

Christ Seen: Moses concludes the prophecy of the Jews rejection, v. 29, as Paul concludes his discourse on the same subject. Rom. 11:33. What shall not the joy be when Christ, the coming King brings back His people to their own land.

CHAPTER THIRTY

Contents: The Palestinian covenant declared.

Conclusion: Those shall have life who choose it. Those who come short of life and happiness must thank themselves. They would have had it, had they chosen communion with God.

Key Word: Choice, v. 19.

Strong Verses: 15, 19.

Christ Seen: Israel has never yet taken the land under the unconditional Abrahamic covenant, nor ever possessed the whole land promised. Gen. 15:18; Num. 34:1-12. The covenant awaits the coming of Christ, the King, for its fulfillment.

CHAPTER THIRTY-ONE

Contents: Moses' last counsel to the priests and instruction to the Levites. Warning of Israelitish apostasy.

Conclusion: It is a great encouragement to God's people that in the place of some useful instrument of His whom He removes, He raises up others to carry on His work.

Key Word: Counsel, (spake these words) v. 1.

Promises: 6, 8.

Christ Seen: (v. 8). When the Good Shepherd puts forth His own, He precedes them (Jn. 10:4), and the iron gates open at His summons (Acts 12:10). "He will not fail thee" reappears in Heb. 13:5 as the right of Christ's people.

CHAPTER THIRTY-TWO

Contents: The song and exhortation of Moses.

Conclusion: The warning and consoling words of God sent down from heaven should sink into our hearts and soften them as the rain softens the earth, and so make us fruitful in obedience.

Key Word: Doctrine, v. 2. (He gave a song of praise, Ex. 15, but this is one of instruction).

Strong Verses: 4, 29, 43.

Christ Seen: vv. 49, 52. Those may die happily whenever God calls them, who have had a believing prospect through Christ and a foregleam of the heavenly Canaan as a well grounded hope of life beyond death. (Jn. 11: 25).

CHAPTER THIRTY-THREE

Contents: Moses' blessing upon the tribes.

Conclusion: It is a very desirable thing to have an interest in the prayers of those who are about to depart for heaven.

Key Word: Blessing, v. 1.
Promises: 25, 27.
Christ Seen: Happy is the people whose Shepherd is Christ (Jno: 10).   They are in His hand, v. 3; at His feet, v. 3; at His side, v. 12; between His shoulders, v. 12; in His arms, v. 27; behind His shield, v. 29, and fitted with His sword, v. 29.

CHAPTER THIRTY-FOUR

Contents: Vision and death of Moses.
Conclusion: Those may leave this world with cheerfulness who have known God face to face through His Son, and who have had the vision of the heavenly Canaan in their eye.
Key Word: Death, v. 5.
Strong Verse: 10.
Christ Seen: It was reserved for Joshua (the Lord Jesus of whom Joshua was a striking type) to do for us that which the law could not do in that it was weak through the flesh.   Through Him we are led into the land of rest—the rest of conscience and the rest of heaven.

We leave Moses, the great law giver, buried in the plains of Moab. We leave our Saviour, who came to fulfill the law, and bear for us its curse, seated at the right hand of God on high, awaiting the hour of His return, when of the increase and peace of His government, there shall be no end.

JOSHUA

Key Thought:	Number of Chapters:	Key Verse:	Christ seen as:
Possessions	24	1:3	Capt. of Lord's Hosts

Writer of the Book:	Date:	Conclusion of the Book:
Joshua	About 1425 B. C.	The faithfulness of Jehovah to His own has been fully demonstrated.

SUMMARY

CHAPTER ONE

Contents: Joshua's commission and command.
Conclusion: Those who make the Word of God their rule and conscientiously walk by that rule will both do well and make great progress. We will be animated and emboldened for God's work as we keep our eyes upon the divine warrant.
Key Word: Strong, vv. 6, 7, 9, 18.
Strong Verse: 8. Promise: 9.
Christ Seen: Joshua, type of Christ as Captain of our Salvation. Heb. 2:10, 11. He comes after Moses, John 1:17. Leads to victory, Rom. 8:37. Our Advocate when we have met defeat, 1 John 2:1. Allots our portions, Eph. 1:11, 14.

CHAPTER TWO

Contents: Rahab and the Jericho spies.
Conclusion: Let not God's people be afraid of their most powerful enemies, for their God can, when He pleases make their worst enemies afraid of them.
Key Word: Spies, v. 1.
Strong Verses: 18, 24.
Christ Seen: v. 21. Rahab's scarlet line speaks, by its color, of the safety that comes to our households through the sacrifice of Christ if it be exhibited by faith in the believer. Heb. 9:19, 22.

CHAPTER THREE

Contents: The passing of Jordan.
Conclusion: The believer is to go on in the way of duty, though foreseeing great difficulties, depending on the divine sufficiency for that which he finds himself not sufficient for. "Is anything too hard for Jehovah?"
Key Word: Pass-over, v. 6.
Strong Verses: 5, 17.
Christ Seen: The passing of the Jordan is a type of the believer's death with Christ (Rom. 6:6-11; Eph. 2:5, 6; Col. 3:1-3) in which we pass from an old world into a newness of life.

CHAPTER FOUR

Contents: The memorial stone.
Conclusion: God's works of wonder on our behalf ought to be kept in everlasting memory and means devised for preserving our memory of them.
Key Word: Memorial, v. 7.
Strong Verses: 22, 24.
Christ Seen: The Lord Jesus, our Joshua, passed through the Jordan of death, opening the Kingdom to all believers. He appointed His twelve apostles according to the tribes of Israel by the memorial of the Gospel to transmit the knowledge of this to the remote places and to the future ages.

CHAPTER FIVE

Contents: Reproach of Egypt rolled away. New food for the new place. The unseen Captain.

Conclusion: (Circumcision, the seal of the covenant in their flesh, was
neglected in the wilderness wanderings. They were hereby owned as
freeborn children of God, the reproach of the bondage in Egypt being
removed.)

God is jealous for the honor of His people and is ready to roll away
whatever reproach they may for a time lie under, if they become "circum-
cised in heart."

Key Word: Reproach (rolled away), 9.

Strong Verses: 14, 15.

Christ Seen: The N. T. uncircumcision is world conformity, the failure openly
to take a believer's place with Christ in death and resurrection. Gal. 6:
14-16; Rom. 6:2-11.

CHAPTER SIX

Contents: Conquest of Jericho.

Conclusion: The victories of faith are often to be won by means, and upon
principles utterly foolish and inadequate in the view of human wisdom.
If faith is obedient to God's precepts, He will certainly confound the
mighty with the weak things.

Key Word: Fall (of Jericho), v. 5.

Strong Verses: 16, 27.

Christ Seen: By the foolishness of preaching the Gospel of Christ, fitly compared to the sounding of the ram's horns, the devil's kingdom is thrown
down and the weapons of our warfare, though not carnal, nor seeming to
a carnal eye able to accomplish anything, are yet mighty through Christ,
to the pulling down of strongholds. 2 Cor. 10:4, 5.

CHAPTER SEVEN

Contents: Sin of Achan and the defeat at Ai.

Conclusion: Let all men know that it is nothing but sin that separates them
from God and if it be not sincerely repented of and put away, it will bring
disaster, not only upon themselves, but those associated with them.

Key Word: Accursed, v. 13.

Strong Verses: 12, 13, 19.

Christ Seen: The story illustrates the truth of the oneness of the church
in Christ. 1 Cor. 5:1-7; 12:12, 14, 26. The whole cause of Christ is
injured by the unspirituality of one believer.

CHAPTER EIGHT

Contents: Conquest of Ai. The blessings and cursing of Ebal.

Conclusion: The believer, clad in the whole armor of God, meeting the
enemy of God as God directs, will see the scale easily and quickly turned
against those who have not God on their side.

Key Word: Victory (took the city), v. 19.

Strong Verses: 26, 35.

Christ Seen: (vv. 30-35). Even when we enter the land of rest through faith
in Jesus, we cannot escape God's holy law. It is even more perfectly fulfilled as we walk in the Spirit (Rom. 8:1-4). As the law was written on
stones, may it be engraven on our hearts. (Heb. 8:10).

CHAPTER NINE

Contents: The league with the Gibeonites.

Conclusion: We make more haste than good progress in any business when
we do not stop to take God along with us and by the Word and prayer to
ascertain His will.

Strong Verse: 25.

Key Word: League, v. 15.

Christ Seen: vv. 4, 5, 12, 13. God's people have often been deceived and im-
posed upon with a show of antiquity. Christ's people usually suffer more
from the devil's wiles than from his direct attacks. Only those who maintain close fellowship with Christ can avoid being caught with the Gibeonit-
ish stratagem.

CHAPTER TEN

Contents: Victory at Gibeon, Makkedah, etc. Sun's action halted.

Conclusion: When enemies set themselves in array against us and threaten to swallow us up, we may by faith and prayer, apply to Christ, our Joshua, for strength and succor and will assuredly receive the answer of victory and faith.

Key Word: Delivered, vv. 8, 30, 32.

Strong Verses: 8, 14. Promise: 25.

Christ Seen: v. 25. A figure of Christ's victories over the powers of darkness and the believer's victories through Him. All enemies shall be made His footstool. Psa. 110:1. All things will be put under Him, Heb. 2:8, and principalities and powers made a show of. Col. 2:15.

CHAPTER ELEVEN

Contents: Final conquest of Canaan.

Conclusion: Those who, through obedience to His precepts, have God on their side, need not be disturbed as to the number and power of their enemies. "More are those that are with us than those that are against us."

Key Word: Delivered, vv. 6, 8.

Strong Verses: 6, 23.

Christ Seen: As Israel, at first forwarded by miracles, and now left to make their own way, so the war carried on against Satan's kingdom was at first advanced by Christ's special miracles, but being sufficiently proved by them to be of God, we are now left to the ordinary assistance of divine grace in Christ in the use of the Sword of the Spirit and need not look for hailstones nor the standing still of the sun.

CHAPTER TWELVE

Contents: The roster of the kings of Canaan.

Conclusion: Fresh mercies must not drown the remembrance of former mercies, nor must the glory of present servants of God be allowed to diminish the honor due those who have gone before them, paving the way for later victories. (v. 6).

Key Word: Kings, v. 1.

Strong Verse: 6.

Christ Seen: vv. 6, 7. The triumphs and grants of the law were glorious but those of the Gospel far exceed in glory. Jesus, the true Joshua, has provided for all the children of promise, spiritual blessings—the privilege of His presence and heaven hereafter.

CHAPTER THIRTEEN

Contents: Joshua instructed concerning the division of the land.

Conclusion: All people, and especially old people, should set themselves to do that quickly which must be done before they die, lest death prevent them. vv. 1, 7.

Key Word: Divide (the land), v. 7.

Strong Verse: 1.

Christ Seen: Joshua had the honor of dividing the land as Christ, the true Joshua, who has conquered for us the gates of hell and opened to us the gates of heaven, purchasing an eternal inheritance for all believers, will in due time, have the honor of putting us in possession.

CHAPTER FOURTEEN

Contents: Land divided, the portion of Caleb.

Conclusion: Whatever we undertake, God's favorable presence with us is all in all to our success, therefore we should make sure of it by conformity to His will and an eye to His favor. vv. 8, 9.

Key Word: Divided (land), v. 5.

Strong Verses: 10, 11, 12.

Christ Seen: v. 12. Because it was formerly in God's promise, Caleb shows how he values the promise and insists on the mountain the Lord had spoken of. The man of faith values that which is given by promise of grace in Christ far above that given by providence only.

CHAPTER FIFTEEN

Contents: Land divisions; the portion of Judah.

Conclusion: It is no breach of God's law moderately to desire those comforts and conveniences of life which are attainable in a fair and regular way and will make us more efficient workmen for God.
Key Word: Borders.
Strong Verse: 19.
Christ Seen: v. 10. The blessings of the upper springs illustrate the spiritual blessings in Christ which relate to our souls, and those of the nether springs speak of those which relate to the body and the life that now is.

CHAPTER SIXTEEN

Contents: Land divisions; portions of Manasseh and Ephraim.
Conclusion: It is a brand of failure upon the Christian, when through carelessness, cowardice or want of faith in God, he fails to drive out the Canaanite (world) as commanded. Covetousness often brings us into compromise and leads eventually to being infected with the world's idolatry.
Key Word: Borders, v. 5.
Strong Verse: 10.
Christ Seen: Christ and worldly desires (typified in Canaanites) cannot dwell side by side in the same habitation. If we would have the realization of His place, the Canaanites must be expelled. (1 John 2:15).

CHAPTER SEVENTEEN

Contents: Land divisions; portion for Manasseh.
Conclusion: (v. 14). Many covet larger possessions who do not cultivate and make the best of what they have. If we would have more talents bestowed upon us, we should trade with those with which we are entrusted.
Key Word: Portions, v. 5.
Strong Verses: 13, 15, 18.
Christ Seen: v. 13. Many Christians try to serve their own ends by conniving with the Canaanites, whom Christ has distinctly commanded must be driven out. To thus court compromise with the world is to court failure, for unless we crown Christ Lord of all we do not crown Him Lord at all.

CHAPTER EIGHTEEN

Contents: Tabernacle set up; apportionment of land to seven tribes.
Conclusion: Many Christians stand in their own light and forsake their own mercies for the sake of lying vanities. With the title to a good land, given us by the sacrifice of Christ, we must not allow ourselves to be slack in possessing it all, because of seeming difficulties that are in the way.
Key Word: Borders, v. 12.
Strong Verses: 1, 3.
Christ Seen: The setting up of the tabernacle (v. 1) in Shiloh, gives a hint that in the coming Shiloh (Christ) of whom Jacob had spoken, all the ordinances of the worldly sanctuary would have their accomplishment in a greater and more perfect tabernacle. Heb. 9:1, 11.

CHAPTER NINETEEN

Contents: Land divisions for six more tribes.
Conclusion: (v. 49. The last served was the eldest and greatest man of Israel). Men in great public places should learn to prefer the common welfare before their own private satisfaction.
Key Word: Inheritance, v. 11.
Strong Verses: 47, 49.
Christ Seen : v. 10. Within the lot of Zebulun were places made illustrious in the N. T. Within it was Nazareth where the Saviour spent so much of His time and mount Tabor on which He was transfigured and the coast of the Sea of Galilee on which He preached so many sermons and wrought so many miracles.

CHAPTER TWENTY

Contents: Cities of refuge.
Conclusion: Other refuge have we none, in any trouble, save Him in whom our trust is stayed.
Key Word: Refuge, v. 2.

Strong Verses: 9.

Christ Seen: Cities of refuge typify the relief which the Gospel provides for poor, penitent sinners and their protection from the curse of the law and the wrath of God, in our Lord Jesus Christ, to whom believers flee for refuge. Heb. 6:18.

CHAPTER TWENTY-ONE

Contents: Land divisions; portions for Levites.

Conclusion: God performs His promises to the utmost (v. 45) and if in anything the promise seems to come short, the saint must confess that upon himself rests all the blame.

Key Word: Inheritance, v. 3.

Strong Verses: 44, 45.

Christ Seen: There is an inheritance provided for all the saints, God's royal, priesthood (Levites) for which they must petition through the true Joshua, Christ who has said, "Ask, and it shall be given you."

CHAPTER TWENTY-TWO

Contents: Two and a half tribes dismissed to their homes. Altar of Reuben and Gad.

Conclusion: Unhappy strifes will be prevented or soon healed by an impartial and favorable inquiry into that which is the matter of the offense. God does, and men MUST often overlook the weakness of an honest zeal.

Key Word: Witness, v. 27.

Strong Verses: 5, 18, 29.

Christ Seen: v. 28. Those who have found the benefits of God's ordinances cannot but desire to perpetuate them upon their children and use all precaution lest their children cease from following the Lord Jesus. To this end the believer should set up a constant witness of Christ in the home.

CHAPTER TWENTY-THREE

Contents: Last counsels of Joshua.

Conclusion: As all good things come upon the believer according to the promise, so long as we have kept close to God, so all evil things will befall, according to His threatenings, if we forsake Him.

Key Word: Counsel (said unto them), v. 2.

Strong Verses: 3, 6, 8, 14. Promise: 10.

Christ Seen: v. 16. The goodness of the heavenly Canaan and the thought of the possession they might have had, will aggravate the misery of those who shall be shut out from that which they might have enjoyed through God's free grace in Christ.

CHAPTER TWENTY-FOUR

Contents: Last charge of Joshua and his death. Eleazar's death.

Conclusion: v. 15. It is the will of God that all should make religion their serious and deliberate choice and to resolve upon a life of godliness because upon honest investigation, it is found to be the best way.

Key Word: Counsel, v. 2.

Strong Verses: 15, 16, 20, 24.

Striking Fact: The book which began with triumphs here ends with funerals by which all the glory of man is stained.

Christ Seen: v. 26. What the stone of witness was to Israel, the ordinances of the Lord's supper and baptism are to Christians and to the world.

JUDGES

| Key Thought:
Failure | Number of Chapters:
21 | Key Verse:
21:25 | Christ seen as:
Messenger of Jehovah |

| Writer of the Book:

Samuel | Date:

About 1410 B. C. | Conclusion of the Book:
Man is prone to wander from God. God's grace ever pursues and seeks to restore the backslider. |

SUMMARY

CHAPTER ONE

Contents: The incomplete victories of Judah, Benjamin and Manasseh.
Conclusion: God appoints service according to the strength He has given (v. 2) but distrust of His power and promise, lose for us our advantages and run us into a thousand troubles.
Key Word: Partial victory, (vv. 19, 21, 27, 29, 30, 31, 33).
Strong Verses: 2, 7.
Christ Seen: v. 2. Judah was the tribe out of which the Saviour sprang. Christ, the Lion of the tribe of Judah, engaged the powers of darkness and in Him we are more than conquerors.

CHAPTER TWO

Contents: Review of Israelitish invasion of Canaan up to Joshua's death. Results of incomplete obedience. Judges instituted.
Conclusion: God never designed defeat for His own; let them be faithful to Him and they will find Him unchangeably constant to them. His covenants never break except on our side.
Key Word: Sold, v. 14.
Strong Verses: 18, 20, 21.
Christ Seen: The Angel of Jehovah, v. 1, was none other than Christ Himself. He seemed to come up from Gilgal, the place where their covenant had been renewed, of which they would be reminded. The remembrance of what we have received and heard from God, prepares us for special messages from Christ to hold fast. (Rev. 3:2, 3).

CHAPTER THREE

Contents: Apostasies of Israel. Deliverances through Othniel, Ehud and Shamgar.
Conclusion: Man's memory is treacherous in that it easily forgets God and he must be repeatedly tested that God might be kept in sight. It often takes affliction to make him cry to God with importunity, when before he would scarcely think of Jehovah.
Key Word: Proved (tested), vv. 1, 4.
Strong Verses: 9, 15.
Christ Seen: Christ is the Christian's Deliverer who is always ready to answer the prayer of a contrite heart.

CHAPTER FOUR

Contents: Victories of Deborah and Barak.
Conclusion: Those who slight God in their prosperity, will find themselves under a necessity of crying mightily to Him when they are in trouble. He is faithful in spite of our unfaithfulness, and when we sincerely turn to Him, He will give the victory.
Key Word: Prevailed, v. 24.
Strong Verse: 14.
Striking Facts: It is a sure mark of apostasy in a nation when a woman is found in the place of leadership.

CHAPTER FIVE

Contents: Song of Deborah and Barak.
Conclusion: When we have received mercy from God, we should be speedy in our returns of praise while the impressions of the mercy are fresh. Song is a good expedient for perpetuating the memory of God's special favors.
Key Word: Song of praise, vv. 2, 12.
Strong Verse: 31.
Christ Seen: v. 20. "Stars fought"—the elements were against Sisera. Those to whom God is an enemy because of rejection of His Son and His Gospel provided at so great a cost are at war with the whole creation.

CHAPTER SIX

Contents: More apostasy in Israel. Call of Gideon.
Conclusion: In times of apostasy, God often calls His mightiest servants from places of obscurity, and inspiring them with the assurance of the divine presence, He works through them great deliverances for His people.
Key Word: Valour, v. 12, (in God's hands).
Strong Verse: 34.
Christ Seen. v. 24. Jehovah-shalom (God our peace). See Eph. 6:15. The peace of God, found alone in Christ who "is our peace," is the only preparation for intense conflict. In the midst of strife, one who has Christ for his peace, may be possessed of perfect tranquility within. If the Christian is called to battle, let him set up the altar of Jehovah-shalom.

CHAPTER SEVEN

Contents: Gideon's three hundred and the victory over Midian and Amalek.
Conclusion: God wants prepared men to fight God's battles with God's weapons in God's way. A Christian's unfitness for the battle is often seen in the unconscious and trifling acts of his life, which betray his utter lack of faith. (v. 5).
Key Word: Victory, v. 15.
Strong Verses: 2, 7.
Christ Seen: Empty pitchers (v. 16) type of earthly body, emptied of self (2 Cor. 4:7) but filled with God's Word, the lamp (Psa. 119:105). The pitcher was not to be spared in the advance, and the lamp was to be held forth (v. 20; Phil. 2:16). With the trumpet, the tidings of victory in Christ were sounded (Mark 16:15).

CHAPTER EIGHT

Contents: Jealousy of Ephraim. Events to the death of Gideon. Apostasy.
Conclusion: Many are led into false ways by one false step of a good man (v. 27). False worship soon makes way for false deities.
Key Word: Snare, v. 27 (whoring, 27,33).
Strong Verses: 23, 34.
Christ Seen: v. 22. The Lord Jesus has delivered us out of the hands of our dangerous spiritual enemies, and it is fitting that He should rule over us. See Luke 1:24, 25.

CHAPTER NINE

Contents: Conspiracy of Abimelech.
Conclusion: Evil pursues sinners and sometimes overtakes them when they are apparently triumphant. The mighty things of the world may be confounded by the weakest, if God so wills.
Key Word: Vengeance, vv. 24, 56.
Strong Verse: 56.
Christ Seen: v. 51. The name of the Lord Jesus is the strong tower (Prov. 18:10) into which the Christian may always go for safety in times of stress.

CHAPTER TEN

Contents: Further apostasy; servitude to Philistines and Amorites.
Conclusion: The pleasures of sense, the gods of this world, cannot be our satisfaction (v. 14). True happiness and safety are only in God, to whom a true penitent will refer himself for correction as God may see fit, owning that his sin is highly malignant in its deserts (v. 10).

Key Word: Vexed, oppressed, v. 8.
Strong Verses: 10, 14, 16.
Christ Seen: vv. 15, 16.   He has taken his first step toward salvation in Christ who has admitted himself a sinner, lost and undone (Rom. 3:23). Christ calls not the righteous but sinners to repentance.

CHAPTER ELEVEN

Contents: Jephthah's awful vow and the victory over the Amorites.
Conclusion: A Christian in the hands of the Spirit is assured of success in the undertaking to which God has called him. v. 29.   One should be cautious and well advised in the making of vows, lest by indulging a present emotion of pious zeal, they ivolve themselves in a great mistake,
Key Word: Subdued (enemy), v. 33.
Strong Verses: 35, 36.
Christ Seen: Jephthah's sacrifice is a figure of the great sacrifice of Christ. The daughter was a chaste sacrifice, devoted to death by the father and so made a curse. She submitted after a period of agony, to her father's will. v. 30.

CHAPTER TWELVE

Contents: Second jealousy of Ephraim.
Conclusion: Proud men think all the honors wasted that they themselves did not win.   Envy brings serious contentions in the ranks of those who should be as one to fight God's battles.
He who rolls the stone of reproach unjustly upon another, let him expect that it will justly return upon himself.
Key Word: Envy, v. 1.
Strong Verse: 3.
Christ Seen: Jephthah here showed a courteous and conciliatory spirit before he would engage in conflict.   This is the spirit Jesus demands of Christians.   (Matt. 18:15).   Yet many Christians ignore Christ's injunction.

CHAPTER THIRTEEN

Contents: Parents of Samson and Samson's birth.
Conclusion: A promise is given to try our faith and a precept to try our obedience—for God requires both faith and obedience from those on whom He would bestow special favors.
(It is desirable that our children be devoted to God even before their birth.)
Key Word: Conceive, 3, 24.
Strong Verses: 18, 23.
Christ Seen: v. 18.   "Secret" is lit. "Wonderful," the name applied to Christ in Isa. 9:6.   v. 22 declares they were face to face with God who is manifested only in His Son.   As the flame ascended from the altar He ascended.   We owe the acceptance of all our praises and prayers to His mediation.   It is Christ in our hearts by faith that makes our offering a sweet smelling savour.

CHAPTER FOURTEEN

Contents: Samson as Judge.   His victory over a lion; his riddles; his wife.
Conclusion: He that in the choice of a wife is guided only by his eye and governed by his fancy must afterward thank himself if he finds a Philistine in his arms.   (v. 3).   We should not be "unequally yoked with unbelievers."
(God often overrules our mistakes to take occasion against the enemies of His Truth).
Key Word: Wife, v. 2.
Strong Verses: 6, 19.
Christ Seen: God sometimes lets lions roar at us to drive us back upon Christ and His infinite resources.   When God, by His providences, brings good out of evil to the followers of Christ—when that which has threatened their ruin turns to their advantage and the wrath of men turns to His praise—then comes meat out of the eater and sweetness out of the strong.

CHAPTER FIFTEEN

Contents: Samson takes vengeance on the Philistines.
Conclusion: There is nothing too hard or too much for him to do on whom
the Holy Spirit comes in power, even though there are only the most
contemptible instruments at hand with which to work (foxes, jawbone).
Key Word: Avenged, v. 7.
Strong Verses: 16, 18.
Christ Seen: In the bursting of Samson's bands, we find an illustration of
the way the Lord Jesus was loosed from the cords of death and came
forth from the tomb and graveclothes.   Thus, He triumphed over the
powers of darkness that shouted against Him.

CHAPTER SIXTEEN

Contents: Samson and Delilah; his fatal error and his death.
Conclusion: Beware of Satan who ruins men by rocking them to sleep, flat-
tering them into a good opinion of their own safety, then robbing them
of their strength and honor, leading them captive at his will.
(God often leaves men to do foolish things to punish them for indulging
in the lusts of uncleanness.)
Key Word: Strength, v. 6, (departed, v. 20).
Strong Verses: 20, 28.
Christ Seen: Samson's strength was not in his hair but in his Nazarite consecration, of which his long hair was but a badge.   Likewise the Christian's
power is not in his outward profession, but in his faith in Christ.   What
was real in Samson was his great faith in times of awful apostasy and
God honored this faith (Heb. 11:32) as He honors the Christian's real dependence on Christ.

CHAPTER SEVENTEEN

Contents: Micah's worship in self will.
Conclusion: The love of money makes much mischief; destroys the duty and
comfort of every relation and frequently leads to the setting up of a false
worship.
Key Word: Graven image, v. 3.
Strong Verse: 6.
Christ Seen: v. 13.   Apostates who please themselves with their own delusions
infer, if providence brings anything to their hands that helps them in their
way, that God is pleased with them.   With all false worship there is usually an exaltation of false priesthood, usurping the place of Christ.

CHAPTER EIGHTEEN

Contents: The Danite invasion.   Civil and religious confusion.
Conclusion: Many seek to justify themselves in their idolatrous impiety by
the prosperity that seemingly attends them, not knowing that many are
brought to destruction by their false security and that departing from the
revealed will of God concerning worship is a dangerous move for a people
to make.
Key Word: Seeking inheritance, v. 1.
Strong Verses: 9, 10.
Christ Seen: v. 24.   An excellent definition of idolatry.   Anything allowed
to take the place of Christ in our lives, and which man is concerned
about as if life and comfort, hope and happiness were bound up in it, is an
idol.

CHAPTER NINETEEN

Contents: The Levite and his concubine.   Wickedness of Gibeonites.
Conclusion: Because men like not to retain God in their knowledge, God
gives them up to vile affection through which they dishonor themselves
and turn His glory into shame.   (Rom. 1:24, 28).   In the miserable end
of this woman, we see the hand of God punishing her for her uncleanness.   v. 2.
Key Word: Abused, 25.
Strong Verse: 30.

CHAPTER TWENTY

Contents: Civil war in which the Benjamites are punished.

Conclusion: We cannot expect the presence of God with us in our enterprises unless we seek it by humbling ourselves before Him. (v. 26). He is not under obligation to prosper us. Men are often so confident that God owes them His favor because they think their cause a good one, that they think it needless to humble themselves before God in penitence.

Key Word: Vengeance, vv. 9, 28.

Strong Verses: 11, 18, 26.

Christ Seen: God's people often in times of stress find their access to Him barred because of sin. We can only approach him by confession (1 John 1:9) and full dependence on the blood of Christ. (1 John 1:7).

CHAPTER TWENTY-ONE

Contents: Mourning for the lost tribe of Benjamin.

Conclusion: There may be overdoing in well doing. Great care must be taken in the government of our zeal, for even necessary justice must be rendered with compassion. Many a war is ill-ended which was well begun. (2, 6, 13).

        v. 25. Men should learn to be thankful for magistrates, both supreme and subordinate for they are ministers for God unto us for good. Any government is better than no government or anarchy.

Key Word: Depleted tribe, vv. 3, 6.

Strong Verses: 2, 13.

Christ Seen: Note that in v. 3 there is no mourning for sin and no humbling because of national transgressions and they get no word from Jehovah. Consequently they act wholly in self will (v. 10). We cannot expect Christ to take the leadership and give us victory until we really return to Him in humble contrition.

RUTH

Key Thought: Kinsman	Number of Chapters: 4	Key Verse: 4:14	Christ seen as: Kinsman Redeemer

Writer of the Book:	Date:	Conclusion of the Book:
Unknown	About 1300 B. C.	True rest comes only through redemption and union.

SUMMARY

CHAPTER ONE

Contents: Naomi departs from Moab and returns with Ruth to Bethlehem.

Conclusion: When we take God for our Father we must take His people for our people though they be poor and despised. Those who forsake the communion of saints and return to the people of Moab will sooner or later break all communion with God and embrace the idols of Moab.

Key Word: Fidelity, v. 17.

Strong Verses: 16, 17.

Christ Seen: Many have a value and affection for Christ yet come short of salvation by Him because they cannot find it in their hearts to forsake other things and attach themselves to Him. If we resolve that nothing shall separate us from our duty to Christ, we may be sure that nothing can ever separate us from happiness in Him.

CHAPTER TWO

Contents: Ruth serves Boaz who exercises a great kindness toward her.

Conclusion: God wisely orders small events and those that seem altogether contingent serve His own glory and supply the needs of His trusting people.

Key Word: Favour, v. 13.

Strong Verses: 12, 20.

Christ Seen: vv. 22, 23. If we would benefit through Christ, we must adhere closely to Him, His fields and His servants. Has the Lord dealt bountifully with us? Let us not be found in any other field seeking happiness and satisfaction in the world.

CHAPTER THREE

Contents: Ruth rests at the feet of Boaz.

Conclusion: The married state should be a state of rest, when wandering affections are fixed in one who is fit, both temporally and spiritually to be a good husband.

Key Word: Rest, v. 1.

Strong Verses: 10, 11.

Christ Seen: The Lord Jesus is our Kinsman Redeemer. Through His incarnation He became kin to us as human beings that we, through the Spirit, might become betrothed to Him.

CHAPTER FOUR

Contents: Ruth finds reward in her marriage to Boaz.

Conclusion: Fair and square dealings in all matters of contract and business are what all those must make conscience of who would approve themselves as "Israelites indeed without guile."

Key Word: Kinsman redeemer, v. 1.

Strong Verse: 14.

Christ Seen: At vast expense, our Lord Jesus, the Bethlehemite Redeemer purchased the heavenly inheritance for us which by our sin was mortgaged and forfeited, and which of ourselves we could never have redeemed.

I SAMUEL

Key Thought: Kingdom	Number of Chapters: 31	Key Verse: 10:25	Christ seen as: Seed of David

Writer of the Book:	Date:	Conclusion of the Book:
Uncertain, Samuel, Nathan or Gad	About 1155 B. C.	Prayer should have a great place in our lives that the power of God may work for and through us.

SUMMARY

CHAPTER ONE

Contents: The vow of Hannah and the birth of Samuel.
Conclusion: Prayer is heart's ease to a gracious soul. If we seek on the basis of God's glory (v. 11) we shall be confident that we do not seek in vain. Prayer smoothes the countenance (v. 18).
Key Word: Bitterness, v. 10.
Strong Verses: 17, 27, 28.
Christ Seen: True prayer may only be offered on the grounds of the sacrifice (v. 3). By Christ's offering,. not only is atonement made for sin, but the audience and acceptance of our prayers is obtained for us. In all our supplications, we must have an eye to the Great Sacrifice.

CHAPTER TWO

Contents: Hannah's prophetic prayer. Evil sons of Eli. Samuel in the tabernacle. The warning to Eli.
Conclusion: Nothing is more provoking to God than the profanation of sacred things and men serving their lusts with the offerings of the Lord. Those who allow and countenance their children in an evil way by not using their authority to restrain and punish them, involve themselves in their guilt and may be expected to be cast off from God's service.
Key Word: Evil sons, v. 23.
Strong Verses: 2, 3, 6, 7, 8, 9, 10, 30.
Christ Seen: v. 35. This had its full accomplishment in the priesthood of Christ, that faithful High Priest raised up of God when the Levitical priesthood was cast aside, who in all things did His Father's mind, and for whom God builds a sure house, built on a rock so that the gates of hell cannot prevail against it.

CHAPTER THREE

Contents: Samuel becomes Jehovah's prophet-priest.
Conclusion: A child may have an ear for God's call; a mind for God's service and a message for God's bidding, for God will not be without a mouthpiece even though the ordained priesthood be deaf to His voice.
Key Word: Called, v. 4.
Strong Verses: 10, 18, 19.
Christ Seen: God's ministers must nourish a holy sensitiveness to sacred things, or callousness will lead them to some sin for which God will be compelled to lay them aside. (v. 13). Learn to say "yes" to Jesus and to receive the discipline of His refining providence (Heb. 12:7).

CHAPTER FOUR

Contents: Ark taken by Philistines.
Conclusion: One may go forth with a Bible under the arm and a shout upon the lips and yet not have God Himself. Many who have estranged themselves from the vitals of religion, putting their confidence in the rituals of religion, find themselves with only a form of godliness without the power thereof.

Key Word: Ark taken, vv. 11, 17.
Strong Verse: 22.
Christ Seen: Farewell, all in this world, if the ark, the token of Christ's presence with us, be lost.

CHAPTER FIVE

Contents: Ark of God a curse to Philistines.
Conclusion: Sacred signs are not things that God is tied to or that man can trust to for blessing.   His presence may be a savour of life unto life or of death unto death.
Key Word: Hand of the Lord, vv. 6, 9, 11.
Strong Verse: 6.
Christ Seen: Those who contend with God, His ark and the followers of His Beloved Son will invariably be ruined at last.   How much better to let Jesus enter, letting the dearest idols yield before Him.

CHAPTER SIX

Contents: Ark brought to Joshua.
Conclusion: The Word of God in the hands of the world brings them condemnation (v. 2) causing them to seek to get rid of it.   By refusing to part with their sins, sinners but lengthen out their own miseries (v. 4).
Key Word: Ark, v. 1.
Strong Verses: 13, 20.
Christ Seen: v. 13.   The return of the ark (token of God's presence) and the revival of holy ordinances after days of restraint and trouble must be a matter of great joy to Christians.   We must reverently use the tokens of God's grace through Christ or we will be made to sink under the tokens of His displeasure (v. 19).

CHAPTER SEVEN

Contents: Ark brought to house of Abinadab.   Revival of Mizpah.   Victory at Eben-ezer.
Conclusion: When we are truly sensible that by sin we have provoked God to withdraw from us and that we are undone if we continue in that state, if we make a solemn business of returning to God we may be assured we are on the way to a renewed prosperity and deliverance.
Key Word: Return, v. 3.
Strong Verses: 3, 8, 12.
Christ Seen: v. 12.   The Christian should, as he passes along, set up his Ebenezers by which he will be reminded that "hitherto the Lord hath helped him" and by which he will give all the glory of his victories to God and His Son Jesus Christ.

CHAPTER EIGHT

Contents: Israel demands a king; theocracy rejected.
Conclusion: When God's people will not accept His best for them, they will get the best they can be persuaded to take and, with the answer to their selfish prayers, will receive also an added judgment.
Key Word: King, vv. 5, 19.
Strong Verses: 7, 9, 18.
Christ Seen: v. 20 .   For a professed Christian to want to live like the world means not only that he is displeasing Christ, but will at last find himself a dupe.
   It was God's will that Israel should have a king but in His own time. He must come of the tribe of Judah (Gen. 49:10).   Because of Judah's sin (Gen. 38, Deut. 23:2) his line was prohibited from office for ten generations.   David is found to be the first one to satisfy these conditions. (Matt. 1).

CHAPTER NINE

Contents: Saul chosen king.
Conclusion: The wise God serves very great and certain purposes by seemingly small and casual affairs.   Let us therefore remember that promotions come not by chance and that faithfulness and humility on the path of present duty are the key to exaltation at the hands of God.

Key Word: Saul, v. 2.
Strong Verses: 21, 25, 27.
Christ Seen: v. 24.   Note the suggestiveness of the dish set before Saul. The shoulder denotes strength; the breast which went with it denotes affection.   Let all who are called to minister to Christ's people be reminded that a great responsibility is upon their shoulders and that the people should be dear to their bosom, as they are to Christ Himself.

CHAPTER TEN

Contents: Saul anointed king.
Conclusion: Whom God calls He qualifies.   When God works in us by His Spirit, it serves to confirm faith and furnish proof of a divine commission, v. 9.
Key Word: Anointed, v. 1.
Strong Verses: 6, 7, 24.
Christ Seen: The sacred unctions point to the Great Messiah, the anointed One who was anointed with the oil of the Spirit without measure, above all priests or princes of earth.
   v. 19.   Their obstinacy was a presage of their rejecting Christ, in the rejecting of whom they cast off God that He should not reign over them.

CHAPTER ELEVEN

Contents: Saul's victories at Jabesh-gilead.   Kingdom renewed at Gilgal.
Conclusion: Unless the Christian has forsaken his covenant with God, there is no occasion for his courting a covenant with the world by compromise. Through our King, we may have the victory.
Key Word: Compromise (covenant) rejected, vv. 1, 13.
Strong Verses: 6, 13.
Christ Seen: The right eye is the eye of faith.   The left eye was covered with the shield.   By the compromise they would be unfitted to fight.   Thus Satan seeks to cripple the follower of Christ in service.   A compromising Christian is always blind in one eye.   Look unto Jesus with both eyes. (Heb. 12:1).

CHAPTER TWELVE

Contents: Samuel's proclamation of the kingdom.   Deliverances of God rehearsed.   The sign of thunder and rain.
Conclusion: Religion has reason on its side (v. 7) which demonstrates that obedience to God is the happiness of men and disobedience to God is the ruin of men.
Key Word: Reason (counsel), v. 7.
Strong Verses: 14, 15, 23-25.   Promise: 22.
Christ Seen: v. 22.   Had God chosen us on our good merits, we might fear He would cast us off for our bad merits, but choosing us in Christ before the foundation of the world, for His name's sake, He cannot lose us.

CHAPTER THIRTEEN

Contents: The self-will of Saul.   He intrudes into the priests' office.   His divine rejection announced.
Conclusion: Some lay great stress upon the external performances of religion, thinking thereby to excuse their ignorance of God Himself.   Though enemies press, we are powerless to engage them without God Himself.   We will make progress if we wait upon Him and become assured of divine power.
Key Word: Disobedience, v. 13.
Strong Verse: 14.
Christ Seen: v. 11.   Scoffers of the latter days think the promise of Christ's return is broken because He does not come in their time, though it is certain that He will come "in such an hour as we think not."

CHAPTER FOURTEEN

Contents: Jonathan's great victory over the Philistines.
Conclusion: Let this strengthen the weak and encourage the timid, that no matter how few and feeble those are who seek to Him for direction and

acknowledge Him in all their ways, God will give the victory. God can not only save us, but save by us, therefore let faith venture.

Key Word: Delivered, v. 12.

Strong Verses: 6, 45.

Christ Seen: To fail to feed upon the honey (Christ in the Word) vv. 25-30, is not time gained but strength lost, unfitting one for the conflicts.

CHAPTER FIFTEEN

Contents: Saul's incomplete obedience and his rejection as king.

Conclusion: Some judge many things in their lives, but spare one Agag which the Lord has condemned. Partial obedience spells disobedience and in the absence of perfect obedience, our sacrifices are worthless, v. 22.

Key Word: Disobedience, vv. 11, 19, (rejected, v. 23).

Strong Verses: 22, 24, 25.

Christ Seen: v. 20. We see how hard it is to convict the children of disobedience of their sin and strip them of their fig leaves, for they ever seek to justify themselves on the ground of their good intentions. Ceremonial observances cannot take the place of humble, sincere obedience to the will of God which requires full yieldedness to Jesus Christ.

CHAPTER SIXTEEN

Contents: Choice of David as king. His anointing and visit to Saul.

Conclusion: Whom God appoints, He anoints, and whom He anoints is truly qualified for service.

Key Word: Chosen, v. 1, (anointed, v. 17).

Christ Seen: David means "beloved" for he was a type of the Beloved Son. As David was called from the place of obscurity and contempt, so Christ came from a humble walk of life. David was first anointed by God and later by the people. (2 Sam. 2:4; 5:3). Christ was anointed at His baptism, and at His coming again, it will be ratified by His brethren, the Jews and all nations.

CHAPTER SEVENTEEN

Contents: Defiance of Israel by Goliath and David's victory over him.

Conclusion: The battle is God's battle. If our confidence is purely in the power of God, rather than in any armor or sufficiency of our own, we may be certain the world's utmost might cannot withstand. God resists the proud and pours contempt upon those who bid defiance to His people, humiliating them by a defeat with the meanest of instruments.

Key Word: Prevailed, v. 50.

Strong Verses: 37, 47.

Christ Seen: David's victory over Goliath is a type of the triumph of the Son of God over Satan. Goliath is also a remarkable type of the anti-Christ (note 6 pieces of armor, vv. 5-7). David anointed for the kingship but not yet in power is defied by the boastful champion whom he overcomes in the name of the Lord of Hosts. When Jesus comes as Lord of Hosts, anti-Christ will be destroyed by the brightness of His coming.

CHAPTER EIGHTEEN

Contents: Love covenant of Jonathan and David. Saul's jealousy and attempts on David's life. Saul's daughter given to David.

Conclusion: The weeds of envy will grow if one thinks more of reputation than of duty. (vv. 7, 8). It is a sign that the Spirit of God has departed from men, if they be continually envious and suspicious of those about them and cannot endure to hear anyone praised but themselves. v. 12.

Key Word: Envy (displeased), vv. 8, 29.

Strong Verse: 14.

Christ Seen: vv. 3, 4. Jonathan's love is an illustration of the love the Lord Jesus has shown to us. He stripped Himself to clothe us; He even clothed Himself with our rags that we might be clothed upon with His glory. Phil. 2:5-7.

v. 23. We should magnify the honor of being sons to the King of Kings. "Behold what manner of love the Father has bestowed upon us."

CHAPTER NINETEEN

Contents: Saul's murderous hate pursues David.

Conclusion: God always raises up a friend for us in time of need. Envy allowed its way becomes murderous. Cut the claws of the tiger pup, lest it become a full grown tiger, when it is too late.

Key Word: Murderous envy, vv. 1, 10, 15.

Strong Verse: 12.

Christ Seen: The murderous attempts on the life of the anointed king by the usurping king, remind us of the repeated attempts of the usurper, Satan, against the life of God's Anointed One, Christ, when He was upon earth.

CHAPTER TWENTY

Contents: Jonathan protects David. Their parting.

Conclusion: Though the believer be despised of many, compelled to leave all comforts and part with best friends for Christ's sake, be this our comfort, that we have made an everlasting covenant with Jehovah who will exalt us in due time.

Key Word: True friend, v. 17, (loved as his own soul).

Strong Verses: 17, 42.

Christ Seen: v. 15. The covenant of Jonathan and David is an illustration of that between God and the Son on behalf of believers. John 10:28; Rom. 8:32-39.

CHAPTER TWENTY-ONE

Contents: David flees to Ahimelech and Achish.

Conclusion: If we would but trust God aright, we would not have to resort to miserable and dishonoring devices for our preservation in times of testing.

Key Word: Afraid, v. 12.

Strong Verse: 9.

Christ Seen: v. 6. Jesus showed from this in Matt. 12:3 that ritual observances must at times give way to moral duties in case of urgent necessity, thus He justified His disciples in plucking corn on the Sabbath day.

CHAPTER TWENTY-TWO

Contents: David in rejection gathers mighty men. His wanderings and dangers.

Conclusion: Those who give way to jealousy are in a continual agitation and torment and show that the Spirit of God is not with them.

Key Word: Suffering with David, v. 22.

Strong Verses: 14, 23.

Christ Seen: v. 23. Those who honor Christ, the true David, must expect to share in His rejection and suffering. As He has been promised that the Father will hide Him in the shadow of His hand (Isa. 49:2) so we, with Him, may be confident of being safeguarded.

CHAPTER TWENTY-THREE

Contents: Wanderings and adventures of David.

Conclusion: Whatever befalls us, if we acknowledge God in all our ways and seek direction from Him, God will baffle the designs of the enemy and turn their counsels in our favor.

Key Word: Hunted (search him out), vv. 14, 23.

Strong Verses: 14, 16.

Christ Seen: As David might justly claim that his enemies rewarded him evil for good and that for his love they were his adversaries, so Christ was basely used. John 10:32.

CHAPTER TWENTY-FOUR

Contents: David's mercy to Saul in En-gedi.

Conclusion: Be not overcome of evil but overcome evil with good.

Key Word: Mercy (dealt well), v. 18.

Strong Verses: 12, 17.

Christ Seen: As David rendered good for evil to him from whom he had received evil for good, he was a type of Christ who saved His persecutors.

CHAPTER TWENTY-FIVE

Contents: Samuel's death; David and Nabal. Abigail becomes David's wife, and also Ahinoam.

Conclusion: Let the believer be encouraged to commit his cause to God when in any way injured, being assured that in His own good time God will redress the wrongs in His own way if we but sit still and leave the matter to Him.

Key Word: God avenges (returned the wickedness), v. 39.

Strong Verses: 28, 29.

Christ Seen: v. 44. Saul's defrauding David of his only rightful wife led him into the irregularity of having several wives. When the marriage knot is once loosed, it is seldom ever tied fast again. See Jesus' teaching in Matt. 19:4, 5.

CHAPTER TWENTY-SIX

Contents: Saul spared by David a second time.

Conclusion: No questionable means need be employed to help out God's plans for our advnacement (v. 10). God can weaken the strongest and befool the wisest on our behalf. Wait His time.

Key Word: Spared, v. 11.

Strong Verses: 9, 10, 24.

Christ Seen: As David's way to the throne lay through multiplied sorrows and difficulties, so does Christ's, who, though the anointed King with undisputed title, yet remains "meek and lowly" awaiting the set time.

CHAPTER TWENTY-SEVEN

Contents: David down in the dumps.

Conclusion: Unbelief is a sin that besets those who have been undergoing long trials. It is no advantage to us when we are in the dumps, to cross over the borders into the world for comfort, for we cannot expect God's protection when we are out of His will.

Key Word: Discouragement (I shall perish), v. 1.

Strong Verse: 1.

Christ Seen: David had every assurance that he would be king, yet concluded that he would perish. In this he was unlike Christ who was born King, was rejected all through His earthly career, yet ascended into heaven declaring the certainty of His second coming as King.

CHAPTER TWENTY-EIGHT

Contents: David among Israel's enemies. Saul consults the witch.

Conclusion: Seek the Lord while He may be found for there is a time when He will not be found (v. 6). To think that any spiritualistic medium can be of help when God has frowned upon us, is to heap contempt upon God, who has expressly forbidden all such recourse.

Key Word: Spiritism, v. 7.

Strong Verses: 15, 16.

Christ Seen: v. 8. The soul cannot live apart from the unseen world, and for this reason God has made every provision for our securing of guidance through Christ who is at His right hand. Never did Saul look so mean as when he went sneaking to a spiritist at night. Such works are of the darkness and cannot bear the light. On this occasion, God actually sent back the spirit of Samuel, that Saul might get an answer to his design and should be given up to strong delusion, but it was the rare exception to His usual order.

CHAPTER TWENTY-NINE

Contents: David saved from fighting against Israel.

Conclusion: God's providence orders wisely and graciously for His children even when they have sadly erred. Even the ill favor of men may turn out to be for our good that a door might be opened for deliverance out of straits our own folly has brought us into.

Key Word: Ill favor, v. 6.

Strong Verse: 6.

Christ Seen: The practice of deceit has forced many Christians to follow Satan, taking up arms even against the Lord's Anointed and His followers. A Christian in such a strait always has a heavy heart.

CHAPTER THIRTY

Contents: David avenges the destruction of Ziglag.

Conclusion: When we go abroad to tarry for a while with the enemies of God's people, we may expect to be met by evil tidings when we return home again. In the mercy of God, we can even then, if called according to His purpose, encourage ourselves in God and be assured that He will overrule and bring light out of darkness and peace out of trouble.

Key Word: Recovered, vv. 8, 18.

Strong Verse: 6.

Christ Seen: What a blessed provision that a wandering Christian with anxiety gnawing at the heart, and with bitter compunction of conscience, can come back to Christ, and through His work as Advocate (1 Jno. 2:1) strengthen himself in the Lord and once more go on with power!

CHAPTER THIRTY-ONE

Contents: Death of Saul and Jonathan.

Conclusion: As men live, so will they die. Those are indeed in a deplorable condition, who, despairing of the mercy of God, would leap into a hell before them thinking to escape the hell within them. We all need to pray, "Lead us not into temptation."

Key Word: Defeat, v. 8.

Strong Verses: 11, 12.

Christ Seen: The only gleam of light in this chapter is the scene of Jabesh-gilead. Like Joseph and Nicodemus at the death of Christ, these men identified themselves with what seemed a lost cause. Are we equally grateful in confessing Christ who delivered us from eternal death?

II SAMUEL

Key Thought:	Number of Chapters:	Key Verse:	Christ seen as:
Kingdom	24	1 Sam. 10:25	Seed of David

Writer of the Book:	Date:	Conclusion of the Book:
Uncertain	About 1155 B. C.	Be sure your sin will find you out.

SUMMARY

CHAPTER ONE

Contents: David mourns the death of Saul and Jonathan.
Conclusion: He that is deeply concerned for the honor of God cannot rejoice in the afflictions that come upon his enemies. In the disgrace that comes upon them, let us not forget their former successes and real service.
Key Word: Mourned, vv. 12, 17.
Strong Verses: 26, 27.
Christ Seen: (v. 17-27). In this noble poem, David forgets all his injuries and considers only the pleasant things. If human love can impute only good to the object of its affections, what will not God's love in Christ impute to believers for whom He gave His precious life! He loved us even when we were dead in trespasses and sins.

CHAPTER TWO

Contents: David received as King of Judah. Abner makes Ish-bosheth king over eleven tribes. Civil war.
Conclusion: We may expect, one upon another, trials of our faith in the promises of God and trials of our patience, whether or not we can wait God's time for the performances of the promises.
Key Word: Anointed, v. 4.
Strong Verse: 1.
Christ Seen: v. 4. Jesus first presented Himself to Judah. Thus, like David, His kingdom is set up by degrees. He is Lord of all by divine designation but we see not yet all things put under His feet, and will not until His second coming.

CHAPTER THREE

Contents: Abner deserts to David. Joab's murder of Abner.
Conclusion: Evil pursues sinners and will overtake them at the last in one way or another. (Illustrated both in the case of Abner and that of Joab, v. 29).
Key Word: Great man fallen, v. 38.
Strong Verse: 39.
Christ Seen: v. 37. The servants of the King of Kings do many things thinking to further His Kingdom, that have not His sanction and will bring trouble upon the heads of those who do them in His name without His leading.

CHAPTER FOUR

Contents: Murder of Ish-bosheth.
Conclusion: The guilt of blood brings a curse, and if men do not avenge it, God will.
Key Word: Murder, v. 11.
Strong Verse: 11.
Christ Seen: v. 9. God had hitherto helped him in his difficulties and in coming to the throne, David would therefore depend upon Him and not the devices of men to complete His purpose. Let this teach us that Jesus Christ is coming to the throne, not by man dragging in the millennium but by the hand of God Himself.

CHAPTER FIVE

Contents: David becomes king over Israel. War with Philistines.
Conclusion: Those who have the Lord of Hosts for them need have no fear

what hosts of men or demons can do against them. If we grow great and win many victories, we can only ascribe our advancement to God's favor with us.

Key Word: Anointed, v. 3, (victory, v. 25).

Strong Verses: 10, 19.

Christ Seen: David was recognized as king on three counts. (1) Of their flesh, v. 1. Christ, Matt. 25:40. (2) Their leader in battle, v. 2. Christ, Josh. 5:13-15. (3) Designated by God, v. 2. So also Christ, Rom. 3:25. As David had three anointings; one by God, one by Judah and one by all tribes, so Christ was anointed at His baptism, will be received of the Jews and later of all nations.

CHAPTER SIX

Contents: David seeks to bring the ark to Jerusalem.

Conclusion: God will have His work done in His own way and cannot bless us if we employ heathen methods (1 Sam. 6:7-8) in doing God's work. We need to seek His directions continually lest we do good things in a wrong way.

Key Word: Ark, v. 2.

Strong Verse: 11.

Christ Seen: If we would only open our homes to God's ark (Christ's presence), there would be similar blessing.

CHAPTER SEVEN

Contents: David's desire to build the Lord's house. The Davidic covenant.

Conclusion: We need no more to make us happy than to have God for a Father to us. If He is our Father, we must be dutiful children, or expect His chastisements, which are an article of the covenant and which flow from His father-love.

Key Word: Established (kingdom), v. 16, (confirmed, v. 24).

Strong Verses: 14, 22, 25.

Christ Seen: The covenant confirmed to David by the oath of Jehovah and renewed to Mary by the angel Gabriel, is immutable, and God will yet give to the thorn-crowned King the throne of His Father David forever. Luke 1:31-33; Acts 2:29-33; 15:1-17.

CHAPTER EIGHT

Contents: Full establishment of David's kingdom.

Conclusion: After the long and frequent struggles which the Christian has with the powers of darkness, he shall at last be made more than conqueror and shall reign with Christ.

Key Word: Reigning, v. 15.

Strong Verse: 14.

Christ Seen: The Son of David shall at length put down all principality and power and take the throne. He has, as David had, a line to kill and a line to save. The Gospel is to some a savor of life unto life and to others a savor of death unto death.

CHAPTER NINE

Contents: David's kindness to Mephibosheth.

Conclusion: Kindness is one of the laws of Christianity and the Christian should seek opportunity of doing good. The most necessitous are generally the least clamorous and the best objects of our kindness and charity are such as will be discovered only through our inquiry.

Key Word: Kindness, v. 7.

Strong Verse: 7.

Christ Seen: The story gives us a picture of salvation by God's grace in Christ. Grace comes to the helpless, those "sold under sin;" invites us to the place of peace and satisfaction; feasts us at God's table; keeps our lame feet out of sight.

CHAPTER TEN

Contents: The Ammonite-Syrian war.

Conclusion: False men are ready to think all others as false as themselves. There is nothing so well meant but that it may be misinterpreted, and is likely to be so by men who love nobody but themselves. "Love thinketh no evil."

Key Word: Kindness misinterpreted, vv. 2, 3.

Strong Verse: 12.

Christ Seen: v. 5. The Christian may learn not to lay too much to heart the reproaches he receives for Christ's sake, for they will soon wear off and turn eventually to the shame of their authors. Contrast Christ's dealings with those who ill-treated Him in the person of His disciples.

CHAPTER ELEVEN

Contents: David's great sin.

Conclusion: A Christian with natural tendencies to sensuality may have cravings even when the general bent of his mind is to live in God's will. The devil finds work for idle hands to do (v. 1) and we should therefore be warned of the danger of having nothing in particular to do. Sin started leads to more sin to hide it. After all, the atmosphere of trial and difficulty is the occasion of highest strength.

Key Word: Adultery, v. 4, (murder, v. 15).

Strong Verses: 11, 27.

Christ Seen: We need to bear in mind that as the chosen seed through which Messiah was to come, David and others of the direct line had the combined forces of evil against them to accomplish, if possible their downfall. Of all men, they should have walked in hourly dependence on God. The best Christian is liable to attack and failure, but if we abide in Christ no weapon that hell can forge can hurt us.

CHAPTER TWELVE

Contents: David's rebuke and repentance. Birth of Solomon. Ammonite victory.

Conclusion: If the believer, brought face to face with his sins sincerely confesses and repents of them, he may be restored to fellowship, although God will not interfere with the consequences in this life, v. 1.

Key Word: Confession and restoration, v. 13.

Strong Verses: 13, 22, 23.

Christ Seen: God always has His man for His work and while it may cost the man nights of pain and prayer to deliver the message of Christ he may be sure that if Christ is with Him, His message will accomplish its purpose. A dogmatic message is truer and more tender than soft speeches that do not arouse conscience.

CHAPTER THIRTEEN

Contents: Ammon's crime. Absalom's vengeance for Tamar's wrong.

Conclusion: Fleshly lusts are their own punishment and not only war against the soul but against the body also, and are the rottenness of the bones. The sin of adultery makes awful mischief in families and the sinner serves a hard master. v. 1. Those who are peculiarly beautiful have no reason on that account to be proud, but great reason to stand upon their guard.

Key Word: Shame, v. 13, (avenged, v. 32).

Strong Verse: 39.

Christ Seen: Except we allow Christ to control the flesh, we cannot be saved from ourselves. There is no knowing to what lengths we might go but for His keeping power.

CHAPTER FOURTEEN

Contents: The recall of Absalom and David's forgiveness.

Conclusion: If we let private affections stand in the way of public duty (See Gen. 9:6) we may justly expect that God will make the one whom our foolish pity spares, a scourge upon us.

Key Word: Forgiven, v. 33.

Strong Verse: 14.

Christ Seen: v. 33. If the compassion of a father prevails to reconcile him to an impenitent son, shall penitent sinners doubt the compassion of God, in His Son, when they truly come to Him?

CHAPTER FIFTEEN

Contents: Absalom steals the love of ten tribes. David's flight.

Conclusion: He who steals one heart away from another by means of innuendos is the vilest of robbers, and especially when professed devotion to God is used as a pretext to carry out the design. (v. 7).

Key Word: Conspiracy, v. 12.

Strong Verses: 25, 26.

Christ Seen: How soon our hearts become alienated from Christ, our rightful King! The Absaloms ingratiate themselves and wean away our love and loyalty to Jesus.

CHAPTER SIXTEEN

Contents: False servant of Mephibosheth. Shimei curses David. Absalom takes Jerusalem.

Conclusion: A humble and tender spirit will turn reproaches into reproofs and so get good by them instead of being provoked at them. The world's smiles are more dangerous than its frowns.

Key Word: Cursed, v. 5.

Strong Verses: 11, 12.

Christ Seen: v. 9. David is herein a type of Christ who rebuked His disciples, who in zeal for His honor, would have used their miraculous powers on the heads of those who affronted Him. (Luke 9:55).

CHAPTER SEVENTEEN

Contents: Conflicting counsel of Ahithophel and Hushai.

Conclusion: It is to the comfort of all who fear God that He has an overruling hand in all counsels and a negative voice in all resolves, and laughs at men's projects against His anointed ones.

Key Word: Counsel, v. 15.

Strong Verses: 27, 28, 29.

Christ Seen: Absalom is a type of the false Messiah, who will gather an army against Christ the Greater David (Rev. 19:19), meeting his defeat in the brightness of Christ's coming.

CHAPTER EIGHTEEN

Contents: Battle of Mount Ephraim. Slaying of Absalom.

Conclusion: Those who exalt themselves shall be abased. It never pays to take counsel against the Lord and His anointed.

Key Word: Avenged, v. 31.

Strong Verses: 31, 33.

Christ Seen: As the false king was cast into a pit, so anti-Christ will be thrown into the bottomless pit at the coming of Christ, and then every tongue shall confess that Christ is King of Kings.

CHAPTER NINETEEN

Contents: Joab reproaches David's return to the throne.

Conclusion: A good man and a good cause will again recover their credit and interest, though, for a time, they may seem to have lost them. The good services done will still be remembered when men come to their right minds.

Key Word: Return, v. 14.

Strong Verses: 22, 23.

Christ Seen: vv. 14, 15. Our Lord Jesus will rule in those who invite Him to the throne of their hearts, and not until He is invited.

CHAPTER TWENTY

Contents: Joab murders Amasa. Suppression of Sheba's revolt.

Conclusion: We must not think it strange while in this world if the end of one trouble be the beginning of another, but God will bring us victoriously through them all, if we but trust in His wisdom.

Key Word: Traitor, v. 1.

Strong Verse: 20.

Christ Seen: vv. 12, 13. Wicked men think themselves safe if they can just conceal their wickedness from the eye of the world. The covering of blood with a cloth cannot stop its cry for vengeance in God's ears. We can-be more willing to part with our sins than our God is to withdraw His judgments and cover our sins with the blood of Jesus.

CHAPTER TWENTY-ONE

Contents: Three years famine. Saul's sons slain. War with Philistines.

Conclusion: When we are under God's judgments, we should enquire the grounds of the controversy, and when the cause is revealed, should go to all lengths to make right the wrongs of the past, that God's full blessing may be renewed upon us.

Key Word: Recompense (atonement) v. 3.

Strong Verses: 3, 7.

Christ Seen: vv. 9, 13, 14. Through Christ who was hanged and made a curse for us to expiate our guilt, though He was Himself guiltless, God is entreated for us. In token of the completeness of the sacrifice they took Him down from the cross and laid Him in the sepulchre.

CHAPTER TWENTY-TWO

Contents: David's song of deliverance.

Conclusion: No believer has so little from God but there is ground for praise, nor so much but that he has need to call upon God. Praise is the blossom of prayer.

Key Word: Praise, vv. 4, 50.

Strong Verses: 2, 3, 4, 31, 33, 48.

Christ Seen: What David here sings concerning Jehovah, we may now ascribe to the Lord Jesus, who through His finished work has become the Deliverer of us all.

CHAPTER TWENTY-THREE

Contents: Last words of David. Deeds of his mighty men.

Conclusion: Those who have ventured themselves for the good of the public are worthy of double honor, both to be respected by their fellow citizens and to be remembered by their posterity. Though our deeds be not recorded by men, they are recorded in heaven.

Key Word: Mighty men, v. 8.

Strong Verse: 2.

Christ Seen: vv. 3, 5. The verses have a prophetic application to Christ who is to be the just ruler, ordering all things according to His Father's will, and who will be as the light of the morning.

CHAPTER TWENTY-FOUR

Contents: David's sin in numbering the people. His choice of punishment.

Conclusion: God does not judge of sin as we do. What appears to us to be but a small offense, may be a great sin in the eyes of God who knows men's principles, being a discerner of the thoughts and intents of the heart. His judgments are according to the truth.

Key Word: Sinned, v. 10.

Strong Verses: 10, 24.

Christ Seen: v. 25. Christ is our altar and sacrifice. Through Him alone may we expect to get favor with God and to escape His wrath for our sins.

I KINGS

Key Thought: Royalty	Number of Chapters: 22	Key Verse: 2:12	Christ seen as: King of Kings

Writer of the Book:	Date:	Conclusion of the Book: Jehovah is the sover- eign ruler of Israel, blessing the obedient, punishing the disobed- ient, and forgiving the penitent.
Uncertain	About 560 B. C.	

SUMMARY

CHAPTER ONE

Contents: David's declining strength. Adonijah plots to seize kingdom. Counter plot of Nathan and Bath-sheba. Solomon anointed.

Conclusion: When men exalt themselves, God very often leaves them to themselves until they are corrected with a scourge of their own making. He that in the morning grasps at a crown, may before night be forced to hold to the horns of the altar and beg for life. God will be consulted.

Key Word: Self-exalted, v. 5 (humbled, v. 50).

Strong Verses: 29, 30.

Christ Seen: v. 39. Solomon is a type of Christ as Prince of Peace, (Isa. 9: 6; 1 Chron. 22:9). Jesus will not fulfill the Solomon type until He has fulfilled the David type. Chosen before born (Isa. 42:1). Rode into Jerusalem on a mule (Jn. 12:14-16). Anointed (Acts 10:38). Peace filled the earth when His reign was finally set up (Zech. 14:9).

CHAPTER TWO

Contents: David's charge to Solomon, David's death. Execution of Adonijah. Abiathar removed. Execution of Shimei.

Conclusion: The punishment of sin may be slow of foot but it is sure of nose and will at length find the offender. Even a hoary head ought not to be any man's protection from justice.

Key Word: Punishment, vv. 5, 8.

Strong Verse: 2. **Promise:** 3.

Christ Seen: (v. 24). The solemn declaration, "As Jehovah liveth," recalls the words of our Lord, "As the living Father sent me and I live because of the Father" (John 6:57). Let us draw daily on His life so that He may live in us (Gal. 2:20).

CHAPTER THREE

Contents: Alliance of Solomon and Pharaoh. Marriage with Pharaoh's daughter. Losses at Gibeon. Solomon's prayer. His wisdom.

Conclusion: The wisdom of God is laid up for those who have the spirit of a child (Lk. 10:21; vv. 8, 9). A knowledge of our own limitations is very essential to true success, if we have learned that the power of the omnipotent God is at our disposal.

Key Word: Wisdom, vv. 9, 28.

Strong Verse: 7.

Christ Seen: Wisdom. Its beginning, Psa. 111:10. Its source, Dan. 2:20-22. Its quality, Jas. 3:17. Way to it, 1 Cor. 3:18. Personification of it, 1 Cor. 1:30. How to obtain it, Jas. 1:5. Who it is for, Mt. 7:24-25.

CHAPTER FOUR

Contents: Princes and commissaries of Israel. Solomon's reign and wisdom.

Conclusion: There is spiritual peace and joy and a holy security for all faithful subjects of God's Anointed One.

Key Word: Safety, v. 25.

Strong Verse: 25.
Christ Seen: Solomon was a type of Christ in whom are hidden all the treasures of wisdom and knowledge—hidden for a use—for "He is made unto us wisdom."

CHAPTER FIVE
Contents: Preparation for building the temple.
Conclusion: Satan does all he can to hinder the work of God's temple, but when he is withheld for a time, we should be extra zealous in that which is good that we might carry it forward to completion. (Acts 9:31).
Key Word: Temple, v. 5.
Strong Verses: 5, 17.
Christ Seen: v. 17. The costly stones speak of Christ who was laid for the foundation of the spiritual temple, an elect and precious stone.

CHAPTER SIX
Contents: Work on the temple begun. Dimensions and materials.
Conclusion: We should not mistake noise and notoriety for spiritual progress (v. 7). Quietness and order both become and befriend the carrying on of spiritual work.
Key Word: Finished, v. 14.
Strong Verse: 12.
Christ Seen: Christ is the true Temple (Jn. 2:21). God Himself prepared Him (Eph. 1:4; Heb. 10:5). In Him all God's spiritual children meet and through Him have access to God.

CHAPTER SEVEN
Contents: Work on the temple and Solomon's house.
Conclusion: God who is best should be served and honored with our best.
Key Word: Work ended, v. 51.
Strong Verse: 51.
Christ Seen: The temple is not only a type of Christ but of the believer who is also spoken of as a temple, or habitation of God. (1 Cor. 3:16-17; 6:19). It should be as beautiful as the Holy Spirit can make it, therefore we should be yielded to His master strokes.

CHAPTER EIGHT
Contents: Ark brought in; Shekinah glory fills the temple. Solomon's sermon.
Conclusion: All cost and pains are lost on stately structures unless God has been in the work, and if He fails to manifest His glory in them, they are after all but a ruinous heap. A temple without the ark and the glory are like a candlestick without a candle.
Key Word: Dedicated (filled with glory) v. 11.
Strong Verses: 10, 27, 57, 58, 61.
Christ Seen: It is a great thing when a nation's ruler can be led of the Spirit in prayer and when he realizes that all answer to prayer is only on the ground of the shed blood of Christ. vv. 22, 62. (Heb. 9:22; 10:19-20).

CHAPTER NINE
Contents: Jehovah appears to Solomon. Covenant made. Solomon's fame.
Conclusion: God deals plainly with men and sets before them blessing or cursing. God never fails to perform His part of a covenant and if we improve the grace He is willing to give, He will confirm us to the end.
Key Word: Covenant, v. 4.
Strong Verses: 9, 25.
Christ Seen: When we yield ourselves to Christ, desiring to be His alone, He takes possession, hallowing, infilling and guaranteeing our security.

CHAPTER TEN
Contents: Solomon and the queen of Sheba. His revenue and splendor.
Conclusion: That fame is true fame which has associated with it the name of the Lord and which challenges inquiry into the means of God's grace.
Key Word: Fame, vv. 7, 23.
Strong Verses: 8, 24.

Christ Seen: Mt. 12:42. Christ mentions this queen's inquiry after God through Solomon as showing the stupidity of those who would not enquire after God through Jesus Christ who was God manifest in the flesh and therefore better able to instruct them than anyone else.

CHAPTER ELEVEN

Contents: Solomon's heart turned. Chastened of God. Rise of Jeroboam. Death of Solomon.

Conclusion: The way of sin is down hill and those who get into it cannot easily get untangled. God at first appointed one woman for one man, and he who thinks one not enough, will not be satisfied with two. When our love is set on the things of the flesh, we may be sure we have lost our love for God and are on the way to trouble.

Key Word: Backslidden, v. 9 (heart turned).

Strong Verse: 9.

Christ Seen: v. 32. The house of David must, in spite of everything, be kept intact, because out of it was to come the Messiah. As it was spared on account of the promise to David, so all God's favors shown to us are for Christ's sake and the covenant made with Him.

CHAPTER TWELVE

Contents: Accession and folly of Rehoboam. Kingdom divided.

Conclusion: Taking the counsel of unspiritual men always spells blunder and a rough answer never fails to bring division. If we make God the source of our counsel (Jas. 3:15) we will avoid all folly.

Key Word: Counsel forsaken, vv. 8, 13.

Strong Verse: 7.

Christ Seen: (v. 7). Here we have the principle underlying the sacrifice of Calvary (Rev. 5:9). Because Jesus girded Himself and washed our sins in His own blood, He ascended to the throne. He teaches us that if we would be great, we must become the servants of all.

CHAPTER THIRTEEN

Contents: Warning of punishment for idolatry. Disobedience and death of the prophet.

Conclusion: If we offer to God that which is an abomination to Him (the worship of the flesh) the offerer will certainly fall under the wrath of God.

Key Word: Warning, v. 2.

Strong Verses: 4, 8.

Christ Seen: v. 9. God would teach His servants not to have fellowship with the works of darkness, lest they fall under their contagion and give them encouragement. The devil always has his snares ready to entrap one who bears Christ's message. God's commands, like His promises, are yea and amen in Christ. Let us not dare to turn aside on advice of others.

CHAPTER FOURTEEN

Contents: Prophecy against Jeroboam and partial fulfillment. Judah's apostacy under Rehoboam. Death of Rehoboam.

Conclusion: Be not deceived; God is not mocked and often He makes quick work of sinners. If men of prominence do wickedly they involve many others who follow their pernicious ways (v. 16) and he who leads many others to hell must answer eternally for it.

Key Word: Cut off, v. 10.

Strong Verses: 9, 16.

Christ Seen: How blind we have become when we get out of fellowship with Christ! (Rom. 1:21). We may disguise ourselves, but we cannot cheat Christ, the Searcher of hearts (Jn. 4:29).

CHAPTER FIFTEEN

Contents: Accession of Abijam and Asa over Judah. War with Baasha. League with Syria. Accession of Nadab over Israel and Baasha over Israel.

Conclusion: Divine threatenings are not bugbears, for no word of God shall fall to the ground. The harboring of evil MUST eventuate in open defeat and ruin.

Key Word: Wars, vv. 6, 16, 20, 29, 32.

Strong Verses: 4, 11.
Christ Seen: v. 14 (Cp. v. 18). A heart perfect with the Lord is not sinless perfection, nor flawless obedience, but sincerity of intent and desire to do Christ's will.

CHAPTER SIXTEEN

Contents: Evil reigns of Baasha, Elah, Zimri, Omri, Ahab—kings of Israel.
Conclusion: Destruction, when it comes, whoever is the instrument of it, is the act of God's justice and the result of sin. Those who resemble others in their sins may expect to get similar plagues.
Key Word: God provoked, v. 2.
Christ Seen: Happy are they who, amid political convulsion, let Christ live in them, and receive the kingdom which cannot be moved (Heb. 12:27).

CHAPTER SEVENTEEN

Contents: Elijah's ministry and prediction of drought. Elijah fed. Raising of the widow's son.
Conclusion: God can wonderfully raise up servants and suit them to the work He designs them for. He can, if He chooses, use one man to arrest the downward movement of a nation, and with no weapon but the Word of God and prayer.
Key Word: Man of God, v. 24.
Strong Verses: 1, 24.
Christ Seen: God marvelously provides for His true servants in times of sore testing. We may be called upon at times to live from hand to mouth, but if it be from Christ's hand (Jno. 6:11) each day's need will be supplied.
v. 13. "Bring it to me." Cp. Mt. 14:18. Herein Elijah is a type of Christ as our provider.

CHAPTER EIGHTEEN

Contents: Elijah goes to meet Ahab and gives challenge. Contests with the priests of Baal.
Conclusion: The man of faith need not be afraid to risk his all on the honor of God (v. 23). Let opposers who talk of the failure of Christianity, do what it does—bring down the consuming, cleansing, illuminating power of God into the lives of men.
Key Word: Challenge, v. 24.
Strong Verses: 21, 37, 39.
Christ Seen: Nothing is needed so much today as the answer by fire. See Mt. 3:11; Lk. 12:49; Acts 2:2-3.

CHAPTER NINETEEN

Contents: God's care of His overwrought prophet. Call of Elisha.
Conclusion: Even though we faint in our faith, God abideth faithful. The best thing for a discouraged man is to get where he can see from God's viewpoint (v. 11) which he can do only by coming before God in prayer.
Key Word: Discouragement, v. 4.
Strong Verses: 7, 18.
Christ Seen: v. 12. Under law God spoke to His people with terror, but in the Gospel of Christ, which was introduced in the spirit and power of Elias, He speaks by a still small voice which makes none afraid. Heb. 12:18.

CHAPTER TWENTY

Contents: Ahab's Syrian campaigns and victories. His sin in sparing Ben-hadad.
Conclusion: Enemies are more than a match for us, but no match for Jehovah. God often uses one wicked man to scourge another.
v. 42. There are times when keeping back the sword from blood is doing the work of God deceitfully. Foolish pity spoils many a victory.
Key Word: Victory, (vv. 13, 28); Disobedience, (v. 42).
Strong Verse: 13.
Christ Seen: (v. 13). Even when we as Christians have sinned, God's love to us in Christ is unchanged (Rom. 8:38-39), and He is constantly devising new ways of expressing it and revealing Jesus to us.

CHAPTER TWENTY-ONE

Contents: Ahab covets Naboth's vineyard.   Elijah announces Ahab's doom.

Conclusions: One may covet and get what it is not God's will for them to have, but he may be sure that with it, he will get a curse.   Covetousness opens the door for all sin.

Key Words: Coveting, v. 4.

Strong Verses: 3, 29.

Christ Seen: (v. 9).   Some who have no real regard for Christ make Christianity a cloak for selfish schemes, and thus sell themselves to the devil (v. 20).   If you want a little corner added to your estate, let Jesus Christ find it for you.

CHAPTER TWENTY-TWO

Contents: Alliance of Ahab and Jehosophat.   Ahab's ultimate defeat.

Conclusion: He who joins himself in affinity with vicious men, rejects the counsels of God and hates the preachers of God's Word, will find that no masquerade will hide him from God's judgment and that no armor is proof against His vengeance.

Key Word: Alliance, v. 4.   (Defeat, v. 37).

Strong Verse: 14.

Christ Seen: v. 14.   The greatest kindness possible to a person going on a dangerous path is to tell them God's truth, as it is in Christ.   Beware of being beguiled by every voice that speaks in the heart.   God's voice always calls us to take up Christ's cross and stand alone against the crowd.

II KINGS

Key Thought:	Number of Chapters:	Key Verse:	Christ seen as:
Royalty	25	10:10	Kings of Kings

Writer of the Book:	Date:	Conclusion of the Book:
		God's Word is certain
Uncertain (Ezra)	About 560 B. C.	of fulfillment to saint and sinner.

SUMMARY

CHAPTER ONE

Contents: Elijah's message to Ahaziah. Elijah's deliverance.

Conclusion: Those who will not inquire of the Word of God for their comfort will be made to listen to it, whether they wish it or not. To consult with the devil's agents as to fortune means departure from God.

Key Word: Prediction, v. 4.

Strong Verse: 15.

Christ Seen: v. 15. All heaven is interested in Christ's true servants. Who can harm those whom God will shelter? Jesus cautioned His followers from attempting to imitate this episode (9-18). We belong to another dispensation which savors of forbearance and meekness (Lk. 9:54).

CHAPTER TWO

Contents: Translation of Elijah. Faith of Elisha. Theological students and their unbelief. Elisha's miracle.

Conclusion: Those who know they are soon going to heaven should be concerned for those they are leaving behind to carry on God's service and to leave with them their experiences, testimonies, counsels and prayers.

Key Word: Translated, v. 11.

Strong Verse: 9.

Christ Seen: Those who ask for the mantle of and walk in the steps of their godly and faithful predecessors will certainly experience the same grace. Jordan means "judgment" Christ and the believer go together (v. 8) through the judgment of the cross. Gal. 2:20; Rom. 6:3.

CHAPTER THREE

Contents: Accession of Jehoram over Israel. Moab rebels against Israel. Elisha's reproof of alliance between Jehoshaphat and Jehoram. Defeat of Moabites.

Conclusion: It would often go hard with us if God did not take more care of us, both for body and soul, than we take for ourselves. For reasons which He alone knows, God sometimes puts victories in the hands of those who are not faithful to Him.

Key Word: Victory, v. 18.

Strong Verse: 18.

Christ Seen: If we are to have the fullness of Christ and the living water He promised, we must co-operate with Him. He alone can send the water, but we must dig the ditches (v. 16).

CHAPTER FOUR

Contents: Increase of the widow's oil. Woman of Shunem and her son restored to life. Noxious pottage healed. A hundred men fed.

Conclusion: Be a man of God and God will give you His work to do. He who has power from God to satisfy the deepest needs of man will never want for applicants.

Key Word: Man of God, vv. 7, 9, 16, 21, 22, 40, 42.

Strong Verses: 6, 7, 40, 41.

Christ Seen: v. 41. When the theological student feeds on the wild gourds of the world, he will find himself in the grip of spiritual death. The meal, made of bruised corn, speaks of Christ in the Gospel. If the results of the cross are put in the pot, it will take away its poison.

CHAPTER FIVE

Contents: Naaman the Syrian healed by obeying Elisha's word.
Conclusion: There is little hope for one who is more concerned about his dignity than his disease, but full blessing is assured to one who will humble himself as a little child and walk in the light of God's commands.
Key Word: Leper cleansed, vv. 1, 14.
Strong Verses: 13, 15.
Christ Seen: Leprosy is an intense symbol of sin. 1. Circulates in the blood, hereditary. 2. Contagious. 3. Subtle, at first concealing its presence. 4. Unclean, a state of living death. 1 Tim. 5:6. 5. Banishing, Rev. 21:27. 6. Incurable by human power, Jer. 13:23. 7. Its only cure, the power of Christ.

CHAPTER SIX

Contents: Elisha recovers the lost axe. Seige of Samaria by Syrians.
Conclusion: The Christian on his knees can see more than the philosopher on his tiptoes. They who fight against God are given up to delusions, not knowing that the believer has God, (Rom. 8:13) Christ, (Mt. 28:20) the Holy Spirit, (Jn. 16:16-17) and angels (Heb. 1:14) on his side.
Key Word: Man of God, v. 9 (Prayer, v. 17).
Strong Verse: 16.
Christ Seen: v. 6. The God of nature is not tied up to its laws. As He raised the iron against the natural laws, so His grace can raise the iron heart which has sunk into the mud of this world and raise up affections naturally earthly to things above. Hearts may be as heavy as lead at the bottom of the river, but let a splinter of Calvary's Cross be inserted, and they rise to the surface and swim.

CHAPTER SEVEN

Contents: Jehovah's terror upon the Syrians.
Conclusion: Faith expects from God what is beyond all human expectation. They who cannot find it in their hearts to take God at His Word, forfeit all benefits of His promises.
Key Word: Promise fulfilled, vv. 1, 16.
Strong Verses: 6, 7.
Christ Seen: The lepers were first in the deserted camp. Abundance was awaiting the starving people, but only a few outcasts tasted it. Christ's abundance is for all, but often the outcasts procure more than the children of the church.

CHAPTER EIGHT

Contents: Famine predicted. Jehoram restores the Shunanmite land. Reigns of Jehoram and Ahaziah of Judah and Joram of Israel.
Conclusion: God through His ministers, calls for reformátion and obedience, and if the calls be not regarded, men may expect plagues and evil days to come, for He WILL be heard. (vv. 1, 12). Men often think themselves sufficiently armed against those sins by which they are afterward entirely overcome. (v. 13).
Key Word: Prediction, vv. 1, 10.
Strong Verse: 19.
Christ Seen: The king had a wonderful memory for those who fed him when he was hungry and ministered to him when he was in need, recalling Jesus' words in Matt. 25:37.

CHAPTER NINE

Contents: Jehu annointed king of Israel. Slays Jehoram, Ahaziah and Jezebel.
Conclusion: God doesn't always pay up for sin every week, but in the end, He pays. He is known by His judgments.
Key Word: Sin requitted, vv. 26, 36.
Strong Verse: 26.
Christ Seen: v. 11. Men who have no religion commonly look upon followers of Christ as mad. Of the Savior they said, "He is beside himself." Of John, "He has a devil." Of Paul, "Much learning hath made thee mad."

CHAPTER TEN

Contents: Judgment on house of Ahab. Princes of Judah slain. Baal worship put out. Jehu's reign and death.

Conclusion: God is not the author of any man's sin, but even by that which men do from bad principles, He serves His own purposes and takes vengeance on those who have defied Him.

Key Word: Judgment, vv. 10, 17.

Strong Verse: 10.

Christ Seen: v. 16. If we aim at the applause of men and make their praise our highest aim, instead of the honor of Christ, we are upon a false bottom. An upright heart approves itself to God and covets no more than His acceptance. (Gal. 6:14).

CHAPTER ELEVEN

Contents: Royal seed of Judah destroyed. Joash becomes king. Execution of Athaliah. Revival through Jehoida.

Conclusion: All attempts to frustrate God's revealed purpose are foolish and bound to be fruitless. Who can disannul what God has purposed? Though the promise be bound up in one life, yet will it not fail.

Key Word: Preserved, v. 3.

Strong Verse: 17.

Christ Seen: Three times the royal line was all extinct except for one babe. Moses, Heb. 11:23; Joash, v. 3. Christ, Mt. 2:12-16. The hidden king in type may represent the hiding of Christ in our hearts, while we give some Athaliah (evil) the real government of our lives. The Athaliah must be stoned.

CHAPTER TWELVE

Contents: Reign of Joash over Judah and his death. Repair of the temple.

Conclusion: Those who are entrusted with public money for the carrying on of God's work should learn to deal faithfully, as those who know God will reckon with them, if men do not. Loose financial methods in the church dishonor God.

Key Word: Repairing temple, v. 5.

Strong Verses: 2, 15.

Striking Facts: v. 9. This is the first mite box mentioned in the Bible. The last one is in Mk. 12:4.

Christ Seen: When our lives are yielded to Christ, His power is with us. This makes our enemies His enemies. He shows Himself strong on behalf of those whose hearts are perfect toward Him.

CHAPTER THIRTEEN

Contents: Reign of Jehoahaz over Israel and his death. Accession of Jehoash and his death. Elisha's death and the miracle at his tomb.

Conclusion: The slowness of God's processes against sinners must be construed to the honor of His mercy, not to the impeachment of His justice (v. 23). It is of the Lord's mercies, that they are not consumed.

Key Word: Gracious, v. 23.

Strong Verses: 4, 23.

Christ Seen: (v. 20-21). Contact with Elisha, even when his body lay in the grave, caused the dead to revive. Compare Matt. 27:52-53; Jn. 5:25-29).

CHAPTER FOURTEEN

Contents: Reign of Amaziah over Judah. War between Israel and Judah. Reign of Jeroboam in Jerusalem.

Conclusion: Those who are too eager, through pride, to fight, may get enough of it in quick order. Many would have honor and wealth enough, if they but knew when they had enough.

Key Word: Defeat, v. 12.

Strong Verses: 26, 27.

Christ Seen: (v. 26-27). God could not forget the time when Israel was a child in His love, and He brought him out of Egypt (Hos. 11:1). If we as children, saved through the sacrifice of Christ, wander away from Him, is not the memory of our first love, with its holy promise, cherished by the Father? He will draw us back by the hand of some Jeroboam (Heb. 12).

CHAPTER FIFTEEN

Contents: Reign of Azariah and Jotham over Judah and Zechariah, Shallum, Menahem, Pekahiah, Pekah over Israel.
Conclusion: God may for a time suffer wickedness to prosper that it may of itself carry away the wealth and honors that might have been kept if God had been recognized. One wicked man is made the scourge of another and every wicked man sooner or later ruins himself.
Key Word: Reigns.
Strong Verse: 12.
Christ Seen: Azariah suffered an eclipse because he persisted in the sacreligious endeavor to be both King and Priest. This is the exclusive prerogative of Christ (Zech. 6:13).

CHAPTER SIXTEEN

Contents: Reign of Ahaz over Judah. Assyrians take Damascus.
Conclusion: That religion is of no worth which is guided by fancy instead of faith (v. 10). The hearts of idolaters walk after their eyes.
Key Word: Abominations, v. 3.
Christ Seen: (v. 10-20). Ahaz displaces the ancient brazen altar of Jehovah for an imitation of one he saw at Damascus. Thus men today are going back from the simplicity and spirituality of Christ to exploded systems that have failed in the past to satisfy the souls of men.

CHAPTER SEVENTEEN

Contents: Reign of Hoshea in Israel. Israel becomes tributary to Assyrians. The sins of Israel.
Conclusion: Those who forget God may themselves expect to be forgotten. Those who try to be like the world may expect to be swallowed up by the world. Those who will not serve God in their own land need not be surprised if they are forced to serve enemies in a strange land.
Key Word: Carried away, vv. 6, 18.
Strong Verses: 13, 14, 37. Promise: 39.
Christ Seen: From this captivity Israel has never been restored. (Deut. 28: 15-68). A remnant of Judah returned, and many Hebrews became believers in Christ and were added to the Church (1 Pet. 1:1-2). Paul gives us a far horizon in Rom. 11:25-27. The national restoration is near at hand.

CHAPTER EIGHTEEN

Contents: Reign and revival of Hezekiah over Judah. Victory over Phillistines. Invasion of Sennacherib. Insolence of Rab-shekeh.
Conclusion: Santanic suggestions are always artful and cleverly managed and well sprinkled with pride, malice, falsehood and blasphemy. Thus Satan steals a man's watch and explains it so well, the victim gives him his coat and vest.
Key Word: Seducers, v. 30.
Strong Verses: 6, 7.
Christ Seen: v. 36. We are bidden to follow the steps of Jesus (Isa. 53:7) silently committing our cause to Him Who never fails to vindicate those who trust Him.

CHAPTER NINETEEN

Contents: Hezekiah's message to Isaiah and the answer. Sennacherib defies God. Hezekiah's prayer and the answer through Isaiah.
Conclusion: Prayer changes things. If the motive of our prayer is the honor of God, we may be sure He will graciously and copiously answer, being able to do exceeding abundantly above all that we ask or think.
Key Word: Prayer answered, vv. 19, 34.
Strong Verses: 15, 34.
Christ Seen: v. 30. The remnant shall yet again be planted in their own habitations and shall take root there and grow rich. That soul is indeed prosperous who takes root downward by faith in Christ, and then becomes fruitful upward in righteousness.

CHAPTER TWENTY

Contents: Hezekiah's illness and recovery.

Conclusion: Neither greatness nor goodness can exempt us from sickness, yet often when the death sentence has apparently been received within the body, it is reversible through Spirit-born, faith-filled prayer.

Key Word: Healed, v. 5.

Strong Verse: 5.

Christ Seen: (v. 2). Compare Hezekiah's attitude to death with that of Paul. Let Hezekiah's action remind us how much we owe to the Lord Jesus, who abolished death for those who trust in Him, and took the sting out of it.

CHAPTER TWENTY-ONE

Contents: Evil reigns of Manasseh and Amon in Judah.

Conclusion: Those have much to answer for who not only are wicked themselves but help to make others so. v. 16.

Key Word: Evil reigns, vv. 2, 20.

Strong Verses: 11, 12.

Christ Seen: (v. 16-26). Christ's heaviest denunciations were against those who deliberately cause others to fall (Mt. 18:6). No man sins to himself.

CHAPTER TWENTY-TWO

Contents: Reign of Josiah. Repairing temple and finding of the book of the law.

Conclusion: An unread Bible is a lost Bible and a lost Bible always means spiritual degeneracy and its accompanying curses. When man finds the Word, the Word is quick to find him and convict him of sin. Either sin keeps one from the Book or the Book keeps one from sin.

Key Word: Bible found, v. 13.

Strong Verses: 13, 19.

Christ Seen: Christ is the Living Word revealed in the written Word (Jno. 1:1). What havoc is wrought when God's Word drops out of sight, and there is no vision of the Living Word!

CHAPTER TWENTY-THREE

Contents: Law read to the people. The king's covenant and reformations.

Conclusion: We should put ourselves heartily into God's hands for service and as far as our influence goes, our endeavors should go to do good and bring the wickedness of the wicked to an end.

Key Word: Covenant, v. 3.

Strong Verses: 3, 25.

Christ Seen: There are times when we need to carefully examine ourselves, not in the light of our own ideas of right and wrong, but by the example and precepts of our Lord Jesus Christ.

CHAPTER TWENTY-FOUR

Contents: Jehoikim tributary to Nebuchadnezzar. Reigns of Jehoikim, Jehoichin and Zedekiah. Deportation to Babylon.

Conclusion: Time will not wear out the guilt of sin. Threatenings will be fulfilled as certainly as promises if the sinner's repentance prevent not.

Key Word: Judgment, vv. 3, 14.

Strong Verse: 3.

Christ Seen: (v. 1-9). God, here, like the Saviour in the New Testament, would have gathered Israel under His protecting wings, but they would not (Mt. 23:37); therefore the times of the Gentiles began, and are still running their course (Lk. 21:24).

CHAPTER TWENTY-FIVE

Contents: Seige of Jerusalem and final deportation.

Conclusion: Those who have by sin provoked God to leave them may expect ultimately to be encompassed about with innumerable evils.

Key Word: Broken up, v. 4.

Christ Seen: Thus ended the kingdom of Judah, and from that time the Jews have been a scattered people whose only real hope, though they know it not, is the second coming of Christ, the Messiah whom they rejected. Amid all the catastrophe, recall the tears of the book of Lamentations, like those of Jesus afterward (Mt. 23:37).

I CHRONICLES

Key Thought: Temple	Number of Chapters: 29	Key Verse: 2 Chron. 15:2	Christ seen as: God's true King

Writer of the Book: Uncertain (Ezra)	Date: About 1000 B. C.	Conclusion of the Book: Jehovah is the sovereign Lord blessing the obedient and punishing the disobedient.

SUMMARY

CHAPTER ONE

Contents: Genealogy: Adam to dukes of Edom. The patriarchal line.
Conclusion: We are all by nature the seed of Adam. Let us see to it that by faith we become the spiritual children of Abraham. Rom. 4:11-12.
Key Word: Genealogy.

CHAPTER TWO

Contents: Genealogy, sons of Judah.
Conclusion: The best and most honorable families may have those belonging to them who are black sheep.
Key Word: Genealogy.

CHAPTER THREE

Contents: Genealogy of David's line.
Conclusion: Since piety and devotion are not hereditary, it behooves all parents to consecrate their children to God long before they are born and to do their best to bring them up in the nurture and admonition of the Lord, praying for the coming generations.
Key Word: Genealogy.
Christ Seen: From David's line our Lord came, as regards the flesh, as appears from Lk. 3:31.

CHAPTER FOUR

Contents: Posterity of Judah and Simeon.
Conclusion: If we set ourselves to acknowledge God in all our ways we put ourselves under the divine blessing and protection and will be prospered accordingly. (v. 10).
Key Word: Genealogy.
Strong Verse: 10.

CHAPTER FIVE

Contents: Line of Reuben, Gad, half of Manasseh. Captivity for their sins.
Conclusion: In all conflicts we must look up to heaven for strength and it is believing prayer that will be prevailing prayer.
Key Word: Genealogy.
Strong Verses: 20, 22.
Striking Facts: v. 22. If we depend upon a commission from God to wage war upon another country we may depend upon His providence to give success.

CHAPTER SIX

Contents: Sons of Levi. Cities of the priests and Levites.
Conclusion: There is always abundance of service to be done by God's children in His house. As everyone has received the gift, therefore let him minister according to all that God has commanded.
Key Word: Genealogy.
Strong Verse: 49.
Christ Seen: (v. 49). The burnt offerings implied confession of sin and of its due deserts, in anticipation of Christ's sacrifice which did finally put away sin (Rom. 3:25; Heb. 9:15).

CHAPTER SEVEN

Contents: Sons of Issachar, Benjamin, Naphtali, Manasseh, Ephriam, Asher.
Conclusion: (v. 22). It is often the burden of those who live to be old that they see their children go before them. It is a brotherly and friendly office on the part of the Christian, to comfort such in their afflictions with the Word of God.
Key Word: Genealogy.

CHAPTER EIGHT

Contents: Sons of Benjamin. The stock of Saul and Jonathan.
Conclusion: (v. 40). It is much to a man's praise that he is qualified to serve his country being mighty in valor, even though not a child of God.
Key Word: Genealogy.

CHAPTER NINE

Contents: Record of the Israelites. The charge of certain Levites.
Conclusion: God's work is likely to be done well when each knows the duty of his place and makes a business of it. That which is everybody's work in the church will generally be nobody's work.
Key Word: Inhabitants.

CHAPTER TEN

Contents: Saul's overthrow and death. Triumph of the Philistines. Saul's sin.
Conclusion: Those who abandon themselves to the devil's leading will be abandoned by God and their doom will be according to their transgressions.
Key Word: Retribution, v. 13.
Strong Verse: 13.
Striking Facts: v. 6. Those who love their children will avoid sin lest they bring ruin on their children with themselves or entail a curse upon them in later years.

CHAPTER ELEVEN

Contents: David becomes King of Israel. Catalog of his mighty men.
Conclusion: God's counsels will be fulfilled at last, whatever seeming difficulties lie in the way.
Key Word: Annointed (king). v. 3.
Strong Verse: 9.
Christ Seen: v. 10. The honors of Christ's kingdom are prepared for those who fight the good fight of faith and are willing to venture even life itself for Christ's sake.

CHAPTER TWELVE

Contents: David's army at Ziglag. The leaders who made David king.
Conclusion: It is good to take sides with those who take sides with God and have God with them. Let us therefore testify our allegiance to the Lord Jesus and make ourselves His helpers without reservation.
Key Word: Helpers, vv. 1, 21.
Strong Verses: 22, 38.
Christ Seen: vv. 38-39. When Christ is enthroned in a soul, there is bound to be great joy, and a great feast begins, to last not merely for a few days but throughout eternity.

CHAPTER THIRTEEN

Contents: David's attempt to bring the ark to Jerusalem. The ark left at the house of Obed-edom.
Conclusion: Beware of presumption, rashness and irreverence in dealing with holy things and think not that a good intention will always justify a rash action. We must not trifle in our approaches to God.
Key Word: Ark. v. 3.
Strong Verse: 14.
Christ Seen: There are preachers who lay hands on the ark of God's Word, thinking to save Christianity from overthrow. It is dangerous to put unsanctified hands on the person of Christ, His virgin birth, atonement, resurrection, and other fundamentals of God's Word.

CHAPTER FOURTEEN

Contents: The prosperity of King David. Double defeat of the Philistines.
Conclusion: David's frequent inquiry of God should direct us in all our ways to acknowledge Him and in all our perplexities to fly to Him that we might perceive God to go before us.
Key Word: Kingdom exalted, v. 2.
Strong Verse: 16.
Christ Seen: v. 17. God has highly exalted our Redeemer, David's greater Son and given Him a name above every name (Phil. 2:9).

CHAPTER FIFTEEN

Contents: Ark brought to Jerusalem in the appointed way.
Conclusion: It is not enough that we seek God in a due ordinance, but we must seek Him in due order. When those who have suffered for their irregularity learn from God's Word to be obedient in all details, the correction is well bestowed.
Key Word: Ark brought, vv. 15, 25.
Strong Verses: 13, 28.
Christ Seen: v. 26. Those who bear the vessels of the Lord have great need of divine help in their ministrations, that Christ may be glorified in them and the churches edified through them.

CHAPTER SIXTEEN

Contents: David's festival and psalm of thanksgiving. The ark established in Jerusalem.
Conclusion: Though God's Word may be clouded and eclipsed for a time, it will at length shine out of obscurity, wherefore let us encourage ourselves to triumph and trust in God and glorify Him continually by our praises.
Key Word: Praise, v. 4
Strong Verses: 8, 15, 31, 34.
Christ Seen: v. 10. Ceremonial worship was a divine institution containing the types of the mediation of Christ and could not therefore be omitted. So the church should keep up the appointed ordinances in which Christ is remembered, until He comes.

CHAPTER SEVENTEEN

Contents: David's desire to build the temple. The Davidic covenant and David's prayer.
Conclusion: Thrice happy is that people whose God is Jehovah, for He will be to them a God all-sufficient (v. 27). Whom He blesses are truly and eternally blessed, therefore let our desires and hopes be for things eternal.
Key Word: Covenant, v. 23.
Strong Verses: 20, 27.
Christ Seen: v. 7. David is here a type of Christ in the flesh, the Shepherd King. At His first coming He took the Shepherd's place. At His return He will take the place of ruler over Israel.

CHAPTER EIGHTEEN

Contents: David's kingdom fully established.
Conclusion: Those who take God along with them whithersoever they go may expect to prosper and be preserved whithersoever they go.
Key Word: Judgment and justice, v. 14.
Strong Verses: 6, 13.
Christ Seen: All opposing rule will eventually be put down by the Son of David and the most inveterate enemies shall fall before Him, acknowledging that He is Lord to the glory of the Father.

CHAPTER NINETEEN

Contents: Ammonite-Syrian war.
Conclusion: Those who design ill themselves are apt to be jealous and to suspect ill of others without cause, but the hearts of such are marked for ruin. Right will prevail at last.
Key Word: Misjudged, v. 3.
Strong Verse: 13.

Christ Seen: v. 19. Let those who in vain have stood out against Christ, the greater David, be wise for themselves and agree with Him quickly while they are in the way.

CHAPTER TWENTY

Contents: Joab and David take Rabbah. War with Philistines.

Conclusion: The power and pride of great men against us need not terrify us if we have the power and peace of God with us. God takes pleasure in abasing lofty looks and mortifying the giants who array themselves against Christianity.

Key Word: War, v. 4.

CHAPTER TWENTY-ONE

Contents: David's sin in numbering the people. Joab's faithful protest. David's choice of punishment.

Conclusion: God does not judge of sin as we do. What appears to man to be but a small offense may be a great sin in the eyes of God who knows men's principles, being a discerner of the thoughts and intents of the heart. His judgments are according to the truth.

Key Word: Sin, v. 8.

Strong Verses: 8, 13.

Christ Seen: v. 18. If we have sinned, the safest thing to do is to flee to Christ, who is an altar and sacrifice, for through Him alone there is hope of winning back the joy of salvation and getting favor with God.

CHAPTER TWENTY-TWO

Contents: Material prepared for the temple. David instructs Solomon in God's promises. Princes charged to assist Solomon.

Conclusion: Nothing is more powerful to engage us in any service for God than to know that hereunto we were appointed by God. Where God gives rest He expects work (v. 9-10) let us therefore be invigorated for Christian service.

Key Word: Temple, v. 10.

Strong Verses: 13, 19.

Christ Seen: Everything about the temple was to be stately and magnificent, being a type of Christ in whom all fullness dwells and in whom are hid all treasures.

CHAPTER TWENTY-THREE

Contents: Number and distribution of the Levites.

Conclusion: There is a place in the service of God for every Christian and God would have each at his own post, for of all men an idle Christian makes the worst figure. No place in God's service is commonplace unless it be made so by an unworthy spirit.

Key Word: Service, v. 4.

Strong Verse: 25.

CHAPTER TWENTY-FOUR

Contents: The divisions of the priests and Levites for the temple service.

Conclusion: God was, and is still, the God of order, particularly in the things of His worship. Every Christian should therefore pray to know his place in the work of God and should keep to it.

Key Word: Service, vv. 3, 19.

Christ Seen: In the mystical body of Christ every member has its use for the good of the whole. Rom. 12:4-5; 1 Cor. 12:12.

CHAPTER TWENTY-FIVE

Contents: The offices of the temple singers.

Conclusion: The glory and honor of God should be extolled in the music of the church whether vocal or instrumental, making melody from the heart as to the Lord. (Eph. 5:19.)

Key Word: Sacred song, v. 6.

CHAPTER TWENTY-SIX

Contents: The division of the temple porters. Levites as treasurers. Officers and judges

Conclusion: Whatever service God wishes men for, He either finds them fit or makes them so. All service for God is honorable, and happy will be that man who is faithful to his appointed part.

Key Word: Ministry, v. 12.

Christ Seen: The temple treasuries illustrate the plenty there is in our Father's house, enough and to spare. In Christ, the true Temple, are hid all treasures of wisdom and knowledge and riches to supply all the believer's needs. (Phil. 4:19).

CHAPTER TWENTY-SEVEN

Contents: The captains for each month. Princes of the twelve tribes. David's several officers.

Conclusion: It is the wisdom of rulers in providing for public safety to seek to make it effectual and yet easy and as little as possible burdensome to the people.

vv. 23-24. A good man cannot, if he stops to reflect, be pleased with that which he knows displeases God, nor take comfort in that which is obtained through unbelief in God's promises.

Key Word: Officers, v. 1.

CHAPTER TWENTY-EIGHT

Contents: David counsels Israel and Solomon concerning the temple.

Conclusion: As the time apparently draws nigh for God's servants to die, they should put forth every effort to counsel and encourage their successors, calling attention to the patterns God has given in His Word.

Key Word: Counsel, v. 2.

Strong Verses: 8, 9, 20.

Christ Seen: The Gospel temple of Christ, being builded of living stones, is all being framed according to the divine counsels, ordained before the foundation of the world for God's glory. In bringing it to completion we should cling to the plans given in the New Testament.

CHAPTER TWENTY-NINE

Contents: David exhorts the people. The princes and people willingly offer. David's thanksgiving and prayer. Solomon made king. David's death.

Conclusion: Those whose affections are set upon the service of God will think no pains nor cost too much to bestow upon it and God loveth a cheerful giver.

Key Word: Willing offerings, v. 6.

Strong Verses: 9, 11, 12.

Christ Seen: v. 25. Solomon's glorious and peaceful kingdom is a type of the coming kingdom of the Messiah on earth. His will be indeed "the throne of the Lord" (v. 23) for the Father will commit all judgment to Him.

II CHRONICLES

Key Thought: Temple	Number of Chapters: 36	Key Verse: 15:2	Christ seen as: God's true King.

Writer of the Book:	Date:	Conclusion of the Book: Seeking and serving
Uncertain (Ezra)	About 530 B. C.	the Lord is the secret of a vital religion and a life of victory.

SUMMARY

CHAPTER ONE

Contents: Solomon's sacrifices at Gibeon. His vision and prayer and God's answer.

Conclusion: Those who make this world their end come short of the other and are never satisfied with this. Those who make the other world their end and seek spiritual gifts, not only obtain these with full satisfaction, but enjoy much of this world on their way there.

Key Word: Prayer, v. 7.

Strong Verses: 11, 12.

Christ Seen: (v. 6). We may be thankful that the one offering of Christ has now done away with the many individual offerings. We may learn this lesson—that which is laid out in promoting fellowship with God is never wasted.

CHAPTER TWO

Contents: Preparation to build the temple.

Conclusion: (vv. 4-6) It becomes us to go about every work for God with a due sense of our utter insufficiency for it and our incapacity in ourselves to do anything adequate to the divine perfections.

Key Word: Temple, v. 4.

Strong Verse: 6.

Christ Seen: The artificer was a Gentile, a good omen of uniting Jew and Gentile in the Gospel temple, which is Christ, v. 14.

CHAPTER THREE

Contents: Temple begun. The materials and dimensions.

Conclusion: God's Word prescribes all the details of how His work is to be carried on. Nothing can be added to or subtracted from God's perfect plans.

Key Word: Temple, v. 1.

Christ Seen: The temple was built at Jerusalem (v. 1). As it typified Christ it was fitly built there; since it was there He raised up the temple of His body.

CHAPTER FOUR

Contents: Further details about the temple.

Conclusion: The typology of the temple is obscure and is not expounded in the N. T. as is the tabernacle. In many ways the temple, while manifesting outward splendor, also manifests spiritual deterioration of the people.

Key Word: Temple.

Christ Seen: Everything in the temple directed the worshipper to the great propitiation. So should we in all our devotions keep the eye of faith upon Jesus Christ who was the fulfillment of all.

CHAPTER FIVE

Contents: The ark brought in. The glory fills the house.

Conclusion: When God's work is carried out according to His revealed will and done in the spirit of unity with praise, He is certain to own it and to give a special manifestation of His presence.

Key Word: Glory, v. 14.
Strong Verse: 14.
Christ Seen: The ark was a type of Christ, and as such a token of the presence of God.   The temple would be a desolate place indeed if Christ was not in it to glorify it.

CHAPTER SIX

Contents: Solomon's sermon and prayer.
Conclusion: Those who set God before them and walk before Him with all their hearts, will find Him as good as His word and better.   He will both keep covenant with them and show mercy to them.   (v. 14.)
Key Word: Dedication, v. 12.
Strong Verses: 14, 41.
Christ Seen: v. 20.. We may with confidence pray to God to be well pleased with us because we are in Jesus Christ in whom God is well pleased. He says not now of any house "this is my beloved place," so there is but one safe shelter—Christ.

CHAPTER SEVEN

Contents: Divine acceptance.   Sacrifice and rejoicing.   God appears to Solomon.
Conclusion: The surest evidence of God's acceptance of our prayers is the descent of His holy fire upon us.   The heart to which God manifests Himself is thereby owned as a living temple.
Key Word: Accepted, vv. 1, 12.
Strong Verses: 1, 14.
Christ Seen: v. 1.   Christ, our sacrifice, was made sin and a curse for us and the sacrifice was consumed by the fire of God's wrath against sin that we might escape, and inherit His perfect righteousness.

CHAPTER EIGHT

Contents: The energy and fame of Solomon.
Conclusion: When our hearts are truly set on God's work, we find our Father in heaven ready to indulge us in many innocent desires and to give us success in our undertakings.
Key Word: Solomon's work, v. 16.
Christ Seen: v. 16, cp. Eph. 2:20-22.   So Christ's temple being built in this age was foreplanned and is step by step coming to its completion as the living stones are added.   (1 Pet. 2:5).

CHAPTER NINE

Contents: Solomon and the queen of Sheba.   His revenue and splendor.
Conclusion: Those who honor God, He will honor.   The best way to get the credit of our endowments as well as the full enjoyment of them is to consecrate them to God and use them for Him.
Key Word: Fame, v. 1.
Strong Verse: 8.
Christ Seen: The lustre of Solomon's kingdom was typical of the glory of the coming kingdom of Christ and a faint representation of His throne to be set up when He returns.

CHAPTER TEN

Contents: Accession and folly of Rehoboam.   Division of the kingdom.   Accession of Jeroboam over Israel.
Conclusion: Taking counsel of men who know not God is sure to mean serious blunders, and a rough answer never fails to bring division.   Good words cost nothing and purchase great things.
Key Word: Foolish counsel, v. 8.
Christ Seen: Wise is the man who knows enough to let Christ be "made wisdom unto him," rather than to turn to the conceited counsels of young men.

CHAPTER ELEVEN

Contents: Rehoboam returns to Jerusalem.   Jeroboam rejects the worship of God.

Conclusion: It is dangerous to undertake anything contrary to the will of God, and he is wise who, when he finds himself going contrary to God's plans, lets his own plans drop.

Key Word: Deterred, v 4.

Christ Seen: v. 14. Christ's representatives should never allow a secular advantage to keep them among worshippers of the devil or in any place where they are in danger of making shipwreck of faith and conscience.

CHAPTER TWELVE

Contents: Rehoboam defeated by Shishak. Death of Rehoboam.

Conclusion: It becomes us, when we are under the rebukes of providence, to justify God (v. 6) and humble ourselves (v. 12), thereby we may be saved from total ruin, though we have to bear a part of God's judgment.

Key Word: Humbled, v. 7.

Strong Verse: 12.

Christ Seen: (v. 12). It is only those who humble themselves as little children, at the foot of the cross, who may have God's wrath turned from them. (John 3:18, 36).

CHAPTER THIRTEEN

Contents: War between Abijah and Jeroboam. Death of Jeroboam.

Conclusion: Right may indeed suffer the worst for a time, but it will prevail at last. The battle is ours, if God be for us.

Key Word: Reliance (on God), v. 18.

Strong Verses: 10, 12.

Christ Seen: v. 18. The prayer of faith is the prevailing prayer and it is by faith in Christ's mediation that we overcome the world. 1 John 5:4.

CHAPTER FOURTEEN

Contents: Death of Abijah. Accession of Asa. Asa's victory over Zerah.

Conclusion: He who has sought God in the day of peace and prosperity can with holy boldness cry to Him in the day of testing and God will have delight in giving him a great victory.

Key Word: Rest (on God) v. 11.

Strong Verse: 11.

Christ Seen: v. 7. Those have rest indeed who have the peace of Christ, for He gives not as the world gives. John 14:27.

CHAPTER FIFTEEN

Contents: Warnings of Azariah. Reform under Asa.

Conclusion: If we turn aside from God and His ordinances, He is not tied to us, but will certainly cease to act for us, when we will discover that present triumphs are no security to us. If we keep praying we will keep prevailing.

Key Word: Reform, v. 8.

Strong Verses: 2, 15. Promise: 7.

Christ Seen: v. 8. Attachment to Christ means detachment from idols. 1 Thes. 1:9.

CHAPTER SIXTEEN

Contents: War between Asa and Baasha. Asa's rebuke and death.

Conclusion: God is much displeased when He is distrusted and when the arm of flesh is relied on more than His power and goodness. Since we have the Rock of Ages to rely upon, let us not lean upon broken reeds.

Key Word: Unbelief, vv. 7, 12.

Strong Verse: 9.

Christ Seen: v. 12. (Physicians) Egyptian healers whose methods were demonical, answering to spiritualism, Christian Science, New Thought, clairvoyancy, etc., of our own time. The help of physicians is good if our trust is not in the physician but in Christ, the Great Physician.

CHAPTER SEVENTEEN

Contents: Accession of Jehoshaphat and his growing power.

Conclusion: True religion and obedience to God are the best friends to outward prosperity.

Key Word: Obedience, v. 4.
Strong Verses: 3, 4.
Christ Seen: v. 3 (ways of David). Note that Jehoshaphat followed David as far as David followed God. Paul exhorts us to be followers of him, but only as far as he followed Christ. 1 Cor. 11:1.

CHAPTER EIGHTEEN

Contents: Jehoshaphat's alliance with Ahab. Ahab's lying prophets. Micaiah's true prophecy. Defeat and death of Ahab.
Conclusion: Some men's kindnesses are dangerous and their society infectious. There can be no surety of being in familiar converse with wicked people and yet getting no hurt by them.
Key Word: Ungodly alliance, v 1.
Strong Verse: 13.
Christ Seen: v. 21. One evil spirit can make use of 400 prophets to deceive those who will not receive the love of the truth. Remember Jesus' words (Matt. 7:15-20) "Beware of false prophets."

CHAPTER NINETEEN

Contents: Jehu rebukes Jehoshaphat's alliance with Ahab.
Conclusion: Rebuke a wise man and he will take warning (Prov. 9:8-9) and if he truly repents, he will be particularly concerned to recover those who have fallen into sin or been hardened in it by his example.
Key Word: Returned, v. 4.
Strong Verse: 7.
Christ Seen: v. 7 may well be taken in connection with the offer of salvation through Christ in this age. We have no perfection to offer God, and there is no iniquity with Him. We must therefore take heed to Christ's sacrifice and become identified with Him, the perfect One.

CHAPTER TWENTY

Contents: Jehoshaphat's prayer for deliverance and its answer. Invading armies stricken.
Conclusion: Faith takes God's bonds, knowing they are as good as ready money (v. 19). If the battle is God's and we are on God's side, we may be certain of shortly being made more than conquerors through Him that loved us. This is the victory, even our faith.
Key Word: Believing, v. 20.
Strong Verses: 9, 17
Christ Seen: v. 26. The valley of Berachah, lit. "blessing" (modern Bible class name—Baraca) was perpetuated for the encouragement of succeeding generations to trust in God and to remind us that our praises should be as oft repeated as our prayers. Let the cross of Christ be such to us, for to His work thereon we owe everything.

CHAPTER TWENTY-ONE

Contents: Jehoram's wicked reign over Judah and its accompanying disasters.
Conclusion: Bad men bring judgment upon themselves and all about them. Wickedness makes men despicable even in the eyes of those who have little religion, and the name of the wicked shall rot. (v. 19).
Key Word: Evil, v. 6.
Strong Verse: 7.
Christ Seen: (v. 7). It is well for Christians that they have a covenant with God by sacrifice, else every fresh mistake would bring upon them instant judgment. If God should mark iniquities, who could stand?

CHAPTER TWENTY-TWO

Contents: Accession of Ahaziah over Judah. Athaliah's wicked plot.
Conclusion: The counsel of the ungodly is the ruin of many. Those who forsake the divine guidance of the Holy Spirit and the Word debase and destroy themselves.
Key Word: Evil, v. 4.
Christ Seen: Three times the royal seed was extinct except for a single babe whom God preserved. 1. Moses, Heb. 11:23. 2. Joash. 3. Jesus, Matt. 2:12, 16.

CHAPTER TWENTY-THREE

Contents: Joash becomes king of Judah. Execution of Athaliah. Revival through Jehoiada.

Conclusion: Some who are themselves most guilty are commonly most forward to cry "treason" at others. Evil doers will surely be cut down like the grass and wither as the green herb, then shall the righteous shine forth as the noonday.

Key Word: Execution, v. 15.

Strong Verse: . 16.

Christ Seen: v. 21. When the Lord Jesus is enthroned upon the heart and the usurper of the life put down, all is quiet and springs of joy are opened.

CHAPTER TWENTY-FOUR

Contents: Reign of Joash. Temple repaired. Zechariah stoned. Judah defeated by Syrians.

Conclusion: It is easier to build temples than to be a temple of the Holy Spirit. Outward religious zeal is no substitute for inward spiritual vision. (vv. 4, 24.)

Key Word: Repaired (temple), v. 6; judgment, v. 24.

Strong Verses: 10, 20.

Christ Seen: vv. 24-26. If vengeance pursues men, the end of one trouble will be but the beginninng of another, until divine wrath finally completes their doom. In like manner God's wrath pursues every rejector of His Son. (John 3:36).

CHAPTER TWENTY-FIVE

Contents: Reign of Amaziah over Judah. War between Judah and Israel.

Conclusion: Trust in God means to be willing to venture the loss of anything for Him, knowing that He can more than make up any damage we sustain in obeying His commands. A firm belief in God's all-sufficiency to bear us out in our duty, will make His yoke easy and His burden light.

Key Word: Counsel despised, v. 16.

Strong Verse: 8.

Christ Seen: v. 2. Amaziah is an illustration of many today, who live moral lives, yet not enemies to Christ. He that is not with Christ is counted against Him.

CHAPTER TWENTY-SIX

Contents: Accession of Uzziah. His successes and fame.

Conclusion: The world's smiles are the devil's darts and prosperity ruin as many as adversity. It is dangerous to be strong except in the Lord and the power of His might.

Key Word: Pride, v. 16.

Strong Verse: 5.

Christ Seen: Humility is always the safest plan for it brings Christ's successes into our lives. Psa. 105:4. Whatever we have must be viewed as a talent given us for helping forward Christ's Kingdom.

CHAPTER TWENTY-SEVEN

Contents: Reign of Jotham in Judah and his death.

Conclusion: The more steadfast we are in religion, the mightier we shall be for the resistance of evil and the performance of good.

Key Word: Mighty, v. 6.

Strong Verse: 6.

Christ Seen: Jotham became mighty because he ordered his way before the Lord. Those who make themselves felt in the world are those who take Christ into all their plans. Through Him we are made more than conquerors. (Rom. 8:39).

CHAPTER TWENTY-EIGHT

Contents: Reign of Ahaz. War with Rekah. Intercession of Oded. Edomite and Philistine invasion.

Conclusion: If men will not be humbled by God's judgments, God will find means to bring them low and will make them as despicable as they have been formidable.

Key Word: Brought low, v. 19.
Christ Seen: v. 16.   Estrangement from Christ is generally followed by seeking protection from the enemies of Christ, v. 20, but no enemy of Christ can strengthen the people of God.

CHAPTER TWENTY-NINE
Contents: Hezekiah's reign in Judah and the revival.   Temple restored.
Conclusion: Those who begin with God begin at the right end of their work and will prosper accordingly.   Let us do our part to revive the work of God and ascribe to Him all the glory of what is done.
Key Word: Cleansed, v. 15.
Strong Verses: 11, 27.
Christ Seen: v. 22.   Even repentance and reformation will not obtain pardon, but through Christ, who was made our sin offering, we may find peace.   With our offering, our praises should ascend, because Christ has been made unto us righteousness.

CHAPTER THIRTY
Contents: Preparations for the passover and its observance.
Conclusion: In every true reformation, the doctrine of the atonement must be emphasized.   God's grace will meet us in our deepest difficulties if they are felt and confessed and if we approach Him by the blood-sprinkled way.
Key Word: Passover, v. 1.
Strong Verses: 8, 9.
Christ Seen: v. 15.   Christ our passover was sacrified for us. 1 Cor. 5:7. When He is trusted as the Lamb of God who beareth away sin, God is in a position to heal us and to give us the joy of salvation.

CHAPTER THIRTY-ONE
Contents: Idols destroyed and other reforms of Hezekiah.
Conclusion: Vital communion with God on the ground of the shed blood will kindle in us a holy zeal and an indignation against sin and all that is offensive to God.
Key Word: Prospered, v. 21.
Strong Verses: 10, 21.
Christ Seen: v. 10.   If one has tasted the sweetness of the passover Lamb, which is Christ, he will never grudge the expenses of carrying on His work, but will freely give as he has freely received.

CHAPTER THIRTY-TWO
Contents: Invasion of Sennacherib.   His army defeated in answer to prayer.
Conclusion: A believing confidence in God will raise us above the prevailing fear of man.   The good soldier of Jesus Christ can always say "If God be for us, who can be against us?"
Key Word: Trust, v. 8.
Christ Seen: Satan is ever determined to destroy the believer's faith in Christ's all-sufficiency, knowing that if he can but scare him, his point is won.   When thus tempted, we should betake ourselves immediately to Christ who will instantly give the victory.

CHAPTER THIRTY-THREE
Contents: Manassah's accession and evil ways.   Reign and death of Amon. Accession of Josiah.
Conclusion: In prosperity men forget God, but in adversity they can find no other refuge.   Blessed be the affliction that brings one to his knees, for the divine mercy far exceeds the divine vengeance.
Key Word: Sin, v. 2; repentance, v. 12.
Strong Verses: 12, 13.
Christ Seen: v. 16.   God is ever ready to accept and welcome returning sinners who entreat Him on the grounds of Christ's atoning sacrifice.

CHAPTER THIRTY-FOUR
Contents: Reign of Josiah.   Book of the law found and read.

Conclusion: When man finds the Word, the Word finds man and reveals to him his true condition. If heartily received, it will lead to cleansing, consecration and continuance in the ways of God.

Key Word: Reform, v. 33.

Strong Verse: 27.

Christ Seen: A lost Bible means a lost Christ. One day our neglect of the Living Word in the Written Word will come suddenly home to us and we will cry out in the agony of conviction. Let us find the Word and let the Christ in it find us.

CHAPTER THIRTY-FIVE

Contents: The passover kept. Death of Josiah.

Conclusion: Religion cannot flourish if the passover is neglected. Christ, our passover, is sacrificed for us and it is well for us to be continually put in mind of His atoning death through the ordinances of the church.

Key Word: Passover, v. 1.

Christ Seen: v. 13. The lamb roast with fire, suggests Christ who was subjected to the fires of God's wrath against sin. He cannot be feasted upon except in view of the substitutionary character of His atoning death.

CHAPTER THIRTY-SIX

Contents: Reign and dethronement of Jehoahaz. Final deportation. Captivity of Judah in Babylon.

Conclusion: God gives sinners both time and inducement to repent and waits to be gracious to them, but if they will profane God's institutions by their sins, it is just with God to suffer them to be profaned by their enemies.

Key Word: Wrath, v. 16.

Strong Verse: 16.

Christ Seen: v. 16. God's methods to reclaim sinners by His Word, by faithful ministers, by providences, by conscience, show His great compassion through Christ and unwillingness that any should perish.

EZRA

Key Thought: Restoration	Number of Chapters: 10	Key Verse: 1:5	Christ seen as: Lord of heaven and earth

Writer of the Book: Ezra	Date: About 536 B.C.	Conclusion of the Book: God's Word should have a place and power in the religious, social and civil life of His people.

SUMMARY

CHAPTER ONE

Contents: Decree of Cyrus for restoration of the temple and preparations for the return of the remnant.

Conclusion: (v. 1) The hearts of kings are in the hand of the Lord and like the rivulets of water, He turns them whatever way He wills. Therefore whatever good offices are done for the church, God must have the glory.

Key Word: Temple, v. 2.

CHAPTER TWO

Contents: The returning remnant.

Conclusion: Sin debases and diminishes a nation but God always has a faithful remnant who love the ceremonies of His house and give liberally and cheerfully for its upkeep.

Key Word: Remnant's return, v. 1.

Strong Verses: 68, 69.

Striking Facts: Persons from all tribes returned under Zerrubabel, but in the broad sense, the dispersion of Israel still continues and the tribes cannot be identified. Only God knows who they are. At the revelation of Jesus Christ they will be made known.

Christ Seen: Each of us should be able to establish his connection with Christ, and to vindicate his claim to be considered a child of God, a joint heir with Christ.

CHAPTER THREE

Contents: Altar set up and temple foundations relaid. Worship established.

Conclusion: To see any branch of God's work reestablished after long desolations cannot but open fountains of joy and praise in those who love God. We should be thankful for even the beginnings of mercy though we have not yet seen the perfection of it.

Key Word: Established, v 11.

Strong Verses: 11, 13.

Christ Seen: v. 3. If we have enemies, the safest course is to keep on intimate terms with God through His Son Jesus Christ who is typified in the daily Lamb and whose righteousness must be our confidence in all our supplications.

CHAPTER FOUR

Contents: Work hindered by adversaries.

Conilusion: God's work cannot be advanced except Satan will rage and the gates of hell will fight against it. Wonder not at the church's enemies but keep an eye single to God who will ultimately give the victory.

Key Word: Hindered, v. 4.

Strong Verse: 3.

Christ Seen: v. 14. A secret enemy to Christ and His Gospel is often guilded over with a pretended affection to Caesar and his power. The worst enemy is one who claims to be a Christian but is not.

CHAPTER FIVE

Contents: Encouragement of the prophets and the work resumed.

Conclusion: It is a sign that God has mercy in store for a people when He raises up men of God among them to encourage and help them in His work. When we cannot do what we would in His service, we should take courage and do all we can.

Key Word: Work resumed, v. 2.

Christ Seen: v. 2. It is the business of Christian ministers to stir up God's people to that which is good, especially to the work of completing the temple of Christ which is being erected out of "living stones."

CHAPTER SIX

Contents: Darius confirms the decree of Cyrus. Temple furnished and worship restored.

Conclusion: When God's time has come for the accomplishment of His gracious purposes concerning His church, He will raise up instruments to promote it and from men of whom good service was not expected. The wrath of the enemy may be made to praise God.

Key Word: Finished, v. 14.

Strong Verses: 10, 21, 22.

Christ Seen: v. 10. Let men in authority despise not the prayers of the meanest saints who know how to approach God on the ground of Christ's sacrifice. Let God's people pray for those in authority.

CHAPTER SEVEN

Contents: Ezra's expedition to Jerusalem and his thanksgiving.

Conclusion: God is able to do for us exceedingly abundantly above all that we ask or think. When magistrates are moved to encourage the work of the church, we should thank God who put it into their hearts to do so.

Key Word: Decree, v. 13.

Strong Verses: 10, 23.

CHAPTER EIGHT

Contents: List of Ezra's companions and his visit to Jerusalem. Treasure placed in the temple.

Conclusion: God's servants have His power engaged for them. Those who trust in God will be ashamed of seeking much to the creature for protection. In carrying out God's commissions, we are safe under the shadow of His wings. (v. 22.)

Key Word: Furthered, v. 36.

Strong Verse: 22.

Christ Seen: v. 23. Even the common dangers of our everyday journeys are such as to oblige us to sanctify our going out with prayer and our return in peace with thanksgiving through Jesus Christ.

CHAPTER NINE

Contents: The remnant loses its separated position. Ezra's prayer and confession.

Conclusion: Let this be the comfort of true penitents, that though their sins have piled up to heaven, God's mercy is in the heavens and if we confess our sins, trusting to the sacrificed One, God is faithful and just to forgive, and to cleanse from all unrighteousness.

Key Word: Confession, v. 6.

Strong Verses: 6, 13, 14.

Christ Seen: v. 5. The evening sacrifice was a type of the propitiation of the Lamb of God, Who, in the evening of the world, took away sin by the sacrifice of Himself. With the eye of faith fixed upon that sacrifice we may confess our sins and hope for full cleansing.

CHAPTER TEN

Contents: Separation restored. Strange wives surrendered.

Conclusion: There is hope concerning people when they are convinced not only that it is good to part with their sins, but indispensably necessary lest they be undone.

Key Word: Separated, v. 11.

Strong Verses: 1, 11.

Christ Seen: v. 19. The only way of obtaining pardon for sin is to seek it on the ground of Christ's sacrifice, who was our trespass offering, so owning our guilt and His blood as that which washes away the stain and guilt of sin.

NEHEMIAH

Key Thought: Political	Number of Chapters: 13	Key Verse: 2:5	Christ seen as: Lord of heaven and earth.

Writer of the Book: Nehemiah	Date: About 445 to 448 B.C.	Conclusion of the Book: Prayer, pains and per- severance are the con- ditions of successful work for God.

SUMMARY

CHAPTER ONE

Contents: Nehemiah learns of distress in Jerusalem. His prayer.
Conclusion: The desolation and distresses of the church should deeply con-
cern the Christian and move him to earnest prayer, for there is no other
method for bringing relief to God's people, or directions for ourselves as
to the way in which we should render help.
Key Word: Fasting and prayer, v. 4.
Strong Verse: 10.
Christ Seen: v. 8. Our best pleas in prayer are those taken from the
Word of God on which He has caused us to hope through Jesus Christ. If
God were not more mindful of His promises than we are of His precepts,
we would be undone.

CHAPTER TWO

Contents: Nehemiah's visit to Jerusalem by permission of Artaxerxes.
Conclusion: The Christian should be concerned in the sorrows and desolations
of others, having a deep concern for God's honor. When prayer is sincerely offered, it is sure to be seconded with serious endeavors to render aid.
Key Word: Arise, build, v. 20.
Strong Verses: 18, 20.
Christ Seen: v. 4. We are not limited to certain moments in our addresses
to the King of Kings but have access to the throne of Grace in every
time of need, being emboldened by His invitation, Who has, by His blood,
made possible our approach into God's holy presence.

CHAPTER THREE

Contents: Wall of Jerusalem built.
Conclusion: What is to be done for the public good, everyone should have a
part in and further to the utmost of his place and power. It is good to
be zealously affected in a good cause.
Key Word: Repaired, v. 4.

CHAPTER FOUR

Contents: Opposition by ridicule, anger and discouragement.
Conclusion: God's people are often a despised people, loaded with contempt,
but the reproaches of enemies should rather quicken them to duty than
drive them from it. Those who cast contempt on God's people, in reality
despise God Himself and prepare for themselves everlasting shame.
Key Word: Opposition, v. 1.
Strong Verses: 6, 9, 20.
Christ Seen: v. 13. Having prayed, they set a watch. Jesus taught us that,
"We cannot secure ourselves by prayer, without watchfulness." Matt.
26:41. Prayer without watchfulness is presumption. Watchfulness without prayer is hypocrisy.

CHAPTER FIVE

Contents: Opposition by greed and heartlessness. Nehemiah's example of
unselfishness.

Conclusion: Nothing exposes Christianity more to the reproaches of its ene-
mies than the worldliness and hard-heartedness of its professors. Fol-
lowers of Christ should be careful, lest by these means, they bring a re-
proach upon their religion.
Key Word: Usury, v. 7.
Strong Verse: 19.
Christ Seen: v. 15. Let us remember the words of the Lord Jesus, how
He said, it is more blessed to give than to receive. Acts. 20:35.

CHAPTER SIX

Contents: Opposition by craft. Nehemiah's manly firmness. The wall done.
Conclusion: Christian fortitude will always be sharpened by opposition.
Every temptation to draw us from duty and into a snare, should drive us
to God and so quicken us the more to duty.
Key Word: Craftiness, v. 8.
Strong Verses: 3, 11.
Christ Seen: v. 3. Let those who are tempted to waste time from the Master's
business by attending idle affairs with vain companions, make use of this
answer—"We have work to do and cannot come down." If we see to
Christ's business, He will see to our safety.

CHAPTER SEVEN

Contents: Jerusalem put in charge of Hanani and Hananiah. Genealogy of
the first remnant.
Conclusion: Those who fear God will evidence it by being faithful to all men
and universally conscientious.
Key Word: Register, v. 5.
Strong Verse: 2.
Christ Seen: We ought to make sure that we and our loved ones and friends are
included in God's register. We cannot lay claim to an inheritance except
through Christ and the new birth. Rom. 8:16, 17.

CHAPTER EIGHT

Contents: The law read and explained. Feast of tabernacles restored.
Conclusion: Reading the Scripture in religious assemblies is an ordinance of
God whereby He is honored and the church edified. It should be delivered
distinctly, for it is a requisite that those who hear the Word should
understand it, else it is to them as an empty sound of words.
Key Word: Bible, v. 8.
Strong Verses: 6, 8.
Christ Seen: v. 14. The feast of tabernacles was a memorial of their dwell-
ing in tents in the wilderness, a representation of our tabernacle state
in this world as followers of Christ, and a type of the Gospel church.

CHAPTER NINE

Contents: The people feast and repent. Confession of the priests and Levites.
Conclusion: When we are seeking to God for mercy and relief in time of
distress, it is an encouragement to faith to look back upon our own and
our fathers' experiences, noticing how all glory belongs to God and all
shame to ourselves. When confessing our sins, it is good to reckon up
God's many mercies that we may see how ungrateful we have been.
Key Word: Confessed, v. 2.
Strong Verses: 6, 17.
Christ Seen: The history of God's dealings with Israel is an epitome of His
dealings with us. Fortunate for us it is that we are not represented
by our promises and prayers but by Jesus Christ, in whom we are accepted.

CHAPTER TEN

Contents: The covenant and the signers.
Conclusion: Conversion means a separating of ourselves from the course and
custom of this world and devoting ourselves to the conduct of the Word
of God.
Key Word: Covenant, v. 29.
Strong Verse: 29.

CHAPTER ELEVEN

Contents: The dwellers at Jerusalem and the cities.
Conclusion: Those who take care of the outward concerns of the church, the common service in connection with it, are as necessary in their place as those who take care of the inward concerns, giving themselves entirely to the ministry of the Word and prayer.
Key Word: Dwellers, v. 1.

CHAPTER TWELVE

Contents: Priests and Levites who went to Jerusalem with Zerubbabel. Dedication of the walls.
Conclusion: Great mercies call for the most solemn returns of praise in the courts of the Lord's house.
Key Words: Dedication, v. 27.
Strong Verse: 43.
Christ Seen: v. 30. The purifying was a type of the blood of Christ (Num. 19:9) by which our consciences are purged from dead works, making us fit to serve the living God. (Heb. 9:14).

CHAPTER THIRTEEN

Contents: Cleansing the temple. Nehemiah's second visit to Jerusalem and his further reforms.
Conclusion: Nothing grieves a godly man more than to see the ministers of God's house practicing things contrary to God's Word. There is sure to be a general decay of religion and corruption of manners when the people forsake the sanctuary and profane the Sabbath.
Key Word: Cleansed, v. 30.
Christ Seen: v. 8. Those who would expel sin out of their hearts, the living temples, must throw out its household stuff and all the provision made for it, taking away those things which are fuel for lust. Let the blood of Christ be then applied by faith, that it be furnished anew with the grace of God's Spirit.

ESTHER

Key Thought:	Number of Chapters:	Key Verse:	Christ seen as:
Providence	10	4:14	Our Mordecai

Writer of the Book:	Date:	Conclusion of the Book:
Uncertain (Mordecai)	464-434 B. C.	The great God takes a real interest in all our affairs and shapes His providences to work out His glory through them.

SUMMARY

CHAPTER ONE

Contents: Ahasuerus' great feast and the story of Vashti.

Conclusion: Better is a dinner of herbs with quietness than the banquet of wine with its tumult and the sin sure to result from it. When wine is in, wit is out.

Key Word: Feast, v. 9.

Striking Fact: v. 12. Whether or not it was the part of wisdom for Vashti to deny obedience to the king, or that the king was ruled by passion, the incident served God's providence making way for Esther to the crown.

CHAPTER TWO

Contents: Esther made queen.

Conclusion: God sometimes raises up the poor out of the dust to set them among princes. Those who make sure of God's favor usually find favor with man, at least so far as it is good for them.

Key Word: Chosen, v. 17.

Christ Seen: v. 3. To what absurd practices do those come who are destitute of the Word of God and given up to their vile affections. It is the Gospel of Christ alone that can purify men from such lusts of the flesh.

CHAPTER THREE

Contents: Conspiracy of Haman. The king's decree to destroy the Jews.

Conclusion: Though religion in no way stands in the way of good manners, but teaches us to render honor to whom honor is due, yet it is the character of a Christian not to hypocritically express respect for one known to be a vile person, merely because he occupies a place of authority. However threatened, it behooves the Christian to be true to conscience, if he is sure his conscience is enlightened by the Holy Spirit.

Key Word: Decree, v. 14.

Strong Verse: 2.

Christ Seen: v. 8. The enemies of the followers of Christ could not give them such bad treatment as they do if they did not first give them a bad name by malicious representations.

CHAPTER FOUR

Contents: Fasting among the Jews. Esther's resolution to defeat the decree.

Conclusion: We should consider for what end God has put us in the place where we are and should study to answer that end lest our opportunity slip.

Key Word: Fasting and weeping, v. 3.

Strong Verses: 14, 16.

Christ Seen: v. 11. We should be thankful that nothing need bar us from the court of our King in time of need, for we are welcome in the very holiest through faith in the blood of Jesus.

CHAPTER FIVE

Contents: Esther's courage in proceeding to obtain favor.

Conclusion: If we have had power with God in prayer we shall find favor with men in the time of need, for God can turn the hearts of men which way He pleases.

Key Word: Favor, v. 2.
Christ Seen: v. 9.   Those who walk in holy sincerity with Christ may walk in holy security and go on in their work not fearing what man can do to them.

CHAPTER SIX
Contents: Haman compelled to exalt Mordecai.
Conclusion: God's wisdom and grace is seen in the way He times the means of deliverance for His people so as to manifest His own glory.   As for God, His way is perfect, and let not enemies think to triumph over those who are in covenant with Him.
Key Word: Honored, v. 11.
Strong Verse: 13.
Christ Seen: When we are suffering indignity at the hands of the rejectors of Christ, let us turn to this story and see how God can cause the wrath of man to praise Him.

CHAPTER SEVEN
Contents: Esther's banquet and the hanging of Haman.
Conclusion: Mischief is sure to return upon the person himself who contrives it.   The wicked shall be snared in the work of their own hands. Psa. 7:15-16.
Key Word: Hanged, v. 10.
Strong Verses: 9, 10.
Christ Seen: v. 7.   The day is coming when those who have persecuted and hated the followers of Christ would gladly be beholden to them, like the rejected virgins (Matt. 25) who cry "give us oil."

CHAPTER EIGHT
Contents: The vengeance order of Ahasuerus.
Conclusion: Let the odds be against God's people, they have but to include God in their faith and He will open ways of deliverance and draw conclusions.
    The holy joy of those who trust in God is a great ornament to their profession and will encourage others to trust in Him.   (v. 16.)
Key Word: Decree, v. 17.
Strong Verse: 16.
Christ Seen: v. 6.   Those who are true followers of Christ had rather die in the last ditch than live to see the desolations of the church of God. The speed with which the royal decree was circulated is a rebuke to the church which has been entrusted with the decree of salvation through Christ, and still great multitudes have never heard.

CHAPTER NINE
Contents: Vengeance executed; the Jews victorious.   Feast of Purim instituted.
Conclusion: When we have received signal mercies from God, we should be quick to return our thanks to Him while the impressions are fresh.   If the favor has extended to the whole people, steps should be taken to perpetuate the remembrance of it for the honor of God and the encouragement of others to trust in Him.
Key Word: Vengeance, v. 5.
Strong Verse: 22.
Christ Seen: The changes recorded in this chapter remind us of the change that Christ's advent made in the world, even among religious people.   Contrast Esther and Mary of Bethany.

CHAPTER TEN
Contents: Mordecai made prime minister.
Conclusion: Men of virtue and true piety may for a time seem to be kept in obscurity, but often by the hand of God they are suddenly discovered to the world and caused to be preferred.
Key Word: Advanced, v. 2.
Strong Verse: 3.
Striking Fact: The name of God nowhere occurs in the book, but in no other book of the Bible is His providence more evident.
Christ Seen: As God exalted Mordecai to honor and glory, so will He work for His Son and all who love Him, and He will ultimately put all enemies under His feet.

JOB

Key Thought:	Number of Chapters:	Key Verse:	Christ seen as:
Testings	42	1:9	Risen Redeemer

Writer of the Book:	Date:	Conclusion of the Book:
		Trial is the school of
Uncertain	During times of Abraham	trust—not always given
(Moses, Elihu or Job)	Oldest Book in Bible	as chastisement, but sometimes for our education.

SUMMARY

CHAPTER ONE

Contents: Job's family and their piety. Satan's challenge and the calamities that befell Job.

Conclusion: God allows Satan power over His saints but it is always limited by the will of God. Nothing shows more accurately what we are than the way in which we stand in the presence of trial and difficulty.

Key Word: Tested, v. 12.

Strong Verses: 8, 21.

Christ Seen: v. 12. The power Satan has over the Christian is bounded by the prayer of the Lord Jesus who "ever liveth to make intercession." No affliction can ever fall upon the believer except by God's permission and when it comes, God has some great purpose in it, which it is our part to ascertain.

CHAPTER TWO

Contents: Job in Satan's seive. Family, property and health gone. His three friends.

Conclusion: One of the greatest evidences of God's love to those who love Him is to send them affliction, with grace to bear it. If trial makes us complain against God, then the devil laughs and is glad. Trial is the school of trust. (1 Pet. 1:7).

Key Word: Afflicted, v. 7.

Strong Verse: 10.

Christ Seen: v. 4. This verse gives the foundation stone of so-called Christian Science. Body healing is the substitute for soul healing through Christ. Men will embrace anything that will relieve pain and distemper of body and hence Satan uses physical ailments to try and draw men from seeing their need of Jesus.

CHAPTER THREE

Contents: Job tells his misery and despair.

Conclusion: "Pity thyself" is the devil's most popular sermon to one who will listen to him, for he delights to embitter the saint by causing him to misunderstand God's providences. Remember that God's worst is better than the devil's best and if our circumstances find us in God, we shall find God in all our circumstances.

Key Word: Curse, v. 1.

Christ Seen: v. 3. Though many, because of distrust, have cursed the day of their birth, yet no one ever curses the day of their "new birth" nor wishes they had never found Christ as their Saviour.

CHAPTER FOUR

Contents: Eliphaz's theory in regard to Job's suffering.

Conclusion: Those who pass rash and uncharitable censures upon their brethren, do Satan's work. We should be careful not to add affliction to saints who are already in grief, unless we are certain we have a God-given message to deliver.

Key Word: Retribution, v. 7.

Strong Verses: 8, 9, 17.

Christ Seen: vv. 14, 15. There are certain dogmatists who have to be listened to because they have had some ONE remarkable experience, and everyone else's case is similar to their own. The best and truest comfort is found in Christ who knows our hearts better than we do ourselves.

CHAPTER FIVE

Contents: Eliphaz's discourse continued.
Conclusion: Even Satan may be God's servant to make better saints of us, the blow at the outward man proving the greatest blessing to the inward man. We should therefore be more desirous of knowing God's purpose in our trouble than of getting out of it.
Key Word: Chastisement, v. 17.
Strong Verses: 2, 8, 17, 18.
Christ Seen: Fellowship in Christ's sufferings is the qualification for sharing His dignity.

CHAPTER SIX

Contents: Job's answer to Eliphaz. His appeal for pity.
Conclusion: No one can judge another justly without much prayer for divine guidance. Affliction does not necessarily prove one to be a hypocrite or a wicked man.
Key Word: Pity, vv. 14, 28.
Strong Verses: 14, 24.
Christ Seen: See 1 Peter 2:20-23.

CHAPTER SEVEN

Contents: Job's answer to Eliphaz continued.
Conclusion: We believe in the sun even when it is hidden behind a cloud, therefore we should not doubt the goodness of God when His face seems for a time to be hidden from us. The Great Physician has never taken down a wrong bottle.
Key Word: Complaint, v. 11.
Strong Verses: 17, 18.
Christ Seen: v. 11. It is better to die praising Jesus and praying than complaining and fretting. The only time our Lord ever asked "why" was when He bore the world's sin and the Father's face was turned away.

CHAPTER EIGHT

Contents: Bildad's theory of Job's affliction.
Conclusion: It is not just or charitable to argue that merely because one is in deep affliction, he is therefore a hypocrite. Let us "judge nothing before the time." A day is coming when the secrets of God's providence will be solved to universal satisfaction.
Key Word: Hypocrisy, v. 13.
Strong Verses: 13. Promises: 20, 22.
Christ Seen: Let the afflicted one include the Lord Jesus in his faith and he will eventually be vindicated in the sight of men.

CHAPTER NINE

Contents: Job answers Bildad, denying he is a hypocrite.
Conclusion: Man is an unequal match for his Maker, either in dispute or combat. If God should deal with any of us according to our deserts, we should certainly be undone.
Key Word: Complaint, v. 17.
Strong Verses: 20, 32.
Christ Seen: 2, 3, 33. While it may be possible for us to vindicate our own integrity to friends, we can never plead our integrity for our justification before God. Were it not that the believer stands in Christ's righteousness, he would have no ground whatever before God.

CHAPTER TEN

Contents: Job's answer to Bildad continued.
Conclusion: Sometimes, when in affliction, the believer is tempted to think that God's providences and His justice cannot be reconciled. Faith and patience would keep us from being weary of our lives and would show

us that when God contends with us, there is always some good purpose
in it.
Key Word: Complaint, v. 1.
Strong Verse: 12.
Christ Seen: v. 2.   The Christian's comfort is that he is "in Christ" and
that although he is afflicted, there is no condemnation. (Rom. 8:1). He
is chastised that he might not be condemned with the world. (1 Cor.
11:32).

CHAPTER ELEVEN

Contents: Zophar's theory of Job's condition.   He thinks Job a hypocrite
and liar.
Conclusion: Those are not always in the right who are most forward to
express their judgment and to conclude that if God should speak, He
would agree with them.   We should seek to put the best possible construc-
tion upon the words and actions of our brethren that they will bear, lest
we add to their afflictions.
Key Word: Liar, mocker, v. 3.
Strong Verses: 7, 14, 15.   Promise: 20.
Christ Seen: Zophar is a type of the religious dogmatist who thinks he knows
all about God's ways and exactly what God will do in each individual case.
Probably there was some truth in his allegations.   Christians are often
filled with self complacency, judging their best by other's worst, instead of
looking at Jesus.

CHAPTER TWELVE

Contents: Job answers his three friends, extolling God's wisdom.
Conclusion: There is a wise providence which guides and governs all things
by rules with which the wisest men are but imperfectly acquainted.   The
afflicted one should learn to acquiesce in His disposals and the one who is
tempted to criticise and censure should learn not to be over-wise in his
expressions of judgment.
Key Word: Hand of God, v. 9.
Strong Verses: 9, 14.
Christ Seen: v. 3.   Nothing is more grievous to one who has fallen from
prosperity into adversity than to be insulted when he is down.   Our Lord
Jesus is the wisest and kindest of comforters.   To Him let us go in all
our troubles.

CHAPTER THIRTEEN

Contents: Job's answer to three friends continued.
Conclusion: We should persevere in the way of duty, though it cost us all
that is dear to us in this world, rejoicing in God when there is nothing
else to rejoice in, knowing that the "sufferings of this present time
are not worthy to be compared with the glory which shall be revealed in
us."
Key Word: Reasoning, v. 6.
Strong Verses: 15, 16.
Christ Seen: v. 15.   Those who walk in unbroken fellowship with Christ,
having assurance there is no unconfessed sin in their lives, may cheerfully welcome every event, being in readiness for it.

CHAPTER FOURTEEN

Contents: Job's answer to his friends continued.
Conclusion: God's providence has the ordering of the period of our lives; our
times are in His hand.   The consideration of our inability to contend with
God, of our sinfulness and weakness, should lead us to throw ourselves
unreservedly into His hands that He might accomplish fully His purposes
in us.
Key Word: Trouble, v. 1.
Strong Verse: 14.
Christ Seen: v. 14.   Though our friends prove miserable comforters, the
believer may rejoice in all circumstances in the comfort that there is a
life beyond, victory over even the grave through our Lord Jesus Christ.

CHAPTER FIFTEEN

Contents: Eliphaz's theory about Job, charging him with foolishly justifying himself:

Conclusion: Those speeches which do no good, being of no service either to God, our neighbors or ourselves, are better unspoken. If in our troubles we give ourselves to prayer and worship, we will be less apt to drop those expressions which cause others to question our sincerity and constancy in religion.

Key Word: Unprofitable talk, v. 3.

Strong Verses: 15, 31.

Christ Seen: v. 15. Although God uses His saints, He places no confidence in them apart from the ability of the Holy Spirit which He imparts to them for service, and the standing they have in Jesus Christ.

CHAPTER SIXTEEN

Contents: Job charges that Eliphaz is but heaping up words.

Conclusion: It is a great comfort to a good man who lies under the censures of brethren who do not understand his case, that there is a God in heaven Who knows his integrity and sooner or later will clear it up.

Key Word: Miserable comforters, v. 2.

Strong Verses: 2, 19, 21.

Christ Seen: v. 2. The best friend to plead for us is the Lord Jesus and it is the Holy Spirit through the Word, Who comforts effectually.

CHAPTER SEVENTEEN

Contents: Job's answer continued. He longs for death.

Conclusion: The believer should recognize that wherever he goes there is but a step between him and the grave and should always be ready. However he should allow no hard providence to deter and discourage him in the service of God, but should be so much the more emboldened to persevere in God's way.

Key Word: Darkness, v. 12.

Strong Verse: 9.

Christ Seen: v. 3. The believer has a surety with God, namely Christ, the heavenly intercessor. He will plead our cause if we look to Him and no one else can lay anything to our charge. (Rom. 8:32, 33).

CHAPTER EIGHTEEN

Contents: Bildad's second discourse on Job's case.

Conclusion: The way of sin is a way of fear and leads to everlasting confusion, of which the present terrors of conscience are but the ernest.

Key Word: The wicked, v. 5.

Strong Verse: 5.

Christ Seen: v. 4. It is not true that all who suffer great distress in this world should, on that account, be judged wicked when no other proof appears against them. Christ's people are usually a suffering, cross-bearing people.

CHAPTER NINETEEN

Contents: Job's answer to Bildad. His sublime faith.

Conclusion: We may easily bear the unjust reproaches of men if we live in expectation of the glorious appearance of the great God, our Saviour, and that we shall be made like Him when we see Him as He is.

Key Word: Hope, v. 27.

Promises: 25, 26, 27.

Christ Seen: Job had very clear beliefs. The brief statement here takes in Christ's redemption, assurance through Him, His second coming and resurrection.

CHAPTER TWENTY

Contents: Zophar's second discourse on Job's case.

Conclusion: Though wicked men may sometimes prosper, their joy is but for a moment and will quickly end in endless sorrow.

Key Word: Portion of the wicked, v. 29.

Strong Verse: 5.

Christ Seen: Zophar was wrong in applying his reasoning to Job's case and wrong in supposing this life to be the place of judgment, but he was right in seeing a real connection between sin and punishment. Sin is sure to become bitter, and eternally so, unless the sinner takes refuge in the finished work of Christ.

CHAPTER TWENTY-ONE

Contents: Job's answer to Zophar in which he denies any secret sin.

Conclusion: The providences of God in the government of this world are sometimes hard to be understood. When we cannot clearly account for the prosperity of the wicked and affliction of the godly, we should silently wait the issue, judging nothing before the time.

Key Word: Prosperity (of wicked), v. 7.

Strong Verse: 22.

Christ Seen: v. 25. If we have eternal life through Jesus Christ, and spiritual blessings, we have no reason to complain of the little suffering we may be called upon to bear for Christ's sake in this world.

CHAPTER TWENTY-TWO

Contents: Eliphaz's third discourse, accusing Job again of hypocrisy.

Conclusion: It is the duty of those especially who are in affliction to keep up a perfect acquaintance with God, accommodating themselves to all the disposals of His providence; thus they shall be possessed of His peace, no matter what the circumstances.

Key Word: Wickedness, v. 5.

Strong Verses: 15, 16. Promise: 21.

Christ Seen: v. 5. Think it not strange, if like the Master, you are misunderstood and blackened, but learn to pass by accusations and commit your cause to Him who judgeth righteously.

CHAPTER TWENTY-THREE

Contents: Job again answers. He longs for God.

Conclusion: Those who keep the way of the Lord may comfort themselves with the thought that they are being tried, that the result will be for their honor and benefit and that when God is through with them they shall come forth as gold (1 Pet. 1:7) pure and precious to the Refiner.

Key Word: Tried, v. 10.

Promise: 10.

Christ Seen: v. 10. Though men do not, can not, or will not understand us, it is a comfort to know that our Lord Jesus, Who was tried in all points as we are, does perfectly understand our hearts.

CHAPTER TWENTY-FOUR

Contents: Job's answer continued. The prosperity of the wicked.

Conclusion: Though wicked men seem sometimes to be under the special protection of divine providence, even dying without any disgrace, yet God keeps account of all their wickedness and will some day make it appear that their most secret sins, which they thought no eye saw, were under His eye and will be called over again.

Key Word: Prosperity (of wicked).

Strong Verse: 23.

Christ Seen: Job's argument proves that the wicked do not get their hell in this life, nor the saints their heaven. God does not have pay-day every day, but in the end He pays. Though Christians suffer now, let them know that their standing in Christ is secure nevertheless, and let them seek to glorify Him in their sufferings, rather than to complain.

CHAPTER TWENTY-FIVE

Contents: Bildad's third discourse on Job's case.

Conclusion: Man cannot, in himself, be justified before God for he has no merit of his own to extenuate his guilt.

Key Word: Justification, v. 4.

Christ Seen: v. 4. Since man, by reason of his fallen state and corrupt nature is odious to God's holiness, even in his best righteousness, we have need to be born again, that being justified by faith in Christ, we may have peace with God. Rom. 5:1.

CHAPTER TWENTY-SIX

Contents: Job's answer to Bildad. His faith in God.
Conclusion: God is infinite and incomprehensible; man's capacities to understand Him and all His ways are weak, therefore the full discovery of God's glory is reserved for the future state. Let us meanwhile be content with His revelations to us.
Key Word: God's power, v. 14.
Strong Verse: 14.
Striking Facts: v. 3. We are often disappointed in the counseling of our friends for they demand what we cannot produce and we need what they cannot give. Our Lord, however, never mistakes in His operations or misses in His ends.

CHAPTER TWENTY-SEVEN

Contents: Job's answer to Bildad continued.
Conclusion: The consideration of the miserable condition of the hypocrite should engage us to be upright.
Key Word: Hypocrites, v. 8.
Strong Verses: 6, 8.
Christ Seen: It is often the lot of upright men to be censured and condemned as hypocrites, but it well becomes them to bear up boldly under such censures, holding fast to Jesus Christ, who will keep from discouragement and eventually vindicate them.

CHAPTER TWENTY-EIGHT

Contents: Job's answer continued. The value of divine wisdom.
Conclusion: To be truly religious is to be truly wise. If we know God, His wisdom will appear in the practice and observance of our religion and we shall be surely guided in our way.
Key Word: Wisdom, v. 12.
Strong Verse: 28.
Christ Seen: v. 12. There is truer satisfaction in the wisdom which God, through Christ, communicates to the Christian, showing the way to the joys of heaven, than in all the natural philosophies and sciences which only help men to find a way into the earth. (1-11).

CHAPTER TWENTY-NINE

Contents: Job's answer continued. He rehearses the story of his life.
Conclusion: A gracious soul delights in God's smiles, not the smiles of the world, although virtue and piety challenge respect and usually have it. Those who are not only good, but DO GOOD are worthy of double honor.
Key Word: The past, v. 2.
Strong Verse: 3.
Christ Seen: We can see in this chapter a familiar type of Christ in His power and goodness. Our Lord Jesus is the poor man's Lord, loving righteousness and hating iniquity. Upon Him the blessing of a world ready to perish comes.

CHAPTER THIRTY

Contents: Job's answer continued. He reviews his present condition.
Conclusion: The best saints often receive the worst of indignities from a spiteful and scornful world, merely because providence appears temporarily to be against them. Our Master Himself was thus abused, therefore we need not deem it strange.
Key Word: Abhored, v. 10.
Strong Verse: 23.
Christ Seen: Those who today cry "Hosannah" may tomorrow cry "Crucify." Job is here a type of Christ who was made the reproach of men and Who hid not His face from shame and spitting.

CHAPTER THIRTY-ONE

Contents: Job's answer continued. He insists on his integrity.
Conclusion: An upright heart does not dread a scrutiny. A good man is

willing to know the worst of himself and will be thankful to those who will faithfully tell him of his faults.

Key Word: Integrity, v. 6.

Strong Verses: 4, 14.

Christ Seen: v. 4. The Lord Jesus keeps account of all and will bring every work into judgment. "If our hearts condemn us not, then have we confidence toward God."

CHAPTER THIRTY-TWO

Contents: Elihu's discourse, stating his reasons for interfering.

Conclusion: One who is jealous of the honor of God cannot be grieved when injury is plainly done. It is time to speak when we hear errors advanced and disputed for under pretense of supporting God's cause with them. (1 Tim. 4:12).

Key Word: Opinions, vv. 6, 17.

Strong Verses: 8, 21.

Christ Seen: Elihu shows a deeper spiritual conception than any of Job's three friends, because he has a higher conception of God. Externalists and moralizers, while they see God in His power through His works, know nothing of His grace toward man in Christ Jesus, but look upon Him as being very exacting in all His relations. He who has seen God in the cross of Calvary will have the highest conception of God.

CHAPTER THIRTY-THREE

Contents: Elihu's discourse continued. Affliction is shown to be discipline.

Conclusion: God often afflicts the body in love and with gracious designs of good to the soul. Wherever God finds a submissive heart, He can do great things for the soul.

Key Word: God's working, vv. 29, 30.

Strong Verse: 4. Promise: 26.

Christ Seen: v. 14. "Ransom." Jesus Christ is our Ransom, the ransom of God's finding. So great was the injury done by sin, that nothing less could atone for it than the blood of the Son of God.

CHAPTER THIRTY-FOUR

Contents: Elihu's discourse continued. He magnifies God's holiness.

Conclusion: It is absurd and unreasonable to multiply words in complaint against God's ways. His Fatherly corrections are a part of our filial education and we should beware of a rebellious heart which only brings added affliction to ourselves and reproach upon God.

Key Word: Rebellious, v. 37.

Strong Verses: 10, 21, 32.

Christ Seen: God's absolute justice should be accepted in spite of human reasonings. The saints, saved by the blood of the Lamb, and most able to pass an opinion, will cry, "Great and marvelous are thy ways . . . Righteousness and true are thy ways. Thy righteous acts have been made manifest." (Rev. 15:3, 4).

CHAPTER THIRTY-FIVE

Contents: Elihu's discourse continued. Job's rash talk reproved.

Conclusion: It is vain to appeal to God to remove affliction, or to try to acquit ourselves, if we have not studied to know the end for which the affliction was sent. It is equally vain to pray for relief when we do not trust our case in God's hands.

Key Word: Vanity, v. 13.

Strong Verse: 14.

Christ Seen: When in deep affliction, Christians often despair and think that their salvation in Christ has brought them nothing. Let us have done with self-will that chafes and argues, yielding ourselves instead into the hands of Him who says, "Casting all your care upon Him for He careth for you."

CHAPTER THIRTY-SIX

Contents: Elihu's discourse continued. God's justice defended.

Conclusion: God does all things well. Though it may seem sometimes that we are neglected and forgotten and that providence has made an oversight, yet the tender eye of the heavenly Father is upon us, and when affliction has accomplished that for which it was sent, we shall be comforted and established.

Key Word: God's discipline, v. 22.

Strong Verses: 11, 22.

Striking Facts: v. 22.   Trial is the school of trust.   Sore distress is a blessing in disguise if it drives one to Christ and teaches the power of faith and prayer.

CHAPTER THIRTY-SEVEN

Contents: Elihu's discourse continued.   God's majesty.

Conclusion: We must all own that our finite understandings cannot comprehend the infinite perfections of God, but we may be sure that because He is infinitely wise, He will do everything for the best.   It therefore becomes us, in whatever circumstances, to reverence Him and patiently wait.

Key Word: Majesty, vv. 14, 22.

Strong Verses: 14, 22, 23.

Christ Seen: Let us look for the rainbow in the clouds.   There is a sure hiding place in every tempest.   Such is Jesus to all who love and trust Him.

CHAPTER THIRTY-EIGHT

Contents: God's challenge to Job.

Conclusion: Those who try to call God to account, will be called to account. Seeking to establish one's own character and darkening the counsels of God's wisdom, is an affront and provocation to God.   Humble faith can know more of God's secrets than human reasonings.

Key Word: Challenge, v. 3.

Christ Seen: v. 4.   Man knows nothing about the making of this world other than what God has revealed in His Word.   It is the honor of Jesus Christ that He was present when this was done.   (Prov. 8:22; Jno. 1:1, 2).

CHAPTER THIRTY-NINE

Contents: God's challenge to Job continued.

Conclusion: When we consider God's wonderful works in all nature about us, and see how wonderfully even the brute creatures are fitted for and inclined to the services for which they were designed, we see how unfit we are to dictate to God.   Those who see God's hand in everything can best leave everything in His hands.

Key Word: Challenge, v. 1.

Christ Seen: vv. 28-30.   The Lord Jesus referred to this instinct of the eagle in Matt. 24:28.   See Rev. 19:17-18.   Every creature will make toward that which is its proper food.

CHAPTER FORTY

Contents: God's challenge to Job continued.   Job's answer.

Conclusion::   A real vision of God's power and wisdom changes men's opinions of themselves and silences their disputes with God.   The valley of humbling is a blessed place, for no one falls there who does not rise to newness of life and service.

Key Word: Challenge, v. 2.

Strong Verse: 4.

Christ Seen: v. 4.   God demands a quality no human being is able to present (not even perfect Job) but by His grace, through Jesus Christ, He bestows upon the yielded believer all that He asks.

CHAPTER FORTY-ONE

Contents: God's challenge to Job concluded.

Conclusion: Man is utterly unable to contend against the Almighty.   If the inferior creatures keep man in awe, how wonderful must the majesty of God be, who has sovereign dominion over all.

Key Word: Challenge, v. 1.

Christ Seen: When we contrast the mighty works of God with the puniness and littleness of man, how can we help but rejoice that God has found a way out to man in the person of His beloved Son?   His works may baffle our minds, but the heart can find perfect peace in Jesus.

CHAPTER FORTY-TWO

Contents: Job's self-judgment, followed by new prosperity.

Conclusion: Righteousness in a man is excellent but when one becomes too much aware of their own goodness, it reveals deep darkness as to their own real condition before God. If we really know God, we will be humble. If we really know ourselves, we cannot be proud.

Christ Seen: There can be no personal acquaintance with God until we have the sentence of death written upon self, realizing that in ourselves there is no good thing. All we are, we have by God's grace in our Lord Jesus Christ.

Striking Facts: The godly suffer that they might come to self-knowledge, 42:3; and self-judgment, 42:6; that they might repent, 42:6; and have greater fruitfulness, 42:7-17; and escape condemnation with the world. 1 Cor. 11:32.

PSALMS

Key Thought:	Number of Chapters:	Key Verse:	Christ seen as:
Praise	150	29:2	Son of God

Writer of the Book:	Date:	Conclusion of the Book:
David, Moses, Asaph Ethan, Sons of Korah.	1500 to 1000 B. C.	Worship the Lord in the beauty of holiness and give to Him the glory due His name.

SUMMARY

CHAPTER ONE

Contents: The two ways of man.
Conclusion: Blessed is the man whose footsteps are ordered by the Word of God for he shall find both peace and prosperity. Those who are without God are being hurried to a terrible doom.
Key Word: Godly and ungodly, vv. 1, 4.
Strong Verse: 2. Promise: 3.
Christ Seen: Our Lord Jesus was the typical "blessed man" who delighted to do the Father's will.

CHAPTER TWO

Contents: The psalm of the king; rejected, established and finally reigning.
Conclusion: The kings of earth are ever setting themselves in array against God and His Annointed King, but in the day when He comes those who will not bend will be broken. Infinitely wise is he who yields his life to Jesus now and dreadful is the folly of those who continue in enmity to Him.
Key Word: God's King, v. 6.
Strong Verse: 12. Promise: 8.
Christ Seen: v. 12. The yoke of Christ is intolerable to a graceless neck but to the sinner, saved by His precious blood, it is easy and light. Matt. 11:29.

CHAPTER THREE

Contents: A prayer of David (when he fled from Absalom).
Conclusion: God is a shield for His trusting people. He wards off the fiery darts of Satan and the storms of trouble, at the same time speaking peace to the tempest within the breast.
Key Word: Sustained, v. 5.
Strong Verses: 3, 5, 6.
Christ Seen: In many of the psalms of David, we can see more of David's Lord than of David himself. The agonies of Christ are wonderfully portrayed in this chapter.

CHAPTER FOUR

Contents: David's exhortation to others to serve God.
Conclusion: The godly are chosen, and by distinguished grace set apart and separated from men, all the longings of the soul being satisfied in God. How rash are they, who by rejecting Christ, hate their own mercies merely that they might discover the vanities of sin.
Key Word: Godliness, v. 3.
Strong Verses: 5, 8.
Christ Seen: v. 5. Let the sinner flee to the sacrifice of Calvary and there put his whole trust, for He who died was none other than the Lord Jehovah.

CHAPTER FIVE

Contents: David's prayer in which he extols God's holiness and asks judgment upon the wicked.
Conclusion: Prayer should be both the key of the morning and the bolt of the evening. If we pledge ourselves to Him at the beginning of day,

taking sides with Him against the things He abhors, we will be apt to find His way straight before our faces throughout the day.

Key Word: Prayer, v. 2.

Strong Verses: 3, 11, 12.

Christ Seen: v. 7. (Worship toward the temple). The temple shadowed forth the body of Christ, our Mediator, in Whom alone our prayers are accepted with the Father. In our praying the soul should ever look toward Him.

CHAPTER SIX

Contents: David in weakness seeks God's help.

Conclusion: Our way often lies through a vale of tears, but there is One Whom we can trust in the greatest straits and difficulties and Who can dry our tears and stop our pains. To Him let us betake ourselves waiting upon Him in earnest prayer.

Key Word: Sore vexed, v. 3.

Strong Verse: 9.

Christ Seen: v. 2. In this psalm of sorrow, David is seen as a type of Christ who wept and cried out "My soul is exceeding sorrowful even unto death," but found strength to sustain in the Father above.

CHAPTER SEVEN

Contents: David prays for deliverance from persecutors.

Conclusion: When the believer is slandered he has the court of heaven to fly to and a righteous Judge who is the patron of oppressed innocency. He will be our defense and will return upon the wicked their shame. Self vindication is not judicious or serviceable.

Key Word: Persecutors, v. 1.

Strong Verses: 9, 10, 16.

Christ Seen: If David needed deliverance from his foes, how much more do we (1 Pet. 5:8-9), and how blessed that Christ has already won the victory, and that we may have it in Him.

CHAPTER EIGHT

Contents: Meditation on the majesty of God's works and the insignificance of man.

Conclusion: When we consider the majesty of God's wonderful works in the universe, we cannot but wonder that He should notice such a mean creature as man, yet we may be sure he takes precedence of all the inhabitants of this world, being made but a little lower than angels.

Key Word: Excellence, vv. 1, 9.

Strong Verses: 4, 5, 9.

Christ Seen: The psalm wonderfully foreshadows Christ. He was the revelation of the Father's excellent name; His glory is set above the heavens; He has sovereign dominion and it is He whom God has clothed with glory and honor. For a little time He was made lower than angels, when He took upon Himself the form of a servant. All creatures are under His feet and will eventually own Him to be Lord of all.

CHAPTER NINE

Contents: Praise for victory over enemies.

Conclusion: In the midst of all distresses, we may by faith find a refuge in God and when victory comes, we should not forget that He expects returns of praise.

Key Word: Praise, vv. 1, 11.

Strong Verses: 16, 18. Promises: 9, 10, 18.

Christ Seen: v. 18 is one of the sweet promises of the Bible. When pleaded before the throne in the name of the Lord Jesus, who is indeed Himself the great Promise of the Bible, it will be found exceedingly precious.

CHAPTER TEN

Contents: The psalmist meditates on the wicked and desires to see them humbled under God's hand.

Conclusion: The Christian cannot but lay to heart that which is offensive to God, feeling a tender compassion for those who are oppressed and a zeal for the honor of God. Let us look to God with a firm belief that He

will at the proper time give redress to the injured and reckon with the oppressors.
Key Word: Wicked, v. 2.
Strong Verses: 17, 18.
Christ Seen: v. 16. We shall speed well if we carry our complaints to the King of Kings, for at the throne of the Lord Jesus, all wrongs will be redressed. "Come quickly Lord Jesus."

CHAPTER ELEVEN

Contents: The doom of the wicked.
Conclusion: If we get the vision of God on His throne, governing all creatures, rendering to all according to their works, we shall then see no reason to be discouraged by the power of oppressors but will rest in Him.
Key Word: Wicked, v. 2.
Strong Verses: 4, 7.
Christ Seen: v. 4. There is One who pleads His precious blood in our behalf in the temple above and an Intercessor at the right hand of the throne Who is never deaf to the cries of His trusting people.

CHAPTER TWELVE

Contents: A prayer for help against oppressors.
Conclusion: The believer is commonly tempted to think that because trouble has lasted long, it will last always, but if he will bring his cares and griefs to the throne of grace, he may go away with praise, being assured that all will be well at last.
Key Word: Oppressors, v. 5.
Strong Verses: 3, 6.
Christ Seen: v. 6. Some see in the seven-fold trying of God's Word, an allusion to the seven dispensations of man or to the seven periods of the church, or to that perfection signified in the number seven to which the Scriptures will have been brought at the Revelation of Jesus Christ.

CHAPTER THIRTEEN

Contents: Prayer for deliverance from enemies.
Conclusion: The believer's desires often turn to impatience, for days seem long when the soul is cast down, but because God's face is hidden, it does not follow that His heart has forgotten. If we hold to God by faith, we will at the same time be assured that victory is coming and that, after all, God has dealt bountifully with us.
Key Word: Supplication, v. 3.
Strong Verse: 6.
Christ Seen: If, after all our pains, we find Jesus Christ in a new way, it will make full amends for all our long patience.

CHAPTER FOURTEEN

Contents: The corruption and foolishness of man.
Conclusion: Man in his natural state has become odious to God, utterly incapable of answering the ends of his creation, until by God's free grace, a change has been wrought.
Key Word: Corrupt, v. 1.
Strong Verse: 3.
Christ Seen: The only perfect goodness is to be found in Jesus Christ. All have sinned and come short of God's standard; all are therefore concluded under sin, in the same state of damnation, until by God's grace and faith in Christ, they are regenerated.

CHAPTER FIFTEEN

Contents: Those who shall dwell with God.
Conclusion: Those who would find their way to heaven must have some of heaven in them on their way there. The child of God will walk in the ordinances of the Lord, abhoring that which dishonors Him.
Key Word: Who shall abide, v. 1.
Strong Verses: 1, 2.

Christ Seen: v. 1. When we are taught of God, we will see that only our spotless Lord can find acceptance before the Majesty on High. Until we are "in Christ," conformed to His image, there is no abiding place for us in His tabernacle.

CHAPTER SIXTEEN

Contents: Meditation on the goodness of God.

Conclusion: Those who commit themselves to God's care and submit themselves to God's guidance will find a blessed portion in Him. If we have the pleasures of His favor, we should not fail to give Him the praise of it.

Key Word: Goodly heritage, v. 6.

Strong Verses: 8, 10, 11.

Christ Seen: It was the Lord Jesus, who in the fullest sense made the Father His portion, the Father's glory His highest end and the Father's will His delight. He Who in soul and body was preeminently God's Holy One was loosed from the pains of death because it was not possible that He should be holden of it. (vv. 8-10.)

CHAPTER SEVENTEEN

Contents: David prays for relief from the pressure of enemies.

Conclusion: If we are abused and misrepresented, we have a righteous God to go to whose judgment is according to the truth and by whose decisions there will be rendered to every man his due. In the prospect of awaking with His likeness, we can cheerfully waive the enjoyments of this life and suffer with patience.

Key Word: Oppressors, v. 9.

Strong Verses: 8, 15.

Christ Seen: v. 15. It is in Christ alone, the first born from the dead, the express image of Jehovah's glory, that the saints will rise immortal, incorruptible, to be eternally satisfied in heaven. We shall see Him as He is and be made like Him.

CHAPTER EIGHTEEN

Contents: Praise for God's marvelous deliverances.

Conclusion: God not only will deliver His trusting people out of their difficulties in due time, but will give them grace to bear up under their trials in the meantime. Give God the glory of all the deliverances and advancements of His Kingdom.

Key Word: Delivered, vv. 17, 50.

Strong Verses: 3, 30, 32. Promise: 2.

Christ Seen: David is here a type of Christ who was brought safely through all conflicts with the forces of evil and given to be head over all. Though He sees not yet all things put under Him, yet He knows that He shall reign until all opposing rule is put down and all men acknowledge Him to be both Lord and Christ.

CHAPTER NINETEEN

Contents: God's revelation of Himself in the book of nature, book of the law and the book of human life.

Conclusion: God makes Himself known through three great books, all of which have as their theme the glory and handiwork of God. The book of nature (vv. 1-6) is read by every human being. The book of the law (vv. 7-14) converts the soul and becomes an unfailing guide. The book of human life (vv. 12-14) is a Bible to the unsaved world and must therefore be maintained with unspotted pages.

Key Word: Glory of God, v. 1.

Strong Verses: 1, 7, 14.

Christ Seen: Christ, the Sun of Righteousness, is the Bridegroom who rejoices to reveal Himself to men and like the champion, wins glory to Himself in His union with His Bride, the true church.

CHAPTER TWENTY

Contents: A prayer for God's anointed people.

Conclusion: The children of this world trust in second causes and rise or fall with them but those who have a believing and obedient trust in God have the sure way to preferment and establishment.

Key Word: Saving strength, vv. 1, 6.
Strong Verse: 7.
Christ Seen: vv. 3, 5. In all our conflicts, we are to have an eye to the sacrifice of Jesus, pausing ever at His cross before we march on to battle. Come what may, having trusted in His finished work, we may then rejoice in His saving arm.

CHAPTER TWENTY-ONE
Contents: Praise for blessing and confidence for further victory.
Conclusion: Let praise be the blossom of prayer. Though we cannot sing a note in honor of our own strength, we can always rejoice in our omnipotent God, if we have trusted all to Him.
Key Word: Answered prayer, v. 2.
Strong Verses: 8, 13.
Christ Seen: vv. 2, 5, 6. The psalm looks forward to Jesus, who is God over all blessed forever; once crowned with thorns but now wearing the glory crown. He is the Pleader whose requests are never withheld. Let us make use of this all-prevailing Intercessor.

CHAPTER TWENTY-TWO
Contents: David in great perplexity cries for help.
Conclusion: Trouble and perplexity drive us to earnest prayer and earnest prayer drives away trouble and perplexity. To fall upon the knees is the surest way to whip the enemy.
Key Word: Trouble, v. 11.
Strong Verses: 22, 24, 27.
Christ Seen: The psalm gives a graphic picture of the death of the Lord Jesus and is called "the psalm of the cross." We see both the sufferings of Christ and the glory to follow. Oh for grace to draw near and see this great sight. (Read Matt. 27.)

CHAPTER TWENTY-THREE
Contents: David sees Jehovah as his good shepherd.
Conclusion: Jehovah is with (v. 1) under (v. 2) beside (v. 2) after (v. 6) before (v. 5) and ahead of (v. 6) all His trusting children. They shall not want for food (v. 2) drink (v. 2) strength (v. 3) guidance (v. 3) comfort (v. 4) satisfaction (v. 5) or life (v. 6).
Key Word: Shepherd, v. 1.
Promises: 1, 4.
Christ Seen: The shepherd psalm follows the psalm of the cross. We must by experience know the value of the blood shed on Calvary's cross and see the sword awakened against the Shepherd before we can truly know the sweetness of the Good Shepherd's care. Psa. 22 is the Good Shepherd dying for His sheep. (Jno. 10:11.) Psa. 23 is the Great Shepherd caring for His sheep. (Heb. 13:20.) Psa. 24 is the Chief Shepherd coming again for His sheep. (1 Pet. 5:4.)

CHAPTER TWENTY-FOUR
Contents: The one who shall stand before Jehovah.
Conclusion: Those who have been made meet for heaven shall be brought safely into God's presence. While none may venture to meet God's standards on the footing of the law, God's grace in Christ can make us meet.
Key Word: Blessing and righteousness, v. 5.
Strong Verses: 1, 3, 4.
Christ Seen: Christ, the ascended Savior, is here seen as Head and Crown of the universe, the King of Glory. He it was who could ascend the hill of the Lord, meeting perfectly all requirements. He has entered there as the forerunner of all who trust Him and shortly is coming out again to be acknowledged King of Kings and Lord of Lords.

CHAPTER TWENTY-FIVE
Contents: Prayer for guidance, forgiveness, mercy and deliverance.
Conclusion: It is our duty and privilege to trustingly wait upon the Lord in adoration, supplication and service all the days of our lives. Those

whose hearts are right with Him, shall not err for want of heavenly direction in any time of perplexity.

Key Word: Prayer, v. 1.

Promises: 9, 14.

Christ Seen: v. 8. Good and upright. God's goodness and uprightness are in perfect union. They were perfectly blended in the sacrifice of the Lord Jesus on Calvary. Because God Himself has paid the price of the cross, He can be just and yet justify the ungodly; His goodness and righteousness are harmonized. Faith in this sacrifice is the sinner's only hope of being delivered.

CHAPTER TWENTY-SIX

Contents: David prays for vindication and deliverance and pledges faithfulness.

Conclusion: It is a great comfort to those who have a clear conscience toward God that He is a witness to their sincerity and as the righteous God will sooner or later vindicate them.

Key Word: Examine, v. 2.

Strong Verses: 6, 7, 11.

Christ Seen: In this chapter is seen a type of Christ Who was made a reproach of men and Who forewarned His followers that it would also be their portion to have all manner of evil spoken against them falsely for His sake.

CHAPTER TWENTY-SEVEN

Contents: David glories in Jehovah's name and expresses triumphant faith.

Conclusion: God is the believer's light and strength by whom and in whom he lives. We should therefore let the heart be fixed in Him and the mind stayed upon Him, waiting His deliverance in all circumstances.

Key Word: God's goodness, v. 13.

Promises: 1, 3, 5, 10, 14.

Christ Seen: v. 12. We get here a picture of Christ against whom false witnesses arose, breathing out cruelty, but though He was delivered into their wicked hands, He was not delivered to their wills, for God exalted Him far above all principality and power.

CHAPTER TWENTY-EIGHT

Contents: Prayer for deliverance from enemies and testimony as to answered prayer.

Conclusion: The Lord is our strength to support us in either service or suffering, as well as our shield to protect us from the designs of the enemy. The heart that truly believes in Him shall in due time greatly rejoice.

Key Word: Supplication, v. 2.

Promise: 7.

Christ Seen: v. 2. The holy place within the veil was the place where the ark and mercy seat were which foreshadowed the Lord Jesus. If we gain acceptance in prayer, we must ever turn ourselves to the blood-springled mercy seat of His atonement.

CHAPTER TWENTY-NINE

Contents: Adoration of God's mighty power.

Conclusion: Let the crowns, the great ones of earth, acknowledge their dependence upon God and join in worship to the blessed and only Potentate of the universe.

Key Word: Power and majesty, v. 3.

Strong Verse: 2. **Promise:** 11.

Christ Seen: v. 11, Peace. Jesus, the mighty God, is our peace. Having purchased the peace of pardon on the cross, He bequeathed it in His promise to His followers, "Peace I leave with you; my peace I give unto you."

CHAPTER THIRTY

Contents: Thanksgiving for answer to prayer.

Conclusion: We should hem all our blessings with praise lest they unravel. Let us never forget to pray, nor ever doubt the success of prayer.

Key Word: Thanks, v. 12.

Strong Verses: 4, 5.
Christ Seen: v. 7.   The Lord Jesus is able to bring substantial consolation to the believer.   He Himself was for a time deserted of the Father
that those who believe on Him might not be deserted eternally.

CHAPTER THIRTY-ONE

Contents: David implores God's help against enemies and extols God for his
preservation.
Conclusion: All our affairs are safe in Jehovah's hands; without reservation
therefore, we should yield ourselves to the Father's hand to be sanctified
by His grace, devoted to His honor, employed in His service and fitted for
His Kingdom.
Key Word: Trouble, v. 9.
Strong Verse: 19.   Promises: 20, 24.
Christ Seen: v. 5.   These living words of David were our Lord's dying words
from the cross when He made His soul an offering for sin.

CHAPTER THIRTY-TWO

Contents: The blessedness of those whose sin is forgiven.
Conclusion: The only cover that will hide our sins forever away from God's
sight is that provided in the atoning death of His Son.   He is blessed
indeed who has a Substitute Who assumes all accounts to stand for him.
If the believer does not humble himself by the confession of his sins to
God, God will humble him by chastisements.
Key Word: Forgiven, v. 1.
Strong Verse: 1.   Promise: 8.
Christ Seen: v. 2.   The righteousness of Christ being imputed to the be-
liever and the believer being made the righteousness of God "in Him"
his iniquity is not set to his account.   Christ took upon Himself the
iniquity of us all and was made sin for us.

CHAPTER THIRTY-THREE

Contents: Praise of God's wisdom and power.
Conclusion: The righteous who know the goodness of God should never be
empty of His praises.   Though the residence of God's glory is in the
highest heavens, yet His eye is upon every inhabitant of earth and no
detail of their lives escapes His observation.
Key Word: Praise, v. 2.
Strong Verses: 4, 10, 12.
Christ Seen: v. 6.   The three persons of the Godhead united in the creation
of all things.   Christ is the Word, (Jno. 1:1) without whom nothing was
made.   The Holy Spirit is the breath.   God made the world, as He rules
it and redeems it, by His Son and Spirit.

CHAPTER THIRTY-FOUR

Contents: David thankfully records God's goodness and invites the praise of
others.
Conclusion: God's people who share His special favor should concur in His
praises and magnify His name together.   Upon every fresh occurence
of His mercies, let us renew our praises, thus encouraging others to trust
Him.   The true and only way to happiness is to walk in the love and favor
of God.
Key Word: Praise, v. 1.
Strong Verses: 1, 19.   Promises: 7, 10, 15.
Christ Seen: v. 20.   Although it is strange that we meet with anything
of Christ here, this Scripture is said to have been fulfilled in Christ.   Jno.
19:36.   The passover lamb of which not a bone was broken prefigured
Jesus and at the same time the complete keeping of His Body, the Church.

CHAPTER THIRTY-FIVE

Contents: An appeal to heaven for the confusion of enemies.
Conclusion: The most righteous men and the most righteous causes may
expect to meet with many mighty and malicious enemies.   The safest
place to leave a righteous cause is with the righteous God Who is able to
give judgment upon it in the right way and at the right time.   If God is
our friend, it does not matter who our enemies are.

Key Word: Persecutors, v. 3.
Strong Verses: 27, 28.
Christ Seen: Herein David was a type of Christ to whom the wicked world was most ungrateful (Jno. 10:32) and who was slandered as no one else ever was (Matt. 26:60). If we are falsely charged, let us remember that so persecuted they the prophets and our Lord Himself.

CHAPTER THIRTY-SIX

Contents: The wicked contrasted with the righteous and the Lord of devout men extolled.
Conclusion: Sinners are self destroyers and when sin is finally made to appear in its true colors to them, they will be made a terror to themselves. But whatever is amiss with the world, we may be sure there is nothing amiss with Jehovah and that those who cleave closely to Him shall be eternally satisfied.
Key Word: Wicked, v. 1 (satisfaction, v. 8).
Strong Verse: 7. Promises: 8, 9.
Christ Seen: v. 9. From the Lord Jesus as the self-sufficient spring (Jno. 4:14), proceeds our life and by Him it is sustained. In His light we see light. We cannot see Jesus by the light of self, but we see self in the light of Jesus.

CHAPTER THIRTY-SEVEN

Contents: The riddle of the prosperity of the wicked and the affliction of the righteous.
Conclusion: The believer should never waste a minute fretting about his enemies, but should look forward with the eye of faith, when he will see no reason to envy wicked people their short-lived prosperity. Those who make God their heart's delight will have their heart's desire and will be fully satisfied in Him.
Key Word: Evil doers, v. 1, and righteous, v. 37.
Strong Verses: 1, 7, 16. Promises: 3, 4, 5, 23, 24.
Christ Seen: Come what may, the saints are safe in Christ Jesus and because He lives, they shall live also. As heirs with Him, heaven and eternity shall be theirs. Who would not be a Christian on such terms, in spite of all the oppression of the godless?

CHAPTER THIRTY-EIGHT

Contents: David's grief, complaints and confession.
Conclusion: God often contends with His children to awaken their consciences and to set their sins in order before them for their humiliation. If we are truly penitent for sin, we will make a particular acknowledgment of what we have done amiss and God will then restore the joy of salvation, with patience to bear our affliction.
Key Word: Bowed down, v. 6.
Strong Verse: 15
Christ Seen: v. 3. This is the condition of every awakened conscience until given relief through the Lord Jesus. When man sees himself in the light of God's Word applied by the Spirit, he must acknowledge his depravity and helplessness to get deliverance apart from Jesus Christ.

CHAPTER THIRTY-NINE

Contents: The psalmist, bowed down with sorrow and sickness, is burdened with unbelieving thoughts and prays for help.
Conclusion: We should not feed the fire of discontent by pouring over our troubles, for we cannot, with all our disquietment, altar the nature of things. Although satisfaction is not to be found at all in the creature, it is always to be found in God, and to Him we should be drawn by our disappointments.
Key Word: Sorrow, v. 2.
Strong Verse: 1.
Christ Seen: How frail we are in our life and in our moods. We have far less excuse than David for fearing man, for the Lord Jesus travels in our company and says, "Lo, I am with you always."

CHAPTER FORTY

Contents: God's salvation extolled and prayer for deliverance.
Conclusion: Those who seek God in all their perplexities shall rejoice and be glad in Him, for He will not only be found of them, but will be their bountiful rewarder, wherefore, they should say continually, "the Lord be magnified."
Key Word: Praise and prayer, vv. 3, 13.
Strong Verses: 2, 16.
Christ Seen: vv. 6-8. The offerings had their worth only as types of the sacrifice of Christ, but when He came, as it was foretold in the volume of the Book, they ceased to be of worth. He alone completely did the will of God. Our expiation from sin is due not to us, but our Substitute's obedience to the will of Jehovah.

CHAPTER FORTY-ONE

Contents: Prayer for relief from sickness and confession of sins.
Conclusion: When we suffer in our reputation, our first concern should be about our integrity and we may then trust our reputation to God. His good will is sufficient to secure us from the ill will of all that hate us.
Key Word: Enemies, v. 5.
Promise: 1.
Christ Seen: v. 9. Betrayal was one of the bitterest drops our Lord Jesus had to take. He applied this passage to Himself (Jno. 18:18, 26) ·as He gave Judas the sop. The believer need not think it strange if he receives abuses from trusted friends.

CHAPTER FORTY-TWO

Contents: The experiences of a much afflicted saint and his confidence in God.
Conclusion: God often teaches His saints effectually to know the worth of His mercies by causing them to feel the want of them. A believing confidence in God is the best antidote against disquietude of spirit. The way to forget our miseries is to rest in the God of our mercies.
Key Word: Hope, v. 5.
Strong Verses: 5, 11.
Christ Seen: v. 7. Our Lord Jesus, for our sakes, was overwhelmed with a deluge of grief, like that of the old world, when the fountains of the deep were broken up. He endured all the billows of God's wrath against sin.

CHAPTER FORTY-THREE

Contents: Prayer for God's help and leading.
Conclusion: We need desire no more to give us satisfaction of heart than the good that flows from God's favor. If we conscientiously follow His light and truth, it will certainly bring us to His holy hill above.
Key Word: Oppression, v. 2.
Strong Verses: 3, 5.
Christ Seen: v. 3. No common light can show us the road to heaven, but only that light sent from heaven, the Holy Spirit, the Spirit of Light and the truth as it is in Jesus, the Light of the world.

CHAPTER FORTY-FOUR

Contents: Complaint of the Lord's apparent forgetfulness and entreaty for His help.
Conclusion: The tokens of God's displeasure are more grievous to those who have been long accustomed to the tokens of His favor, but the remembrance of His former goodness should be a cause of heart searching and a support to faith.
Key Word: Affliction, v. 24.
Strong Verses: 5, 6.
Christ Seen: v. 22. There is a reference here to those who suffer, even unto death, for the testimony of Christ and to whom it is applied in Rom. 8:36.

CHAPTER FORTY-FIVE

Contents: A psalm of the King, looking to His advent in glory.
Conclusion: In the eyes of all those enlightened by the Holy Spirit the Lord

Jesus, the King of Kings, excells all the children of men in His excellencies. How much more worthy is He of our love.

Key Word: King, v. 1.

Strong Verses: 6, 7.

Christ Seen: In Jesus, the Anointed King, we behold every feature of a perfect character in harmonious proportion. He will never be so beautiful as when He is seen in union with His Bride, the Church.

CHAPTER FORTY-SIX

Contents: A psalm of holy confidence in God.

Conclusion: God's people may count themselves safe and make themselves strong in Him in Whom there is always help sufficient, no matter what is the case and exigence.

Key Word: Refuge, v. 1, 11.

Strong Verse: 10. Promise: 1.

Christ Seen: v. 4. God the Father is a river (Jer. 2:13). God the Son is a river, the fountain of salvation (Zech. 13:1, 3). God the Spirit is a river (Jno. 7:38; 4:14). The perfections of the Father, the fullness of Christ, the operations of the Holy Spirit—these make up the great river that makes glad the city of God.

CHAPTER FORTY-SEVEN

Contents: The people exhorted to shout over God's triumphs.

Conclusion: Let all who know God and own His sceptre sing His praises forever; for while we dwell under the shadow of such a throne there is eternal reason for thanksgiving.

Key Word: Praises, v. 6.

Strong Verse: 8.

Christ Seen: The prospect of the coming universal reign of Christ as Prince of Peace is enough to make the tongue of the dumb sing.

CHAPTER FORTY-EIGHT

Contents: Praise of the beauty and strength of Mount Zion, the city of God.

Conclusion: There is one city which is the world's star (Jerusalem), the most precious pearl of all lands, because it is God's city on which His eye is ever resting. (Although it has long been in the dust, it will be restored again as the capital of the whole earth Isa. 62:6-7; Mic. 4:8).

Key Word: Mount Zion, v. 2.

Strong Verse: 1. Promise: 14.

Christ Seen: There is a spiritual Zion equally glorious and which shall never be overthrown, the Church, against which the gates of hell shall not prevail. She is putting on her garments to welcome the King when He comes to reestablish the literal Zion and to rule over the whole earth.

CHAPTER FORTY-NINE

Contents: The despicable character of those who trust in their wealth.

Conclusion: There is no security in the possession and enjoyment of wealth, for money cannot buy the redemption of the soul. God's children, though poor, are truly happy above the most prosperous of this world because they are guarded against the terrors of death and judgment to come.

Key Word: The rich, v. 6.

Strong Verses: 16, 17. Promise: 15.

Christ Seen: v. 7. Christ has done that for us which all the wealth of the world cannot do, redeeming us with His precious blood (1 Pet. 1:18-19). The redemption of the soul is precious because of its tremendous cost. Having been once wrought, it ceases forever, never needing to be repeated. (Heb. 9:25-26; 10:12.)

CHAPTER FIFTY

Contents: The arraignment of the ungodly and the greatness of Jehovah.

Conclusion: Every man shall be called to give an account of himself to God. In that great day, He will make those to hear judgment who would not hearken to His calls in Grace. Those only will be gathered to God who have sincerely covenanted with Him through the sacrifice of His Son.

Key Word: Judgment, v. 6.

Strong Verse: 23, Promise: 12.
Christ Seen: v. 5. It is only by the sacrifice of Christ that sinners can be accepted of God. Those who have so covenanted will be gathered unto Christ at His coming (2 Thes. 2:1) to be assessors with Him in the later judgment of the world (1 Còr. 6:2).

CHAPTER FIFTY-ONE

Contents: The penitential prayer of David.
Conclusion: All the believer's wrong doing comes to a climax at the foot of the throne, being violation of God's law. While the penalty of sin has been blotted out by the blood, the defilement of all subsequent sin remains. Confession brings sin out of its hiding place and enables the sinner to take sides with God against it. See 1 Jno. 1:9.
Key Word: Confession, v. 3.
Strong Verses: 1, 7, 10, 17.
Christ Seen: v. 7. The sinner is purged by blood upon acceptance of Christ (Heb. 1:3; 9:12; 10:14) which takes away the guilt of sin. The washing (v. 2) takes away the defilement of sin in the Christian, being accomplished by the application of the Word by the Spirit. (Eph. 5:25, 36.)

CHAPTER FIFTY-TWO

Contents: The triumph of God's people over all oppressors.
Conclusion: Those who think to support themselves in their own power and wealth without God and His Word, are wretchedly deceived, for their houses are built on sand. The ruin of mighty, yet godless men cannot but be universally noticed when that day comes.
Key Word: Triumph, v. 6.
Strong Verses: 8, 9.
Christ Seen: v. 8. Those whose confidence is in God are compared to green olive trees, which are fat as well as flourishing (92:14). The wicked are compared (37:35) to a green bay tree, which has an abundance of large leaves but no useful fruit. Let us be among God's fruit-bearing trees, rooted and grounded in Christ and drawing our nutriment hourly from Him.

CHAPTER FIFTY-THREE

Contents: The foolishness and iniquity of atheism.
Conclusion: Bad practices are the fruit of bad principles and bad principles are the natural fruit of denial of God. Atheists, whether in opinion or practice, are the biggest fools of earth. There cannot be right living where there is not right believing.
Key Word: Atheist, v. 1.
Strong Verse: 1.
Christ Seen: v. 6. Those who meet the atheism and sinfulness of men cannot but long for the hastening of the glorious return of the Lord Jesus to earth to bring joy to the Church, His Bride, and restoration to His people Israel.

CHAPTER FIFTY-FOUR

Contents: Prayer for rescue from oppressors.
Conclusion: If we are for God, we may be assured God will be for us and that we will have such care from Him that we need never stand in fear of enemies. Let us make His strength our refuge and confidence.
Key Word: Oppressors, v. 3.
Strong Verse: 7.
Christ Seen: v. 6. In all our perplexities, if we have an eye to the Great Sacrifice of Calvary, we can look up and praise God. Apart from our Substitute, we have no ground for prayer.

CHAPTER FIFTY-FIVE

Contents: Complaint concerning false friends.
Conclusion: The best salve for every sore is prayer. One of the greatest griefs is to find ourselves deceived in some who have made great pretentions to friendship in the name of religion, but if our minds are stayed on Christ, we may ever have peace of heart, for His peace passes understanding (Phil. 4:6-7).

Key Word: Complaint, v. 2.
Strong Verses: 16, 17. Promise: 22.
Christ Seen: David's suffering at the hands of false friends is here a type of Christ's sufferings. Ahitiphel, who is undoubtedly referred to, is a type of Judas, for they both hanged themselves.

CHAPTER FIFTY-SIX

Contents: David pours out complaint about enemies.
Conclusion: When we are surrounded on all sides with difficulties and dangers because of enemies, we have but one retreat—the mercy of God. Faith in Him will surely banish fear.
Key Word: Enemies, v. 2.
Strong Verses: 3, 4, 11.
Christ Seen: What can flesh do? Nothing, if we are in Christ. Neither death, nor life, nor angels, nor principalities, shall be able to separate us from God's love in Him (Rom. 8:31).

CHAPTER FIFTY-SEVEN

Contents: David in faith pleads God's mercy in his calamities.
Conclusion: God's glory should be nearer our hearts than any interests of our own. Whatever God performs concerning His people, it will finally appear to have been performed for their benefit. By faith and prayer, let us therefore take refuge in Him in every time of pressure.
Key Word: Calamities, v. 1.
Promise: 3.
Christ Seen: The Psalm may be construed of Christ, who in the days of His flesh was assaulted by the tyranny of enemies. Herod and Pilate, with the Gentiles and Jews furiously raged and took counsel together against Him. The chief priests and princes were like lions in readiness to devour Him. In it all, He taught us that if we seek the Father's glory our interests are safe in His hands.

CHAPTER FIFTY-EIGHT

Contents: Prayer for the defeat of ungodly men.
Conclusion: However wicked people may prosper and bid defiance to divine justice, they will eventually learn that there is a God who judges in the earth. The saints will surely see God's vindication of the righteous.
Key Word: Wicked, v. 3.
Strong Verse: 11.
Christ Seen: Whatever hazard, whatever hardship for Christ's sake, the believer may be assured of being an unspeakable gainer in the issue.

CHAPTER FIFTY-NINE

Contents: Complaint of the malice of enemies and comfort and confidence in God.
Conclusion: Those who are for Christ's sake, harmless and innocent may expect to be hated of wicked men. It is their wisdom and duty in times of such difficulties, to wait upon God, for He is their defense, their refuge in Whom they shall be safe.
Key Word: Enemies, v. 1.
Strong Verses: 9, 16, 17.
Christ Seen: v. 6. The persecutors of our Lord Jesus are compared to dogs (22:16). They ran Him down with barking, for otherwise they could have found no way to take Him. What they lacked in reason and justice, they made up in noise.

CHAPTER SIXTY

Contents: Prayer for the deliverance of God's people from enemies.
Conclusion: God often gives His own people a hard course in this world that they may not take up their rest in the world but may dwell at ease in Him alone.
Key Word: Prayer, vv. 1, 11.
Strong Verses: 11, 12.
Christ Seen: v. 4. Christ, the Son of David, is given for an ensign of the people (Isa. 11:10), a banner to those who fear God. His love is the

banner over them. In His name and power they war against the powers of darkness. Let us unfurl our banners to the breeze in confident joy.

CHAPTER SIXTY-ONE

Contents: Encouraged by experiences and expectation, David calls on God for further deliverance.

Conclusion: Past experiences of the benefit of trusting God implicity should ever engage us to keep close to Him and encourage us to hope for fresh mercies in the time of stress.

Key Word: Prayer, v. 1.

Strong Verses: 3, 4.

Christ Seen: v. 2. The rock is Christ. Those are safe who are in Him, but none can mount this rock except God, by His Spirit, help them to it. The Spirit is able to effect such a leading even in the case of one who is on the border of despair.

CHAPTER SIXTY-TWO

Contents: David professes his confidence in God and encourages himself to wait on God.

Conclusion: Hope in God will always be an anchor to the soul, sure and steadfast. Though enemies be mighty and malicious, if God is for us and we are for God, we need not fear what man can do.

Key Word: Refuge, vv. 7, 8.

Strong Verses: 2, 5, 6, 7, 11.

Christ Seen: Jesus Christ is the channel of God's power and mercy to us. Those who trust in Him will be satisfied, for His riches are open to the poorest.

CHAPTER SIXTY-THREE

Contents: David's desire toward God and joyful dependence upon Him.

Conclusion: The believer need desire nothing more than the favor of God to make him happy and satisfied. The consciousness of communion with God is the sure pledge of deliverance.

Key Word: Longing, v. 1.

Strong Verses: 1, 7.

Christ Seen: v. 11. Those who heartily espouse the cause of Christ Who is to be manifested as King of Kings, shall glory in His victory at last.

CHAPTER SIXTY-FOUR

Contents: David prays for deliverance from the malicious designs of enemies.

Conclusion: God will turn the tables on the adversaries of His people and defeat them at their own weapons, therefore the righteous need not worry about the arts of self defense, but may safely leave their avengement in His hands.

Key Word: Preservation, v. 1.

Strong Verse: 10.

Christ Seen: Those saved through the blood may look forward with quiet confidence to the time when Jesus shall come in power to right the world.

CHAPTER SIXTY-FIVE

Contents: David gives to God the glory of His power and goodness.

Conclusion: Praise is due to God from all the world because of His mighty works, but praise especially waits for Him in His church among His people.

Key Word: Praise, v. 1.

Strong Verse: 4.

Christ Seen: Thunder tones and lightning flashes—such are darker aspects of nature. Beneath all, like a sweet refrain, we hear God praised as the God of salvation.

CHAPTER SIXTY-SIX

Contents: A call to praise God for His sovereign dominion and power in the whole creation.

Conclusion: God's works are wonderful in themselves and if duly considered, will fill the soul with amazement and praise, for it will ever be discovered that His grace and love lay at the bottom of every testing and that everything works for the benefit of His glorious purposes.

Key Word: Praise, v. 2.
Strong Verses: 16, 18, 20.
Christ Seen: v. 13. Even the thankful heart dares not come to God apart from the Great Sacrifice. Never attempt to pray without Jesus.

CHAPTER SIXTY-SEVEN

Contents: Prayer for the prosperity of God's cause in the world.
Conclusion: Those who themselves delight in praising God cannot but desire that others may be brought to praise Him, and long for the day when all nations shall bow before Him.
Key Word: Praise, v. 3.
Strong Verses: 1, 2.
Christ Seen: v. 7. Christ is coming to set up His Kingdom on the earth when all the ends of the earth shall end their idolatry and adore Him. Not until the Lord Himself is made King of Kings will God's love, light, life and liberty reach to all peoples.

CHAPTER SIXTY-EIGHT

Contents: Prayer against enemies and for God's people. All called upon to praise God for His greatness and goodness.
Conclusion: The glory of Zion's King is that He is a Savior and benefactor to all His willing people and a consuming fire to all those who are impenitent and enemies of God's work in the world. He continually furnishes His people with occasion for praise, and His praises shall eventually cover the earth.
Key Word: Praise, vv. 4, 32.
Strong Verses: 19, 34.
Christ Seen: v. 18. This may refer to the triumph of bringing the ark into the hill of Zion, but mystically certainly was penned with foresight of Christ who arose from the dead, with triumph ascended into heaven, taking with Him the captive spirits of the just in Paradise and thence sending the Holy Spirit unto His disciples.

CHAPTER SIXTY-NINE

Contents: David complains of great distress and begs God to succor him.
Conclusion: When the waters of affliction rise about us, the only course is to commit the keeping of our souls to God, that we may be neither soured with discontent nor sink with despair. Our prospects are as bright as the promises of God.
Key Word: Deep waters, vv. 2, 15.
Strong Verses: 13, 30.
Christ Seen: This Psalm has been called the psalm of Christ's humiliation and rejection. vv. 14-20 describe His Gethsemane experience (Matt. 26:36-45). v. 21 describes the cross (Matt. 27:34-48). The present blindness of Israel is pictured in vv. 22-28 (Rom. 11:9-10). v. 25 pictures Judas (Acts 1:20) a type of his generation.

CHAPTER SEVENTY

Contents: Prayer for help for the godly and shame for enemies.
Conclusion: God sometimes delays help to His own people that He might excite earnest desires on their part. A heart to love His salvation and to desire His glory before our own is a good ernest of the answer to prayer and of His good will toward us. Rest assured that the enemies of Christ will have wages for their work.
Key Word: Enemies, v. 2.
Strong Verse: 4.
Christ Seen: v. 3. These exclamations of exulting insolence were hurled at our Lord Jesus as He was accompanied to the cross. Our Savior caught in His ears the distant mutter of all the violent exclamations and felt the keen poisoning edge of every insult in His omniscience, as they cried "aha, aha."

CHAPTER SEVENTY-ONE

Contents: Prayer that enemies might be put to shame. Joyful praise of God's goodness.
Conclusion: Those who live a life of confidence in God and continually resort

to Him by faith and prayer, may promise themselves a strong habitation in Him, such as will never fall of itself, nor can ever be broken down by any invading power.

Key Word: Trust, vv. 1, 5, 14.
Strong Verses: 3, 15, 16.
Christ Seen: Other subjects may soon wear out, but those who make God's righteousness and salvation through Christ their theme, will ever have material for meditation and praise.

CHAPTER SEVENTY-TWO

Contents: The glories of the reign of the coming King.
Conclusion: A day is coming when all shall sing "All hail the power of Jesus name, let angels prostrate fall; bring forth the royal diadem and crown Him King of All."
Key Word: King, v. 11.
Strong Verse: 17.
Christ Seen: v. 11. Jesus Christ is coming to be acknowledged Imperial Lord and King by all men, no matter how high their state. Every knee shall bow to Him and every tongue confess that He is Lord to the glory of the Father. "Come quickly, Lord Jesus."

CHAPTER SEVENTY-THREE

Contents: The temptation to envy the prosperity of wicked people and how to fortify ones self against it. The awful fate of the ungodly.
Conclusion: Observing that many wicked men prosper in their impiety and that many godly people have to drink deeply of the bitter cup of affliction, often brings one the temptation to think that, after all, all is left to blind providence. But the prosperity of the wicked will be found to be short and uncertain and sure to end in destruction and misery. The righteous man's afflictions end in peace and eternal joy.
Key Word: Prosperity of wicked, v. 3.
Strong Verses: 24, 25, 28.
Christ Seen: v. 25. The truly pious soul longs for the Lord Jesus in all places, objects and events. Heaven would be no heaven at all if He were not there. He·is better than all on earth—more excellent than all in heaven.

CHAPTER SEVENTY-FOUR

Contents: The deplorable condition of God's people spread before Him with petition for deliverance.
Conclusion: The desolations of God's house cannot but grieve the believer more than any desolations that might come to his own house. In the time of such distress, he cannot sit still in apathy but will turn to God seeking to know "why?" (v. 1) the desolations have come, looking to Him for deliverance.
Key Word: Desolations, v. 3.
Strong Verse: 12.
Christ Seen: v. 12. The Christian may now plead the ancient work of the Lord Jesus, that which was finished on Calvary, which was the overthrow of Satan, sin, death and hell. He who wrought such a wonderful salvation for us cannot desert the Christian now.

CHAPTER SEVENTY-FIVE

Contents: A rebuke for those who fail to reckon with God.
Conclusion: A word from God soon abases the lofty, and hence failure to reckon on God is madness. Even kings serve His purpose when they rise and when they fall, for He is back of the scenes controlling all things.
Key Word: Promotion, v. 6.
Strong Verses: 6, 7.
Christ Seen: v. 3. This verse may well be applied to Christ. The world's inhabitants were being dissolved by sin and destruction was threatened to the whole creation. Christ bore up the pillars and saved the world from utter ruin by saving His people from their sins. "He upholds all things by the word of His power."

CHAPTER SEVENTY-SIX

Contents: The glory of God's power celebrated.

Conclusion: The hardships which God's people suffer by the wrath of their enemies will be made to redound to the glory of God when He rises to make His judgments heard and sets the bounds to the wrath of man. Force is of no avail when leveled against the God of Hosts.

Key Word: Greatness (of God), v. 1.

Strong Verses: 7, 10.

Christ Seen: This psalm expresses the advantages the Christian enjoys in Jesus Christ through whom God is known, in whom God's name is made great. He has spoiled principalities and powers and will make a show of them openly.

CHAPTER SEVENTY-SEVEN

Contents: Sorrowful complaints followed by encouragement by remembrance of God's former mighty deliverances.

Conclusion: The thoughts of unbelief can always be argued down if we but stop to meditate upon God's great deliverances of former days, for He is a God Who changes not.

Key Word: Remember, vv. 2, 6, 10.

Strong Verses: 10, 11, 12.

Christ Seen: v. 11. Whatever else may be forgotten, the marvelous works of the Lord Jesus in the days of old must not be suffered to be forgotten, for the memory of the cross is always the handmaid for faith and the foundation of all true prayer.

CHAPTER SEVENTY-EIGHT

Contents: Israel's sins wherewith they had provoked God. The tokens of God's displeasure as the result.

Conclusion: God's people limit Him by forgetfulness of His benefits (v. 11) refusing to walk in His commands (v. 10) and by believing not in His promises (v. 22). Yet He is full of compassion, ever waiting to forgive their iniquity and spare them from being cut off entirely.

Key Word: Longsuffering, v. 38.

Strong Verse: 72.

Christ Seen: v. 72. The psalm describing the varying conditions of the people, ends in peace with the reign of the Lord's annointed, David. When the Lord Jesus, the Chief Shepherd, comes, these desert roamings will be ended and we shall enter into the rest of a peaceful Kingdom.

CHAPTER SEVENTY-NINE

Contents: The deplorable condition of God's people and prayer for relief.

Conclusion: If God's people degenerate through sin from what their father's were, they may expect that God will let a just reproach come upon them that they might be brought to true repentance. Those who desire God to avenge them must themselves be upon praying ground.

Key Word: Reproach, v. 4.

Strong Verses: 8, 9.

Christ Seen: v. 10. The day is coming when God will make bare His everlasting arm on behalf of His people, taking glory to His own name by sending back the Lord Jesus, the King of Kings, by the brightness of whose coming the wicked shall be destroyed and God's name glorified.

CHAPTER EIGHTY

Contents: The tokens of God's favor besought and the former blessings cited as a basis for present deliverance.

Conclusion: There is no obtaining favor with God until we are converted unto Him and there will be no turning unto Him except as we submit to His grace, for it is He who turns us. When we confess that it is our own sinful ways which have provoked God to hide His face, we are beginning at the right end and are on the road to victory.

Key Word: Turn us again, vv. 3, 7, 14, 19.

Strong Verse: 17.

Christ Seen: v. 17. Their king is called the man of God's right hand, as he was also under-shepherd under Him who was the Great Shepherd of

Israel (v. 1) Christ is the Great Shepherd to whom we may commit His sheep in faith.

CHAPTER EIGHTY-ONE

Contents: God chides His people for their ingratitude and pictures their happy state had they but obeyed Him.

Conclusion: God gives those up to their own heart's lust who are determined to give themselves up to be led by them. Those who will listen to the counsels of His Spirit will find those joys and consolations which always reward the obedient.

Key Word: Abandoned, v. 12.

Strong Verses: 10, 16.

Christ Seen: v. 16. The honey out of the rock speaks to us of Christ, the Rock of our Salvation (1 Cor. 10:4) and the fullness of grace in Him and the blessings of the Gospel. Those who hearken to Christ are filled and satisfied with all that is good.

CHAPTER EIGHTY-TWO

Contents: Instructions for the judges of the earth.

Conclusion: God judges among the mighty of earth. They have their power from Him and are accountable to Him. Magistrates should therefore do good with all their power, remembering that it is their special office and duty to protect and deliver the poor.

Key Word: Judging, v. 2.

Strong Verse: 3.

Christ Seen: v. 8. This may be taken as a prayer for the hastening of the coming of Christ who is the Judge of the earth, the King by right divine Who is to inherit all nations. When He comes, all unrighteous potentates will be broken like potter's vessels.

CHAPTER EIGHTY-THREE

Contents: An appeal to God's jealousy for His cause and prayer for defeat of enemies.

Conclusion: We cannot but be zealous against those who federate to strike at God, and should earnestly desire and beg of God that such enemies should be brought to confusion, both that He might be glorified and that they might be brought to repentance. (vv. 15-16.)

Key Word: Enemies, v. 2.

Strong Verses: 17, 18.

Christ Seen: The prophecy reaches to all the enemies of Christ's church. Those who have persistently opposed Christ and His Kingdom, may here read their doom.

CHAPTER EIGHTY-FOUR

Contents: Testimony to God's goodness and the happiness of those who put their confidence in Him.

Conclusion: True subjects love the courts of their King. Favored indeed are those who are constantly engaged in His service (v. 4), who find their strength in Him, and who know Him by the life of real faith. (vv. 5, 12).

Key Word: Blessed, vv. 4, 5, 12.

Strong Verses: v. 10. Promise: 11.

Christ Seen: v. 11. God has given both grace and glory, for the Lord Jesus is the fullness of both. In Him we shall find comfort and protection and in Him no good thing may be withheld, for His grace secures every covenant blessing to the believer.

CHAPTER EIGHTY-FIVE

Contents: Prayer for an afflicted people. Remembrance of former mercies and faith for future good.

Conclusion: The sense of present affliction should not be allowed to drown the remembrance of former mercies, but should rather cause us to recall them with praise, and encourage us to look for grace and mercy in reference to present distress.

Key Word: Revive us, v. 6.

Strong Verses: 6, 8.

Christ Seen: v. 10. In Christ the attributes of God meet in perfect unity in the salvation of guilty men by a holy and righteous God. By the gift of Calvary, God is as true as if He had fulfilled every letter of His threatenings and as righteous as if He had never spoken peace to a guilty sinner. Christ, our perfect Substitute, has taken the full penalty of our sins.

CHAPTER EIGHTY-SIX

Contents: The malice of enemies deplored. God's goodness pleaded in prayer for mercy.

Conclusion: The best self preservation is to commit ourselves to God's keeping and by faith and prayer to make Him our preserver.

Key Word: Supplication, v. 6.

Strong Verses: 5, 11, 15.

Christ Seen: In this Psalm we may hear the voice of Christ, who was both Son of God and Son of man, one God with the Father and one man with men. He prays for us as our Priest. He prays in us as our Head through His Spirit. He is prayed to by us, as our God.

CHAPTER EIGHTY-SEVEN

Contents: God's favor to Zion and His great love for it.

Conclusion: God has expressed a particular affection for Jerusalem because there He met and conversed with His people and showed them the great tokens of His favor. Because His love is set upon it, His people also should hold it in reverent regard.

Key Word: Zion, v. 2.

Strong Verse: 3.

Christ Seen: v. 3. Zion may be taken as a type of the Gospel church of which even more glorious things are spoken than of Jerusalem. It is the Bride of Christ, a peculiar people, a royal priesthood, and the gates of hell shall not prevail against it. We need never be ashamed of the church, even in its meanest condition.

CHAPTER EIGHTY-EIGHT

Contents: Lamentation over trouble and pleading with God for mercy.

Conclusion: Sometimes the best of God's saints are severely exercised with the sorest of inward troubles and would be distracted with dismal apprehensions but for the Throne of grace to which they may seek for mercy and strength. Lest there be offenses which prevent the Lord from giving favorable regard to our requests, such times should be times of earnest heart searching.

Christ Seen: The psalmist combats his despair by reminding God he has been a praying soul. That one can pray as David does here is a sure sign that The Holy Spirit is in the heart and faith centered in the divine sacrifice. This proves that God has not forsaken but is working out some purpose.

CHAPTER EIGHTY-NINE

Contents: Joy over and praise of God's greatness. Complaint of the seeming failure of the covenant and prayer for redress.

Conclusion: Though we may find it hard to reconcile some dark providences with the goodness and truth of God, yet we should hold firmly to His promises, knowing that His truth is inviolable, and pleading them in prayer before Him. No matter how serious the situation, there is ever matter for praise and thanksgiving.

Key Word: Covenant, vv. 3, 34.

Strong Verses: 7, 14, 18.

Christ Seen: v. 27. The covenant looks beyond David and Solomon. Isa. 7:13-15; 9:6-7; Mic. 5:2. Jesus has preeminence in all things, having a more glorious name than any other. When He comes, it will be seen what the covenant stores up for the once despised Son of David, but Who is to be exalted as King of Kings and Lord of Lords.

CHAPTER NINETY

Contents: The frailty of man and his consequent need of being submitted to God's sentences.

Conclusion: Men are dying creatures and all their comforts in the world are likewise passing away with time. They should therefore stand in awe of God, walk in His ways, and with the constant apprehension of the uncertainty of life, lest they fail to be diligent and doing their best in His service.

Key Word: Frailty, v. 9.

Strong Verses: 8, 12, 17.

Christ Seen: v. 17. The beauty of the Lord is the beauty of holiness and it shall suffice, if in our lives His holiness is reflected by the Spirit and we are transformed into the image of Christ from one stage of glory to another. That beauty of holiness shone with resplendent lustre in the Lord Jesus, and as He lives in us, it may be reflected in every disciple.

CHAPTER NINETY-ONE

Contents: The preservation of those whose confidence is in God.

Conclusion: Those who live a life of communion with God are constantly safe under His protecting wing and may preserve a holy security of mind at all times. He will be their rest and refuge forever.

Key Word: Refuge, v. 9.

Promises: 1, 2, 3, 4, 7, 11.

Christ Seen: v. 1. Into the secret place those only come who know the love of God in Christ Jesus and those only dwell there to whom "to live is Christ."

CHAPTER NINETY-TWO

Contents: The ruin of sinners and the joy of saints.

Conclusion: Let the Christian not fear the pride and power of evil men nor be in the least discouraged by their impotent menaces. The impenitent workers of iniquity are counted and taken as God's enemies and as such they shall perish and be scattered.

Key Word: Wicked, v. 7.

Strong Verse: 4. Promises: 12 13.

Christ Seen: v. 4. The special work of God which brings to men joy unspeakable and full of glory, is that which He has wrought out on Calvary's cross. Well may we say, "How great are thy works; thy thoughts are very deep."

CHAPTER NINETY-THREE

Contents: The honor of God's kingdom.

Conclusion: The majesty of God's Kingdom eclipses all others. He can do everything; with Him nothing is impossible. Let not the Christian therefore fear the power of man which is borrowed, but fear Him who has power omnipotent and eternal.

Key Word: Majesty, v. 1.

Strong Verse: 5.

Christ Seen: The King Immortal and Almighty will stand upon His glorious throne in the person of the Son of Man. That the Lord Jesus already does reign in the hearts of His own should be our praise. That He may come and set up His Kingdom on earth should be our prayer.

CHAPTER NINETY-FOUR

Contents: An appeal to God to appear for His people against His and their enemies.

Conclusion: There is a God to Whom vengeance belongs Who will certainly call enemies to account. Those who suffer wrong should be encouraged to bear it as His chastisements, committing themselves to Him Who judges righteously and works all things together for the good of those who love Him.

Key Word: Evil doers, v. 16.

Strong Verses: 9, 12. Promises: 14, 22, 23.

Christ Seen: v. 14. God's people in Christ may be cast down but they can never be cast off. They cannot be utterly forsaken because they are God's inheritance in Christ. Eph. 1:18.

CHAPTER NINETY-FIVE

Contents: A call to praise God as our gracious benefactor.

Conclusion: It is due our God and King that we should speak forth and sing forth His praises out of the abundance of a heart filled with love, joy and thankfulness.

Key Word: Thanksgiving, v. 2.

Strong Verses: 1, 2, 7.

Christ Seen: v. 1. Christ is the Rock of our Salvation, therefore we must sing our songs of praise to Him Who sits upon the throne, and to the Lamb. We are His under all possible obligations, being the people of His pasture, the sheep of His hand (v. 7). By His hand we are led into green pastures, protected and provided for. (Jno. 10).

CHAPTER NINETY-SIX

Contents: Call to all people to praise God in view of His glory and greatness.

Conclusion: In God there is everything that is awful, yet everything that is amiable. Those who have come to know Him should go forth in His strength, enamoured with His beauty and to continually praise Him in song, thanksgiving and in service.

Key Word: Praise, v. 4.

Strong Verses: 4, 10.

Christ Seen: vv. 10-13. Let it be told everywhere that Christ's government will be the happy settlement of all things and that it will be incontestably just and righteous. He is coming to judge and to rule and even now is at the threshhold. "Come quickly, Lord Jesus."

CHAPTER NINETY-SEVEN

Contents: The comfort of God's people, arising from His sovereign dominion.

Conclusion: It is enough to make us rejoice in and adore Jehovah that His throne is fixed upon the rock of eternal holiness, that righteousness is His immutable attribute and that judgment marks His every act. Though we cannot see or understand all that He does, we may be sure that when the books of divine providence are opened, no eye will discern a word that should be blotted out.

Key Word: Exalted, v. 9.

Strong Verses: 10, 11.

Christ Seen: Those who rejoice in Jesus Christ and His exaltation have fountains of joy treasured up for them. While they may expect tribulation in this world, the day is coming when they shall see all powers recognize the chief power and Christ's Kingdom victorious among the heathen.

CHAPTER NINETY-EIGHT

Contents: Exhortation to praise. The joy of the redeemed because of the setting up of God's Kingdom.

Conclusion: The setting up of Christ's Kingdom is a matter of joy and praise. He shall be welcomed to the Throne with acclamations of joy and with loud shouts until the earth rings.

Key Word: Victory, v. 1.

Strong Verse: 1. Promises: 10, 11.

Christ Seen: Jesus, our King, has lived a marvelous life, died a marvelous death, risen by a divine power, by the energy of the Spirit has wrought marvelous things and is yet to be openly proclaimed the conquering King, monarch over all the nations at His second coming.

CHAPTER NINETY-NINE

Contents: Call to praise God because of the glories of His Kingdom among men.

Conclusion: The holiness of God's name makes it truly great to His friends and will make it terrible to His enemies. Let those who worship Him in all humility, praise His great Name and give Him the glory due unto it.

Key Word: Jehovah exalted, v. 5.

Strong Verse: 9.

Christ Seen: v. 5. Jehovah has revealed Himself in Jesus Christ as our reconciled God who allows us to approach to His Throne. Jesus is the King, the Mercy Seat is the throne, and the sceptre which He sways is holy like Himself.   As we exalt Him, let us draw near in all humility and adoration.

CHAPTER ONE HUNDRED

Contents: Call to praise God in consideration of His being and His relation to us.

Conclusion: True worshippers should be joyful worshippers.   If we serve Him in uprightness, realizing all His goodness, we cannot but serve Him with gladness, intermixing praise with all our service.

Key Word: Praise, v. 4.

Strong Verse: 3.

Christ Seen: v. 3.   It is the Christian honor to have been chosen out of the world by the Good Shepherd, to be His own special property, and it is his privilege to be guided by His wisdom, tended by His care and fed by His bounty.

CHAPTER ONE HUNDRED ONE

Contents: David's vow to God when he took upon him the charge of the kingdom.

Conclusion: The believer should resolve to walk by the rules of Christian prudence and in the ways of Christian piety, whether he be abroad in public stations, or before his own family.

Key Word: Mercy and judgment, v. 1.

Strong Verse: 2.

Christ Seen: David is here a type of Christ who has His eyes upon the faithful in the land and will ultimately banish the wicked from His presence.   v. 8 will have its larger fulfillment when He comes in judgment.

CHAPTER ONE HUNDRED TWO

Contents: Sorrowful complaint of great afflictions and a believing prospect of deliverance.

Conclusion: The greatest ease to an afflicted spirit is to unburden itself by a humble representation of its griefs before God, who has invited His children to cast all their burdens upon Him, promising to sustain them.

Key Word: Prayer, vv. 1, 17.

Strong Verses: 25, 26, 27.   Promise: 17.

Christ Seen: vv. 25, 26.   The application of these verses to Christ (Heb. 1:10-12) shows that the Psalm has a reference to the days of the Messiah.   The Son of God made the worlds (John 1:1-3; Col. 1:16) yet for our sakes He became a man of sorrows, and acquainted with grief.

CHAPTER ONE HUNDRED THREE

Contents: The psalmist, affected with the goodness of God stirs himself up to praise God.

Conclusion: God is the fountain of all good, whatever may be the channel and to His holy name we should concentrate our praise.   He has crowned us with loving kindness and tender mercies; He has removed our transgressions far from us, therefore blessing His name should be the alpha and omega of all our service.

Key Word: Bless the Lord, vv. 1, 20, 21, 22.

Strong Verses: 2, 13.   Promises: 3, 4, 5.

Christ Seen: v. 4.   Redemption will ever constitute one of the sweetest notes in the believer's grateful song.   Glory be to our Great Substitute Who has delivered us from going down into the pit by giving Himself to be our ransom.

CHAPTER ONE HUNDRED FOUR

Contents: God's greatness, majesty and sovereign dominion celebrated.

Conclusion: It is the joy of the saints that He Who is their God is a great God Who may be seen in all His mighty works in nature, which proclaim Him to be infinitely wise and good.

Key Word: God's greatness, v. 1.

Strong Verses: 24, 34.

Christ Seen: v. 4.   This is quoted by the Apostle (Heb. 1:7) to prove the preeminence of Christ above the angels.   Heb. 1:3 shows us that it is Christ who upholds all things by the word of His power.

CHAPTER ONE HUNDRED FIVE

Contents: Jehovah extolled for His deliverances of Israel. The coming forth from Egypt described.

Conclusion: God's marvelous works will be had in everlasting remembrance by the thoughtful and the grateful, and should be the subject of familiar discourse. We should continually give thanks to Him, for at best we can give but poor returns for such rich receivings.

Key Word: Wondrous works, v. 2.

Strong Verses: 4, 5.

Christ Seen: God is always mindful of the covenant He has made with believers—ratified by the blood of His Son. He shows His independence of human standards in choosing us though we are unworthy. He is ever interposing in our behalf, saying, "Touch not mine anointed."

CHAPTER ONE HUNDRED SIX

Contents: The badness of Israel made heinous by the great goodness of God.

Conclusion: Man's perverseness arises continually from his stupidity toward God. Our understandings are dull; our memories are treacherous, so that we easily lose sight of God's mercies. In spite of our treatment, He is a gracious God Who pities us and is ever making merciful allowances for us, not giving us our full deserts.

Key Word: Long suffering, vv. 43, 45.

Strong Verses: 3, 5.

Christ Seen: The theme of this psalm is God's redeeming grace. Side by side with this catalogue of sin, is the divine mercy. He saved them for His name's sake (v. 8). God has not made a covenant with us who receive His Son, and though we may grieve Him we may claim His special favor and help at all times.

CHAPTER ONE HUNDRED SEVEN

Contents: God's wisdom, power and goodness celebrated. Man's deplorable forgetfulness of His mercies.

Conclusion: Those who have no special matter for praise may furnish themselves with matter enough from God's universal goodness. All receive the mercies of His providence and are therefore called upon to give thanks.

Key Word: Jehovah's goodness, vv. 8, 15, 21, 31.

Strong Verses: 8, 9.

Christ Seen: v. 2. Those who have an interest in the Great Redeemer, being saved by Him from sin and hell, of all people have reason to say that God is good and His mercy everlasting.

CHAPTER ONE HUNDRED EIGHT

Contents: Thanks to God for His mercies and His promises pleaded.

Conclusion: We should praise God publicly as those who are not ashamed of our obligations to Him and our thankful sense of His favors, but desire that others also may be affected with a realization of His goodness and the value of leaning upon His promises.

Key Word: Praise, v. 1.

Strong Verses: 12, 13.

Christ Seen: v. 7. With such assurance, we may speak of the performance of God's promise to the Son of David, who is certainly to have the uttermost parts of the earth for His inheritance. He waits at God's right hand for the hour when He shall come forth to be proclaimed both Lord and King.

CHAPTER ONE HUNDRED NINE

Contents: Complaint of the malice of enemies and appeal to the righteous God for judgment.

Conclusion: When enemies are spiteful and malicious, it is the unspeakable comfort of the Christian that God is for him and that to Him they may apply, knowing that He will concern Himself for them and will visit overwhelming ruin upon the enemy in His own time and way.

Key Word: Adversaries, v. 20.

Promise: 31.

Christ Seen: David is here a type of Christ Who was compassed about with hateful enemies, who persecuted Him, not only without cause, but for His love and His good works (John 10:32) yet He gave Himself to prayer to pray for them. However the imprecations here are not appropriate in the mouth of the Saviour. It is not the spirit of the Gospel, but of Sinai which here speaks out of the mouth of David.

CHAPTER ONE HUNDRED TEN

Contents: The Messiah promised to the fathers and expected by them.
Conclusion: Christ is the rightful Lord whose title is incontestable. He will certainly come to take, and keep possession of, that Kingdom which the Father has promised, and none can hinder.
Key Word: Messiah, v. 1.
Strong Verse: 1.
Christ Seen: This psalm affirms the deity of Jesus, (v. 1) announces His eternal priesthood, (v. 4) and looks to the time when He will appear as the Rod of Jehovah's strength (Rom. 11:25-27) and as the Judge over all powers (vv. 5, 6).

CHAPTER ONE HUNDRED ELEVEN

Contents: Exhortation to praise God for the greatness and glory of His works.
Conclusion: All who love God delight to meditate upon His works. They are all praiseworthy, and if considered, cannot but cause us to adore Him and to express His praise to others.
Key Word: Jehovah's works, vv. 2, 4, 6, 7.
Strong Verses: 4, 10.
Christ Seen: v. 9. The Christian can indeed sing of redemption, for it is an accomplished act, wrought out for us by Jesus on Calvary. All who have received Him are indeed the Lord's redeemed.

CHAPTER ONE HUNDRED TWELVE

Contents: The eternal happiness of the saints.
Conclusion: The truly happy man is he who fears the Lord, for he is given outward prosperity as far as it is good for him, and all spiritual blessings which are true and eternal riches.
Key Word: The upright, v. 2.
Strong Verses: 1, 7.
Christ Seen: Fixedness of heart, the sovereign remedy against all disquieting news is one of the believer's inheritances in Christ, Who has proved Himself the victor over Satan. Looking to Jesus, the author and finisher of our faith is the sure way of establishing the heart.

CHAPTER ONE HUNDRED THIRTEEN

Contents: A call to praise God.
Conclusion: Praise is a duty the believer should much abound in and in which he should be frequently employed, for in every place there appears the manifest proofs of God's wisdom, power and goodness.
Key Word: Praise, v. 1.
Strong Verses: 3, 7.
Christ Seen: What a wonderful God is ours! Heaven cannot contain Him, yet He has given His only begotten Son to lift us out of the mire and to get us in the company of princes (Eph. 2).

CHAPTER ONE HUNDRED FOURTEEN

Contents: The deliverance of Israel out of Egypt.
Conclusion: He who made the hills and the mountains to skip, can when He pleases dissipate the strength and spirit of the proudest of His enemies and make them tremble.
Key Word: Jehovah's presence, v. 7.
Strong Verse: 7.
Christ Seen: Like Israel, believers have come out of Egypt and belong no more to the world, nor do we speak its language. Redeemed by the blood, our exodus has made us temples of Christ.

CHAPTER ONE HUNDRED FIFTEEN

Contents: Indignation against the makers and worshippers of idols and exhortation to trust in God.

Conclusion: The creatures of men's vain imaginations and the works of men's hands have no divinity in them and to worship such things is the heighth of absurdity. It is wisdom to trust in the living God who proves Himself the help and shield to all who humbly put their confidence in Him.

Key Word: Idols, v. 4.

Strong Verses: 11, 12.

Christ Seen: Jehovah has no outward semblance save that which He has taken in the person of His Son (Jno. 1:14). Having Him we may say we are blessed of the Lord Who made heaven and earth (v. 15; Jno. 1:1-3).

CHAPTER ONE HUNDRED SIXTEEN

Contents: Thanksgiving for the many gracious deliverances God had wrought.

Conclusion: The experiences we have had of God's goodness in answer to prayer are great encouragements to us to continue praying and should cause us to praise Him continually.

Key Word: Jehovah's benefits, v. 12.

Strong Verses: 1, 15.

Christ Seen: A psalm of thanksgiving in the person of Christ. He proclaims the mercies He experiences from His Father in the days of His incarnation and the glories He has received in the Kingdom above.

CHAPTER ONE HUNDRED SEVENTEEN

Contents: A solemn call to the nations to praise God.

Conclusion: The Lord is kind to us as His creatures and merciful to us as sinners, therefore praise is due Him from all peoples.

Key Word: Praise, v. 1.

Strong Verse: 2.

Christ Seen: In Jesus Christ God has shown to the world mercy mixed with kindness to the very highest degree. The tidings of His gospel to all nations should cause them to glorify God.

CHAPTER ONE HUNDRED EIGHTEEN

Contents: Cheerful acknowledgement of God's goodness and dependence upon that goodness for the future.

Conclusion: Never failing streams of mercy flow from our God. The more our hearts are impressed with the sense of His goodness, the more we are bound to praise Him and the more our hearts will be enlarged in all manner of obedience.

Key Word: Thanks, vv. 1, 29.

Strong Verses: 6, 8 (middle verse of Bible).

Christ Seen: v. 22. Jesus Christ is the tried stone, elect, precious, which God Himself appointed. While the Jews could not see the excellence in Him that they should build upon Him, in raising Him from the dead God made Him the headstone of the corner, the foundation of the church. To the rejector He is now a stumbling stone. At His second coming He is the stone cut out without hands which is to fall upon and crush the unbelieving nations.

CHAPTEN ONE HUNDRED NINETEEN

Contents: The excellency and usefulness of the divine revelation set forth and exhortation to all to make it their meditation and to be governed by it.

Conclusion: Great blessing belongs to those who read and understand the Word of God, and more blessed is the man whose life is the practical transcript of the will of God as revealed in the Scriptures.

Key Word: The Word, v. 11.

Strong Verses: 11, 18, 27, 89, 130, 160. Promise: 165.

Christ Seen: v. 99. The disciples of Christ who sit at His feet and let Him interpret the Word to them are often better skilled in divine things than the doctors of divinity. The best way to find "the wondrous things" is to saturate the study of the Word in prayer (v. 18) which makes it possible for Christ to speak to us out of the Word, through the Holy Spirit. John 16:13, 14.

CHAPTER ONE HUNDRED TWENTY

Contents: Prayer for deliverance from the mischief designed by false and malicious tongues.

Conclusion: It is often the lot of the innocent that there are those who carry on malicious designs against them under the color of friendship. In such distresses we always have recourse to God, Who, being the God of Truth, will certainly be the protection of His people from lying lips and will baffle the enemy at last.

Key Word: Lying lips, v. 2.

Strong Verse: 1.

Christ Seen: David is herein a type of Christ Who was greatly distressed by lying lips and deceitful tongues, and found sufficient grace to bear in silence by waiting upon His heavenly Father.

CHAPTER ONE HUNDRED TWENTY-ONE

Contents: The guardian care of the Lord and the peace of His house.

Conclusion: The Christian may stay himself upon Jehovah as a God of power, a God all-sufficient for us. Our safety is in putting ourselves under His protection.

Key Word: Keeper, v. 3.

Strong Verse: 2. **Promise:** 7, 8.

Christ Seen: v. 2. Help cometh (lit) "from before the Lord." This suggests Christ incarnate through Whom God has made Himself our help and Who helps us constantly by His intercession at God's right hand.

CHAPTER ONE HUNDRED TWENTY-TWO

Contents: Prayer for the welfare of Jerusalem.

Conclusion: When peace comes to Jerusalem there will be peace for all the world, therefore the saints should earnestly pray for it.

Key Word: Peace of Jerusalem, v. 6.

Strong Verse: 6.

Christ Seen: v. 5. The thought of God reigning in the Son of David, avenging the just cause, is cheering for disconsolate hearts. Christ's throne is set and truth and righteousness shall be manifested on tne throne with the King when He comes.

CHAPTER ONE HUNDRED TWENTY-THREE

Contents: Expectation of mercy from God in the day of contempt.

Conclusion: When man's eyes are toward God, he will always see God's mercy coming toward him. He Who dwells in heaven beholds all the calamities of His people and thence will send to save all trusting ones.

Key Word: Mercy, v. 3.

Strong Verse: 1.

Christ Seen: As the Oriental servant was an adept at reading the meaning of his master's slightest gesture (v. 2) so let us live, as our Lord did, with the eye keen to see the least indication of God's will.

CHAPTER ONE HUNDRED TWENTY-FOUR

Contents: David gives to God the glory of the deliverances of His people.

Conclusion: God sometimes suffers the enemies of His people to prevail very far against them, that His own power may appear the more illustrious in their deliverance. Happy be the people whose God is Jehovah and who commit themselves to His keeping.

Key Word: Our help, v. 8.

Strong Verse: 8.

Christ Seen: "Why were we chosen in Christ when others were overwhelmed by sin and carried down," is a question that comes to many Christians (Rom. 9:18). (See Rom. 11:33).

CHAPTER ONE HUNDRED TWENTY-FIVE

Contents: The security of God's people because of His promises, and the jeopardy of the wicked.

Conclusion: There is no gap in the hedge of God's protection which He makes round about His trusting people. The happiness of God's people will be the vexation of those who perish in their wickedness.

Key Word:　Security, v. 2.
Promise:　1.
Christ Seen:　Those who trust in God live within ramparts of His loving care forever, for His Son is made our High Priest while the Holy Spirit is made our constant companion.

CHAPTER ONE HUNDRED TWENTY-SIX

Contents:　Thanksfulness for deliverance from captivity.
Conclusion:　The long want of mercies greatly sweetens them when they are returned to us.　When God appears for His people they should give Him the glory and give notice to all about them what wonders He has wrought for them.
Key Word:　Deliverance, v. 3.
Strong Verse:　3.　Promises:　5, 6.
Christ Seen:　The return out of captivity may be taken as typical of the sinner's redemption by Christ.　Surely He has done great things for us, whereof we should be glad and should give Him glory continually.

CHAPTER ONE HUNDRED TWENTY-SEVEN

Contents:　The vanity of worldly care and the wisdom of dependence on God for all things in the home.
Conclusion:　The best designed home will be a failure unless God crowns it with His favor.　He would have us keep our eyes upon Him in all the affairs of the family that we might avoid excessive care.　He would have us realize that our children are a trust from Him and will be most our honor and comfort if they are dedicated to Him.
Key Word:　Home, v. 1.
Strong Verses:　2, 3.
Christ Seen:　Happy are they who have brought up their children to know that Christ is the unseen Host of the home, the silent listener to every conversation.

CHAPTER ONE HUNDRED TWENTY-EIGHT

Contents:　The prosperity of those who live in the fear of God and in obedience to Him.
Conclusion:　Those who are truly holy are truly happy.
Key Word:　Prosperity, v. 2.
Strong Verse:　1.
Christ Seen:　Those may be assured of a prosperous and happy life who make Christ Lord of their lives and evidence it by constant conformity to His will.

CHAPTER ONE HUNDRED TWENTY-NINE

Contents:　Prayer for destruction of all the enemies of Zion.
Conclusion:　God has many ways of disabling men to do their mischief against His people and of bringing their counsels to naught.　He is righteous in allowing His saints for a time to be afflicted and He is righteous in reckoning with all persecutors in the end.
Key Word:　The wicked, v. 4.
Strong Verse:　4.
Christ Seen:　The sufferings of Christ were a prophecy of what His church would be called upon to endure for His sake.　The true church has ever had fellowship with Him under His cruel flagellations.

CHAPTER ONE HUNDRED THIRTY

Contents:　The Psalmist's desire toward God and his repentance before God.
Conclusion:　Those who cry to God out of a sincere heart when they are in the depths of despair will soon sing of His mercy in the heights of His love.
Key Word:　Supplication, v. 2.
Strong Verses:　3, 5, 6.
Christ Seen:　There is but one solution to the sin question since all our transgressions are recorded. God has provided a sacrifice—Christ, through Whom there is redemption for all.　Our transgressions will not be acted upon if we are in Christ, since He has borne the penalty for us.

CHAPTER ONE HUNDRED THIRTY-ONE

Contents: The lowliness and humility of a sanctified heart.
Conclusion: The love of God reigning in the heart will subdue all inordinate self love.   To know God and our duty toward Him is the highest learning to be had in this world.
Key Word: Humility, v. 1.
Christ Seen: v. 2.   The Lord Jesus teaches us humility by this same comparison.   Matt. 18:3.   We must become, not childish, but as little children, childlike in our confidence toward God.

CHAPTER ONE HUNDRED THIRTY-TWO

Contents: A pleading of the divine covenant and its promises.
Conclusion: Those who have the immutable promises of God for their foundation stand upon a sure rock.   God has given us His promises that our faith might have strong confidence at all times, and that we might know That His Anointed will sit upon the throne of earth to reign eternally.
Key Word: Remember David, vv. 1, 10.
Christ Seen: v. 11.   Peter applies this to Christ and tells us that David himself so understood it.   Acts 2:30.   Christ fulfilled all the conditions and the Father has given Him the throne of His father David.   Luke 1:32. He is now at the right hand of His Father's throne and when the fullness of the Gentiles is gathered in, the promise of the Davidic throne will be made good, and He will come to reign over all.   The saints shall sit with Him upon this eternal throne.   Rev. 3:21.

CHAPTER ONE HUNDRED THIRTY-THREE

Contents: The happiness of brotherly love.
Conclusion: To live together in peace, love, concord and mutual agreement, not only in occasional meetings, but all through the course of our lives, is indeed a great blessing and is very pleasing to our heavenly Father.
Key Word: Unity, v. 1.
Strong Verse: 1.
Christ Seen: The finest unity is that which the saints have in Christ.   John 17:21.   If we are in tune with Christ, we will be in tune with all His. While there may not always be oneness of view, there can always be oneness of spirit and object in Christ.

CHAPTER ONE HUNDRED THIRTY-FOUR

Contents: Exhortation to, and prayer for, those who are constantly ministering before the Lord.
Conclusion: Even by night, God's servants are under His eye and have access to Him.   Let them therefore bless the Lord, that spiritual blessings out of Zion might come upon them.
Key Word: Bless the Lord, v. 1.

CHAPTER ONE HUNDRED THIRTY-FIVE

Contents: A call to the servants of God to praise Him for His mighty works.
Conclusion: Jehovah is great indeed, Who knows no limits of time or place, Who works in all the universe as He pleases.   His name should endure forever in the constant and everlasting praises of His people.
Key Word: Jehovah's greatness, v. 5.
Strong Verses: 6, 13.
Christ Seen: We have here arguments for praise, but how many more reasons are there than the psalmist had, for us to praise Him, who have been taken into God's family and made joint heirs with Jesus Christ!

CHAPTER ONE HUNDRED THIRTY-SIX

Contents: Call to praise God as the great Benefactor of the whole creation.
Conclusion: We should give thanks to God, not only for the mercies which are handed out to us here on earth, but for that which endures forever in the glories and joys of heaven to follow this life.
Key Word: Everlasting mercy, v. 1.
Strong Verse: 26.

Christ Seen: vv. 23-24. In our lost estate, God has extended His great mercy toward us in the gift of His Son to redeem us from sin, death and hell and save us from all spiritual enemies.

CHAPTER ONE HUNDRED THIRTY-SEVEN

Contents: Lamentation over the sad condition of God's people in captivity.

Conclusion: Those who are glad at the calamities that sometimes in God's providence come to His people, shall not go unpunished, for those who mock their grief shall endure eternal grief.

Key Word: Captivity, v. 3.

Strong Verse: 4.

Christ Seen: The Christian is not tied to Jerusalem and the temple for he finds acceptance with God anywhere and always through His Son. Christ is our joy, not Jerusalem.

CHAPTER ONE HUNDRED THIRTY-EIGHT

Contents: Thankfulness for the experience of God's goodness.

Conclusion: Praising God is work of which the greatest of men need not be ashamed. A debt of gratitude is due Him for the wonders of His grace, the revelation of His Word, and the confidence derived from the promises that there is no experience that can overwhelm us if we look toward Him.

Key Word: Jehovah's loving kindness, v. 2.

Strong Verses: 2, 6, 7, 8.

Christ Seen: v. 2. Christ is the essential Word, John 1:1. He and His gospel are magnified above all the discoveries God had made of Himself to the fathers.

CHAPTER ONE HUNDRED THIRTY-NINE

Contents: Meditation upon the doctrines of God's omniscience and omnipresence.

Conclusion: The God with whom we have to do has a perfect knowledge of us and all the motions and actions, both of our outward and inward man. We should therefore desire of Him that when He sees sin in our hearts, He might discover it to us that we might walk in the perfect enjoyment of His presence.

Key Word: Omnipresence, v. 7.

Strong Verses: 17, 23, 24.

Christ Seen: v. 7. No one can escape the all-pervading Being and observation of the Holy Spirit. We are, whether we will it or not, as near to God as our soul is to our body, for the Holy Spirit, the Vicar of Christ, dwells within the Christian (1 Cor. 6:19). This makes it dreadful work to sin, for it is insulting God to His face.

CHAPTER ONE HUNDRED FORTY

Contents: The malice of enemies and prayer for preservation.

Conclusion: Those are safe whom God preserves. In Him believers may count upon security against all real enemies.

Key Word: Preservation, vv. 1, 4.

Strong Verses: 7, 12.

Christ Seen: David is here a type of Christ in that he suffered before his reign and was humbled before he was exalted. As there were many who valued Him, so there were many who hated Him, and those who could not agree in anything else joined themselves faithfully together to persecute Christ.

CHAPTER ONE HUNDRED FORTY-ONE

Contents: Prayer for God's favorable acceptance and powerful assistance.

Conclusion: Though the snares be placed by the enemy with ever so much subtlety, God can, and will, secure His praying people from being taken in them.

Key Word: Keeping, v. 9.

Strong Verses: 3, 8.

Christ Seen: v. 2. Christ in the evening of the world, offered up Himself a sacrifice that a way of approach might be made for the believer into the Holy of Holies. It was the fire under the incense that brought out its sweetness—it is the Holy Spirit who offers fragrant prayer to God. Rom. 8:26-27. The fire, however, was from the blood-sprinkled altar, and apart from Christ's atonement, no acceptable prayer can be offered. Heb. 10:19-20.

CHAPTER ONE HUNDRED FORTY-TWO

Contents: The malice of enemies and expectation of God's deliverance.
Conclusion: There is no cave so deep or dark but that out of it we may send up our souls in prayer to God, with expectation of being brought out of all our perplexities.
Key Word: Trouble, v. 2.
Strong Verse: 5.
Christ Seen: v. 4. David is here a type of Christ, Who in His suffering for us was forsaken of all men and trod the winepress alone.

CHAPTER ONE HUNDRED FORTY-THREE

Contents: Complaint of great distresses and dangers and prayer that persecutors might be reckoned with.
Conclusion: If we look with earnest desire toward God, we need not let our heart be troubled, no matter what troubles we are in. John 14:1.
Key Word: Overwhelmed, v. 4.
Strong Verses: 8, 10.
Christ Seen: v. 3. There is no judgment or condemnation for those who are in Christ. They have been judged in Him once for all. John 5:24; Rom. 8:1.

CHAPTER ONE HUNDRED FORTY-FOUR

Contents: Acknowledgment of the great goodness of God and prayer for the prosperity of the kingdom.
Conclusion: Happy is the people whose God is the Lord, for even when they are weak, they may be made strong in the Lord and in the power of His might.
Key Word: Our strength, v. 1.
Strong Verses: 3, 15.
Christ Seen: vv. 12-14. David as king is here a type of Christ Who provides effectually for the good of His chosen and who will remove every hurtful thing from earth when He comes to reign.

CHAPTER ONE HUNDRED FORTY-FIVE

Contents: David engages himself and others to praise God.
Conclusion: Praising God should be our daily work, for God is every day blessing us. His greatness and goodness cannot be comprehended, and when we have said what we can in praising Him, there is more to be said.
Key Word: Great goodness, v. 7.
Strong Verses: 3, 8, 14, 16. Promises: 18, 19.
Christ Seen: v. 18. The Lord Jesus has promised to be always nigh to His own. To utter these words often during the day is to practice the presence of Christ.

CHAPTER ONE HUNDRED FORTY-SIX

Contents: The psalmist engages himself to praise God and exhorts others to trust and praise Him.
Conclusion: There should be no exemption from the service of praising God. So long as He lets us breathe, we should bless Him for His goodness and mercy.
Key Word: Praise, v. 1.
Strong Verses: 5, 9.
Christ Seen: The psalm is very applicable to Christ, by whom God made the world; Who caused the blind to receive their sight and the lame to walk; He will subvert all the counsels of hell and earth that militate against His church and will exercise full judgment at His coming again.

CHAPTER ONE HUNDRED FORTY-SEVEN

Contents: A call to praise God. The greatness and condescending goodness of the Lord celebrated.

Conclusion: Praise is comely—it becomes us as reasonable creatures on account of God's manifest greatness and goodness in all nature and much more as a people in special covenant relations with Him.

Key Word: Jehovah's greatness, v. 5.

Strong Verses: 5, 11.

CHAPTER ONE HUNDRED FORTY-EIGHT

Contents: A call to all living things to praise God.

Conclusion: No place is too high for the praises of the Most High. All creatures on earth should also speak the Lord's praise, for He is Creator and Preserver; Maker and Ruler.

Key Word: Praise, v 1.

Strong Verse: 13.

Christ Seen: v. 14. The blessing of nearness to God has now, through Christ, come upon the Gentiles. Those who were afar off are now made nigh by His blood. Eph. 2:13.

CHAPTER ONE HUNDRED FORTY-NINE

Contents: Triumph in the God of Israel.

Conclusion: Our praises of God should flow from a heart filled with delight and triumph in His attributes and our relation to Him.

Key Word: Praise, v. 1.

Strong Verse: 4.

Christ Seen: vv. 7-10. Our Lord Jesus is coming as King to overthrow all evil, to display His justice against evil-doers, and with Him, the saints shall judge the world.

CHAPTER ONE HUNDRED FIFTY

Contents: The psalmist would fill all the world with God's praises.

Conclusion: What have we our breath for but to spend it in praising God and how can we spend it better? Since we must shortly breathe our last, while wᵣ have breath, let us praise the Lord.

Key Word: Praise, v. 1.

Strong Verse: 6.

Christ Seen: The first psalm began with "blessed" and ended with "blessed." The fruit of the blessedness of meditating on God's Word, is now shown in the last psalm which begins and ends (lit.) with "Hallelujah.". Those who are blessed with all spiritual blessings in Christ Jesus will end their course on earth with one abounding and unhesitating hallelujah.

PROVERBS

Key Thought:	Number of Chapters:	Key Verse:	Christ seen as:
Wisdom	31	9:10	Wisdom

Writer of the Book:	Date:	Conclusion of the Book:
Solomon	990 to 995 B. C.	The most intensely practical thing in the world is godliness.

SUMMARY

CHAPTER ONE

Contents: Wisdom's reasoning with the children of men and the certain ruin of those who turn a deaf ear to Wisdom's call.

Conclusion: Of all things to be known, the most important is that God is to be reverenced and served, and those know little who do not know this. All true knowledge takes rise from reverence of God and tends to it as its perfection and center.

Key Word: Wisdom, v. 2.

Strong Verse: 7. Promise: 33.

Christ Seen: v. 20. It is Christ Who pleads with sinners and passes sentence on them. He calls Himself Wisdom, Luke 7:35. In Him are hid all the treasures of wisdom and knowledge. He is the center of all divine revelation—the eternal Word by Whom God speaks to men.

CHAPTER TWO

Contents: How wisdom is to be obtained and used. The unspeakable advantage of true wisdom.

Conclusion: God has provided that those who are sincerely disposed to do His will shall have that knowledge and understanding necessary for them. His wisdom will preserve us from men of corrupt principles whose business it is to debauch lives, and from women of corrupt practices.

Key Word: Wisdom, v. 7.

Strong Verses: 6, 7. Promises: 21, 22.

Christ Seen: v. 7. Wisdom is laid up for the righteous, in Christ, Who is made unto the believer, wisdom and knowledge.

CHAPTER THREE

Contents: The power of true wisdom to make men both blessed and a blessing.

Conclusion: Those who have a continual regard to God's precepts and put themselves under divine guidance by acknowledging God and praying in faith to Him, shall find health of soul, good habits of body and true success in life.

Key Word: Favor, vv. 4, 33.

Strong Verses: 5, 11, 26. Promise: 6.

Christ Seen: vv. 13-14. In all the wealth of the world is not to be found a taste of that transcendant happiness which is gained in Christ, in whom are stored the treasures of wisdom, which consist in the knowledge and love of God.

CHAPTER FOUR

Contents: Earnest exhortation to the study of true wisdom.

Conclusion: True wisdom from God is the principle thing. It is that which recommends us to God, which beautifies the soul, which enables us to answer the ends of our creation, to live to some good purpose in the world and which makes our path brighter and brighter until we get to heaven at last.

Key Word: Wisdom v. 5.

Strong Verses: 18, 23.

Christ Seen: v. 18. The Christian walks in a way of light. Christ is their way and Christ is the light. They are guided by the Bible which is a light to their feet.

CHAPTER FIVE

Contents: Caution against the sin of whoredom.

Conclusion: We ought industriously to avoid everything that might be an occasion of the sin of adultery or a step towards it, for it is destructive of all the seeds of virtue of the soul and those who are entangled in it have but a step between them and hell.

Key Word: Strange woman, v. 3.

Strong Verses: 21, 22.

Christ Seen: v. 21. Those who practice adultery promise themselves secrecy (Job 24:15). All the workings of the heart and all the outgoings of the life are wide open to God, Christ and the Holy Spirit. Every action will be brought into judgment when Jesus comes.

CHAPTER SIX

Contents: Caution against rash suretyship, slothfulness, forwardness, and whoredom.

Conclusion: Suretyship is to be avoided, because by it poverty and ruin are often brought into families. Poverty and want will certainly come upon those who are slothful. The froward man who devises mischief will surely fall into mischief. Adultery is to be looked upon with utmost dread and detestation as a sin that impoverishes men, debauches their consciences, threatens death and brings infamy upon the reputation.

Key Word: Warnings (5:1).

Strong Verses: 6, 23, 32.

CHAPTER SEVEN

Contents: Warning against all approaches to the sin of adultery.

Conclusion: The Word of God, if used for a defense and armor, will keep one from the strange woman and the destroying sin of adultery. Let the Word therefore discover to us the fallacies of this sin and suggest to us the answers to all its flatteries.

Key Word: Strange woman, v. 5.

Strong Verse: 2.

CHAPTER EIGHT

Contents: Praise of divine wisdom. Christ, the Wisdom of God, speaks to men.

Conclusion: Right knowledge of the divine will concerning us is to be preferred above all the wealth of this world, for it brings favor with God, and eternal life.

Key Word: Wisdom, v. 1.

Strong Verse: 36. Promise: 35.

Christ Seen: v. 22. Wisdom here is certainly more than the personification of an attribute of God, or the will of God, but is a distinct representation of Christ. John 1:1-3; Col. 1:17.

CHAPTER NINE

Contents: Wisdom (Chr'st) and sin, as rivals for the soul of man.

Conclusion: Christ and sin are both seeking to have the uppermost place in the soul of man. We are therefore concerned to put a value upon our own souls and to sit down at the rich feast provided at Wisdom's table. There is no true wisdom but in the way of Christ and there is no true life but in the end of His way.

Key Word: Wisdom.

Strong Verse: 10.

Christ Seen: vv. 1-5. Heaven is the place where Wisdom (Christ) has prepared many mansions. Christ Himself is the sacrifice which has been killed and it is His flesh that is meat indeed. His disciples have gone forth with the invitation to the Gospel feast, even the simple being freely invited.

CHAPTER TEN

Contents: The blessedness of the ways of righteousness and the folly of the ways of wickedness.

Conclusion: The head of the just man will be crowned with the blessings both of God and man, and they shall leave behind them blessed memories. The wicked man's ways will turn out to be his shame and when his body is in the grave, his name will be spoken only with contempt.
Key Word: Wickedness and righteousness, v. 2.
Strong Verses: 7, 9, 19, 22, 28.

<h3 align="center">CHAPTER ELEVEN</h3>

Contents: Proverbs contrasting good and evil.
Conclusion: The ways of righteousness are plain and safe and in them we may enjoy a holy security. The ways of wickedness are dangerous and those who indulge themselves in sin are fitting themselves for destruction.
Key Word: Righteousness and wickedness, v. 5.
Strong Verses: 24, 30. Promise: 25.

<h3 align="center">CHAPTER TWELVE</h3>

Contents: Proverbs contrasting good and evil.
Conclusion: In the life of the righteous, there is all true comfort and satisfaction and at the end of life there is eternal joy. The man who devises wickedness is under condemnation and all his triumphing on earth is but for a moment.
Key Word: Goodness and wickedness, v. 2.
Strong Verse: 28. Promise: 21.

<h3 align="center">CHAPTER THIRTEEN</h3>

Contents: Proverbs contrasting good and evil.
Conclusion: The destruction of sinners is unavoidable, for God's wrath pursues them, and whom God pursues is sure to be overtaken. The happiness of the saints is indefeatable, for God has promised that they shall be abundantly recompensed for all the good they have done and the ill they have suffered.
Key Word: Righteousness and wickedness, v. 5.
Strong Verse: 7. Promise: 13.

<h3 align="center">CHAPTER FOURTEEN</h3>

Contents: Proverbs contrasting good and evil.
Conclusion: The house of the wicked, though built ever so strong and high, shall be brought to disgrace and at length made extinct. The tabernacle of the upright, though moveable and despicable shall, at all events have grace and comfort, and shall be eternally established.
Key Word: Righteousness and wickedness, v. 2.
Strong Verses: 11, 12, 16, 26, 27.

<h3 align="center">CHAPTER FIFTEEN</h3>

Contents: Proverbs contrasting good and evil.
Conclusion: The course of the wicked man is an abomination to God, neither is there any offering he can make to God that can be accepted, as long as the heart is resolved to go on in sin. The upright man is regarded as the friend of God, whose prayer is God's delight, and to whom He is very near.
Key Word: Righteousness and wickedness, v. 6.
Strong Verses: 3, 8, 9, 16, 33.
Christ Seen: The fruits of a right and holy life listed here are all by-products and experiences of those whose "life is hid with Christ in God."

<h3 align="center">CHAPTER SIXTEEN</h3>

Contents: Proverbs contrasting good and evil.
Conclusion: The safest way in which to travel is the way of the upright, a way which God makes plain to those who desire to walk in it. We should take heed of deceiving ourselves by resting in that which seems right, but is not really so.
Key Word: Righteousness and wickedness.
Strong Verses: 7, 8, 18, 25, 31, 32.
Christ Seen: v. 4. God makes no man wicked, but He made those whom He foreknew would be wicked of their own choice, because He knew how

to get glory to Himself and honor upon them (Rom. 9:22) by the display of His grace in Christ Jesus.

CHAPTER SEVENTEEN

Contents: Proverbs contrasting good and evil.
Conclusion: About the most satisfactory substitute for wisdom is silence. Discretion of speech is better than fluency of speech.
Key Word: Wicked and unjust, v. 15.
Strong Verses: 3, 13.

CHAPTER EIGHTEEN

Contents: Proverbs contrasting good and evil.
Conclusion: The only zone of safety is the name of the Lord which is the strong tower in which one may find rest and be fortified against the evil one, if they will but come into it by faith in God's Word.
Key Word: Wicked and righteous, v. 5.
Strong Verse: 24. Promise: 10.
Christ Seen: v. 24. Christ is the true friend to all believers, who sticks closer than a brother. To Him therefore let us show ourselves friends.

CHAPTER NINETEEN

Contents: Proverbs contrasting good and evil.
Conclusion: If we keep God's Word, God's Word will keep us from all things that are really hurtful. Those who despise the ways of His Word are on the high road to ruin.
Key Word: Goodness and wickedness, vv. 16, 28.
Strong Verse: 16. Promises: 17, 23.
Christ Seen: v. 17. What is given to the poor out of love for Christ, God places to our account as lent to Him. Jesus said "Inasmuch as ye have done it unto one of the least of these, my brethren, ye have done it unto me."

CHAPTER TWENTY

Contents: Warnings and instructions regarding the ways of folly.
Conclusion: Here in this imperfect state, no person can claim to be sinless, but the just man, walking by the rule of God's Word may have the comfort of a good conscience, and his children will fare the better for his sake.
Key Word: Counsel, v 5.
Strong Verses: 1, 7, 9. Promise: 22.
Christ Seen: v. 9. This is a challenge to any man in the world to prove himself sinless. Only saints in heaven, who "have seen Him as He is" and been made like Him, can say it. Though the believer, through the work of the Spirit, is pure from the sins of many others, yet each one still has sins that easily beset him—sins of omission and sins of commission which they have to continually confess in order to maintain unbroken fellowship with Christ.

CHAPTER TWENTY-ONE

Contents: Warnings and instructions.
Conclusion: Those who follow after righteousness, shall find righteousness, honor and life.
Key Word: Counsel (20:5).
Strong Verses: 3, 13, 21, 30.
Christ Seen: v. 3. The sacrifice which typified the great sacrifice of Christ, was a divine institution. Religious ceremonies based upon Christ's sacrifice are pleasing to God when offered in faith and repentance, but when not backed by true devotion, are an abomination.

CHAPTER TWENTY-TWO

Contents: Warnings and instructions.
Conclusion: Those who walk humbly with God in obedience to the commands of His Word and in submission to the disposals of His providence, shall find true riches, honor, comfort and long life in this world, and eternal life at last.
Key Word: Counsel (20:5).
Strong Verses: 1, 4.

CHAPTER TWENTY-THREE

Contents: Warnings and instructions.
Conclusion: The indulgence of the appetites is a sin that easily besets us. We should apprehend ourselves to be in danger when in the presence of luxury, gluttony and sensuality, and should restrain ourselves from such gratifications, lest our hearts be overcharged with surfeiting and that day come upon us unawares.
Key Word: Instruction, v. 12.
Strong Verses: 17, 23.

CHAPTER TWENTY-FOUR

Contents: Warnings and instructions.
Conclusion: If wicked people prosper, we should not be inclined to do as they do, nor complain of what God does in His providence. They have no real happiness of heart, their prosperity is only for the present and there is no good for them in the world to come. Let us therefore honor and reverence God and be dutiful to the government God has set over us.
Key Word: Counsel, v. 6.
Strong Verses: 16, 19, 20, 24.

CHAPTER TWENTY-FIVE

Contents: Warnings and instructions.
Conclusion: (Principal lesson, vv. 21, 22.) The way to turn an enemy into a friend is to act friendly towards him. If it does not gain him it will aggravate his sin and punishment, and will heap the coals of God's wrath upon his head.
Key Word: Proverbs, v. 1.
Promises: 21, 22.
Christ Seen: v. 1. Herein Christ is greater than Solomon for John 21:25 tells us that if we had on record all the good things that Christ said the world could not contain the books.

CHAPTER TWENTY-SIX

Contents: Warnings and instructions.
Conclusion: (Principal lesson, vv. 20-25.) God gives us two ears and two eyes, but only one tongue. We should therefore see and hear more than we speak, for we cannot recover our words.
Key Word: Proverbs, v. 1 (25:1).
Strong Verses: 12, 20, 27.

CHAPTER TWENTY-SEVEN

Contents: Warnings and instructions.
Conclusion: (Principal lesson.) Use the present time with diligence and wisdom and presume not upon tomorrow. We should speak of the morrow as those who are submitted to the will of God, knowing the uncertainty of one moment, except as God allows it to us.
Key Word: Proverbs (25:1).
Strong Verses: 1, 6.
Christ Seen: (v. 9). Human friendships are often sweet, but the greatest sweetness and confidence will be found in Jesus, the greatest Friend of all.

CHAPTER TWENTY-EIGHT

Contents: Warnings and instructions.
Conclusion: True religion is true wisdom, making men wise in every relation. Those who make conscience of God's law will find a security in the worst of times and will always be found vigorously opposing sin.
Key Word: Proverbs (25:1).
Strong Verses: 4, 6, 9. Promises: 13, 26.

CHAPTER TWENTY-NINE

Contents: Warnings and instructions.
Conclusion: Those who never regard the Word of God are an easy prey to the enemy of souls. A confidence in God and His Word enables one to look with gracious contempt upon the most formidable designs of the devil, and will keep one in the way of duty, and above the fear of man.

Key Word: Righteous and wicked, v. 2.
Strong Verses: 1, 18.   Promise: 25.

CHAPTER THIRTY

Contents: The words of Agur.
Conclusion: God's Word is sure and pure, and venturing our souls upon it, we shall find it a shield against temptations, a safe protection in the midst of greatest dangers.   God will certainly reckon with any who presume to add to His Word, or advance anything in competition with it.
Key Word: Proverbs, v. 1.
Strong Verses: 5, 6.
Christ Seen: v. 4.   It is God Who has gathered the winds in His fists and His name is "I am that I am" (Ex. 3:14), a name to be adored, not to be understood.   He has a Son, Jesus Christ, whose name was to be called "Wonderful, Counsellor, the Mighty God, Prince of Peace."   By Him, God made all that was made, and by Him He controls all things.

CHAPTER THIRTY-ONE

Contents: Words of King Lemuel on the dangers of intemperance and the worth of a godly woman.
Conclusion: A virtuous woman who has command of her own spirit, who is pious and industrious, who is firm for the principles of God's Word, is a rare prize.   Such a one is of unspeakable worth, and he who has such a wife, should show to her great kindness and respect, and to God, thankfulness of heart.
Key Word: Virtuous woman, v. 10.
Strong Verses: 10, 30.
Christ Seen: The scope of each of the various proverbs of this book is one and the same—to direct our manner of life aright and to point us to the Lord Jesus Christ, Who is "made unto us Wisdom and Righteousness."

ECCLESIASTES

Key Thought:	Number of Chapters:	Key Verse:	Christ seen as:
Vanity	12	2:11	Above the Sun

Writer of the Book:	Date:	Conclusion of the Book:
Solomon	980 to 985 B. C.	Apart from God, life is full of weariness and disappointment.

SUMMARY

CHAPTER ONE

Contents: The doctrine of the vanity of the creature, and the impossibility of finding satisfaction without God.

Conclusion: All things, considered as abstract from God, and apart from Him, all worldly employments and enjoyments, are vanity of vanities, and if there were no supernatural method of giving peace to the heart and another life to follow, were indeed made in vain.

Key Word: Vanity, v. 2.

Strong Verse: 8.

Christ Seen: All is indeed vanity if Christ is not in the heart nd if there be no hope of eternal life through acceptance of Him. The th ags of earth are pass ng away and hence are vanity if they be trusted in. There is a kingdom coming in which believers shall inherit substance and where there is no vanity. Matt. 11:28-29; 1 Cor. 15:19.

CHAPTER TWO

Contents: Solomon shows that there is no true happiness and satisfaction to be had in mirth, pleasure and the delights of sense.

Conclusion: True and lasting happiness and satisfaction consist not in mirth, the gratifying of appetites, the spending of money or the getting of wisdom. Only he who sets God always before him and employs himself for God may find heart rest in this world and that joy which He alone can give.

Key Word: Vanity, v. 1.

Strong Verse: 26.

Christ Seen: The pleasures of this world are indeed emptiness. In the light of these things ponder Christ's words in Lk. 12:33.

CHAPTER THREE

Contents: The mutability of all human affairs and the unchangeableness and unsearchableness of the divine counsels.

Conclusion: We live in a world of changes. The events of time and the conditions of human life are continually passing and repassing, yet every change is determined by the supreme power and we should therefore accommodate ourselves to His purposes. The only true pleasure of life is in making good use of the things God has given us, making ourselves serviceable to those about us.

Key Word: Man's portion, v. 22.

Strong Verses: 12, 14, 17.

Christ Seen: v. 17. In the midst of all the inequalities of human affairs it is a great comfort to know that the eye of faith can see that Jesus Christ, the Judge, stands before the door and that when He comes, He will reward the righteous and punish the pride and cruelty of oppressors. Though the day of affliction may seem long, we may patiently wait His coming, when there will be an examination into every purpose and every work done under the sun.

CHAPTER FOUR

Contents: Discontent and impatience because of the oppressions and iniquities of life.

Conclusion: The world is full of trouble. By reason of man's perversity, he is ever disturbed and perplexed by social conditions around him. If Christ and the hope of heaven were not taken into account, to die as soon as possible would be desirable.

Key Word: Vanity, v. 7.

Strong Verses: 6, 13.

Christ Seen: v. 4. For every right work, the Christian is remembered by the Lord Jesus, and at His coming will be rewarded. Though he be hated by a neighbor for a right work, the Christian will always be abounding in the work of the Lord knowing his labor will not be in vain in the Lord.

CHAPTER FIVE

Contents: Warnings against a vain religion. The vanity and vexation attending the possession of wealth.

Conclusion: We should address ourselves to the worship of God with all possible seriousness and care, for religious exercises if not rightly directed, may become empty ceremony, and we will miss our end in coming into His presence.

Key Word: Vanity, v. 10.

Strong Verses: 1, 2, 12.

Christ Seen: Those who labor only for the world, to fill their hands with that which they cannot take away, will not only die an uncomfortable death, but will miss the only satisfaction of life—heart peace in Jesus Christ. (v. 12.) The sleep of the diligent Christian is sweet, for having spent his strength and time in Christ's service, he can cheerfully return to Him and repose in Him Who gives rest. Matt. 11:28-29.

CHAPTER SIX

Contents: The vanity of worldly wealth as pertaining only to the body.

Conclusion: Man deprives himself of the good he might have had of his worldly possessions by not consecrating them to God. If one does not have the will to serve God with what he has, God may deny him the power to even serve himself with it.

Key Word: Vanity, v. 2.

Strong Verse: 2.

Christ Seen: v. 7. Those who have ever so much, yet do not know Christ, are ever craving. Wealth to a worldling is like drink to one who has dropsy, which only increases the thirst. Christ is the true Bread which satisfies; the Water of life which quenches all thirst of the soul.

CHAPTER SEVEN

Contents: Prudence recommended as a means of avoiding much of the vanity and vexation of the world.

Conclusion: The best way to save ourselves from the vexation which the vanity of the world creates, is to make use of wisdom, maintaining strict government of the passions. Wisdom is a defense (v. 12).

Key Word: Wisdom, vv. 11, 19.

Strong Verses: 9, 29.

CHAPTER EIGHT

Contents: Wisdom recommended as an antidote against the temptations and vexations arising from the vanity of the world.

Conclusion: Heavenly wisdom makes a man a good man, emboldening him against his adversaries, their attempts and their scorn. It teaches him that sentence is passed by a righteous Judge against all evil works, even though the execution of sentence is long delayed, and that it shall be well in the end with those who fear God.

Key Word: Wisdom, v. 1.

Strong Verses: 11, 12.

CHAPTER NINE

Contents: The universality of death and the need of minding the business of life and using wisdom.

Conclusion: While there is life there is opportunity of preparing for death, and since death is certain, it is our wisdom to make the best possible use of life while it lasts, cheerfully taking our share of life's enjoyments, applying ourselves diligently to life's business, and being governed by divine wisdom in all its affairs.

Key Word: Vanity, v. 9.

Strong Verses: 10, 16.

Christ Seen: v. 1. Regardless of how the outward condition of men may seem to us, let it be remembered that all men's affairs are in God's hand and that prosperity is not necessarily a sign of God's love or affliction of His hatred. If a man has Christ as His Savior, he may be happy though the world frowns upon him, and if he is without Christ, he may be miserable, though the world smiles upon him.

CHAPTER TEN

Contents: Proverbs recommending wisdom as of great use for the right ordering of our lives.

Conclusion: Fools are apt, at every turn, to proclaim their folly, for if one is lacking in true wisdom, it cannot be concealed. True wisdom is true honor and will gain a man a reputation which is very valuable.

Key Word: Wisdom and folly, vv. 6, 10.

Strong Verses: 8, 10.

Christ Seen: v. 1. Those who profess to be followers of Christ, Who is said to be "made unto us wisdom," have need to walk very circumspectly lest they be guilty of any instance of folly, for many eyes are upon them.

CHAPTER ELEVEN

Contents: Exhortation to works of charity and right living.

Conclusion: Since we have death and judgment to prepare for, we should do good to others and abound in liberality to the poor, which will (if we are in Christ) abound to our account.

Key Word: Give, v. 2.

Strong Verse: 9. **Promise:** 1.

Christ Seen: The casting of bread upon the waters is an allusion to the Oriental custom of casting rice grains on the fields when they lie submerged. The seed will be met again with abundant returns. So may we say of all service, great or small, done in the name of Jesus Christ. We shall abundantly reap, either in this world or the next.

CHAPTER TWELVE

Contents: Exhortation to the young to be religious. The vanity of the world.

Conclusion: The great antidote against the diseases of youth, the love of mirth, the indulgence of sensual pleasures, and the vanities to which youth is subject, is the reverence of God reigning in the heart and a respect to His commandments. To reverence God is the summary of religion.

Key Word: Fear God, v. 13.

Strong Verses: 1, 13, 14.

Christ Seen: v. 13. This is on the ground of law, not grace. To fear God and keep the commandments is the best that man, apart from redemption, can do. The Christian, under the Gospel, has Christ living in Him (Gal. 2:20) and his body is a shrine of the Holy Ghost (1 Cor. 6:19).

SONG OF SOLOMON

Key Thought:	Number of Chapters:	Key Verse:	Christ seen as:
Love	8	6:3	Altogether Lovely One

Writer of the Book:	Date:	
Solomon	980-985 B. C.	**Conclusion of the Book:** Christ covets the full communion of His people and ˙ blessedness comes to all who walk in His fellowship.

SUMMARY

CHAPTER ONE

Contents: The Bride and Bridegroom in joyful communion.

Conclusion: Those who are full of Christ earnestly desire the manifestations of His love to their souls, with humble professions of love to Him and complacency in Him above all.

Key Word: Love, v. 2.

Strong Verse: 4.

Christ Seen: The spiritual and larger interpretation of this book is of Christ, the Son and His heavenly Bride, the Church (2 Cor. 11:1-4). The Church is beautiful to Christ as Christ is beautiful to the Church.

CHAPTER TWO

Contents: The Bridegroom speaks concerning himself and his Bride. The Bride speaks remembering her satisfaction in her beloved.

Conclusion: Humble souls see the most beauty in the Bridegroom. To them He is the rose and He is the lily, and all excellency is in Him in the highest degree. Those are made like Him in whose hearts His love is shed abroad.

Key Word: Beloved, v. 8.

Strong Verses: 4, 16.

Christ Seen: Those whose hearts are filled with love to Christ and the hope of heaven, know best the meaning of this chapter—the rejoicing in Him and the longing to see Him.

CHAPTER THREE

Contents: The Bride seeking the favor of the Bridegroom. She calls upon all to admire Him.

Conclusion: Those who are truly of the Bride, will evince the sincerity of their love to Christ by continual and solicitous enquiries after Him and will not be satisfied until Christ Himself is apprehended by faith.

Key Word: My beloved, v. 1.

Strong Verse: 2.

Christ Seen: Under the figure of Solomon, his bed and his guards about it, the Church here admires Christ, the true Bridegroom. Solomon is used as an illustrious type of Christ because of his wisdom and wealth and the fact that he built the temple.

CHAPTER FOUR

Contents: The Bridegroom commends the beauty of the Bride and delights in her affection.

Conclusion: Whatever others think of the Bride of Christ, she is amiable and beautiful in His eyes because of the comliness of grace which He has put upon her. All the beauty of saints is derived from Him.

Key Word: My love, v. 1.

Strong Verse: 7 (See Eph. 5:27).

Christ Seen: The representations here made of the beauty of the Church, do not represent external beauty but the beauty of holiness, the hidden man of the heart as seen by heaven through the blood of Christ.

CHAPTER FIVE

Contents: The distress of the Bride because of the temporary withdrawal of the groom, due to the Bride's neglect.

Conclusion: The slights which careless souls put upon Christ are grievous to Him and He suspends the communication of His comfort to those who are remiss and drowsy in His service. The loss of the sense of His presence is a matter of great grief to the believer.

Key Word: Beloved withdrawn, v. 6.

Strong Verse: 10.

Christ Seen: v. 6. Rev. 3:20 describes the state of the Church in coldness toward Christ. He has knocked for entrance, but in their drowsiness and coldness, they have not responded. They find themselves at last deserted by Him.

CHAPTER SIX

Contents: The Bridegroom applauds the beauty of the Bride, preferring her before all others.

Conclusion: Christ takes delight in His redeemed and in the workings of His own grace in them, notwithstanding their weaknesses, and though He often has to hide His face temporarily, yet He gathers them back to His heart when they return to their.duty, and He always prefers His own to the best of the unsaved of the world.

Key Word: My love, v. 4.

Strong Verse: 3.

Christ Seen: v. 3. Though Christ may have justly hid His face from His Bride for a time, yet His covenant continues firm, and true believers may always say, "I am His and He is mine."

CHAPTER SEVEN

Contents: Further description of the beauties of the Bride.

Conclusion: The Bride of Christ bears the image of the King of Kings and in the beauty of holiness, is beyond anything nature can reach. In answer to the expressions of Christ's regard for His own, the believer should triumph in his relation to Him and rejoice in the hold He has of him.

Key Word: Beauty, v. 1.

Strong Verse: 10.

Christ Seen: v. 11. Those who love Christ will go forth from the amusements of the world, contriving to attend upon Him without distraction. If we keep our eyes upon Christ, we may have the realization of His presence with us wherever we go ("I walk with the King, hallelujah!")

CHAPTER EIGHT

Contents: The affections between the Bridegroom and His Bride.

Conclusion: Those who are espoused to the Lord Jesus, should desire constant intimacy and freedom with Him. Let us be ready to own our relation to Him and affection for Him, never fearing being despised by the world for it.

Key Word: Love, v. 7.

Strong Verse: 7.

Christ Seen: v. 14. "Even so come, Lord Jesus: come quickly." Only those who can in sincerity call Christ their beloved, can desire Him to hasten His second coming. Let believers long for it, pray for it and work for it.

ISAIAH

Key Thought:	Number of Chapters:	Key Verse:	Christ seen as:
Salvation	66	53:5	Suffering and glorified prophet.

Writer of the Book:	Date:	Conclusion of the Book:
Isaiah	766 to 679 B. C.	Salvation is by the grace of God and through the vicarious suffering of Christ.

SUMMARY

CHAPTER ONE

Contents: Charge against Israel for their ingratitude and degeneration. Call to repentance and reformation.

Conclusion: The backslidings of those who have professed relations to God are very provoking to Him and all departures from Him and opposition to Him are aggravated by the constant manifestation of His goodness and mercy toward the backslider. Those who will break off their allegiance with sin are always welcome to come back to fellowship with Him.

Key Word: Sinsick, v. 5.

Promise: 18.

Christ Seen: v. 11. The costly devotions of those who have not apprehended Christ, He of whom the sacrifices were but a faint shadowing, are an abomination to God. The ceremonial observances were all done away with by the death of Christ.

CHAPTER TWO

Contents: The coming glory of Jerusalem and Israel. The humbling of the haughty and the shame of sinners in that day.

Conclusion: In view of the terribleness of that day when Christ shall come to shake the earth and to judge among men, we should shun the ways of sin. In view of the privilege the righteous have of sharing in His universal Kingdom, we should seek to walk in the light of the Lord all our days.

Key Word: Last days, v. 2.

Strong Verses: 11, 22.

Christ Seen: vv. 19-21. Rev. 6:12-17 shows that the reference here is to the time of Christ's return to judge in terrible majesty. Those who do not flee to Christ before that day will flee from Him then. The prophecy of this chapter relates entirely to Christ's kingdom, still future, when once more the laws of God shall go forth out of Zion.

CHAPTER THREE

Contents: The coming desolations of Jerusalem because of sin and the judgment of sinners.

Conclusion: Whatever evil befalls sinners, it is of their own procuring. Those who provoke God make Him their enemy and bring sure misery upon themselves. The greatest of men cannot secure themselves from the sentence of the judgment day.

Key Word: Judgment, v. 13.

Promises: 10, 11.

Christ Seen: v. 10. Whatever becomes of an unrighteous nation, those who are "in Christ" will be "safe by the blood of the Crucified One."

CHAPTER FOUR

Contents: The coming restoration of Jerusalem's peace and purity.

Conclusion: The issue of all the troubles of this present dispensation is to be in happy days for the righteous, when Christ's kingdom will be set up universally, and He will be exalted as its beauty, glory and joy in the esteem of all the living.

Key Word: That day, v. 1.
Strong Verse: 2.
Christ Seen: v. 2.   "Branch" is a name used of Christ, because He was planted by God's power and flourishes to His praise.

CHAPTER FIVE

Contents: Parable of Jehovah's vineyard and the six woes upon Israel.
Conclusion: God expects vineyard fruit from those who enjoy vineyard privileges, not the mere leaves of profession, or the wild grapes of hypocritical performances in religion.   God will deny His grace to those who have long received it in vain.   The curse of barrenness is the punishment of the sin of barrenness.
Key Word: Woe, v. 8.
Strong Verses: 20, 21.
Christ Seen: v. 4.   Some believe Christ thought these words when He beheld Jerusalem and wept over it (Luke 19:41), and had reference to it in the parable of the vineyard.   Matt. 21:33.

CHAPTER SIX

Contents: Isaiah's transforming vision and his new commission.
Conclusion: Those who are to teach others the knowledge of God must themselves have the vision of God.   Those are fittest to be employed for Him who, having heard His voice, have been humbled before Him in the sense of their own vileness and are made deeply sensible of their own weakness.
Key Word: Vision, v. 5.
Strong Verse: 8.
Christ Seen: vv. 9-10.   These verses are referred to six times in the N. T. It pictures the attitude of the Jews especially toward Christ, a condition which still remains with them, and with all who wilfully reject Him.

CHAPTER SEVEN

Contents: Evil confederacy of Rezin and Jekah.   The sign of the Virgin's Son.   Prediction of impending invasion of Judah.
Conclusion: The sin of a land is sure to bring foreign invasion and all kinds of trouble, but to those who will trust Him, God sends seasonable comforts, and the strongest consolations in times of trouble are those which come from expectation of and from Christ.
Key Word: Sign, v. 11.
Strong Verse: 14.
Christ Seen: v. 14.   The Virgin's Son, Immanuel, God with us, was fulfilled in Jesus.   Matt. 1:21-25.   If He had not been Immanuel, God with us, He could not have been Jesus (A Savior).

CHAPTER EIGHT

Contents: Predictions of the Syrian invasion and of the desolations of Judah and Israel.
Conclusion: If a nation insists on rejecting God's.counsels, it is just with God to apply the scourge.   However in the deluge of trouble that may come to a nation, God will keep the heads of His trusting people above water, if they will make His statutes, rather than those having familiar spirits, their counsellors.
Key Word: Trouble and darkness, v. 22.
Strong Verses: 9, 10, 19, 20.
Christ Seen: v. 14.   When Israel rejected Christ, He became to them a stone of stumbling.   This passage is quoted in application to all those who persist in their unbelief of the Gospel (1 Pet. 2:8).   Being disobedient to God's Word, men stumble at it.

CHAPTER NINE

Contents: A divine child, the only hope of Israel.   Vision of the outstretched hand.   The unavailing chastisement.
Conclusion: In the worst of times, God's people have a "nevertheless" to comfort them (v. 1) and balance their troubles.   As the saints then comforted

themselves with the hope of Christ's first coming, so now His second coming is the great hope of every dark day.

Key Word: Great light, v. 2.

Promises: 6, 7.

Christ Seen: vv. 6-7. Christ was Wonderful in His earthly ministry (Luke 24:19); is Counsellor in His priestly service (1 John 2:1); will be Mighty God in His coming manifestation (Psa. 45:36); Everlasting Father in His ultimate relation (Prov. 8:23); Prince of Peace in His kingdom (Acts 10:36).

CHAPTER TEN

Contents: The commission to invade Judah and its execution. Threatening of the invaders ruin after serving God's purpose. New encouragement given to God's people.

Conclusion: God sometimes makes an idolatrous nation that serves Him not at all, a scourge to a hypocritical nation that serves Him not in sincerity and truth. Yet when God has done His work through the idolatrous nation, He will certainly do His work upon them and their day will come to fall because they have not had God in all their thoughts.

Key Word: Indignation, v. 25.

Strong Verse: 33.

Christ Seen: The fearful judgments of the past and those here prophesied as yet future, convince us of the hopeless condition of those who have heard of the way of life and yet refused forgiveness in Christ.

CHAPTER ELEVEN

Contents: Prophecy of the Davidic Kingdom and restoration of Israel.

Conclusion: The great comfort in days of distress is the hope of the coming universal kingdom of righteousness and peace, when Christ, Who is in every way qualified to be King of earth, shall take the throne. Then God's people shall be delivered, not only from evil, but from the fear of it forever.

Key Word: Kingdom.

Promises: 4, 5, 9.

Christ Seen: Nothing of this chapter occurred at Christ's first coming. Israel was then dispersed and Christ was killed. The Messiah was then rejected, but His glorious earth-kingdom is the next step in His program and will be fulfilled when He returns in glory. Luke 1:31-32; Acts 13:15-16.

CHAPTER TWELVE

Contents: The worship of the coming Kingdom.

Conclusion: When Jesus comes to set up His Kingdom, God's regathered people Israel and all the redeemed, shall as one man, with one mind and mouth, praise Him, who is One and His name one.

Key Word: Joy, v. 3.

Strong Verses: 2, 3.

Christ Seen: The Christian does not have to wait until the Kingdom is set up to joy in His praises, for by Jesus Christ, the root of Jesse, God's anger has been turned away, and the believer can say "He is my peace."

CHAPTER THIRTEEN

Contents: Prophecy concerning last days, when punishment will be visited upon the nations, and Israel shall pass through the Great Tribulation.

Conclusion: Men have their day now, and many think to carry the day, but God's day is coming, and His day of reckoning will be cruel with wrath and fierce anger.

Key Word: Day of the Lord (vv. 6, 9) (fierce anger, v. 13).

Strong Verses: 9, 11.

Christ Seen: The chapter looks forward to the apocalyptic judgments centering around Christ's second coming (Rev. 6 to 13). Babylon has never yet been destroyed in the way here foretold, and many believe Babylon will in the last day be rebuilt, and the everlasting destruction here predicted will then fall upon it.

CHAPTER FOURTEEN

Contents: Christ's Kingdom set up on earth with Israel restored. The Beast in hell.   Satan's fall and doom.   Babylon's final judgment.

Conclusion: It is the comfort of God's people that God has purposed through the exaltation of His Son to set up a righteous and eternal Kingdom on earth, when Israel shall have rest from their wanderings and the days of affliction of all His people shall have an end forever.   The rod of the wicked shall be broken, and Satan and all his followers shall be cast into hell.

Key Word: Rest, v. 7.

Strong Verses: 7, 27.

Christ Seen: vv. 12-14.   This is a reference to Satan, the real, though unseen ruler of successive world powers.   This tells the story of the beginning of sin in the universe.   The universal catastrophe here predicted has never occurred and has to do with the close of the times of the Gentiles and the setting up of Christ's Kingdom.

CHAPTER FIFTEEN

Contents: The burden of Moab.   Prophecy of great desolations upon the earth.

Conclusion: Great and dismal changes may in the providence of God be made within a very short time.   Let us therefore live as those who know not what an hour may bring forth.

Key Word: Desolation, v. 6.

CHAPTER SIXTEEN

Contents: Women of Moab anticipate the Davidic Kingdom and lament the pride of Moab.

Conclusion: Those who will not yield to the fear of God, will be made to yield to the fear of everything else.

Key Word: Stricken, v. 7.

Promise: 5.

Christ Seen: v. 5.   Though the thrones of earth be overturned, the throne of David will surely be established in mercy and Christ will sit upon it and will be a protector to all who have been a shelter to the people of God. (Especially Israel.)

CHAPTER SEVENTEEN

Contents: The burden of Damascus, foretelling destruction of cities of Syria and Israel.

Conclusion: The God of our salvation is the rock of our strength.   It is our forgetfulness of Him that is at the bottom of all sin, and brings great calamities upon us.

Key Word: Woe, v. 12.

Strong Verses: 12, 13.   Promises: 7, 8.

CHAPTER EIGHTEEN

Contents: Woe of the land beyond the rivers of Ethiopia, in the day of Israel's regathering.

Conclusion: Though God's covenant people are trampled on as a nation, scattered and abused, no nation, however formidable, will be able to swallow them up.   Though they are cast down, they are not utterly forgotten of God.

Key Word: Woe, v. 1.

CHAPTER NINETEEN

Contents: Burden of Egypt, looking forward, through desolations, to Kingdom blessing with Israel.

Conclusion: The barbarous usage which the enemies of God have given His people, even of long ago, will be remembered against them and they will be paid in their own coin.   Let not the bold be secure, for God can easily cut off their spirit and bring their land to nothing.

Key Word: Egypt, v. 1.

Strong Verse: 20.

Christ Seen: v. 20.   Jesus Christ is the Savior and the Great One here spoken of, Who will eventually bring about the conversion of such perverse nations as Egypt. At His coming, they will receive the light and submit themselves to His rule.

CHAPTER TWENTY

Contents: Prophecy of the wasting of Egypt and Ethiopia by Assyria.

Conclusion: Those who make the creature their expectation and glory and so put it in the place of God, will sooner or later be brought to shame for it and will be utterly disappointed in creature confidences.

Key Word: Shame, v. 5.

Christ Seen: v. 2.   This would be a great hardship upon God's servant, exposing him to ridicule and endangering his health.   When we are obeying some of Christ's hard commands, however foolish it may seem in the eyes of the world, we may trust Him with our credit and safety.

CHAPTER TWENTY-ONE

Contents: Four burdens anticipating Sennacherib's invasion.

Conclusion: Neither the skill of archers nor the courage of mighty men can protect a people from the judgments of God.

Key Word: Grievous vision, v. 2.

CHAPTER TWENTY-TWO

Contents: The burden of the valley of vision, telling of coming grievous distress.

Conclusion: When God threatens His people with judgment, He expects and requires that they will humble themselves under His mighty hand, and if they do not do so, His judgments will follow them to the grave.

Key Word: Treading down, v. 5.

Strong Verse: 22.

Christ Seen: vv. 22-23.   Jesus Christ describes His own power as Mediator by allusion to this.   (Rev. 3:7) He has the key of David.   He opens and no man shuts.   He shuts and no man opens.   He is also a nail in a sure place.   His Kingdom cannot be shaken, and He Himself is "the same yesterday, today and forever."

CHAPTER TWENTY-THREE

Contents: Burden of Tyre.   Desolations preceding the final deliverance of Israel.

Conclusion: The proud boasts of worldly nations, who bid defiance to their neighbors, will surely be silenced by the judgments of God in due time. Pomp and splendor are no guarantee against His judgments.

Key Word: Contempt, v. 9.

Strong Verse: 9.

CHAPTER TWENTY-FOUR

Contents: Looking through national troubles to the Kingdom age.   The coming tribulation for the Jews, destruction of Gentile powers and opening of the Kingdom.

Conclusion: Earth, polluted by the sins of men, will at last be made utterly desolate and empty by the judgments of God.   Satanic hosts and anti-Christian world powers will be cast into the pit.   Then it shall appear that Jehovah is King above all and He shall reign gloriously in the earth.

Key Word: Dissolved, v. 19.

Strong Verses: 4, 21, 23.

Christ Seen: v. 23.   The Lord Jesus Christ will appear as King and Judge in that day and the earth shall shine forth in His glory.   Rev. 21:2, 3.

CHAPTER TWENTY-FIVE

Contents: Triumphs of the coming Kingdom age.

Conclusion: God should be exalted by His people for the wonderful things He has done, and is to do, according to His promises, for these are proofs of His power beyond what any creature could perform, and of His goodness, beyond what such sinful creatures could expect.

Key Word: Wonderful things, v. 1.

Strong Verses: 1, 4.   Promise: 8.

Christ Seen: This chapter looks forward to the coming glorious Kingdom of Christ when all evil shall be put down, death shall be swallowed up in victory and all tears wiped away. Then indeed, His saints will exalt Him for His wonderful works and for fulfilling all His counsels.

CHAPTER TWENTY-SIX

Contents: Worship and testimony of restored and converted Israel in the Kingdom age.

Conclusion: God's people Israel, banished and driven out by the iniquity of the former times will yet be restored as a nation to God's favor. When the Deliverer comes out of Zion, they will join in the song of all the redeemed, rejoicing that the days of distress are over and that God has ordained peace on earth forever.

Strong Verse: 21. Promises: 3, 4, 12.

Christ Seen: v. 21. The Father has given to Jesus Christ authority to execute judgment because He is the Son of Man. John 5:27. At His coming, at the close of the Great Tribulation, the blood of thousands of martyrs will be brought to light and to account.

CHAPTER TWENTY-SEVEN

Contents: Punishment of the proud enemy of God's people. Israel restored and fruitful.

Conclusion: When the Lord comes to punish the inhabitants of the earth, He will first of all punish the serpent, and his proud oppressing tyrants. In that day the sins of Israel will be purged and they will again bring forth fruit to God. Jerusalem will again be a great center of worship, when out of all countries Israel shall be led forth by God's hand.

Key Word: Gathered, v. 12.

Promise: 6.

Christ Seen: While these chapters have to do primarily with events, yet future, in connection with Israel, they are also suggestive of some New Testament truths in connection with Christ's church. The church is a vineyard kept by Him and He never relaxes His care. Those opposing His purposes in this age will be trampled down like briars.

CHAPTER TWENTY-EIGHT

Contents: Woe of Ephriam due to drunkenness. Prediction of Assyrian captivity of Ephriam. Ephriam's fate a warning to Judah.

Conclusion: The glorious beauty and the plenty of the land is but a fading flower to those who indulge themselves in sensuality and drunkenness. God will throw it to the ground to be broken in pieces with a hand they are powerless to oppose and will not suffer either His providences or His ordinances to be brought into utter contempt.

Key Word: Woe, v. 1.

Strong Verse: 16. Promise: 5.

Christ Seen: v. 16. This is expressly applied to Christ in the N. T., 1 Pet. 2:6-8. He is that stone which has become the head of the corner.

CHAPTER TWENTY-NINE

Contents: Warnings to Judah and Jerusalem of impending discipline. The blessing after the final deliverance.

Conclusion: Those who are formal and hypocritical in their exercises of devotion, without spiritual vision, thinking to hide their counsels from the Lord, do but invite His judgments upon themselves.

Key Word: Woe, v. 1.

Strong Verse: 15. Promises: 18, 19, 24.

Christ Seen: vv. 18, 19. This portion of the chapter looks forward to the happy settlement of the affairs of Jerusalem and Judah after the second coming of Christ. Then those who understood not the prophecies shall see God's hand in all events, and will rejoice in Him.

CHAPTER THIRTY

Contents: Warnings against alliance with Egypt against Sennacherib and exhortation to turn to the Lord for help.

Conclusion: When sin has brought men into distress, it is their wisdom, in repentance, to turn to God for deliverance, but those who think to prosper in their sin, by the help of man, add sin to sin and invite worse disaster upon themselves. If we would be saved from the evil of every calamity and secured from the curse of it, we should turn to Jehovah and repose in Him.

Key Word: Shame and confusion, v. 3.

Promises: 15, 18.

Christ Seen: In v. 26 we come to the light of the millennial dawn when Christ shall have come to put down all opposing rule. The welcoming gladness of the people is compared in v. 29 to the songs of the Hebrew festivals.

CHAPTER THIRTY-ONE

Contents: Judah again warned against the Egyptian alliance. Jehovah's defense of Jerusalem.

Conclusion: It is gross absurdity to forsake the Rock of Ages for broken reeds. If men will not court God's wisdom and power to act for them in the time of danger, they will find it to act against them, though they have the strongest of men to aid them. Make not man your confidence, for man can do nothing without God.

Key Word: Trust in man, v. 1.

Strong Verse: 1.

CHAPTER THIRTY-TWO

Contents: Promise of coming Kingdom. Warning of great tribulation. The King Deliverer.

Conclusion: Wasting and desolating judgment upon the land and people of Israel was pronounced because they lived in pleasure and wanton, ignoring God's commands, and all who set their hearts upon the world will meet like wretched disappointment. It is the comfort of the faithful few that blessed times of righteousness and eternal rest are promised when the Prince of Peace shall come forth to reign.

Key Word: Tribulation and kingdom, vv. 10-15.

Strong Verse: 1. Promises: 17, 18.

Christ Seen: v. 1. This Scripture certainly looks forward to the Day of the Lord (2:10-22; Rev. 19:11-21) and the Kingdom blessing to follow when Christ shall return to reign.

CHAPTER THIRTY-THREE

Contents: The distress of Judah and Jerusalem because of coming woes.

Conclusion: The righteous God pays sinners in their own coin. When they have filled up the measure of their iniquity, God will begin, for the sinner's day is sure to come. The godly man's comfort is that he shall, in any event, have communion with God in this life, and afterward look upon the King in His beauty.

Key Word: Judgment, v. 5

Promises: 6, 15, 16, 17, 22.

Christ Seen: v. 17. Those who walk uprightly shall not only be preserved through the judgments that visit mankind upon the earth, but shall with the eye of faith, ever see the King in His beauty, and shall at last stand in His presence, when His beauty shall be upon them. 1 John 3:2.

CHAPTER THIRTY-FOUR

Contents: Prophecy of the Day of the Lord and Armaggedon.

Conclusion: There is a day fixed in the divine counsels for the deliverance of God's people and cause in the earth and the destruction of all enemies —a year of recompense for the controversy of Zion. Those who make the Book of the Lord their meditation and rule of life, will have complete deliverance from the coming judgment of nations (v. 16).

Key Word: Day of vengeance, v. 8.

Strong Verses: 16, 17.

Christ Seen: v. 5. It is Christ Who will come in the clouds of heaven to execute judgment, and out of whose mouth goes a sharp sword, as He judges and makes war upon the nations. Rev. 19:11, 15.

CHAPTER THIRTY-FIVE

Contents: The coming Kingdom blessing and regathering of Israel.
Conclusion: The precious promises of peace in the Gospel will shortly culminate in the endless joys and rest of the coming Kingdom when the saints shall reign with Christ. Vengeance will then be taken on the powers of darkness and recompense will be made to the saints for all injuries and losses. All the earth shall break forth in beauty and great wonders will be wrought among men.
Key Word: Everlasting joy, vv. 1, 10.
Promises: 1, 4, 5, 6, 10.
Christ Seen: It is Christ Who is coming in the fullness of time in flaming fire, to spoil and make an open show of all evil powers and to set up the millennial Kingdom, to which all the prophets bear witness.

CHAPTER THIRTY-SIX

Contents: Sennacherib's invasion and Jehovah's deliverance. The threats of Rabshakeh.
Conclusion: The enemies of God's people are ever trying to frighten them from their confidence in God. That we may keep our ground against the enemies of our souls, it concerns us to keep a firm hope in God that we may not lose spirit in the day of trial.
Key Word: Confidence unshaken, vv. 4, 21.
Strong Verse: 21.

CHAPTER THIRTY-SEVEN

Contents: Jehovah's message to the people by Isaiah. Sennacherib's message to Hezekiah. Hezekiah's prayer and Jehovah's answer. Destruction of Assyrians.
Conclusion: The best way to baffle the malicious designs of the enemy of our souls, is to be driven by them to God in prayer. When dangers are most pressing, it is fitting that prayer should be most lively, for God will be a defense to those who truly look to Him.
Key Word: Jehovah a defense, v. 35.
Promises: 31, 35.

CHAPTER THIRTY-EIGHT

Contents: Hezekiah's sickness and recovery in answer to prayer.
Conclusion: Neither men's greatness nor goodness will exempt them from the arrests of sickness. If one is sick, let him pray (Jas. 5:13) for God's love is sufficient to bring one from the very pit of corruption, if it be His will. Those whose life is as from the dead are in a special manner obliged to praise God all their days.
Key Word: Healing, v. 9.
Strong Verses: 17, 19.
Christ Seen: Some think that in turning his face toward the wall, he was turning, as was customary, toward the temple, which was a type of Christ. To Him we must look, by faith, in every prayer.

CHAPTER THIRTY-NINE

Contents: Hezekiah's folly. Babylonian captivity of Judah foretold.
Conclusion: It is folly for one whom God has dignified to be overproud of the respect paid him by unbelieving princes. We have need to watch our own spirits when showing another what we have done and what we have gotten, as if our own merit had secured it. God will take that from us on which we build a carnal confidence.
Key Word: Impending captivity v. 6.
Strong Verses: 8.

CHAPTER FORTY

Contents: Joyful prospect given to the people of God of the happiness of coming redemption. Reproof for their despondencies.
Conclusion: Nothing can be spoken more comforting to those who realize themselves undone, than the coming of the Redeemer as the Lamb of God and as the Good Shepherd. Those who are ready to acknowledge they have no might, may wait upon Him, for He will be their help if they will humbly depend on Him.

Key Word: Comfort, v. 1.
Strong Verses: 26, 28, 29. Promises: 5, 8, 11, 31.
Christ Seen: v. 11. Christ is the Good Shepherd. John 10:11. He has
a special care for the lambs that are weak and cannot help themselves,
gathering them into the arms of His power and carrying them in the
bosom of His love.

CHAPTER FORTY-ONE

Contents: Greatness of God and weakness of man. Admonition to shun
idols and encouragement to trust in God.
Conclusion: Jehovah is infinite, eternal and unchangeable. He has governed
the world from the beginning and will until the end of time. Let the
believer therefore depend upon Him as the God sufficient for him in the
worst of times. He would not have His people to be a timorous people,
for His grace can silence fears, even when there is the greatest cause for
them.
Key Word: Fear not, vv. 10, 13, 14.
Promises: 10, 13, 17.
Christ Seen: v. 14. Christ is the Redeemer and the Holy One of Israel
engaged by promise of God's people. In Him is help found, therefore let
Him be worshiped in the beauty of holiness.

CHAPTER FORTY-TWO

Contents: Christ, servant of Jehovah. Chastening of Israel and the final
restoration.
Conclusion: A day is coming when all who have contradicted and blasphemed
the Gospel of Christ shall be put-to silence and shame, and when all the
oppositions of the powers of darkness shall be thrown down. Let the
believer therefore delight in Christ, rely upon Him and rejoice in Him,
for all who are "in Him" will be well-pleasing to God.
Key Word: Judgment, vv. 1, 4.
Strong Verses: 1, 4.
Christ Seen: vv. 1-7. Fulfilled in Christ (Matt. 12:17-21). Note the two-
fold account of the coming servant. 1. As weak, despised, rejected and
slain. 2. As mighty conqueror taking vengeance. The former class of
passages were fulfilled in the first advent. The second await His return
for fulfillment.

CHAPTER FORTY-THREE

Contents: The chosen nation redeemed and restored.
Conclusion: Israel is God's peculiar people, distinguished from all others,
and having the promise that they shall never be absorbed and that nations
shall be sacrificed to their welfare. They will be finally gathered from
all the earth to their own land, and when Christ shall appear as King of
Kings, their sins will be blotted out, and they shall be restored to full
favor.
Key Word: Gathered, v. 5.
Strong Verses: 10, 11. Promises: 2, 25.
Christ Seen: Christ, the Great Redeemer, will appear for Israel (Rom. 11:
25). At His coming, the spiritual seed of Israel (through the Gospel
of grace) will be gathered to heaven as their home and given glorified
bodies. Believers under the Gospel are the Bride of Christ who will
"reign with Him" in His coming Kingdom on earth.

CHAPTER FORTY-FOUR

Contents: The promise of the Spirit and the coming restoration. The folly
of idolatry.
Conclusion: There is no God besides Jehovah. He is infinite and therefore
there can be no other. He is sufficient, and therefore no other is needed.
It is foolishness to expect any good from gods of man's own making and
only the blind and ignorant can look to graven images.
Key Word: Ashamed, restored (vv. 11, 22, 26).
Strong Verses: 6, 8, 22.
Christ Seen: vv. 23-27. When Christ returns and is received by Israel,
their idolatry and sin will be remembered no more, and recognizing Him

whom they pierced, they will be restored to a place of great fruitfulness. (Rom. 11:25.)

CHAPTER FORTY-FIVE

Contents: Promises to Cyrus for Israel's sake. Proof of God's eternal power and sovereignty. Encouragement to believing Jews. Doom of idol worshippers.

Conclusion: Beside Jehovah there is no God. He alone is self-existent, self-sufficient, being infinite and eternal. Those are in woeful condition who strive with their Maker and give honor to images which cannot give good. Those who trust in God will never be made ashamed of their confidence in Him.

Key Word: Jehovah omnipotent.

Strong Verses: 9, 18, 22, 24.

Christ Seen: v. 22. This verse has a further reference to the conversion of the Gentiles that live in the ends of the earth through the lifting up of Christ on Calvary's Cross. As the stung Israelites looked to the brazen serpent, so all were invited to look to Christ and be saved.

CHAPTER FORTY-SIX

Contents: Israel exhorted to remember the power of God and powerlessness of idols.

Conclusion: False gods will certainly fail the worshippers when they have most need of them. It is absurd to think of making any creature equal with the Creator, Who is infinitely above all He has created. Let all remember that they have been the constant care of His kind providence and are absolutely dependent upon Him.

Key Word: Remember, vv. 8-9.

Strong Verses: 8, 9, 10.

Christ Seen: vv. 12-13. This may be applied to the Jews in their rejection of Christ, for they thought to establish their own righteousness, and would not accept the righteousness of God in Christ, by faith.

CHAPTER FORTY-SEVEN

Contents: Judgment pronounced upon Babylon.

Conclusion: Those who abuse their honor, or power provoke God to deprive them of it utterly and to make them sit in dust. While God often makes use of evil men for the correction of His people, He always breaks the rod of His wrath because of their boastfulness and cruelty.

Key Word: Vengeance, v. 3.

Strong Verse: 4.

Christ Seen: v. 4. Christ is the Great Redeemer, Who as the Holy One of Israel, saves His people, and as Lord of Hosts will take vengeance upon the wicked.

CHAPTER FORTY-EIGHT

Contents: The dullness of Israel. Restoration under the Servant of Jehovah. Israel reminded of the promises.

Conclusion: God often finds His people obstinate and perverse, but for all that He makes it redound to the honor of His mercy to spare and reprieve them, refining them in the furnace of affliction, rather than cutting them off. O, that men would own Him as the true and only God, receiving His promises and looking to His Redeemer.

Key Word: Anger deferred, v. 9.

Strong Verses: 12, 17, 22.

Christ Seen: vv. 16-17. The Spirit of God is here spoken of as a person distinct from Father and Son, as that which is said to the same purpose with this (61:1) is applied to Christ (Luke 4:21), so may this be. Christ the Redeemer was sent by the Father and He had the Spirit without measure.

CHAPTER FORTY-NINE

Contents: Israel's coming Redeemer. Preservation and restoration of Israel and judgment on oppressors.

Conclusion: God, of old, promised a Redeemer to His people Who would also become a Light to the Gentiles. Through Him, the souls of those looking to Him were to be set free from the bondage of guilt and corruption; His own should be wonderfully provided for, and through Him, at length, Israel would be restored and the earth established in righteousness, peace and joy.

Key Word: Redeemer, v. 7.
Strong Verse: 6.
Christ Seen: v. 7. Christ was the Redeemer Who was despised and rejected of men, and abhorred by nations, who cried "crucify Him." But God promised Him exaltation in the depths of His humiliation, and at His return He will be acknowledged King of Kings and Lord of Lords.

CHAPTER FIFTY

Contents: The humiliation of the Holy One of Israel.
Conclusion: The Lord Jesus, our Redeemer, was to be wise above all men, able to speak the word of comfort to every heart; He was to have the ear of the learned to receive instruction in all things from His Father. In spite of this, He was to be smitten and insulted by men, yet unshaken in constancy and resolution, suffering all patiently and voluntarily for the salvation of the world. Let all who fear God, build their hopes upon Christ Who has proven Himself the Savior of mankind.

Key Word: Smitten Redeemer, v. 6.
Strong Verse: 10. Promise: 7.
Christ Seen: v. 3. Here we see Jesus in creative power; v. 4 as the dependent teacher; v. 5 as the faithful servant; v. 6 as the patient sufferer; v. 8 as the justified Redeemer.

CHAPTER FIFTY-ONE

Contents: Final redemption of Israel and punishment of oppressors.
Conclusion: Although God's people are called upon to suffer much upon earth, they have an eternal cause to rejoice, in that all who trust in His salvation have the approbation of the living God and may therefore despise the censures of dying men who will shortly be punished.

Key Word: Zion's comfort, vv. 3, 11.
Strong Verses: 5, 7. Promises: 12, 13.
Christ Seen: v. 5. Christ brought an everlasting righteousness and salvation. Those whose happiness is bound up in His righteousness, will have the comfort of it eternally.

CHAPTER FIFTY-TWO

Contents: Vision of Jerusalem in the Kingdom age. Jehovah's servant marred and afterward exalted.
Conclusion: Let God's people prepare for eternal joy, for His Word shall without fail have its accomplishment in due season. Jerusalem shall be made a praise and all the earth shall break forth in joy when He Who was rejected and despised of men shall come forth as Lord and King.

Key Word: Jerusalem redeemed, v. 9.
Strong Verses: 7, 11, 14.
Christ Seen: vv. 7, 14. v. 7 has an application to the preaching of the Gospel, a message indeed of good news and victory over spiritual enemies (Rom. 10:15). v. 14 points plainly at Jesus (Acts 8:34-35). Never was man so barbarously treated as was the Son of God. When He returns in glory the kings of the earth shall shut their mouths at Him, and the Jews will look with mourning upon Him whom they pierced.

CHAPTER FIFTY-THREE

Contents: The vicarious sacrifice of Christ, the servant of Jehovah.
Conclusion: The whole race of mankind lies under the stain of original corruption, all gone astray from God. God, in love sent His only begotten Son into the world, Who voluntarily made Himself an offering for sin. He submitted Himself to the disgraces and afflictions due to the worst of men, that those who should believe on Him, might have the joy and glory due to Him as the one perfect man.

Key Word: Man of sorrows, v. 3.
Strong Verses: 3, 4, 5, 6, 7, 10, 11.

Christ Seen: Christ rose in the world as a tender plant. The greater part of those among whom He lived saw none of His beauty. Because He announced Himself as the Savior of the world, He was abandoned and abhorred. Nevertheless God highly exalted Him, and He appears in heaven to make intercession for all who accept His sacrifice.

CHAPTER FIFTY-FOUR

Contents: Israel as the restored wife of Jehovah in the Kingdom age.

Conclusion: We may with greatest assurance depend upon God for the keeping of His covenant with His people (especially Israel) for He will not keep His anger against them forever, but will gather them out of their dispersions that they may return in a body to their land, where He will again be a husband to them.

Key Word: Restored Israel, v. 7.

Promises: 4, 17.

Christ Seen: As Israel is spoken of as the wife of Jehovah, so the church of the present dispensation is called "the bride of Christ" (the Lamb). However this chapter has wholly to do with the fulfillment of God's covenant with Israel.

CHAPTER FIFTY-FIVE

Contents: Jehovah's everlasting salvation.

Conclusion: All are invited to partake of God's salvation provided through Christ. All the world's wealth and pleasure cannot satisfy the soul, but God's eternal salvation brings true life and peace. It is man's wisdom, therefore, to seek Christ while He may be found, forsaking sin and dislodging all preconceived notions contrary to God's truth, for God will then abundantly pardon.

Key Word: Come, vv. 1, 3, 6.

Strong Verses: 1, 6, 8, 9. Promises: 7, 11.

Christ Seen: vv. 4, 5. Christ was given to the world for a witness of God's love and mercy (John 3:16). He is the true leader and commander to show man what to do and enable him to do it. Through Him the door was opened to the Gentile nations to enter into God's eternal salvation.

CHAPTER FIFTY-SIX

Contents: Solemn instruction given to all to make conscience of duty. Charge against the careless and unfaithful.

Conclusion: The more assurance God gives us of the performance of His promises, the stronger obligations He lays us under to obedience to His commands. Righteousness and justice on our part, are required to evidence the security of our faith and repentance, and to open the way of mercy.

Key Word: Justice and righteousness, vv. 1, 2.

Promise: 7.

Christ Seen: v. 1. The great salvation announced and wrought out by Christ was preceded by the call to repentance and faith. In Christ, the righteousness of God was revealed (Rom. 1:17) and He is "made righteousness" unto all who receive Him.

CHAPTER FIFTY-SEVEN

Contents: Further ethical instructions. Sins of the people denounced.

Conclusion: God is justly displeased when the voice of His rod is not heard, much more, when sin and idolatry are knowingly rejoiced in. Sinners shall find no quietness or satisfaction in their own hearts and will be made to feel the full force of His anger if sin is not repented of and forsaken.

Key Word: Wicked, v. 21.

Strong Verse: 21. Promise: 15.

Christ Seen: The remedy held out to Isreal is for all. We may have deserved wrath and chastisement, but if we humble ourselves and return to Him, He will heal where He has wounded and bring us near through the blood of the cross (Eph. 2:16-17).

CHAPTER FIFTY-EIGHT

Contents: Hypocritical professions of religion. Instructions how to keep fasts aright.

Conclusion: It is common for unhumbled hearts, while they perform the external services of religion, to promise themselves acceptance with God, which He has promised only to the sincere. God will not be cheated by hypocritical fasts and ceremonies. Those who fast and pray, yet go on in sin, mock God and cheat themselves.

Key Word: Hypocritical fasts, v. 4.

Strong Verses: 6, 7. Promises: 10, 11.

Christ Seen: v. 14. When we cease to follow our own ways and let the divine peace rule within (Col. 3:15; Phil. 4:7) then do we sit with Christ in heavenly places and feed at the heavenly table.

CHAPTER FIFTY-NINE

Contents: Sins which prevented the bestowal of God's blessing and caused chastisements to fall upon Israel.

Conclusion: If prayers are not answered and the salvation we wait for is not wrought for us, it is not evidence that God is weary of.hearing prayer, but that, for some reason, He cannot answer. Sin hides His face from us, provokes Him to withdraw His gracious presence and suspend the tokens of His favor.

Key Word: Iniquities, v. 2.

Strong Verses: 1, 2.

Christ Seen: v. 20. Christ was the kinsman Redeemer Who came to His own and was rejected. (John 1:11-12.) He is coming a second time to receive His own and to give full deliverance to Israel. (Rom. 11:25-26.)

CHAPTER SIXTY

Contents: The Deliverer out of Zion and the peace and joy of His coming.

Conclusion: When the Redeemer shall appear in glory to be received as the Light of Israel, the knowledge of Him shall fill the whole earth and all the Gentile nations will honor them and flock to them. Wasting and destruction shall be no more and all will be filled with praise to God.

Key Word: Israel's light, vv. 1, 3, 19.

Strong Verse: 19.

Christ Seen: v. 1. This had a near fulfillment in the first advent of Christ, Who came as the Light of the world. However, He was rejected and the Church came in as a parenthesis. Christ is coming again, first for His Church as "the bright and morning star," and then to Israel and all the world, as the "sun of righteousness."

CHAPTER SIXTY-ONE

Contents: Two advents of Christ in one view. Kingdom blessing after the day of vengeance. Israel's restoration.

Conclusion: After the day of Christ's vengeance, comfort will be given to restored Israel. The setting up of the Kingdom in the earth will mean the repairing of all the waste places and all the ends of the earth shall see God's great salvation.

Key Word: Universal righteousness, v. 11.

Strong Verse: 10. Promise: 11.

Christ Seen: v. 2. See Luke 4:16-21 and note that Jesus suspended the reading of this passage at the comma, after the word "Lord." The first advent opened the day of grace "the acceptable year of Jehovah," but does not fulfill the day of vengeance. When He returns this will be fulfilled being followed by the Kingdom of righteousness (4, 11).

CHAPTER SIXTY-TWO

Contents: Restoration of Israel to God's favor, and honor with the nations.

Conclusion: Israel's full salvation is sure to come when they are regathered and their Redeemer recognized. In that day their land will no longer be called "desolate" but "Beulah land," and Jerusalem will be a praise in the earth. All the ends of the earth will know that God has pleaded Israel's cause and fulfilled His prophecies concerning them.

Key Word: Israel's salvation, v. 11.

Strong Verse: 11.

Christ Seen: This prophecy was not fulfilled in the first advent and the preaching of the Gospel of grace. God has made definite promises to

Israel, before whom Christ will yet appear again, to be recognized. We have no right to put the church in Israel's place in the promises.

CHAPTER SIXTY-THREE

Contents: Day of vengeance, and the fear and hope of the remnant of Israel.
Conclusion: Christ is coming to tread the winepress of the wrath of God (Rev. 19:14-15) to take fierce vengeance on all sinners. In that day the remnant of Israel will remember their days of rebellion and will see how God has nourished them through the ages.
Key Word: Day of vengeance, v. 4.
Strong Verse: 1.
Christ Seen: v. 1. Rev. 19:11-21 describes this same day of vengeance, when Christ shall come forth in power, wearing vesture dipped in blood, crowned with many crowns and revealing Himself as King of Kings.

CHAPTER SIXTY-FOUR

Contents: Fear and hope of remnant of Israel in day of vengeance.
Conclusion: The remnant of Israel in the day of Christ's vengeance will bewail their sins, thereby justifying God in all their afflictions, owning themselves unworthy of His mercy and thereby preparing for the deliverance He has promised them.
Key Word: Mercy implored, vv. 9, 12.
Strong Verses: 4, 6.
Christ Seen: v. 4. This is likewise true of those saved under the Gospel of grace (1 Cor. 2:9) to whom is revealed by the Spirit the deep things of God as the result of their acceptance of the crucified and risen Savior.

CHAPTER SIXTY-FIVE

Contents: Answer of Jehovah to remnant of Israel. Eternal blessing in the renovated earth.
Conclusion: Although Jehovah has long stretched forth His hand to a disobedient and gainsaying people, Israel, yet He will spare the remnant at Christ's return, purging them from their sins, establishing them in a purified earth.
Key Word: Israel's hope, v. 8.
Promises: 17, 24.
Christ Seen: Chap. 21 and 22 of Rev. look also to this same time of restoration of all things. The church appears then with Christ, as His Bride, to rule with Him, not as subjects of the earthly kingdom. Israel's glory in the prophecies is always an earthly glory.

CHAPTER SIXTY-SIX

Contents: Blessings of the coming universal Kingdom.
Conclusion: Following the day of Christ's vengeance the sorrows of Israel will be turned into abundant joys. All the Gentiles spared shall rejoice in her salvation. All nations will look upon the glory of God as it shines in the face of Christ, the King, and worship will be carefully and constantly attended upon by all the peoples of the earth.
Key Word: Universal kingdom, v. 23.
Strong Verses: 15, 16, 23.
Christ Seen: The Christian watches with great interest the providences of God towards the Jews, knowing that their return to their land is a preparation for the fulfillment of much prophecy, a sign of the approach of the close of the age and Christ's coming. "Come, Lord Jesus."

JEREMIAH

Key Thought:	Number of Chapters:	Key Verse:	Christ seen as:
Warning	52	7:28; 46:1	Lord of Righteousness.

Writer of the Book:	Date:	Conclusion of the Book:
		Judgment is the certain result of sin. God is
Jeremiah	About 580 to 600 B. C.	longsuffering, not willing that any should perish.

SUMMARY

CHAPTER ONE

Contents: Jeremiah's call and enduement. The sign of the almond rod and seething pot.

Conclusion: God, by His special counsel and foreknowledge designs certain men for certain work for Himself, and whom He calls He fits for their work. Those having His message to deliver, while they should feel their own insufficiency, should not be afraid of the face of man, for God has pledged Himself to be with them.

Key Word: Called of God, v. 5.

Strong Verses: 8, 17, 19.

Christ Seen: The promises of vv. 18, 19 are precious to all who are called as ambassadors of Christ, to stand in the breach and charge men with their sins. Christ in giving His commission assumes responsibility and furnishes all powers of utterance.

CHAPTER TWO

Contents: First message to backslidden Judah concerning their ingratitude to God and wickedness against Him.

Conclusion: It is a great affront to God to neglect Him and forget Him, failing to acknowledge His kindnesses, withholding the tributes of love and praise due Him, and worst of all, to turn to idols which cannot possibly do one any good. Such backslidings are invariably followed with severe corrections that the backslider might read his sin in the punishment.

Key Word: Jehovah forgotten, v. 32.

Strong Verses: 13, 32.

Christ Seen: Israel's failure to respond to God's calls must remind us that we ourselves were marvels of perversity. Who can explain the reason of his poor response to Christ's yearning love? V. 31 will explain. We like to be lords of our own lives.

CHAPTER THREE

Contents: Jeremiah's message concerning the impenitence of Judah. Encouragement to backsliders to return and repent.

Conclusion: Those will justly be divorced from God who join themselves to such as are rivals with Him, but God is ever ready to pardon sin and receive those who will return to Him humbly confessing their sins and acknowledging their dependence upon Him for salvation.

Key Word: Backsliding Israel, v. 11.

Strong Verses: 4, 23.

Christ Seen: The invitation and promise of vv. 12, 13 is the same to backslidden followers of Christ in this age. Confession is an essential condition that must be fulfilled in us (1 Jn. 1:7).

CHAPTER FOUR

Contents: Jeremiah's second message, continued. Warning of the consequences of sin and exhortation to return to God.

Conclusion: It is the evil of men's doings that kindles the fires of God's wrath against them and brings destruction upon the land. That which is to be before He moves, which makes a way of escape for those who will sincerely turn to Him and receive His mercy.
dreaded above everything else is the wrath of God, but God always warns
Key Word: Desolations, v. 7.
Strong Verse: 22.
Christ Seen: The return of Israel to the God of their fathers at the revelation of Jesus Christ (Zech. 12:10) will be the cause of the quickening and service throughout the whole earth. Cf. v. 2 with Rom. 11:12.

CHAPTER FIVE

Contents: Jeremiah's second message, continued. God's charges against them and the judgments threatened.
Conclusion: Sinners have reason to expect punishment on account of God's holiness to which sin is highly offensive. Sin will not go unpunished, else the honor of God's government cannot be maintained, and sinners will be tempted to think Him altogether such a one as themselves.
Key Word: Vengeance, vv. 9, 29.
Strong Verse: 22.
Christ Seen: The words of v. 5 have a striking application in our day when so many religious leaders have "departed from the faith" and are "denying the Lord that bought them."

CHAPTER SIX

Contents: Jeremiah's second message, continued. The terrors that should come because of sin.
Conclusion: The God of mercy is loath to depart even from a provoking people, and earnestly entreats them by true repentance to prevent the necessity of His fierce judgments. Those who perish in their sin will be utterly forsaken of Him, and whom He forsakes is certainly undone.
Key Word: Desolations, v. 8.
Promise: 16.
Christ Seen: v. 16. The old path and the old way is the way of the blood. There is no soul rest except as confidence is fixed in Christ's finished atoning work.

CHAPTER SEVEN

Contents: The message in the gate of the Lord's house. Coming desolations because of sin.
Conclusion: It is common for those who are furthest from God to boast themselves most of being in the Church, but God is holy and will not be the patron of sin even though it be covered up in a form of godliness. When His anger breaks upon them, such sinners have only themselves to thank.
Key Word: Abominations, v. 30.
Strong Verses: 9, 10, 11. Promise: 23.
Christ Seen: v. 11. These words were used by our Lord Jesus. In Jn. 2:13-25 He used them in the temple in connection with His first offer to the Jews. In Matt. 2:13 He uses them in His closing offer.

CHAPTER EIGHT

Contents: Message in the temple gate continued. Terrible judgments impending.
Conclusion: Impenitence brings certain ruin. All the boasted wisdom of man cannot serve to keep him from the consuming judgments pronounced upon those who mock at God's Word and take their own course.
Key Word: Consuming judgment, v. 12.
Strong Verses: 7, 9.
Christ Seen: v. 22. The blood of Christ is a balm from Gilead for the healing of the sin-sick heart, and He is the great Physician who is all-sufficient for any case however difficult.

CHAPTER NINE

Contents: Message in the temple gate continued. Detestation of the sins of the people. The vanity of trusting in anything but God.

Conclusion: Those who will not know God as their law giver will be made to know Him as their Judge. If the furnace of affliction will not purify them from their dross, He will cut them off with terrible desolations.

Key Word: Vengeance, v. 9.

Strong Verses: 23, 24.

Christ Seen: See 1 Cor. 1:18 which belongs to this chapter and learn how little this world's wisdom can avail us in the hour of desolation. Stand with the Crucified and glory in His cross, thus shall ye be counted worthy to escape these things and to stand before Him.

CHAPTER TEN

Contents: Message in the temple gate concluded. Greatness of the true God. Coming distresses in the land because of sin.

Conclusion: Jehovah is the one only living and true God, and to set up any other in competition with Him is the greatest affront. Those who will not believe His Word nor recognize His power will be made to feel His judgments to their ruin.

Key Word: Distress, v. 18.

Strong Verses: 6, 7, 10, 12, 23, 24.

Christ Seen: To be "hid with Christ in God" is the one sure defense from all that man can do for our hurt. In the wounds of our living Saviour, faithful souls may be made strong and courageous.

CHAPTER ELEVEN

Contents: Jeremiah's message on the broken covenant.

Conclusion: Those who enter into solemn covenant with God must expect on their part to fulfill the conditions, else He cannot on His part fulfill the promise. If we do not by obedience meet our end of the contract, we will by disobedience bring ourselves under its curses, and it is just with God to inflict heavy penalty.

Key Word: Broken covenant, 8.

Christ Seen: Jeremiah's Amen ("So be it," v. 5) reminds us of Him Who is God's Amen and in Whom all the promises of God are ratified forever (2 Cor. 1:20).

CHAPTER TWELVE

Contents: Message on the broken covenant concluded. Jeremiah's complaint to God and God's rebuke.

Conclusion: When we find it hard to understand God's providences toward wicked men, we should remember His sure Word that "what a man soweth that shall he also reap." God often lets wicked men have a time of prosperity that by their pride and luxury they might fill up the measure of their iniquity, and so be ripening for a terrible destruction.

Key Word: Prosperity of wicked, v. 1.

Strong Verses: 1, 13.

CHAPTER THIRTEEN

Contents: Sign of the linen girdle and sign of the bottles filled with wine.

Conclusion: Those who persist in sin, ignoring God's Word, make themselves vessels of wrath fitted to destruction. If one judgment does not do the work, God will send one upon another until they are utterly brought to ruin.

Key Word: Punishment, v. 21.

Strong Verses: 16, 23.

Christ Seen: v. 23. There is no hope in "reformation." Only Christ can change the fallen nature. His grace can cause the leprosy of inbred sin to instantly cease its hold.

CHAPTER FOURTEEN

Contents: Message on the drought.

Conclusion: Man's sins bring those judgments upon the earth which make even the inferior creatures to groan. There will come a time when the sinners' expectation from God will utterly fail them. We should dread nothing more than God's departure from us.

Key Word: Drought, v. 1.

Strong Verse: 22.

Christ Seen: v. 21. God has but one covenant with men in this age and that is in the person and work of His Son. Asking "in His name" and on the ground of His redemptive work, God is bound to honor our petitions.

CHAPTER FIFTEEN

Contents: Message on the drought concluded. The people abandoned to ruin. Jeremiah complains of his hardships.

Conclusion: Miserable is the case of those who have sinned so long against God's mercy that at length they have sinned it away. There is no mercy for those who persist in apostasy.

Key Word: Destruction, v. 6.

Strong Verse: 16. Promise: 21.

Christ Seen: v. 16. Christ is the living Bread (Jn. 6:51) that partaken of becomes the joy and satisfaction of our lives.

CHAPTER SIXTEEN

Contents: Sign of the unmarried prophet, forecasting coming calamities.

Conclusion: God often makes men's sins their punishment and fills the backslider in heart with his own ways. Those have cut themselves off from all true peace who have thrown away the favor of God by persisting in wilful sin and idolatry.

Key Word: v. 10.

Strong Verse: 17.

Christ Seen: There is but one way to have our sins effectually and forever put out of God's sight and that is to have them covered with the blood of Calvary.

CHAPTER SEVENTEEN

Contents: Sign of the unmarried prophet concluded. Message in the gates concerning the Sabbath.

Conclusion: The heart of man, out of communion with God, is wicked and deceitful above all things. Those who have wedded themselves to sin invite God's judgments upon their own heads. There is only disappointment and vexation for those who depend upon the arm of flesh instead of God, but those who by faith derive strength and grace from God will be enabled to do that which will redound to God's glory, the benefit of others and their own account.

Key Word: v. 1.

Strong Verses: 5, 7, 9, 10.

Christ Seen: v. 5. Those who trust to their own righteousness and strength, thinking to get salvation without the merit and grace of Christ, thus make flesh their arm and fail of God's salvation.

CHAPTER EIGHTEEN

Contents: Sign of the potter's house. Declaration of God's ways of dealing with nations. Jeremiah's complaint.

Conclusion: Jehovah has incontestable and irresistible ability to form (frame) and fashion nations as He pleases. If they do not turn from evil ways, He will turn His hand against them. Sin ruins the comforts of nations, prolongs their grievances, and at length brings total ruin upon them.

Key Word: Potter and clay, vv. 6, 7.

Strong Verses: 6, 7, 8.

CHAPTER NINETEEN

Contents: Sign of potter's house concluded. Coming calamities.

Conclusion: Let men great and small know that the Lord of Hosts is able to do what He threatens, and will therefore sorely punish those who have persisted in wickedness in spite of all His entreaties. They will be abandoned to utter ruin.

Key Word: Broken, v. 11.

CHAPTER TWENTY

Contents: Jeremiah's first persecution. His complaint to God and encouragement in God.

Conclusion: Those who declare the whole counsel of God may expect to be plotted against, ridiculed and represented as dangerous to the government, which presents a strong temptation to stop preaching or tone down the message. However, the faithful preacher can successfully set all enemies at defiance, for Jehovah has promised to take his part, and to make the Word preached answer the end of its designs.

Key Word: Persecution, v. 11.
Strong Verses: 9, 11.
Christ Seen: vv. 7, 8. Thus our Lord Jesus on the cross was reviled by priests and people for nothing but His faithful witness to God's Word.

CHAPTER TWENTY-ONE

Contents: Message to King Zedekiah. Babylonian captivity foretold.
Conclusion: If God be for us, none can be against us, but if He be against us, who can be for us to stand us in any stead? Our God is a consuming fire, and when once He is angry because of men's sins, no one can stand in His sight.
Key Word: Jehovah's fury.
Strong Verse: 8.
Christ Seen: Christ's great commission to His disciples is an echo of this passage. We are His witnesses setting before men the way of life and the way of death. They that receive Him are saved. Those who believe not shall be damned.

CHAPTER TWENTY-TWO

Contents: Message to Zedekiah concluded. The King exhorted to execute judgment.
Conclusion: God never casts one off until they cast Him off, but when men revolt from their allegiance to Him and trample under foot their covenants with Him, He gives them up to destruction, and who can contend with the destroyers of His preparing?
Key Word: Desolations, v. 5.
Strong Verses: 13, 29.
Christ Seen: vv. 28, 30. Coniah was of David's line through Solomon, and the throne rights were cut off with Coniah. Joseph, the husband of Mary, was of this line. Had Jesus been born in the natural way, He would have had no title to the Davidic throne. However, Mary was of David's line through Nathan, the first born of David, and Jesus being conceived of the Holy Ghost, holds the royal title to the throne, which He will possess at His return.

CHAPTER TWENTY-THREE

Contents: Future restoration and conversion of Israel. Message against the faithless shepherds.
Conclusion: Woe be to those who are commanded to feed God's people and pretend to do it, but instead drag them from God, speaking messages that are the product of their own invention, and slighting the authority of His Word. God disowns all prophets who soothe people in their sins.
Key Word: Lying prophets, v. 25.
Strong Verses: 5, 24, 29, 32.
Christ Seen: vv. 5, 6. Jesus is spoken of as the branch from David, small in His beginnings, but growing to be great and loaded with divine fruits. He is the Lord our righteousness (especially to be manifested before the Jews at His coming again). He is the Lord (Jehovah), denoting eternity and self-existence. As Mediator, He is our righteousness.

CHAPTER TWENTY-FOUR

Contents: Sign of the figs. Judah's restoration, but not those of the second deportation.
Conclusion: The same providence which to some is a savour of death unto death may by God's grace be made to others a savour of life unto life. God knows all who are His, and will protect and deliver them whatever may come.
Key Word: Good and evil figs, v. 3.
Christ Seen: No better proof of the inspiration of the Bible is needed than the prophecies of this chapter concerning Israel's present condition. Not until

the day when they look upon Him whom they pierced will they have a heart to know God.

CHAPTER TWENTY-FIVE

Contents: Prophecy of seventy years' captivity. Sign of the wine cup of fury.

Conclusion: Men would never receive from God the desolating punishments did they not provoke Him by the evil of their persistent sin. That which is provocation to God will prove in the end at least the utter ruin of man, for the day of His fierce wrath is coming upon all the earth.

Key Word: Desolations, v. 11.

Strong Verse: 31.

Christ Seen: vv. 29, 33. This prophecy leaps to the end of the age, the day of the Lord, when Christ will return to execute God's wrath. Rev. 19: 11-21: 14:14.

CHAPTER TWENTY-SIX

Contents: Message in the temple court. Spiteful treatment of Jeremiah and his brave stand. Martyrdom of Urijah.

Conclusion: God's ambassador must keep close to divine instructions, not compromising to please men or to save himself. If he speaks what God appointed him to speak, he will be under God's protection, and whatever affront the people offer to the ambassador, it will be resented by God Himself.

Key Word: Faithful prophet, vv. 14, 15.

Strong Verse: 13.

CHAPTER TWENTY-SEVEN

Contents: Sign of the yokes, to surrounding Gentile kings. Warning of great calamity.

Conclusion: Those who refuse to serve the God Who made them may be justly made by God to serve their enemies who sought to ruin them. God has an indisputable right to dispose of kingdoms as He pleases.

Key Word: Yoke of Babylon, v. 11.

Strong Verse: 5.

CHAPTER TWENTY-EIGHT

Contents: Sign of the yokes continued. False prophecy and death of Hananiah.

Conclusion: Those have a great deal to answer for who tell sinners that they shall have peace in spite of their contempt of the admonitions of God's Word and the exhortations of His true prophets. It is no new thing for lying prophets to father their message upon the God of truth, but they will surely be brought to shame.

Key Word: False teachers, v. 16.

Strong Verse: 9.

Christ Seen: There is only one true messenger of peace—he who carries the tidings of peace through our Lord Jesus Christ. Christ's representatives may be known by the results of their peace offer.

CHAPTER TWENTY-NINE

Contents: Message to the Jews of the first captivity. Action against false prophets. Destruction foretold.

Conclusion: As long as we have God's sure Word before us, it is our own fault if we be deceived, for by it we may be undeceived. If vengeance shall be taken on those who rebel against God's Word, much more on those who teach rebellion by their destructive doctrines.

Key Word: True and false prophecies, vv. 20, 21.

Strong Verse: 11. Promises: 12, 13.

Christ Seen: v. 13. Heart praying was one of the great laws of prayer laid down by the Lord Jesus, the Master prayer teacher. Many prayers offered in Christ's name are lost in the dead letter office for want of sufficient direction.

CHAPTER THIRTY

Contents: Jeremiah's first writing. Summary of Israel in the coming great tribulation.

Conclusion: Israel, after many years of wandering among all nations, is to be finally purified in a season of tribulation such as the world has never known nor ever shall know thereafter. The purposes of God's wrath will all be fulfilled, and then Israel shall be gloriously restored as a nation.

Key Word: Jacob's trouble, v. 7.

Strong Verse: 24.

Christ Seen: The time of Jacob's trouble is a period of seven years coming at the close of the present dispensation, followed immediately by the return of Christ in glory to set up His kingdom. See Christ's own Word: Matt. 24:15-31.

CHAPTER THIRTY-ONE

Contents: Israel in the last days.

Conclusion: God will again at the end of the age take Israel into new covenant relation with Himself, from which they have for hundreds of years been cut off because of rebellion against His Word. At that time, all shall come to the knowledge of God, and the earth shall be filled with songs of joy.

Key Word: New covenant, v. 31.

Strong Verse: 3. Promises: 33, 34.

Christ Seen: vv. 33, 34. This can be applied in the Gospel dispensation to those who have accepted Jesus Christ, those who are yielded to the Holy Spirit to have God's will revealed to them, and have the assurance that their sins through Christ are remembered no more.

CHAPTER THIRTY-TWO

Contents: Sign of the field of Hanameel. Jeremiah's second persecution, his prayer and Jehovah's answer.

Conclusion: When we are perplexed about the methods of God's providence, it is good to go to Him in prayer, by which we shall be taught that not one word of all His counsel shall fail. Though we cannot reconcile one word with another, we may be sure both words are true and both will be made good.

Key Word: Chastisement and promises, v. 42.

Strong Verses: 17, 19. Promise: 27.

Christ Seen: v. 2. God, Who has been faithful to His threatenings against Israel throughout the centuries, will just as certainly fulfill His promise to the remnant of them in His own good time when Christ returns. They will surely be re-gathered as a nation and made fruitful unto God (v. 42).

CHAPTER THIRTY-THREE

Contents: Prophecy concering the Davidic kingdom.

Conclusion: The Davidic covenant will in God's own time be literally fulfilled, to the great joy of the remnant of Israel when Christ shall come to execute judgment in righteousness in the earth. Their sins will be purged away, their nation will be honored by all nations, and to crown all their blessings, they will recognize Christ as their righteousness and worship Him as their King and Lord.

Key Word: Israel's joy, v. 11.

Promise: 3.

Christ Seen: v. 15. Christ is the Branch of righteousness, born of David's line and holding legal title to the promised throne. While under the gospel He is made "righteousness unto all true believers," at His return He will be acknowledged by Israel who rejected Him as their righteousness.

CHAPTER THIRTY-FOUR

Contents: Message to Zedekiah concerning the coming captivity. Zedekiah's ineffectual decree.

Conclusion: God's compassion toward us should engage our compassion toward our fellow-men, and in any case the plain statement of His Word should be obeyed. Those who will not be in subjection to God's law put themselves under His wrath and curse.

Key Word: Desolations, v. 22.

CHAPTER THIRTY-FIVE

Contents: Obedience of the Rechabites in the reign of Jehoiakim.
Conclusion: The obedience of many unsaved people to the moral laws laid down by wise men of the world should put to shame many professing Christians who are disobedient to an infinite God and utterly forget His precepts.
Key Word: Obedience, v. 8.

CHAPTER THIRTY-SIX

Contents: Jeremiah's writing in the days of Jehoiakim. Reading on the fast day. Burning of the roll and orders to persecute Jeremiah.
Conclusion: Though the attempts of those who despise the Word of God are very daring, yet not one tittle of it shall fail. Though many a Bible be burned, this cannot abolish it nor deter the accomplishment of its prophecies.
Key Word: Book burned, vv. 2, 23.

CHAPTER THIRTY-SEVEN

Contents: Jeremiah's imprisonment in the days of Zedekiah.
Conclusion: It is no new thing for those who have faithfully declared the Word of God and are the best friends of the Lord, to be represented as enemies, imprisoned and persecuted. When God's servants are accused, they may boldly deny the charge, commit their cause to Him who judges righteously, and continue to contend for the faith.
Key Word: Imprisonment, v. 15.

CHAPTER THIRTY-EIGHT

Contents: Jeremiah's imprisonment continued. His private conference with the king.
Conclusion: God's faithful ministers, who show men what enemies they are to themselves, are often looked upon as enemies of the country, and are wickedly abused. They may, however, commit the keeping of their spirits to God, their Rewarder, Who can even raise up friends for them in their distress (vv. 8, 9), if it be for His glory.
Key Word: Persecuted, v. 6.
Strong Verse: 20.

CHAPTER THIRTY-NINE

Contents: Final captivity of Judah in accordance with the prophets.
Conclusion: Truly there is a God Who judges in the earth in this world as well as in the next. When sin has provoked Him to withdraw His protection, the greatest city is helpless (the false prophets fell by those judgments which they said would never come. The true prophet Jeremiah escaped those judgments which he maintained would come).
Key Word: Broken up, v. 2.
Promises: 17, 18.

CHAPTER FORTY

Contents: Jeremiah discharged. The Jews under Gedeliah as Governor. Ishmael's design against Gedeliah.
Conclusion: Sooner or later God's true prophets will be justified before the persecutors, and they will be made sensible that their sin is the cause of all their misery. (God in His wrath still remembers mercy and admits a remnant upon a further trial of their obedience.)
Key Word: Jeremiah loosed, v. 4. Remnant of Judah, v. 11.

CHAPTER FORTY-ONE

Contents: Gedeliah slain, and many Jewish captives released by Johanan.
Conclusion: God sometimes permits bloody work to be done for the completing of the ruin of an unhumbled people and the filling up of the measure of their judgments. Murderous work should inspire us with awe of God's judgments, as well as with indignation at the wickedness of men.
Key Word: Murder, v. 2.

CHAPTER FORTY-TWO

Contents: God's answer to the inquiry of the people and Jeremiah concerning the calamities recently befallen. God's charge to the people in the land.

Conclusion: In very difficult circumstances, our eyes must be upon God for direction, and our hearts much be intent on obeying His voice. It is folly to quit the place where God has put us merely because we have met with trouble in it. The difficulty we think to escape by disobeying God's voice we will inevitably run ourselves into.

Key Word: Admonished, v. 11.

Strong Verse: 6.

CHAPTER FORTY-THREE

Contents: Jeremiah carried to Tahpanhes in Egypt. Sign of the hidden stones.

Conclusion: It is common for unhumbled men who persist in sin to represent those who speak God's word as grafters having designs for themselves. However, this does not change the Word of God, and those who think to better themselves by going contrary to the Scriptures will come to ruin.

Key Word: Disobedience, v. 4.

CHAPTER FORTY-FOUR

Contents: Message to the Jews in Egypt. Further judgments threatened. Contempt of the people for the admonitions.

Conclusion: God's past dealings with sinful people should be a warning to us of the danger of sin and the fatal consequences of it. To those who are impenitent sinners God will be found an implacable Judge. In a contest between God's Word and man's word, God's Word will be sure to stand.

Key Word: Jehovah provoked, v. 8.

Strong Verse: 28 (b).

CHAPTER FORTY-FIVE

Contents: Message of Baruch in the days of Jehoiakim.

Conclusion: God takes notice of the frets and discontents of His people and is displeased with them. To seek great things for ourselves when the public is in danger is unbecoming. We should count even the preservation of our lives in such times a great mercy, and continue faithful to our service.

Key Word: Impending evil, v. 5.

CHAPTER FORTY-SIX

Contents: Prophecies against Egypt.

Conclusion: When men think to magnify themselves by pushing on unrighteous enterprises, let them expect that God will sooner or later glorify Himself by blasting them and making an end of them, for He has numberless hosts at His command.

Key Word: Day of vengeance, v. 10.

Promise: 28.

Striking Facts: vv. 27, 28, certainly look forward to the judgments of the nations at the coming of Christ (Matt. 25:42) after Armageddon, (Rev. 16:14), and the deliverance of Israel.

CHAPTER FORTY-SEVEN

Contents: Prophecies against Philistia and Tyre and Zidon.

Conclusion: The sword of the Word, as it is charged from the Lord of Hosts to punish the crimes of nations, cannot be sheathed until it has accomplished that for which He has sent it.

Key Word: Cut off, v. 4.

Strong Verses: 6, 7.

CHAPTER FORTY-EIGHT

Contents: Prophecy against Moab.

Conclusion: Jehovah has all armies at His command. He will in His own time plead the cause of His people against a people that have always been vexatious to them and rebellious toward Him, and will punish them until there is nothing left of them.

Key Word: Spoiling and destruction, v. 3.

Strong Verse: 10.

CHAPTER FORTY-NINE

Contents: Prophecies against the Ammonites, Edom, Damascus, Kedar, king-doms of Hazor, Elam.

Conclusion: Nations that despise and persecute God's people may make a mighty figure for a time, but their pride shall deceive them, for God will surely visit them with desolations, and they themselves shall be despised among men.

Key Word: Desolations, v. 2.

Strong Verse: 16 (a).

CHAPTER FIFTY

Contents: Prophecies against Babylon and Chaldea.

Conclusion: The pride of men's hearts sets God against them and ripens them in due time for utter ruin. Whatever wrong is done against God's people will certainly be reckoned, for though God may have used their persecutions for the good of His people, God has a variety of instruments at command in the earth, and when He opens His armories, all enemies will find themselves overmatched.

Key Word: Vengeance, v. 28.

Strong Verses: 6, 25.

Christ Seen: v. 34. It is the comfort of Christians in distress that they have a Redeemer, Jesus Christ, Who is strong, and will thoroughly plead their cause and give them rest.

CHAPTER FIFTY-ONE

Contents: Prophecies against Babylon continued.

Conclusion: Let no nation think it will exempt them from God's judgment that they have been executing God's judgments on others. Those who have proudly carried everything before them will at length meet with their match, and their day will come to pass.

Key Word: Judgment, v. 9.

Strong Verses: 5, 15.

CHAPTER FIFTY-TWO

Contents: A retrospect: overthrow and capture of Judah. The latter days of Jehoiachin.

Conclusion: Iniquity leads to the certain ruin of those who follow it, and if it be not forsaken will certainly end by the sinner being cast out of God's presence. The unbelief of man shall not make God's threatenings of no effect, but events will fully answer the predictions of His Word.

Key Word: Behold His anger, v. 3.

LAMENTATIONS

Key Thought:	Number of Chapters:	Key Verse:	Christ seen as:
Chastening	5	2:11	Man of Sorrows

Writer of the Book:	Date:	Conclusion of the Book:
		Sin brings misery. The
Jeremiah	About 588 B. C.	compassion of Jehovah for the subjects of His wrath is marvelous.

SUMMARY

CHAPTER ONE

Contents: Jeremiah's first complaint of the calamities of Judah. Appeal to God for deliverance.

Conclusion: Whatever our troubles are which God is pleased to inflict upon us, we must own that therein He is righteous and we are sinful. Our fetters are usually of our own making, and it is with our own rod that we are beaten. Those who are without God's presence are without all true comfort.

Key Word: Comforters, vv. 2, 17, 21.

Strong Verse: 18.

CHAPTER TWO

Contents: Lamentation on the effect of the calamities of Judah. God's passionate consideration appealed to.

Conclusion: The wormwood and gall in affliction is the thought that God has become one's enemy in His hot displeasure at sin. In all sore providences, it is well to reflect that God has fulfilled His Word, for there will be found to be a perfect agreement between the judgments of God's hand and those threatened by His Word upon the unrepentant.

Key Word: Swallowed up, v. 5.

Strong Verse: 17 (a).

CHAPTER THREE

Contents: Complaint of God's displeasure and comfort to God's people. Appeal to God's justice against persecutors.

Conclusion: Bad as things may be, it is owing to the mercy of God that they are not worse, for if we had been dealt with according to our sins, we should have been consumed long ago. Since we are dealt with according to God's mercy, we should acknowledge it to His praise.

Key Word: Bitterness, v. 15.

Strong Verses: 22, 23, 24, 25, 26, 31, 32, 33.

Christ Seen: v. 24-26. If the Lord Jesus is our portion, we always have hope in Him. We cannot be cast off, let us therefore take His yoke and learn of Him and quietly wait in submission and faith.

CHAPTER FOUR

Contents: Lamentation on the direful effects of calamities of Judah. Sins of the leaders acknowledged.

Conclusion: Nothing ripens a people more for ruin, nor fills the measure faster than the sins of the priests and prophets (v. 13), by which they are led blindly away from God and into His judgments.

Key Word: Devoured, v. 11.

Strong Verse: 9.

CHAPTER FIVE

Contents: Lamentation of the state of Judah in captivity. Supplications for the return of mercy.

Conclusion: All our woes are owing to our own sin and folly, and God is therefore righteous in it. Though we may not quarrel with God, we may yet plead with Him and hope for mercy even when He seems to have utterly forsaken.

Key Word: No rest, vv. 7, 15.

Strong Verses: 7, 19.

Christ Seen: The book ends in darkness.   If only we would turn from our griefs to the mercies, goodness and compassions of God expressed in the gift of His Son for our redemption, there would be light in our darkest dungeons.

EZEKIEL

Key Thought:	Number of Chapters:	Key Verse:	Christ seen as:
Visions	48	1:1	High Priest of God

Writer of the Book:	Date:	Conclusion of the Book:
		God is marvelously good to those who show a
Ezekiel	About 570-590 B. C.	desire to walk with Him, and terribly severe upon those who persistently rebel against Him.

SUMMARY

CHAPTER ONE

Contents: Vision of the glory.

Conclusion: While no man has seen God at any time, many have had visions of Him, displays of divine glory, which prostrated man before Him in humbled sense of his own unworthiness, and of the infinite distance between man and God. The more God is pleased to make known to us of His glory, the more humble we should be before Him.

Key Word: Visions of God, v. 1.

Christ Seen: v. 26. We have here a glimpse of the glory and dignity of Christ at His incarnation, a hint of what His condescension was in taking upon Himself the form of a servant and giving Himself to the death of the cross.

CHAPTER TWO

Contents: Ezekiel filled with the Spirit, and his divine command.

Conclusion: If we stand ready to be used of God, we may expect that He will give us a commission. He is pleased to work that in us which He requires of us. Those who will do anything to purpose in His service must not be afraid of the voice of man, but faithfully deliver the message regardless of its reception.

Key Word: Called, v. 3.

Strong Verse: 6.

Christ Seen: v. 1. It is Christ's prerogative to call ministers, enjoin them in their work, and fill them with the Spirit for it (John 15:16).

CHAPTER THREE

Contents: Ezekiel's commission continued. Again filled with the Spirit. His dumbness.

Conclusion: Ministers are God's mouth to the children of men, but must not undertake to preach the things of God until the Word of God has become part of themselves. Those who keep close to Him need not fear the proud looks of men. If the minister is not faithful to his trust, a loss of souls will be charged upon him in the day of account. Though ministers do not faithfully warn the wicked, it shall not be admitted as an excuse for sin—the wicked will die in their iniquity.

Key Word: Watchman, v. 17.

Strong Verses: 8, 9, 18, 19, 27.

Christ Seen: vv. 1-3. We must eat the flesh and drink of the life of the Son of Man if we would be able to deal aright with the needs of the sons of men (Jn. 6:53).

CHAPTER FOUR

Contents: The sign of the tile. Typical representations.

Conclusion: If men will not serve God with cheerfulness in the abundance of all things, God will make them serve their enemies in the want of all things. In times of public distress, God's ministers must be willing to endure hardness that they may evidence the sincerity of their faith and serve the glory of God.

Key Word: Israel's iniquity, v. 5.

CHAPTER FIVE
Contents: Sign of the sharp knife. Famine, pestilence and the sword impending.

Conclusion: When nations (or persons) are made great, it is with design that they may do good, and that they may be as a light to other nations. Contempt of God's Word opens the door to all manner of iniquity, and brings judgments that utterly destroy. Those who refuse God's terms of prosperity cannot expect the continuance of His favor.

Key Word: Judgments, v. 8.

Strong Verses: 7, 8.

CHAPTER SIX
Contents: Message against the mountains of Israel. Remnant to be spared. Desolations upon the land.

Conclusion: If men do not destroy idolatry, as they ought, God will first or last find a way to do it, for idolatry is spiritual whoredom, and therefore a great wrong to God's honor.

Key Word: Desolations, v. 4.

Strong Verse. 10.

CHAPTER SEVEN
Contents: Miserable end of Judah because of sin.

Conclusion: The ruin of sinners comes slowly but surely, but when it comes, it will be total. In the heaviest judgments God inflicts, He does but recompense to sinners their own ways. They are beaten with a rod of their own making.

Key Word: Day of trouble, v. 7.

Strong Verses: 4, 19.

CHAPTER EIGHT
Contents: Third vision of the glory. The former profanation of the temple and God's anger because of sin.

Conclusion: Those are ripe indeed for ruin who have given themselves over to idols, turning their backs upon God and His Word. When their punishment comes, God will be as deaf to their cries as their own idols, to which they vainly cried before.

Key Word: Abominations, v. 6.

Christ Seen: These visions of Israel's sinfulness are interspersed with promises of restoration and blessing to be fulfilled at the coming of the Lord (Rom. 11:26; Zech. 12:8).

CHAPTER NINE
Contents: Visions of the slaying in Jerusalem.

Conclusion: Those who live in sin and hate to be reformed, despising God's Word, will perish in sin, and deserve not to be pitied, for they could have prevented their ruin, but would not. None of those, however, shall be lost whom God has marked for life and salvation.

Key Word: Day of recompense, v. 10.

Strong Verse: 10.

Christ Seen: v. 2. The man clothed in fine linen certainly represents Christ as Mediator, saving those who are His from the flaming sword of vengeance coming upon the earth. This He will do at the end of the age.

CHAPTER TEN
Contents: Visions of the altar fire scattered over Jerusalem. Description of the cherubim.

Conclusion: God's glory and government infinitely transcend all the brightest ideas our minds can receive concerning them. The wheels of His providence move with steadiness and regularity, and all His disposals may be looked upon with wonder, for whatever He pleases He does.

Key Word: Glory, v. 4.

Christ Seen: v. 2. The man in fine linen (same as Chap. 9). The same Jesus Who is the Saviour and Protector of those who believe, as all judgment is committed to Him, will come in flaming fire to take vengeance upon sinners.

CHAPTER ELEVEN
Contents: Vision of wrath against lying princes. Promise to spare the rem-

nant. Israel's coming restoration and conversion. Departure of the glory from Jerusalem.

Conclusion: The fear of the wicked shall come upon him, and there is no fence against the judgment of God. Woe to those entrusted with God's message, who have hidden from the people the things belonging to their peace, for in the day of recompense God will lay at their door the guilt of souls perishing on their account.

Key Word: Judgment, v. 10. (Remnant, v. 13.)

Strong Verse: 21. Promises: 19, 20.

Christ Seen: vv. 17, 21. At the Second Coming of Christ, the Jews will be given a new heart, not divided as it has been through the ages among many gods, a new spirit agreeable to Christ, Whom they hated. They will look upon Him Whom they pierced and will mourn.

CHAPTER TWELVE

Contents: Vision of the prophet as a sign. Full captivity near at hand.

Conclusion: Sinners often try to think their works are not evil because sentence upon them is not executed speedily. Putting the evil day far off only provokes God to bring it sooner, and to make it so much the sorer, and so much more a surprise and terror.

Key Word: Captivity (vv. 7, 11) at hand (v. 23).

Strong Verse: 25 (a).

CHAPTER THIRTEEN

Contents: Message against lying prophets.

Conclusion: Since the devil is the father of lies, those put the highest affront upon God who, claiming to be His prophets, tell lies and father them upon God. A thousand woes upon those who have thus deceived the people and made God their enemy. Though they had claimed to be favorites of heaven, they will in the last day be shown to be the favorites of the devil.

Key Word: False prophets, v. 3.

Strong Verses: 3, 9.

Christ Seen: Matt. 7:22-23. It is Christ Who will say to the false preachers in that day, "I never knew you."

CHAPTER FOURTEEN

Contents: Vision of the elders of Israel. Jerusalem on no account to be spared.

Conclusion: Many who have no idols in their sanctuary have idols in their hearts, which is no less a usurpation of God's throne. Those who have made gods of money and sensual pleasure cannot expect an answer of peace from God, but on the contrary are ripening for utter ruin.

Key Word: Heart idols, v. 3. (Sore judgments, v. 21.)

Strong Verse: 3.

Christ Seen: It is of little use to approach God with requests for guidance, for no prayer can truly be made in the name of Jesus so long as the heart is filled with secret sins and cherished idols, nor can the Spirit of God indict such a prayer.

CHAPTER FIFTEEN

Contents: Vision of the burning vine.

Conclusion: Those who set their faces against God to contradict His Word and defeat His purposes will find His face set against them to their ruin. Though they may come out of one trouble with little hurt, they will soon fall into another and another until they are entirely devoured by the fires of His wrath.

Key Word: Devour, v. 7.

CHAPTER SIXTEEN

Contents: The harlotry of Jerusalem, and threatening of destroying judgments. Promises of future blessing under the new covenant.

Conclusion: Let not men flatter themselves with a conceit that because God has hitherto continued His favors to them, notwithstanding their provocations, He will continue to do so, for ultimately as they have forsaken God, they will be utterly forsaken to ruin by God. If sin is not cast off by repentance, it must be borne to eternal confusion.

Key Word: Jerusalem's harlotry. vv. 16, 35.
Strong Verse: 59.

CHAPTER SEVENTEEN

Contents: Parable of the great eagle. Rebellion of Zedekiah and its results.
Conclusion: He who breaks covenant with God, and tramples the directions of His Word under foot, cannot hope to be delivered from that vengeance which is the just punishment of such treachery. God can without any difficulty root up sinful men and whole kingdoms.
Key Word: Broken covenant, vv. 18, 19.

CHAPTER EIGHTEEN

Contents: Ethical instructions for Israel in captivity.
Conclusion: He who makes conscience of conforming in everything to the will of God, who makes it his business to serve God, and his aim to glorify God, shall without fail be happy here and hereafter, and wherein he comes short of his duty, it shall be forgiven him. Let the impenitent thank themselves if they fall under God's curse, for the soul that sinneth shall neither have peace in this life nor salvation in the next. The God of heaven has no delight in man's ruin.
Key Word: Righteousness and wickedness, v. 20.
Strong Verses: 4, 9, 20, 21, 22, 23, 32.
Christ Seen: In vv. 21, 22. God pledges Himself that forgiven sin shall not be even mentioned. The ground of our present confidence, however, is not the righteousness that we have done (Tit. 3:6) but that of the Lord Jesus in Whom we trust for the putting away of sin.

CHAPTER NINETEEN

Contents: Lamentation for princes of Israel.
Conclusion: God's ministers who have foretold His judgments upon sinners should bitterly lament the destruction of sinners when it comes, as those who have not desired the woeful day. Sinners may thank themselves for the fire that consumes them, for they have by their wickedness made themselves like tinder to the sparks of God's wrath.
Key Word: Lamentation, vv. 1, 14.

CHAPTER TWENTY

Contents: Jehovah vindicated in the chastising of Israel. Israel's future judgment. Parable of the forest of the south field.
Conclusion: God takes it as an affront when those come to inquire of Him who are resolved to go on in their trespasses. He is indeed long-suffering with sinners, and it is owing purely to His mercy, which guards His own glory, that they are not immediately made an end of. If men will not acknowledge God as their ruler, they will have to face Him as Judge when it is too late.
Key Word: Jehovah's long-suffering, vv. 9, 14, 17, 22.
Strong Verses: 19, 20.
Christ Seen: vv. 33-44. This prophecy has to do with the future judgment of Israel at Christ's Coming. The issue determines who of Israel in that day shall enter the land for kingdom blessing. (Ezekiel 20:38; Psalm 50:1-7; Malachi 3:2-5; 4:1, 2.)

CHAPTER TWENTY-ONE

Contents: Parable of the sighing prophet, and of the sword of God. No king for Israel until Messiah comes to reign.
Conclusion: When the sword is unsheathed among nations, God's hand must be owned in it, for His wrath against sin often puts an edge upon the sword, and the instruments He uses in executing judgments, He fills with strength and fury according to the service they are employed in.
Key Word: Jehovah's sword, v. 3.
Strong Verse: 27.
Christ Seen: v. 27. Jesus Christ has incontestable title to the kingship, not only of Israel, but the whole world, and in due time He will have the possession. Until that time, there will be a general and continual overturning of kingdoms.

CHAPTER TWENTY-TWO

Contents: Sins of Israel enumerated.   Parable of the dross in the furnace. Sins of priests, prophets and people.
Conclusion: Whatever God's wrath inflicts upon a people, it is their own way that is recompensed upon their heads, and God deals with them much better than their iniquity deserves.
Key Word: Abominations, v. 2.
Strong Verses: 14, 30, 31.

CHAPTER TWENTY-THREE

Contents: Parable of Aholah and Aholibah.   Sentence passed upon Judah.
Conclusion: Whatever creature we dote upon we make an idol of, and what we make an idol of, we defile ourselves with.   Forgetfulness of God is at the bottom of all such adulterous departures from Him.
   If men will not part with their spiritual whoredoms, they must bear the consequences of them.
Key Word: Whoredoms, v. 8.
Strong Verse: 49.

CHAPTER TWENTY-FOUR

Contents: Parable of the boiling pot.   Ezekiel again made a sign to Israel.
Conclusion: There is a day coming when it will be said, "He that is filthy, let him be filthy still."   The declarations of God's wrath against sinners are as inviolable as the assurances He has given His people of His favor.
Key Word: Vengeance v. 8.

CHAPTER TWENTY-FIVE

Contents: Prophecy against the Ammonites, Moabites, Edomites and Philistines.
Conclusion: Those who glory in any other defence than divine power and promises will sooner or later see cause to be ashamed of their glory. Those who rejoice in the calamities befalling God's people will shortly be reckoned with.
Key Word: Judgments, v. 11.

CHAPTER TWENTY-SIX

Contents: Coming judgment upon Tyre.
Conclusion: It is just with God to blast the designs and projects of those who contrive to raise themselves upon the ruin of others, and let them not expect to prosper long, for the Lord of Hosts is against them to bring them down to the dust.
Key Word: Tyrus' destruction, v. 17.

CHAPTER TWENTY-SEVEN

Contents: Lamentation for Tyre.
Conclusion: God takes notice of the vain conceits men have of themselves in their prosperity.   When they pride themselves on pomp and pleasure, and think themselves perfect, because of their worldliness, He will find a way to bring down their estate to the dust.
Key Word: Lamentation, vv. 2, 32.

CHAPTER TWENTY-EIGHT

Contents: Rebuke of the King of Tyre, and the fate of Satan who inspired him.   Zidon's judgment and Israel's re-gathering.
Conclusion: Those who pretend to be rivals with God will certainly be shown that they are but men—weak, timorous, trembling and perishing men.
Key Word: Brought down, vv. 8, 17.
Strong Verse: 17 (See Rev. 20:10).
Christ Seen: vv. 12-18 go beyond the King of Tyre to Satan, the real but unseen ruler of Tyre.   His unfallen state is here described.   For his fall see Isa. 14:12-14.   The destruction of the serpent at the hands of the seed of woman (Christ), Gen. 3:15, is thus fulfilled.

CHAPTER TWENTY-NINE

Contents: Prophecy against Egypt.

Conclusion: Those who abuse their power will justly be stripped of it. Those who pride themselves in prosperity, forgetting that God is proprietor of the earth, will be forced out of it. God may even use bad men as tools to bring about His purposes.
Key Word: Desolations, v. 9.

CHAPTER THIRTY

Contents: Egypt in the day of Jehovah. God against Pharaoh in the war with Babylon.
Conclusion: Nothing can protect a provoking people when God comes forth to contend with them. God often makes one wicked man a scourge to another for the executing of His judgments upon sin.
Key Word: Judgments, v. 19.

CHAPTER THIRTY-ONE

Contents: Prophecy against Pharaoh.
Conclusion: It is rare to find a humble spirit in the midst of great advancement. God can easily expel those who think themselves, and seem to others, to have taken deepest root. Pride goeth before a fall.
Key Word: Pride punished, vv. 10, 11.

CHAPTER THIRTY-TWO

Contents: Lamentation for Pharaoh and Egypt.
Conclusion: Great potentates, if they be tyrannical and oppressive, are in God's account no better than beasts of prey, and will be shortly devoured. The nation that has terrorized others will eventually be made a terror to itself. (God's messengers should sympathize with the miseries which sinners bring upon themselves. It becomes them to weep for sinners who will not weep for themselves.)
Key Word: Lamentation, vv. 2, 16. Terrors, v. 32.

CHAPTER THIRTY-THREE

Contents: Ethical instructions for the captivity. Rebuke to those who are not sincere in their professions.
Conclusion: God warns sinners of the wrath to come that they may flee from it. Those who go promiscuously into the mouth of judgment, though they hear the warnings of God's servants against the dangers of sin, have destroyed themselves.
Key Word: Warning, v. 3.
Strong Verses: 8, 9, 11, 12, 13, 31, 32.
Christ Seen: vv. 12-13. Many have been ruined by trusting to the merit of their own righteousness, and thinking that God is so much their debtor that they may therefore venture to commit a little sin. "The righteousness of the righteous shall not deliver him." (Rom. 4:5-8; 10:1). Happy is the man who is clothed with the righteousness of Jesus Christ and in whom Christ lives. (Gal. 2:20.)

CHAPTER THIRTY-FOUR

Contents: Message to the faithless shepherds of Israel. Promise of restoration of Israel, and setting up of the kingdom.
Conclusion: Those will have a great deal to answer for in the day of judgment who took upon them the care of souls as under-shepherds, yet never took any care of them. Happy are they who know Christ, the Good Shepherd, being fed in His pastures and blessed with all spiritual blessings in Him.
Key Word: Shepherds, v. 2.
Strong Verse: 31. Promise: 12, 15.
Christ Seen: vv. 23, 29. Jesus is coming as the Great Shepherd (Heb. 13:20) to gather His people and make a final covenant of peace with Israel. He is the "plant of renown," far above all principalities and might and power and dominion, and every name that is named, not only in this world, but that which is to come.

CHAPTER THIRTY-FIVE

Contents: Prophecy against Mount Seir.

Conclusion: Those who have a perpetual enmity to God and His people must expect eventually to be made a perpetual desolation. Those who have lived to shed blood will be given blood to drink.

Key Word: Desolations, vv. 3, 9, 14.

Strong Verse: 6.

CHAPTER THIRTY-SIX

Contents: Message to the mountains of Israel. Restoration of Israel predicted. Israel's past sins.

Conclusion: Those who put shame and reproach upon God's people, though God may have made it serve a purpose to His end, will sooner or later have it turned upon themselves. God takes occasion from the insolence of enemies to show Himself concerned for His people, ready to do them good.

Key Word: Mountains of Israel, v. 1. Restoration, v. 24.

Strong Verse: 23 (b). Promises: 26, 27.

Christ Seen: The restoration of Israel is yet future. The remnant and their posterity which returned after the seventy years were continually under Gentile yoke. In A. D. 70 they were driven into dispersion, which still continues, and never will be brought to its full end until the glorious coming of Christ.

CHAPTER THIRTY-SEVEN

Contents: Vision of the valley of dry bones. Sign of the two sticks.

Conclusion: He Who made man so fearfully and wonderfully can in like manner make him new. Scattered atoms can be marshalled in their proper place and every bone can be made to come to its place by the same wisdom and power by which bones were first formed in the womb.

Key Word: Dry bones, v. 4.

Promises: 5, 6, 28.

Christ Seen: v. 22. As bone came to bone, so the Israelites scattered over the earth will come to their respective families and tribes in the millennial day. Then Christ will come to be recognized as King, in allegiance to Whom all will cheerfully unite. (Many believe David will sit upon the literal throne of Jerusalem as representative of Christ, the great Ruler in the air above.)

CHAPTER THIRTY-EIGHT

Contents: Prophecy against Gog.

Conclusion: God does not only see those who are now the enemies of His people, but foresees those who will be so in the last days, and lets them know by His Word that He is against them, and will make their movements to serve His own purposes.

Key Word: Gog, v. 3. (Latter days, v. 16.)

Christ Seen: This prophecy should be read in connection with Zech. 12:1-4; 14:1-9; Matt. 24:14-30; Rev. 14:14-20; 19:17-21. Many see a reference to the northern European powers headed by Russia in the last days to wage a great war. The reference to Mesheck (Moscow) and Tubal (Zobolsk) is thought to be clear identification. The prophecy belongs to the future battle of Armageddon which is about to take place when Christ returns with all His saints in power and great glory.

CHAPTER THIRTY-NINE

Contents: Prophecy against Gog, continued. Vision of restored and converted Israel.

Conclusion: The powers in the last days that rise up to oppress Israel and work havoc in the earth will be made to know by dear-bought experience that Jehovah is the God of power and the Saviour of Israel, even though they seem long to have been neglected by Him. In that day the slaughter will be so great that there will not be a sufficient number of the enemies left alive to bury their dead.

Key Word: Gog, v. 1.

Strong Verse: 24. Promises: 21, 23.

Christ Seen: God will in the day of Christ's glorious coming let all nations know the meaning of all Israel's troubles, and will get glory to Himself, in their cleansing and restoration.

CHAPTER FORTY

Contents: Vision of the man with the measuring reed. The future temple and its service.

Conclusion: A great and beautiful temple, framed in detail in the counsel of God, is to be set up in Jerusalem in the millennial age, for the setting forth of the truths of God's Word.

Key Word: Temple.

CHAPTER FORTY-ONE

Contents: Further description of the temple.

Conclusion: Same as Chap. 40.

Key Word: Temple.

CHAPTER FORTY-TWO

Contents: Further description of the temple.

Conclusion: Same as Chap. 40.

Key Word: Temple.

CHAPTER FORTY-THREE

Contents: Vision of God's glory filling the temple. Place of the throne of the future kingdom. The altar and offerings.

Conclusion: The glory of God shall return to earth in the kingdom age, filling the new temple, and Israel will once more offer their appointed and acceptable sacrifices in praise to God.

Key Word: Temple, glory (v. 2), throne (v. 7), offerings (vv. 18-27).

CHAPTER FORTY-FOUR

Contents: Gate for the prince. God's glory filling the temple. The priests.

Conclusion: In the great temple of Jehovah in the kingdom age, Israel shall worship with a new heart, and every detail of the temple services will be carried out according to God's appointment.

Key Word: Temple services.

CHAPTER FORTY-FIVE

Contents: Jehovah's portion of the land and the prince's portion.

Conclusion: In the kingdom age Israel will honor Jehovah with portions of land set apart for divine service. Sin offerings will be offered according to God's appointment, for while sin will be suppressed, the tendency to sin is not removed until the new heaven and new earth are established.

Key Word: Portion of land, v. 1.

CHAPTER FORTY-SIX

Contents: Worship of the prince and people, and the offerings.

Conclusion: Israel will acknowledge their dependence upon Jehovah in the kingdom age with many offerings according to a divine plan for that period, by which perfect fellowship may be maintained.

Key Word: Offerings, v. 4.

CHAPTER FORTY-SEVEN

Contents: River of the new sanctuary. Borders of the land.

Conclusion: Rev. 22:1-2; Zech. 14:8-9.

Key Word: River of sanctuary, v. 1; borders, v. 13.

CHAPTER FORTY-EIGHT

Contents: Division of the land. The city and its gates.

Conclusion: The tribes of Israel will in the kingdom age be distributed according to the divine counsels by a plan different from that previously known. The chief glory of the land will be the manifestations of Jehovah's presence in the city of His choice.

Key Word: Borders, v. 1.

Strong Verse: 35 (b).

Christ Seen: The name of the future city (v. 35) suggests Rev. 22:3 which tells us that the throne of God and of the Lamb shall be in it. Not only will the power of God be manifested there but the Lord Jesus Himself will be present.

DANIEL

Key Thought:	Number of Chapters:	Key Verse:	Christ seen as:
Kingdom	12	2:22	King

Writer of the Book:	Date:	Conclusion of the Book:
Daniel	About 534 B. C.	

God is universal sovereign of all—and is yet to be acknowledged as such by all men.

SUMMARY

CHAPTER ONE

Contents: Personal history of Daniel. Reason for appearance of Daniel and his friends before Nebuchadnezzar.

Conclusion: Plain living and high thinking go together. When God's people are in Babylon, they should take special care that they partake not of her sins (Psa. 141:4). It is to the praise of God's people not to relish the delights of sense, but to look upon them with indifference.

Key Word: Heart purpose, v. 8.

Strong Verse: 8.

Christ Seen: This book is written by a man "greatly beloved" (9:23) and deals with much the same prophecies as those of the Revelation of Jesus Christ written by "the beloved disciple," (John). Note similarity between the two:
1. In captivity. Dan. 1:6; 8:2; Rev. 1:9. 2. Beloved. 10:11; John 13:23. 3. Heard the Lord's voice. 8:16; 10:9; Rev. 1:10. 4. Saw the Lord's face. Dan. 10:6; Rev. 1:14. 5. Prostrated. 10:8-9; Rev. 1:17. 6. Quickened. 10:10, 18; Rev. 1:17. 7 Angel taught. 10:11, 12; Rev. 1:1.

CHAPTER TWO

Contents: Visions of Nebuchadnezzar and their results. The forgotten dream and the failure of the astrologers. Daniel's interpretation after prayer for wisdom.

Conclusion: The wisest of men are clouded with a veil of flesh which confounds their understanding of divine things. The sacred things belong to the Lord our God, but believers by prayer are let into His mysteries concerning the last days. The kings of earth have no power but what is given them from above, and in due time all earth kingdoms will be done away and replaced by the eternal kingdom of Christ on earth.

Key Word: Dreams, v. 1.

Strong Verses: 20, 21, 22. **Promise:** 44.

Christ Seen: The vision has to do with the course of the times of the Gentiles, during which four great world kingdoms would succeed each other. The last of the four (Rome) would divide into legs and then into ten toes 7:27). (Gentiles world powers of the last days). The smiting stone (7:34-35) is to destroy this system of kingdoms in its final form by a sudden blow from heaven (not by gradual process). (See Dan. 7:1-28; Rev. 13-19.) When this destruction comes it will be immediately followed by the kingdom of Christ, which will fill the whole earth at once. Christ is the stone cut out without hands, Who will smite the nations, and then become a great mountain, filling the earth with His glory.

CHAPTER THREE

Contents: Pride of Nebuchadnezzar and his punishment. The image of gold. The three Jews refuse to worship the image. Fiery furnace proven harmless. The king convinced.

Conclusion: We should obey the powers that be until they tell us to disobey and dishonor God (Rom. 13:1), then we should obey God rather than man (Acts 5:29). If we are called to pass through the fire, Christ

walked there before us, and will walk there with us (John 15:20), and nothing will be lost by being true to Him.
Key Word: Deliver, vv. 17, 28.
Strong Verses: 17, 28.
Christ Seen: v. 25. Many think this was the eternal Son of God, not a created angel. Hereby Christ shows that what is done against His people He takes as done against Himself. Whoever throws them into the furnace do in effect throw Him in (Isa. 63:9). Those who suffer for Him are therefore assured of His precious presence with them.

CHAPTER FOUR

Contents: Nebuchadnezzar's proclamation. The true vision and its interpretation. Vision fulfilled; the restoration of Nebuchadnezzar.
Conclusion: God has power to humble the haughtiest of men who would in their pride act in competition with Him. Those so confident of their own sufficiency will be brought sooner or later to own God's dominion over them and their own utter weakness. Many have been brought to themselves by being made beside themselves.
Key Word: Pride abased, v. 37.
Strong Verses: 35, 37.
Christ Seen: v. 17. We learn that destinies are not decided in the council chambers of kings but in the celestial council chamber above. Where would we stand apart from the pleading of Christ, our great High Priest?

CHAPTER FIVE

Contents: Daniel's personal history under Belshazzar and Darius. The pride of Belshazzar and his downfall. The writing on the wall. Its interpretation and fulfillment.
Conclusion: God expects from the greatest of men that their hearts will be humbled before Him by acknowledgment that, great as they are, to Him they are accountable. If they persist in their pride and impenitence, they will be made to know that the Most High God rules.
Key Word: Found wanting, v. 27.
Strong Verse: 21.
Christ Seen: Gold and glitter, splendor and mirth cannot add weight to a soul in the balances of God. Those who are in the balances without Christ will be found wanting in the great day of God's wrath.

CHAPTER SIX

Contents: Daniel's history to the accession of Cyrus. Decree of Darius. Daniel's steadfastness. Daniel in the lion's den and his deliverance. Darius' new decree.
Conclusion: "God first" means "safety first." That which believers do faithfully in conscience toward God may often be represented as done with obstinate motives by men, but God knows the heart, and whatever the test, will give peace and deliverance, and will clear the integrity of His trusting child.
Key Word: Delivered, vv. 16, 20, 23.
Strong Verses: 5, 10, 16 (b), 23 (b), 26.
Christ Seen: The Jews, in praying turned their faces toward the holy city. With us, the upturned face and our dependence upon the great High Priest are significant of a posture of soul analagous, yet superior to the open window. Let the windows be open toward the heavenly city from which, for a time, we are exiled.

CHAPTER SEVEN

Contents: The beast vision of Daniel, forecasting the four world empires and the final heading up under anti-Christ. Vision of Christ coming in glory. Interpretation of the beast vision.
Conclusion: The thrones of the kingdoms of this world in their final heading up will be thrown down. The people of God in every age should be encouraged under their troubles with the prospect of Christ's coming in glory, for God has sworn that He will in due time put His King upon the throne of earth and make an end of all unrighteous rule.
Key Word: Kingdom and visions, v. 1.

Strong Verses: 9, 14. Promise: 27.
Christ Seen: vv. 13, 14; identical with Rev. 5:6-10. The order of events will be:
    1. Investure of Christ's earthly kingdom (13, 14; Rev. 5:6-10).
2. The vexing of Psa. 2:5. See also Matt. 24:21, 22; Rev. 6:18. 3. Return of Christ in glory to deliver the smiting blow of 2:45; 7:9-11; Rev. 19:11-21. 4. Judgment of nations and setting up of kingdom (7:10, 26, 27; Matt. 25:31-46; Rev. 20:1-6).

CHAPTER EIGHT

Contents: The ram and rough goat vision, and its interpretation.
Conclusion: Out from the kingdoms of the last days a king of fierce countenance, the anti-Christ, will arise, and acting by the power of Satan, will bring transgression to the full. Though he will for a time prosper in his hellish schemes, the sudden brightness of Christ's coming will utterly destroy him.
Key Word: End-time indignation, v. 19.
Strong Verses: 23, 24, 25.
Christ Seen: Two ends are in view in this chapter—historically the end of the Grecian empire of Alexander; prophetically, the end of the times of the Gentiles (Luke 21:24; Rev. 16:14), when the "little horn" of 7:8, 24-26, the beast, will arise, followed by the return of Christ.

CHAPTER NINE

Contents: Vision of the seventy weeks. Daniel's prayer and confession.
Conclusion: God's Word is intended to encourage our prayers, and when we see the day of the performance of His prophecies approaching, we should the more earnestly confess our sins and pray, not only being forward to speak to God, but as forward to hear what He has to say to us.
Key Word: Prayer, v. 3. Vision, v. 21.
Christ Seen: vv. 24-27. Reduced to calendar years, this 69 weeks of years (v. 25) is 476 years. The edict to restore Jerusalem was issued 446 B. C. Applying 476 to this point brings us to Christ's birth and 30 years over, the very time of the cutting off of Messiah by His crucifixion (v. 26). Luke 3:23 says that Jesus began His ministry at 30 years and an error is imagined by some, but Scripture is accurate, for when in the sixth century, the time A. D. and B. C. was divided, an error of four years was made in the calendar so that really 30 A. D. is 34. Christ's ministry extended nearly four years; thus 30 A. D. in our chronology was the time of Christ's death. At the close of the age, the other week of years will be fulfilled in awful tribulation, after which Christ will appear suddenly in the clouds to set up His eternal kingdom.

CHAPTER TEN

Contents: Visions of the glory of God. The heavenly messenger detained, but comes at last to show Daniel things to come, in answer to prayer.
Conclusion: From the day that we begin to look toward God in the way of duty, He is ready to meet us in the way of mercy. When we rightly understand the methods of God's providence and grace concerning us, we will be better reconciled to them. Failure to complete transactions with God is responsible for many unanswered prayers.
Key Word: Great vision, v. 8.
Strong Verses: 12, 19, 21.
Christ Seen: vv. 6, 16, 17. Christ here appears in the same resemblance wherein He appeared to John in Rev. 1:13-15, viz., in His priestly dress, girded ready to His work on behalf of His people.

CHAPTER ELEVEN

Contents: Prophecy covering the period from Darius to anti-Christ, showing the conflicts of nations, and final heading up for destruction.
Conclusion: That which God has declared in His Word concerning the end of kingdoms shall surely come to pass, and then the sins of men and the wickedness of anti-Christ and Satan shall be made to serve His purposes and contribute to the bringing of his counsels to birth in their season. Though

sin comes to an awful heading up under anti-Christ, it will surely come to
eternal destruction when Christ comes to set up His glorious kingdom.
Key Word: Time of the end, v. 40.
Strong Verses: 32, 33.
Christ Seen: v. 45.   This was not fulfilled in Antiochus, for he died in Tabal,
Persia.   This man, the anti-Christ, will come to his end in Judea be-
tween Jerusalem and the Mediterranean, and it is the brightness of
Christ's coming only that will bring him to his doom (2 Thess. 2:8; Rev.
19:20).

CHAPTER TWELVE

Contents: The great tribulation of the last days, and the resurrection foretold.   The last message to Daniel.
Conclusion: The present age is to close in a time of tribulation such as the
world has never known.   Christ will come to save His people and to raise
the bodies of many from the dust.   Glorious rewards will be conferred
upon those who have themselves been wise and have instructed others
in the way of salvation.
Key Word: Time of the end, vv. 4, 9.
Promises: 2, 3.
Christ Seen: The time of the end or day of Jacob's trouble (Jeremiah 30:7),
will be a time of tribulation such as was not from the beginning of the
world, nor ever shall be (Matt. 24:21).   The New Testament adds
many details concerning it.   But for the appearing of Christ in glory
no flesh would be spared through it.   Those who know Christ as their
Saviour will not be called upon to pass through it (Rev. 3:10), but will
be caught up before it begins (1 Thess. 4:16-18).

HOSEA

Key Thought:	Number of Chapters:	Key Verse:	Christ seen as:
Return	14	14:9	Risen Son of God

Writer of the Book:	Date:	Conclusion of the Book:
Hosea	790-725 B. C.	God longs for the return of backsliders, pleads with them and makes every inducement for their repentance.

SUMMARY

CHAPTER ONE

Contents: Israel, Jehovah's dishonored wife, repudiated, but to be restored.
Conclusion: Giving glory to any creature which is due to God alone is as much an injury and affront to God as for a wife to embrace the bosom of a stranger, is to her husband. Thus many who have been in covenant relation with God have broken their marriage bond, turning away the mercy of God from their houses.
Key Word: Israel—whoredom, v. 2.
Promise: 10.
Christ Seen: v. 11. The day will come (Rom. 11:25) when Israel will come forth out of the lands, acknowledging Jesus Christ Whom they crucified, as their head (Zech. 12:10).

CHAPTER TWO

Contents: The chastisement of adulterous Israel. Lsrael yet to be restored.
Conclusion: Those who exchange the service of God for the service of the world and the flesh will sooner or later be made to own that they have changed for the worse, finding themselves cast off of God and hedged about with thorns. Woe unto us, if God will not own Himself in relation to us.
Key Word: Israel's harlotry, restoration, vv. 5, 18.
Promises: 18, 19, 20.
Christ Seen: vv. 14-23. In the final day of Israel's despair, God has promised to revive her with comforts—the sight of their coming Messiah. In that day they will be betrothed to Him anew forever, and the earth shall be filled with His eternal peace and righteousness.

CHAPTER THREE

Contents: Jehovah's undying love to Israel. The future kingdom on earth.
Conclusion: God's people (Israel) who have gone awhoring from Him must take upon themselves the shame of their apostasy and submit to the punishment of their iniquity. If God dealt with them according to the strict rigor of the law, He would have no more to do with them, but He will deal with them according to the multitude of His mercies, and not according to their iniquities. The remnant of Israel will yet seek the Lord and receive their King.
Key Word: Israel's harlotry, restoration, vv. 3, 4.
Strong Verse: 4. Promise: 5.
Christ Seen: vv. 4-5. The reference may be to the Lord Jesus Christ, the Son of David, to Whom God gave the throne of His father David—Luke 1:32. The Chaldee translates it, "they shall seek the service of the Lord their God, and shall obey Messiah, the Son of David, their King."

CHAPTER FOUR

Contents: Charges against Israel for their sinfulness, idolatry and ignorance.
Conclusion: It is a sad and sore judgment for men when God has to say, "let them alone"—giving them up to their own heart's lust to walk in their

own counsels until the measure of their iniquity is filled. Man's doings will surely return upon him, and his sins against God will be called over to him, either to his humiliation or to his condemnation.

Key Word: Jehovah's controversy, v. 1.

Strong Verses: 9, 17.

Christ Seen: Apart from the restraints of Christianity, the awful condition here portrayed would be that of the whole world today. Truly, the whole creation groaneth and travaileth, waiting the day of Christ's coming and the full deliverance from the curse (Rom. 8:22).

CHAPTER FIVE

Contents: Jehovah's face withdrawn from Israel.

Conclusion: There is a time when Jehovah will not be found—when it is time for His judgments to fall on a rebellious, sinful people. He will take no notice of their troubles or prayers, until they become sensible of their guilt, and are brought to humble themselves before Him for it.

Key Word: Jehovah's withdrawal, vv. 6, 15.

Strong Verse: 15.

Christ Seen: The dry rot of a nation cannot be stopped by grand alliances. Only a wholesale turning to Christ can save nations, and the horrors of this war-torn world would come to a speedy end were He recognized.

CHAPTER SIX

Contents: The voice of the remnant of Israel in the last days. Jehovah's response.

Conclusion: The consideration of God's judgments upon us because of sin should awaken us to return to God by repentance, prayer and reformation. He Who has smitten us will bind us up if we humbly return to Him.

Key Word: Return, v. 1.

Strong Verses: 1, 3, 6.

Christ Seen: vv. 1-3. This will be Israel's resolve in the last days, as the result of the "time of Jacob's trouble." The Lord Jesus will be to them as a refreshing rain after a long drought, and Israel shall be revived.

CHAPTER SEVEN

Contents: Jehovah's response to Israel's cry, continued. Israel's sad state.

Conclusion: If sinful souls are not healed and helped, but perish in their sin and misery, they cannot blame God, for He could and would have healed them. They are not healed because they will not be, refusing to look to God even when they are reaping the sore results of sin. Let all such remember that all their works are remembered and will have to be faced.

Key Word: Wickedness, v. 2.

Strong Verse: 2.

Christ Seen: v. 9. Thus strangers steal away the strength of our affections to Christ and deterioration creeps steadily over our religious life. Let us cleave to Christ lest our power ebb away as did that of Ephraim.

CHAPTER EIGHT

Contents: Jehovah's response, continued. Sins denounced and captivity foretold.

Conclusion: Those who sow to the flesh must reap corruption. All the hopes of sinners are cheats, and their gains are snares. Those who break friendship with God make themselves an easy prey to all about them.

Key Word: Sowing, reaping, v. 7.

Strong Verses: 7 (a), 11.

Christ Seen: Many like Israel turn from the living Christ to the likeness of a calf, then when trouble comes, find themselves left powerless. How different it is when we walk with Him who said, "Lo, I am with you always."

CHAPTER NINE

Contents: Jehovah's response, continued. Israel's coming distress because of sin.

Conclusion: Joy is a forbidden fruit to those who have broken covenant with God, until they return and make their peace with God. If men make things of the world and flesh their portion, it is just with God to deny them the comfort of them—to bring man to a sense of his folly. The day of recompense hastens on apace toward all who go a whoring from God.

Key Word: Days of recompense, v. 7.

Strong Verses: 5, 17.

Christ Seen: v. 8. As a watchman of God, Ephraim had a great privilege within grasp. It is to this privilege also that Christ calls each of His own, for He says, "Tarry ye and watch with me." Beware of failure to heed the gracious challenge!"

CHAPTER TEN

Contents: Jehovah's response, continued. Further reproof for Israel's impiety.

Conclusion: If the grace of God prevail not to destroy the love of sin in us, it is just that the providence of God should destroy the fuel of sin about us, and that what men have made idols of should be spoiled. Because God does not desire the ruin of sinners, He does desire their chastisement.

Key Word: Chastisement, vv. 10, 15.

Strong Verses: 12, 13.

Christ Seen: Those who say "We fear not the Lord" will surely go on to say, "We fear not the King." It is "an evil and bitter thing, to forsake Jesus Christ.

CHAPTER ELEVEN

Contents: Jehovah's response, continued. His tender love for Israel.

Conclusion: Though men who have had relationship with God are ripe for ruin because of following their own counsels, instead of God's, God is slow to anger, loth to abandon them, longing to draw them with the cords of His love.

Key Word: Jehovah's love, vv. 1, 4, 8.

Strong Verses: 3, 4, 8, 9.

Christ Seen: v. 1. These words have a double aspect, being applied to Christ (Matt. 2:15). They speak historically of the calling of Israel out of Egypt, and prophetically of the bringing of Christ from Egypt, the former being a type of the latter. Christ's calling out of Egypt is likewise a figure of the calling of all who are His out of spiritual slavery.

CHAPTER TWELVE

Contents: Jehovah's response, continued. Further reproof of Israel's sins.

Conclusion: Those who make creatures and things their confidence, put a cheat upon their own souls, and prepare vexation for themselves. God has His eye even upon the merchant weighing his goods, and knows his methods and the idols of his heart. If men put contempt upon God, God will let their neighbors look with contempt upon them.

Key Word: Recompense, vv. 2, 14.

Strong Verse: 6.

Christ Seen: vv. 9-10. As great an offense as Israel has been to God throughout the centuries, God's Word assures us that the prophecies regarding their restoration to glory in the earth will be certainly fulfilled in His own time. That time is connected with the time of Christ's Second Coming.

CHAPTER THIRTEEN

Contents: Jehovah's response, continued. Israel's ruin. Ultimate blessing in the kingdom age.

Conclusion: Worldly prosperity, which feeds men's pride, makes them forgetful of God, and sends them on a downhill course in which they cannot easily stop themselves. Those whom God has in vain endured with long-suffering, and appealed to with much affection, will finally be made the vessels of His wrath.

Key Word: Ruined (vv. 8, 16), ransomed (14).

Strong Verses: 4, 6. Promise: 14.

Christ Seen: vv. 9-11. God will yet give Israel a King, whom they will receive as God-appointed, a Saviour to their nation. Israel, becoming weary of the theocracy, or divine government, rejected Samuel, crying, "Give us a king." God gave them a king and plenty of trouble with him. Christ is the true heavenly King, and He will at His Second Coming take the throne of His father David.

CHAPTER FOURTEEN

Contents: Entreaty and promise to Israel. Restoration foretold.

Conclusion: Though backslidings from God are dangerous diseases of the soul, yet they are not incurable, for God graciously promises that if backsliders will return to be reconciled to Him and to His whole will, He will heal their backslidings and make them conscious of His love.

Key Word: Backsliding healed, v. 4.

Strong Verse: 9. Promise: 4.

Christ Seen: vv. 5-7. God will yet be as the dew unto Israel, refreshing them with His comforts, but not until they see it descending upon them in the person of Jesus Christ, their rejected King, when He comes in the clouds of heaven with great glory. Then their branches indeed shall spread, and they shall grow as the vine.

JOEL

Key Thought:	Number of Chapters:	Key Verse:	Christ seen as:
Judgment	3	2:13	Outpourer of the Spirit.

Writer of the Book:	Date:	Conclusion of the Book:
Joel	Either 860-850 B. C. or 400-380 B. C.	Repentance, a heart broken for sin and from sin, is necessary, if the judgments of God are to be averted.

SUMMARY

CHAPTER ONE

Contents: Joel's warnings of desolation upon Israel, and call to repentance. The plague of insects.

Conclusion: Those who will not be aroused out of their security by the Word of God will finally be aroused by His rod, for He has the meanest of His creatures at His command, and if He pleases can humble and mortify a rebellious people by the most contemptible creatures. Even locusts become as lions when armed with a divine commission.

Key Word: Destruction, v. 15.

Strong Verse: 15.

Christ Seen: This prophecy looks for its complete fulfillment to the endtime of the present age (Rev. 14, 16, 19). Joel gives the fullest view of the consummation of all written prophecy concerning Israel's woes and final glory under Christ.

CHAPTER TWO

Contents: Day of vengeance upon Israel. Invading hosts and awful scourges. Repentance of the Jewish remnant and Jehovah's response and deliverance.

Conclusion: There is a great and terrible day of the Lord coming upon the world, to be ushered in with wonders in heaven and earth, blood and fire and pillars of smoke. Woe to those who are not prepared for that day when it comes unawares upon them. Those who are able to pass through it will be given a change of heart through the universal outpouring of the Holy Spirit, and God will reign gloriously in all the universe, restoring to great favor in the earth the remnant of Israel.

Key Word: Day of the Lord, vv. 1, 31.

Strong Verse: 10. Promises: 28, 29.

Christ Seen: v. 28. This has a partial and continuous fulfillment during "the last days" (Heb. 1:2), which began with the first advent of Christ (Acts 2:17), but the greater fulfillment awaits the "last days" as applied to Israel, when Christ shall come to be recognized as Lord of Lords and King of Kings.

CHAPTER THREE

Contents: Restoration of Israel, and judgment of all nations in regard to Israel. Full kingdom blessings under Christ.

Conclusion: Though God has suffered the enemies of His people (Israel) to prevail very far and for a long time, they will, in the day of decision, be called to account for it. To those who have repented and looked toward God as their salvation, that day will be a joyful day, for the Lord will be the strength of Israel, and all the earth shall be filled with the knowledge of Him thereafter.

Key Word: Day of the Lord, v. 14.

Strong Verses: 14, 16.

Christ Seen: v. 2. All nations that wrong the Jews lay themselves open to God's vengeance, especially those in the last days who persecute the Jews. The coming of Christ will be the day of decision for them. The remnant of Israel will then be cleansed and restored, Jerusalem once more being made a praise in the earth.

AMOS

Key Thought:	Number of Chapters:	Key Verse:	Christ seen as:
Punishment	9	4:12	Thy God, O Israel.

Writer of the Book:	Date:	Conclusion of the Book:
Amos	870-783 B. C.	National sin inevitably spells national judgment.

SUMMARY

CHAPTER ONE

Contents: Judgments pronounced upon surrounding peoples—Syria, Tyre, Edom, Ammon.

Conclusion: The God of Israel is the God of all the earth, and the nations that refuse to worship Him, and who persecute His people will be made to know that they are accountable to Him as Judge.

Key Word: Punishment, vv. 6, 9, 11, 13.

Christ Seen: Might may assert its claims to be right, but it endures only for a little time. The very constitution of the universe is in harmony with Calvary, and only a Christian civilization can be permanent.

CHAPTER TWO

Contents: Judgments pronounced upon Judah, Moab and Israel.

Conclusion: To keep not the commandments of God's Word, making no conscience of them, is to despise the wisdom, justice and goodness of the Author. Those who will not submit to the convictions of the Word will have to sink under the weight of God's punishments.

Key Word: Punishment, vv. 1, 4, 6.

Strong Verse: 16.

Christ Seen: v. 13. Here is a graphic picture of the way God bears up the world. Thus did Jesus stoop and sweat great drops of blood in carrying the sins of the world.

CHAPTER THREE

Contents: Jehovah's controversy with Israel.

Conclusion: Judgment begins at the house of God. The nearer men are to God in profession, and the kinder notice God has taken of them, the more quickly and severely will He reckon with them if they by wilful sin disgrace their relation to Him. We cannot expect God to act for us unless we are reconciled to Him.

Key Word: Punishment, v. 2.

Strong Verses: 2, 3, 6.

Christ Seen: v. 6. We may profess to be walking with Christ, but we are not unless we agree with Him as to the sinfulness of sin, the need of cleansing, the hopelessness of our old nature.

CHAPTER FOUR

Contents: Threatening against the oppressors in Israel. Israel reminded of God's chastening in the past.

Conclusion: God designs all His providential rebukes to influence men to turn to Him. The reason God sends worse troubles is because former and lesser troubles have not done their work. If men continue obstinate, they force God to do what He does not willingly do, but what is necessary to bring men to their senses.

Key Word: Israel's stubbornness, vv. 6, 8, 9, 10, 11, 12.

Strong Verses: 12 (b), 13.

CHAPTER FIVE

Contents: God's lamentation over Israel and captivity foretold. The day of the Lord.

Conclusion: If men will not take a right course to obtain the favor of God, God will take an effectual course to make them feel the weight of His displeasure. Our transgressions do not pass Him unobserved, and He knows all hypocrisy in worship, and the punishment will be in proportion to the profession made.

Key Word: Lamentation, vv. 1, 16.

Strong Verses: 8, 9, 14, 15.

Christ Seen: vv. 22-23. Religious ceremonies are of no account with God, except as they express from the heart that for which they stand. "No man cometh to the Father but by Christ." Those ceremonies designed to set forth Christ are an abomination to God if the offerer does not from the heart recognize Christ in them and yield himself to Him. Though ritual sacrifices may be dispensed with, spiritual sacrifices in Christ cannot.

CHAPTER SIX

Contents: Woe pronounced upon those at ease in sin—abandoned by God.

Conclusion: Many are puffed up and rocked to sleep in carnal security by the position they occupy in the world—set upon their own pleasure and careless of the afflictions of others. Those who thus give themselves to mirth when God calls them to mourning will find it a sin that will be punished with terrible woes.

Key Word: Woe, v. 1.

Strong Verse: 1 (a).

Christ Seen: National dissolution is not far away when palaces are filled with riot, while the poor rot in neglect. Many professed followers of Christ are similarly "at ease," indifferent to their brother's woe. The best evidence of sonship in Christ is an active passion for His service.

CHAPTER SEVEN

Contents: Threatening judgments. The prophet's intercession no longer to prevail. Amos charged before the king and his answer.

Conclusion: God's patience, which has long been sinned against, will at length be sinned away—for to be often reprieved yet never reclaimed; often reduced to straits, yet never brought to God—is a great insult to God and merits His rejection. Those who have faithfully declared the counsel of God may expect to be misrepresented as enemies, and often by men in high religious standing.

Key Word: God-abandoned, v. 8.

Christ Seen: The prophet may here be taken as a type of our great Intercessor, but for whose intercession Christians would receive many just blows for their wrong doings.

CHAPTER EIGHT

Contents: The basket of summer fruit foretelling Israel's near ruin. Summary of the case against Israel.

Conclusion: The time of God's patience draws surely to a conclusion, and if men do not make an end of sin, God will make an end of them, even though they be His professing people. To continually trample under foot the Word of God will end in a famine of the Word of God, which in a time of trouble will be the sorest judgment.

Key Word: The end, v. 2.

Strong Verses: 7 (b), 11.

Christ Seen: This chapter may well remind us of another day that is coming (Mt. 13:30), when the harvest has come. Separation between good and bad is inevitable.

CHAPTER NINE

Contents: Final prophecy of dispersion of Israel and their ultimate restoration and blessing in the kingdom age.

Conclusion: The sword of war is the sword of divine vengeance, for God will thoroughly sift His people who ignore His constant pleadings. Evil is often nearest those who put it at the greatest distance from them (v. 10).

Key Word: Israel's sifting, v. 9.

Strong Verses: 6, 10. Promise: 11.

Christ Seen: vv. 11-15. The bringing again of dispersed Israel to their own land is the sure promise of God's Word. In the coming Kingdom of Christ, the Messiah, Israel shall take deep root in the world, never to be rooted out of it. They shall find in Him the happiness and rest they have so long sought, and God's favor shall again be with them to give abundance of all good things.

OBADIAH

Key Thought:	Number of Chapters:	Key Verse:	Christ seen as:
Edom	1	21	"The Lord in His Kingdom."

Writer of the Book:	Date:	Conclusion of the Book:
Obadiah	900-880 B. C.	We should take solemn warning against the perils of pride and anti-Semetism.

SUMMARY

CHAPTER ONE

Contents: Edom's humiliation because of sin against God's people.

Conclusion: If men in their pride and carnal security dare to challenge omnipotence, their challenge will be taken up, and God will promptly lay them low. God will not suffer men to be puffed up by the humiliation of His people, nor to gloat over them in their afflictions.

Key Word: Edom, v. 1.

Strong Verses: 4, 15.

Christ Seen: v. 17. Following the day of recompense, for which Christ is coming to the earth, the promise of deliverance and holiness for the people shall be fulfilled. The kingdoms of the world shall then become the kingdoms of the Lord and His Christ. Who will take to Himself great power, and reign.

JONAH

Key Thought:	Number of Chapters:	Key Verse:	Christ seen as:
Repentance	4	3:2	Risen Prophet

Writer of the Book:	Date:	Conclusion of the Book:
Jonah	825-790 B. C.	God is the God of the Gentiles as well as of the Jew.

SUMMARY

CHAPTER ONE

Contents: Jonah's commission and effort to avoid God's will. Swallowed by a great fish.

Conclusion: Men may be distinctly called of God to proclaim His message, yet refuse to obey, but indisposition to preach will not rid one of the obligation to preach. God will send His storms to teach the wisdom of obedience.

Key Word: Fleeing prophet—v. 3.

Strong Verse: 9.

Christ Seen: Typically Jonah foreshadows Israel out of their own land, a trouble to the Gentiles, cast out but miraculously preserved. In the future, in their hour of deep distress, they will cry out to God, will be delivered and will go forth to the Gentiles as originally commanded, announcing the kingdom of Christ at hand and His Second Coming.

CHAPTER TWO

Contents: Jonah's prayer out of the depths and its answer.

Conclusion: Though we bring affliction upon ourselves by our sins, yet if we pray in humility and godly sincerity, we shall be heard at the throne of grace and God will speak the word of deliverance.

Key Word: Prayer—v. 1.

Strong Verses: 1, 7, 8, 9(b).

Christ Seen: v. 10. Israel swallowed up by the Gentiles in the sea of the nations must go down to the "bottom" before they will cry out to God and look to the One they pierced as their Saviour. When that hour comes, the nations will vomit them out upon their own land, where they will come face to face with Christ.

CHAPTER THREE

Contents: Jonah's second commission. Ninevah's repentance because of his obedience.

Conclusion: Those who would not destroy their souls must afflict their souls. God threatens so He will not have to punish, and makes His judgments conditional upon true repentance. There is mercy for those who will, before it is too late, confess and forsake their sin.

Key Word: Repentance, vv. 8, 10.

Strong Verses: 2(b), 10.

Striking Facts: v. 10. God is unchangeable in character, but He may change His conduct toward men as they change their attitude toward Him. Repentance in man is a change of will. Repentance in God is God willing a change.

Christ Seen: v. 2. Suggests Christ's great commission to His disciples. Let His ambassadors know that they are not mere coiners of phrases, but that they have a message defined by the Lord Jesus Himself (Mt. 28:19-20), and are responsible to proclaim it, no matter how men may receive it.

CHAPTER FOUR

Contents: Jonah's displeasure over God's action toward Nineveh. The sheltering gourd.

Conclusion: Though there be those who find it in their hearts to quarrel with the goodness of God and His sparing, pardoning mercy to others (to which we all owe it that we are out of hell), yet God will justify Himself in the methods of His grace toward repenting sinners. As God values a human soul, so should we look upon it as worth more than all the world.

Key Word: Displeased, v. 1.

Strong Verses: 4, 2(b).

Christ Seen: Jonah (Matt. 12:40) is used as an illustrious type of Christ who was buried and arose (1 Cor. 15:4) after three days. As God prepared Jonah's grave, so He prepared Christ's. Both were buried in order to their rising again for the bringing of the doctrine of repentance to the Gentile world.

MICAH

Key Thought: Controversy	Number of Chapters: 7	Key Verse: 1:8-9	Christ seen as: The Bethlehemite

Writer of the Book: Micah	Date: 758-710 B. C.	Conclusion of the Book: God abhors injustice and ritualism. He takes delight in pardoning penitent sinners.

SUMMARY

CHAPTER ONE

Contents: Jehovah's case against Israel. Impending judgment.

Conclusion: There comes a time when men who have persisted in sin must face ruin without remedy. God cannot help them because they will not by repentance and reformation help themselves.

Key Word: Incurable, v. 9.

Strong Verses: 3, 4.

Christs Seen: vv. 6-16, describes the Syrian invasion. This gives rise to the prophecy of the greater invasion in the last days (4:9-13), and of Christ's deliverance at Armageddon (Rev. 16:14; 19:17).

CHAPTER TWO

Contents: Jehovah's case against Israel, continued. Future deliverance of a remnant.

Conclusion: Sinners cannot expect to rest in a land which they have polluted by their sins against God, for He will certainly cause it to spew them out with terrible judgments. With every threatening of judgment, however, there is a promise of mercy for a remnant who will acknowledge their King and walk in His ways.

Key Word: Sore destruction, v. 10.

Strong Verses: 1, 7.

Christ Seen: v. 13. Christ is the King Who will, after the great Armageddon, pass before Israel to bring them into the land of their rest. While there is in this age an election out of Israel, the promises of restoration to the land here given will only have their accomplishment at Christ's Second Coming.

CHAPTER THREE

Contents: Coming judgments of the captivities. The priests and prophets rebuked.

Conclusion: Men cannot expect to do ill and fare well simply because they are recognized as religious. The time will come when those who have shown no mercy shall have judgment without mercy, for God will hide His face when they are sorely in need of His favor.

Key Word: Israel's sin, v. 8.

Strong Verse: 4.

Christ Seen: v. 8. Oh, that every ambassador of Christ could utter the words of this verse. It is ours by the promise of Christ—Acts 1:8.

CHAPTER FOUR

Contents: The future kingdom of Christ on earth and Israel's happy regathering. Battle of Armageddon.

Conclusion: In the last days of the age, the Kingdom of Christ shall be manifested in the earth with a lustre no earth kingdom has ever had. It will be a kingdom universal, peaceful, prosperous, and of the increase of Christ's government, and peace there shall be no end. Israel, long dispersed and cast off, will have a place of glory in the earth, recognizing Christ as King and Lord.

Key Word: Mountain of the Lord, v. 1.

Promises: 1, 2, 3, 4, 5.

Christ Seen: vv. 1, 2. A mountain in Scripture is a symbol of great earth power (Dan. 2:35). The ultimate establishment of Christ's earthly kingdom is here foretold. Christ will be the King (v. 7) to protect and govern it and to order its affairs for the best to the end of time.

CHAPTER FIVE

Contents: The birth and rejection of Christ foretold. His ultimate eternal kingdom after His rejection.

Conclusion: Christ, who existed from eternity as Son of God, was to be born into the world as the child of woman, to be the Saviour of the world. Rejected, except by a remnant, He would await the consummation of the age, when He will be given a kingdom glorious to Himself; happy for His subjects; disastrous to sinners.

Key Word: Israel's ruler (Christ), v. 2.

Strong Verse: 2. Promise: 4.

Christ Seen: v. 2. See Isa. 7:13, 14; 9:6, 7. Note that the "child" was born in Bethlehem, but the "Son" was "from everlasting." Christ was pre-existent, else He could not have by His atonement made propitiation for the sin of the world.

CHAPTER SIX

Contents: Jehovah's controversy with Israel's past and present.

Conclusion: God issues a challenge to all who have ever professed belief in Him, but have wandered from Him, to testify against Him, if they have found His demands unreasonable, or if He has not fully paid His accounts. If our ceremonies be accepted of Him, they must be backed by lives conformed to His will and in communion with Him, for He cannot be deceived by external ceremonies. If professors of religion ruin themselves by sin, it will be the most terrible of any ruin.

Key Word: Controversy, v. 2.

Strong Verses: 3, 7, 8.

Christ Seen: v. 7. Sacrifices and ceremonies have their value from the reference they have to Christ, the great propitiation, but if the believer disregards their meaning, they are an abomination. Thousands of rams and rivers of oil cannot take the place of one little stream of the blood of Christ, the power of which is truly appropriated to the heart.

CHAPTER SEVEN

Contents: Israel's sad present condition. The voice of the remnant in the last days.

Conclusion: When a child of God has much occasion to cry "Woe is me"— when it seems that all flesh has corrupted their way—it is a great comfort that he has a God to look to, in Whom there is rejoicing and satisfaction always. He cannot but marvel at God's pardoning mercy to men and rejoice at the promise that He shall yet reign supreme in the earth.

Key Word: God, my salvation, v. 7.

Strong Verses: 7, 9, 18, 19.

Christ Seen: v. 19. The gracious God is ready, because of the sacrifice of His Son, to pardon and pass over the iniquity of His people upon their repentance and turning to Him. Let the pardoned sinner remember that if he has not been dealt with according to his deserts, it is because Jesus Christ bore his sins on the cross, and made it possible for God to put His sins in the depths of the sea.

NAHUM

Key Thought: Nineveh	Number of Chapters: 3	Key Verse: 1:8-9	Christ seen as: Bringer of Good Tidings.

Writer of the Book: Nahum	Date: About 660 B. C.	Conclusion of the Book: An awful doom awaits the apostate.

SUMMARY

CHAPTER ONE

Contents: Jehovah's holiness and power.   Nineveh's destruction forecasted.

Conclusion: The wrath of God is revealed from heaven against His enemies, and His favor and mercy are assured to His faithful, loyal subjects.   His mighty power makes His wrath very terrible and His favor very desirable.

Key Word: Vengeance, v. 2.

Strong Verses: 3, 7.

Christ Seen: v. 15.   These words are quoted by the apostle both from Isaiah and Nahum, and applied to the great redemption wrought by the Lord Jesus and the publishing of His gospel to the world (Romans 10:15).

CHAPTER TWO

Contents: The battle in the streets of Nineveh.

Conclusion: God has a quarrel with those who have done violence to His people, and when the measure of their iniquity is filled up, He will fill them with terror, while the fire of His indignation shall utterly consume all in which they have placed their confidence.

Key Word: Nineveh emptied, vv. 2, 10.

CHAPTER THREE

Contents: Nineveh reaps what it has sown—destruction and violence.

Conclusion: The people that have with their cruelties been a terror and destruction to others, will eventually have terror and destruction brought home to them.   They are but preparing to themselves terrible enemies against the day of their own fall.

Key Word: Woe, v. 1.

Christ Seen: The great lesson of Nahum is that the character of God makes Him not only a stronghold to all who trust Him, but One Who "will not at all acquit the wicked."   He can be "just and yet the justifier of him which believeth in Jesus" (Romans 3:26), but only because His law has been fully vindicated in the cross.

HABAKKUK

Key Thought: Faith	Number of Chapters: 3	Key Verse: 2:4	Christ seen as: The Lord in His Holy temple.

Writer of the Book: Habakkuk	Date: 608-590 B. C.	Conclusion of the Book: God is perfectly consistent with Himself, even though evil is long permitted.

SUMMARY

CHAPTER ONE

Contents: Habakkuk's prayer concerning evil in dispersed Israel. God's voice to Israel and Habakkuk's testimony to God.

Conclusion: We must not think it strange if God sometimes suffers wickedness to prevail far and to prosper long, for He has good reasons for His attitude, and He cannot be the author or patron of sin. He takes full account of all sin committed, and will surely make men answer for it in His own time.

Key Word: Israel's iniquity, v. 3.

Strong Verses: 12, 13.

Christ Seen: v. 5. Acts 13:37-41 interprets this prediction of the redemptive work of Christ with Israel in dispersion. God did "work a work" which Israel did not believe. Paul quoted this to the Jews of the dispersion in the synagogue at Antioch.

CHAPTER TWO

Contents: Jehovah's response to Habakkuk's testimony. Vision of coming woes.

Conclusion: The lusts of the flesh, the lusts of the eye and the pride of life are the entangling snare of men, which, if yielded to, bring woes upon them. Those who will not be taught the knowledge of God's glory by the judgments of His mouth will be made to bear the judgments of His hand.

Key Word: Woe, vv. 9, 12, 15, 19.

Strong Verses: 4, 12, 15, 20. Promise: 14.

Striking Facts: v. 14. Isa. 11:9 fixes the time when the earth will be filled with the knowledge of the glory of the Lord—when the Righteous Branch of David, Christ, has come and set up His kingdom. The knowledge of the "glory" of the Lord cannot be until He is manifested in glory (Matt. 24:30; 25:31; Luke 9:26; 2 Thess. 1:7; 2:8; Jude 14).

CHAPTER THREE

Contents: Habakkuk's answer of faith to Jehovah. The terror of God's wrath against sinners.

Conclusion: The God of nature can alter and control all the powers of nature to make earth, sea and heavenly bodies carry out the purposes of His judgment against sinners, or for the salvation of His people. His true children can, in the midst of earth's distresses, rejoice in Him Who is the God of their eternal salvation, since by them, their salvation cannot be hindered but only furthered.

Key Word: Jehovah's wrath, vv. 2, 8.

Strong Verses: 2(b), 18, 19.

Christ Seen: vv. 17-19. This sublime refrain has been the solace of many who have suffered for Christ's sake. If all God's gifts fail, we still possess the divine Saviour and eternal salvation in Him.

His presence is often more apparent when the fields are bare, and we have no one else to whom we can turn.

ZEPHANIAH

Key Thought:	Number of Chapters:	Key Verse:	Christ seen as:
Remnant	3	1:4; 3:13	The Lord in Israel's midst.

Writer of the Book:	Date:	Conclusion of the Book:
Zephaniah	639-609 B. C.	Our God is a jealous God.

SUMMARY

CHAPTER ONE

Contents: Coming judgment on Judah prefiguring the coming day of the Lord.

Conclusion: Those who will not improve the presence of God with them as a Father, may expect His presence with them as a Judge, to call them to account for all their contempt of His grace. The day of His wrath will strip sinners of all that they have and will leave them nothing but distress and pain with no way of helping themselves.

Key Word: Day of wrath, v. 15.

Strong Verse: 18.

Christ Seen: vv. 7, 14. The day of the Lord here is a small specimen of the great "day" that is to come, in which all earth judgments will culminate, to be followed by Israel's restoration and blessing under Christ.

CHAPTER TWO

Contents: Call to remnant of Israel in the day of the Lord. Judgment threatened upon Assyria, Philistia and other nations.

Conclusion: The nations that rebel against the precepts of God's Word have the threatenings of His Word against them, and the effect will be no less than their total destruction in the day of His fierce anger. It concerns each one to make it sure to themselves that they shall be hid in the day of God's wrath, in a hiding place of God's providing.

Key Word: Jehovah's anger, v. 2.

Strong Verse: 3.

Christ Seen: v. 3. The only safe hiding place from the wrath of God against sin is the righteousness of Christ (1 Cor. 1:30; Rom. 10:1-3). To be "hid with Christ in God" (Col. 3:2) is to be in the chambers of safety.

CHAPTER THREE

Contents: Jerusalem's moral state in time of Zephaniah. The coming judgment of nations and kingdom blessing for restored Israel.

Conclusion: The end of nations that have continued to be of the earth and of the devil, when Christ comes to set up His kingdom, shall be destruction. The reproach of Israel shall then be removed, and all who are permitted to enter that Kingdom will have occasion, with all their hearts, to eternally rejoice in Him, for God will have forever removed calamities from them, the noise of war will be silenced, sinful nature put under control and God and His Christ made all in all.

Key Word: Judgment of nations, v. 8. (Kingdom blessing, 14-20.)

Strong Verse: 8. Promises: 9, 17.

Christ Seen: v. 15. It is the Lord Jesus, the rejected and glorified King, Who will be in the midst forever, to receive the homage of His subjects and to give out His favors.

HAGGAI

Key Thought: Build	Number of Chapters: 2	Key Verse: 1:8	Christ seen as: The Desire of all nations.

Writer of the Book: Haggai	Date: About 520 B. C.	Conclusion of the Book: God demands first place in life and in service.

SUMMARY

CHAPTER ONE

Contents: Jehovah's chastening because of the interrupted work on His house. The work on the temple recommenced.

Conclusion: Those are strangers to their own interests who prefer the conveniences and ornaments of the temporal life before the carrying on of God's work in the community. If we would have the real comfort and continuance of temporal enjoyments, we should make God our friend by putting His interests first, otherwise that which we gain is put into a bag with holes.

Key Word: Temple, vv. 2, 14.

Strong Verses: 6, 7.

CHAPTER TWO

Contents: The various temples. Chastening because of priest's impurity and the peoples' delay. Future destruction of Gentile power.

Conclusion: If we take no care of the interests of God's work, we cannot expect that He should take care of all our interests. If we are employed in His work, we should be jealous over ourselves, lest we spoil it by going about it with unsanctified hearts and hands.

Key Word: Jehovah's house, v. 3.

Strong Verses: 6, 8. Promises: 7, 9.

Christ Seen: v. 7. Christ is the desire of all nations, for in Him shall all the families of the earth be blessed with the best of blessings. The shaking of nations will take place in the great Tribulation, which will be followed by Christ's coming in glory.

ZECHARIAH

Key Thought:	Number of Chapters:	Key Verse:	Christ seen as:
God's Ways	14	8:2	Prophet, Priest and King.

Writer of the Book:	Date:	Conclusion of the Book:
Zechariah	520 B. C.	The infinite care and love of God is over His people through the centuries.

SUMMARY

CHAPTER ONE

Contents: Zechariah's symbolic visions, warning of Jehovah's displeasure with the nations.

Conclusion: The judgments of God which those who went before us were under should be taken as warnings not to tread in their steps. A speedy reformation, while the mercy of God is extended, is the only way to prevent an approaching ruin.

Key Word: Jehovah's displeasure, vv. 2, 12, 15.

Strong Verse: 3.

Christ Seen: v. 17. The visions reveal Judah in dispersion, Jerusalem under adverse possession, and the Gentile nations at rest about it, the conditions that have prevailed throughout the present age. God's answer to the angel's intercession sweeps on to the end time, when the Lord shall yet comfort by the return of Christ in glory.

CHAPTER TWO

Contents: Visions of Zechariah. Jerusalem in the kingdom age.

Conclusion: Jerusalem is the apple of Jehovah's eye, jealously guarded by His angels and marked out for a glorious place in the earth in the day when Christ returns to dwell among men upon the earth.

Key Word: Jerusalem, v. 2.

Strong Verse: 8. Promises: 10, 11.

Christ Seen: v. 11. He Whom the Lord of Hosts will send in the latter days to dwell among men can be no other than the Lord Jesus. All nations will at that time own Him as the one sent of Jehovah, which was not fulfilled in His first coming.

CHAPTER THREE

Contents: Visions of Zechariah. Joshua and Satan before the angel of the Lord. Jehovah's servant, The Branch.

Conclusion: By the guilt of our sins we are obnoxious to God's justice, and by the power of our sins we are odious to His holiness. Those who would belong to Christ will be enabled to cast off the filthy rags of corrupt affections and lusts, and will be clothed with the spotless robe of His righteousness. Only such can He place in positions of honor and trust in His service.

Key Word: Garments, v. 3.

Strong Verse: 4. Promise: 7.

Christ Seen: v. 8. Christ is the "Servant, the Branch," Who was long hid, but in the fullness of time was brought forth into the world. His beginning was as a tender branch, but He will yet become a great tree filling the earth.

CHAPTER FOUR

Contents: Vision of the golden candlestick and two olive trees. Zerubbabel designated to finish the temple.

Conclusion: God will carry on and complete His work, not by human might or power, but by the power of His Spirit, working in those designated and called by Him. For those thus called, all difficulties shall be gotten over.

Key Word: Temple's completion, v. 9.
Strong Verse: 6 (b).
Christ Seen: v. 14. Some think Christ and the Holy Spirit are here meant.
From Christ, the olive tree, by the Spirit, the olive branch, all the golden
oil of grace is communicated to believers.

CHAPTER FIVE

Contents: Vision of the flying roll and the ephah.
Conclusion: God's holy law reveals the righteous wrath of God against those
who by swearing, affront God's majesty and who by stealing, set aside
their neighbor's rights.
Key Word: Curse, v. 3.

CHAPTER SIX

Contents: Vision of the four chariots. The symbolic crowning of Joshua.
Conclusion: Following the day when God's judgments go forth to all the
earth, Christ shall be manifested in His kingdom glory as the Priest-King
on His own throne.
Key Word: The Branch, v. 12.
Promises: 12, 13.
Christ Seen: v. 13. Christ is now a Priest, but still in the holiest within
the veil (Lev. 16:15; Heb. 9:11-14, 24), seated on the Father's throne
(Rev. 3:21). He will yet sit upon His own throne (Heb. 9:28), a Priest
—upon His throne.

CHAPTER SEVEN

Contents: The mission from Babylon, and Jehovah's answer to the question
of fasts. Why prayer was not answered.
Conclusion: When we offer up our requests to God, it must be with readiness
to receive instructions from Him. God is not made men's debtor by fasts
which are not observed with self-examination and a purpose to put away
their sins.
Key Word: Fasts, v. 5.
Strong Verses: 9, 10, 13.

CHAPTER EIGHT

Contents: Jehovah's unchanging purpose to restore Jerusalem and bless
Israel in the Kingdom.
Conclusion: Jerusalem, the city of God, and Israel, the people of God, have
God to plead their cause until the day when the dispersion shall be ended,
Israel again is made fruitful, and Jerusalem a praise in the earth. In
that day all men shall honor a Jew as one of the chosen people of God.
Key Word: Zion's restoration, vv. 2, 12.
Strong Verses: 16, 17, 22. Promise: 23.
Christ Seen: In the days after the coming of Christ in glory, Jerusalem
will be made the center of earth's worship, and the Jew will be the mis-
sionary to all nations, bearing the messages of Christ.

CHAPTER NINE

Contents: Burden upon the cities surrounding Palestine. Christ presented
as King-Savior in His first advent.
Conclusion: Christ, Israel's King, Who came as the meek and lowly One,
riding upon an ass, will yet be recognized by Israel, and will bring them
deliverance, slay all enmities and extend His kingdom to all the earth.
Key Word: Zion's King, v. 9.
Strong Verse: 9. Promise: 10.
Christ Seen: v. 9. Having introduced the King, which was Christ in vv.
9-10, the verses which follow look to the end time and the kingdom when
He will come in glory. Except in v. 9, the present age is not seen in
Zechariah.

CHAPTER TEN

Contents: The future strengthening of Judah and Ephraim. Israel's dispersion and regathering in one view.
Conclusion: God has a hand in all the events concerning Israel, and they shall
finally have His favor and presence, being owned and accepted of Him.
The people long dispersed shall be brought together, purified and strengthened in the Lord.

Key Word: Israel's strengthening, vv. 6, 10, 12.

Promise: 12.

Christ Seen: v. 12. It is Christ Whom Israel will recognize as the crucified King, Who will strengthen them, and cause them to bestir themselves to go up and down the land in His name.

CHAPTER ELEVEN

Contents: First advent of Christ foretold and His rejection. God's wrath against Israel as the result. The rise of anti-Christ and his judgment.

Conclusion: Those who will not open the door to let the King in, but sell Him for a paltry price, will sooner or later have to open the door to let ruin in. (This is the desperate case of Israel in the present age.)

Key Word: Jehovah's wrath, v. 6.

Strong Verses: 12, 13.

Christ Seen: v. 7. Beauty and Bands—literally "graciousness and union" —signifying God's attitude toward Israel in sending His Son (Matt. 21:37), and His purpose to reunite Israel (Ezek. 37:15-22). Christ in His first advent came with grace (John 1:17) to offer union (Matt. 4:17), but was sold for 30 pieces of silver (vv. 12, 13). Beauty (graciousness) was thereby "cut in sunder." Bands (union) was broken, God's purpose to reunite Israel being for this age abandoned.

CHAPTER TWELVE

Contents: Jerusalem's coming siege by the Beast and his armies. Deliverance of Judah by the Lord Himself. The Spirit poured out and the pierced One recognized.

Conclusion: Jerusalem, following the awful days of the end-time, shall be repeopled and replenished, but it will not be until Christ returning in glory is recognized by Israel as He whom they have pierced. He will put down all enemies and work a gracious work in His people.

Key Word: Jerusalem's Deliverer, v. 10.

Promise: 10.

Christ Seen: v. 10. The pouring out of the Spirit upon all who receive the Crucified One as Lord and Saviour in the present age is an earnest of what Israel shall receive when Christ's Kingdom comes.

CHAPTER THIRTEEN

Contents: Repentant remnant of Israel in the last days. Refined by great tribulation. Israel again restored to God's favor.

Conclusion: Israel, at the end of the age, will pass through a period of fiery trial for purification, after which they will find Christ to be the Lamb slain for the putting away of sin. Their sin and uncleanness finally put away, they shall be restored to Jehovah's favor.

Key Word: Israel's refining, vv. 1, 9.

Strong Verse: 6. **Promise:** 1.

Chrsit Seen: v. 1. The fountain opened is the pierced side of Jesus Christ. for thence came there out blood and water—precious blood, the price of our redemption. Those who now look to Christ pierced are saved—but this Israel does not see and will not until His Second Coming (v. 6).

CHAPTER FOURTEEN

Contents: The return of Christ. Armageddon. The changes in Palestine. The kingdom established on earth.

Conclusion: In the last days, Christ shall return in glory, His feet touching in that day upon the Mount of Olives. All opposing powers shall be put down, Israel shall be gloriously established, Christ shall be owned by all as King and Lord forever, and all men will serve and worship in the beauty of holiness.

Key Word: Kingdom, v. 9.

Strong Verses: 4, 9, 20.

Christ Seen: v. 9. The prayer (Matt. 6:10) "Thy kingdom come, Thy will be done on earth as it is in heaven," will have its final answer in the coming of the King in the power of His might. It will not be a spiritual and gradual coming, the effects of preaching, but a personal, literal coming in the clouds of heaven (v. 4).

MALACHI

Key Thought:	Number of Chapters:	Key Verse:	Christ seen as:
Robbery	4	3:8	Sun of Righteousness

Writer of the Book:	Date:	Conclusion of the Book:
Malachi	440-410 B. C.	Remember Jehovah, repent toward Him, return to Him and render to Him that which is His due.

SUMMARY

CHAPTER ONE

Contents: Jehovah's love for Israel. The sins of the priests and hypocrisy of the people.

Conclusion: God would have His people know that He loves them, therefore justly takes it very ill to have His favors slighted and His ordinances partaken of in hypocrisy. Those who come to holy ordinances irreverently, going away from them never the better, and under no concern, in effect say, "The table of the Lord is contemptible."

Key Word: Jehovah's displeasure, vv. 10, 13.

Strong Verse: 13.

CHAPTER TWO

Contents: The message to the priests concerning their sins. The evils among the people.

Conclusion: Woe to those appointed to be God's mouth to the people, but who instead are a stone of stumbling. All who rest in external performances of religion will not only come short of acceptance with God in them, but will be filled with shame and confusion.

Key Word: Israel's abominations, v. 11.

Strong Verses: 7, 10, 17.

Christ Seen: v. 10. Cp. Acts 17:24-29. The reference in both instances is to God as "Father of our spirits"—or creation. It has no reference to salvation. "We are children of God by faith in Christ Jesus."

CHAPTER THREE

Contents: Mission of John the Baptist, and Christ's first advent foretold. Israel exhorted to return to God.

Conclusion: Those who deny God His part of their estates may justly expect a curse upon their own part of them. Those who rob God rob themselves of His benefits and protection. In view of the imminence of Christ's coming, we should see to it that our accounts with God are balanced.

Key Word: Return, vv. 7, 18.

Strong Verse: 1. Promises: 10, 11, 17.

Christ Seen: v. 1. The first "messenger" is a prophecy of the appearing of the forerunner, John the Baptist (Matt. 11:10; Mark 1:2), which Isaiah had foretold (40:3). "The messenger of the covenant" is Christ Himself, but for its final fulfillment looks to the second coming of Christ, the messenger having been rejected at His first advent. His sudden coming to the temple, connected with judgment, awaits fulfillment (Heb. 2:20). Malachi, like other O. T. prophets, saw both advents of Messiah blended in one horizon, but not the separating interval.

CHAPTER FOUR

Contents: The day of the Lord and coming of Christ as "sun of righteousness." Elijah to be forerunner of the day of the Lord.

Conclusion: The great day of the Lord is impending, a time of terror and destruction upon all whose hearts have been stout against God, but followed by the coming of Christ as the sun of righteousness with healing in His wings for all who have looked to Him. "Come quickly, Lord Jesus."

Key Word: Day of the Lord, v. 5.

Strong Verses: 1, 2.

Christ Seen: v. 2. The Old Testatment closes with the promise of the rising of the "sun" of righteousness. The New Testament closes with the promise of the rising of the "morning star" (Rev. 22:16). The morning star precedes the coming of the sun, which finally ushers in the day. Christ is coming to the Church as the "morning star" in the last dark hours of the age (1 Thess. 4:13-16—prior to the great tribulation). At the close of the tribulation He is coming as the "sun" ushering in the Millennial day, and Israel's history will then be resumed.

NEW TESTAMENT

MATTHEW

Key Thought:	Number of Chapters:	Key Verse:	Christ seen as:
Savior of the Jews	28	27:37	King and Savior of the Jews.

Writer of the Book:	Date:	Conclusion of the Book:
Matthew	A. D. 37	Jesus, the Messiah-King, was rejected and killed but His wounding was for our transgressions, and He was bruised for our iniquities. He is coming again to rule and judge.

SUMMARY

CHAPTER ONE

Contents: Generations of Jesus Christ. His conception and birth.

Conclusion: Jesus Christ was, in accordance with the prophecies, conceived of the Holy Ghost, born of a virgin. He was both Son of Man and Son of God, thereby being qualified to save His people from their sins.

Key Word: Genealogy, vv. 1, 17.

Strong Verses: 21, 22, 23.

Christ Seen: v. 10. See Gen. 3:15; Isa. 7:14, 8:8, 10; Mic. 5:2, 3. Jesus was not begotten of natural generation. Note v. 16, "Mary, of whom was born Jesus." A feminine form for the word "born" being used, indicates that Jesus was born of Mary, not of man. He was without a sinful nature, for the reason that He had the Holy Spirit for His Father.

CHAPTER TWO

Contents: Visit of the Magi, flight into Egypt, Herod's slaughter of the innocents. Return of Joseph and Mary to Nazareth.

Conclusion: The light of the Scriptures and the light of nature are calculated to lead the seeking soul to Christ, the Savior. Those who follow their light to Him will find in Him joy unspeakable. Those who spurn their light will have in this life only dread of Him and hereafter naught but misery.

Key Word: Star of Bethlehem, vv. 2, 9, 10.

Strong Verses: 6, 9, 10, 11.

Christ Seen: v. 12. This is the first of 21 unsuccessful attempts on the life of Jesus which mark the enmity of Satan and his desire to cut Him off before His appointed work could be done. That enmity was manifested in O. T. times against the royal line, and now that Christ's sacrifice has been made, it is shown in the blinding of the hearts of men lest they see Him as their Savior, and against Christians that their testimony for Him might be hindered.

CHAPTER THREE

Contents: Ministry of John the Baptist and baptism of Jesus.

Conclusion: To follow Jesus in the waters of baptism is to publicly acknowledge our separation from sin, determination to bring forth fruit unto God, and consecration to His service.

Key Word: Baptism, vv. 6, 13.

Strong Verses: 8, 16, 17.

Christ Seen: When John announced (v. 2) the "kingdom of the heavens at hand," he announced that the Christian dispensation was the next thing to come. He presented Jesus not as King Who would at that time set up

His earthly throne, but as "the Lamb of God that taketh away the sins of the world" (the true prophetic order). By Israel's rejection of Him as such they have been nationally set aside until the "fullness of the Gentiles be come in," after which Jesus as King will return to earth in glory to rule. (Matt. 24:29; 25:46; Luke 19:12-19; Acts 15:14-17.)

CHAPTER FOUR

Contents: Temptation of Jesus. Jesus' public ministry begun. Call of first disciples.

Conclusion: The Word of God is the Sword of the Spirit, which if rightly handled, will deal defeat to Satan in his attempts to snare the believer by tempting suggestions. Beware of Satanic twisting of Scripture—"rightly divide the Word of Truth."

Key Word: Temptation.

Strong Verses: 4, 10. Promise: 6.

Christ Seen: v. 1. It is sometimes asked "If Jesus was without a sinful nature, how could He be tempted?" May not a city be besieged, though impregnable? Acid will corrode some metals—others it will not. The devil applied his test to Christ—it did not corrode. Note comparison of Jesus' temptations with those of the first Adam. (1). Gen. 3:6 lust of the flesh (tree good for food); Jesus to turn stones into bread. (2). Lust of the eyes (tree pleasant to the eyes); Jesus—glory of kingdoms of the earth—to take them in a way not appointed by the Father. (3). Pride of the life—(desired to make one wise); Jesus—to throw Himself from pinnacle to be hailed by crowds below as the long expected Messiah.

CHAPTER FIVE

Contents: Sermon on the mount. Beatitudes. Believer as salt and light. Christ's relation to the law. Divorce.

Conclusion: The relationship of a child of God will be manifested in the world by his shining and burning as a light for Christ, by his quiet and savory influence in society, and by his conformity to the Word of God in all things.

Key Word: Sermon on the Mount, vv. 1, 2.

Strong Verses: 16 (b), 18, 28, 32, 39, 44, 48. Promises: 3-12.

Christ Seen: v. 3. Some teach that Christ's words in the sermon on the mount are applicable only to the future earthly kingdom of Christ, not the present age, and as such are postponed until Christ's second coming. However we think of the "kingdom of the heavens" as the church age, during which Christ, through regeneration, is peopling the heavens, and these principles seem to have clearer application to the present age than to that time when righteousness shall cover the earth as the waters cover the sea.

CHAPTER SIX

Contents: Sermon on the Mount, continued. Formalism condemned. The new revelation of prayer (disciples prayer). The law of riches. Cure of anxiety.

Conclusion: True relationship to God will be manifested by a motive of heart devotion to God back of all charity to men, by absolute sincerity and humility in the prayer life, by laying up heavenly treasures and by absolute confidence in the Heavenly Father to supply all real needs and overcome all troubling circumstances.

Key Word: Sermon on the Mount, 5:2.

Prayer, 6:5.

Strong Verses: 1, 8, 9-13, 19, 20, 21, 34. Promises: 6, 14, 33.

Christ Seen: vv. 8-13. Rather than the "Lord's prayer," this should be designated as "the diciple's prayer," for Jesus could not pray this prayer as the expression of His own needs. It is a Christian's prayer beginning "Our Father."

The work of the cross, which at the time the prayer was given, was yet future, should be thought into this prayer. It is a model of what true prayer is—(1) Puts the Father's interest before personal interests. (2) Puts earthly needs in right proportion to spiritual needs. (3) Bases prayer upon relationship. (4) Trusts God for present needs, not worrying about the morrow.

CHAPTER SEVEN

Contents: Sermon on the Mount, continued. Encouragement to prayer. The two ways Warnings against false teachers. Danger of profession without faith. The two foundations.

Conclusion: True disciples of Christ will be men and women cautious in their judgment of others; conscious of their own faults; confident and earnest in prayer; wary of false teachers and hypocritical profession; building all eternal hopes upon the firm Rock, faith in the Word of God and Christ Jesus.

Key Word: Sermon on the Mount, 5:2. (Two ways, vv. 13, 24, 26.)

Strong Verses: 1, 2, 12, 15, 21, 24. Promises: 7, 8.

Christ Seen: v. 22 shows that there will be among those rejected by Christ in the last days, many preachers, so-called soul winners and good moral men, simply because devoid of true faith in Christ Who alone is the foundation of salvation. Beware of mere lip-devotion to Christ which signifies nothing, either here or hereafter.

CHAPTER EIGHT

Contents: Jesus heals a leper, the centurion's servant and Peter's wife's mother. Professed disciples tested. Stilling of the waves. Casting-out demons at Gadara.

Conclusion: Jesus is the divine Son of God, sovereign over all physical ailments, over all circumstances, over the powers of nature, over the evil emissaries of Satan and over sin (9:5). Faith takes Him at His word and finds rest and deliverance at all times in His Word of power.

Key Word: Sovereign Christ, vv. 17, 27.

Strong Verses: 13 (a), 27.

Christ Seen: v. 29. Men may deny the deity of Christ, but demons know better. His divine Sonship is proven amply by the demonstration of His power in all spheres. He was not only Son of God, but Son of Man (vv. 20, 24) and having been subjected to all human testings, He became a perfect sacrifice and substitute for the believer on the Cross.

CHAPTER NINE

Contents: Healing of the palsied man. Call of Matthew. Answering the Pharisees. Healing of woman with issue of blood. Daughter of a ruler raised from the dead. Two blind men healed. A demon cast out. Preaching and healing in Galilee.

Conclusion: All power is given unto Jesus Christ, both in heaven and in earth. Degradation and disease, demons and death are subject to His rebuke, and faith in Him is the most priceless treasure on earth. vv. 2, 22, 29.

Key Word: Power, vv. 6, 8.

Strong Verses: 6, 12, 13, 37, 38.

Christ Seen: v. 3. Either Christ was the Son of God with power to forgive sins and those who claim He is a mere man with no such power, are themselves blasphemers—or else He was, as they charged, a blasphemer. His deity is fully established by His deliverances from sin, and the consciousness of forgiveness which He has given to millions of people throughout the age.

CHAPTER TEN

Contents: The twelve instructed and sent out.

Conclusion: The call of Jesus to His service is His enabling for that service. He stands with His servants in all their trials, takes notice of every insult they are called upon to endure, honors them in this life for their witness of Him and will abundantly reward them in the next life for all their faithfulness. No cross, no crown. No gall, no glory.

Key Word: Calling and enduement, v. 1.

Strong Verses: 16, 24, 25, 28, 30, 33, 37. Promises: 32, 37, 42.

Christ Seen: v. 32. Confession of Christ is the normal answer of a new born soul to God. "Out of the abundance of the heart the mouth speaketh." To evidence the sincerity of our faith by boldly witnessing for Him gives us One in heaven Who speaks a good word to the Father for us.

CHAPTER ELEVEN

Contents: Answer to questions sent Jesus by John the Baptist. Judgment predicted as result of rejection of Christ. Rest for individuals who put their trust in Him.

Conclusion: The miracles of Christ are the seal of heaven upon Him, evincing His divine commission, and proving to this day the truth of His doctrine. Those who will not be prejudiced against Him nor scandalized in Him, cannot but be blessed in Him. Those who will be yoked with Him in His burdens, will by Him, be lifted out of all their burdens.

Key Word: Offended in Christ, vv. 6, 19, 25.

Strong Verses: 6, 25, 30. Promises: 28, 29.

Christ Seen: v. 28. This is a pivotal point in the ministry of Jesus. The Savior-King being spurned by the Jews, now offers rest and service to all who are conscious of their need. To these He will GIVE rest (peace with God, Rom. 5:1, the rest of salvation), and in His service they shall continually FIND rest (the peace of God, Phil. 4:7).

CHAPTER TWELVE

Contents: Jesus announces Himself Lord of Sabbath. Controversy with Pharisees. Healing of the withered hand. A demoniac healed. The unpardonable sin. Death and resurrection foretold. Deficiency of self-reformation. Jesus' new relationships.

Conclusion: Jesus Christ is Lord of the Sabbath day, giving us the true example of the acceptable use of that day, spending it with and for God.

Ascribing the word which Christ does in the power of the Holy Spirit to Satan, is a sin unpardonable here or hereafter.

Key Word: Lord of Sabbath, v. 8.

Strong Verses: 8, 30, 32, 36, 50.

Christ Seen: The Sabbath (v. 1) commemorates a finished creation. The Lord's day (see v. 40) commemorates a finished redemption, for Christ arose from the grave on the first day. The seventh day was a day of legal obligation. The first day is a day of voluntary worship.

CHAPTER THIRTEEN

Contents: Mysteries of the Kingdom of Heaven. The sower, tares and wheat, grain of mustard seed, leaven, hid treasure, pearl, drag net.

Conclusion: The present age will be marked to its end by the presence of both professors of religion and possessors—sinners and saints. The believer's work is to sow the Word of God in faith, not expecting thereby to convert the whole world, but in expectation of Him, Who at the end of the age, will come with His angels to separate the good and the bad—to make an end of sinners and set up His glorious Kingdom.

Key Word: Kingdom mysteries, v. 11.

Strong Verses: 12, 41, 42.

Christ Seen: Some make the parables of the mustard seed and the leaven to teach the conversion of the whole world to Christ in this age by the preaching of the gospel. This view is explicitly contradicted by Jesus' interpretation of the parables of the wheat and tares and the drag net—therefore there is something wrong with the popular interpretation of the leaven and mustard seed. Leaven means "corruption" and is always used in Scripture as a symbol of evil. The mustard seed parable pictures an abnormal and unsubstantial growth of the outward church. See Dan. 4:20-22.

CHAPTER FOURTEEN

Contents: Herod's troubled conscience and the murder of John the Baptist. The 5000 fed. Jesus walks on the water.

Conclusion: That will be multiplied and blessed to the service of men which is by faith passed through the hands of Christ. Faith and love with little can do much. (v. 18.) The steps of faith fall on a seeming void but always find a rock. No sea is too rough on which to venture if the eyes are on Christ and He has bidden us "come" (vv. 29, 30).

Key Word: Lord of nature, vv. 18, 25, 33.

Strong Verses: 18, 27.

Christ Seen: Note v. 33. The sure cure for the unitarian belief about Christ, is to be out on a boisterous sea where no human power can help, and then see Him come forth to quiet the boisterous winds and save the sinking soul.

CHAPTER FIFTEEN

Contents: Scribes and Pharisees rebuked. Syrophonecian's daughter healed. The multitude healed. 4000 fed.

Conclusion: The Christian life is not a label to put on, but a life to be put in; not a system of doctrine to be quibbled about but a great principle to be lived out. Genuine faith overcomes all obstacles. His compassion meets all needs.

Key Word: Hypocrites, v. 7.

Strong Verses: 8, 28.

Christ Seen: v. 28. This was the first time the rejected Christ ministered to a Gentile (cf. Matt. 12:18). When a Gentile addressed Him as "Son of David" (v. 22) He made no reply, but when she acknowledged Him as "Lord," He answered immediately (v. 25). The Gentile has no claim under the covenant rights and promises of Israel.

CHAPTER SIXTEEN

Contents: Jesus' rebuke of blind Pharisees. The symbol of leaven interpreted. Peter's confession of the deity of Jesus. Jesus foretells His death and resurrection.

Conclusion: Jesus is the Son of God, the foundation stone of the church. He died for the sin of the world, arose for the justification of the believer and is coming back in glory to reward His own. The cross of Calvary was God's program for Him, essential for the salvation of men and all attempts to turn Him from it were Satan-inspired (as are all denials of its necessity today).

Key Word: Deity (v. 16); Death (v. 21); Resurrection (vv. 4, 21); Descent (v. 27).

Strong Verses: 15, 24, 26.

Christ Seen: Note vv. 17, 18. Jesus does not here infer that the church was to be built upon Peter but upon Himself, as just confessed by Peter (v. 16) (Cf. 1 Peter 2:4-9). In the Greek, the word "Petra" is in feminine form, denoting that the reference was not to Peter, but to his confession. The deity of Christ is the foundation doctrine of Christianity.

CHAPTER SEVENTEEN

Contents: The transfiguration of Jesus Christ. The powerless disciples, unable to heal a lunatic, and the mighty Christ. Resurrection again foretold. Miracle of the tribute money.

Conclusion: Jesus Christ is sealed of heaven as the beloved Son of God, glorious and mighty in His person, possessed of all power in heaven and earth, the Victor over death and the grave, yet to reign in glory. Genuine faith in Him and yieldedness to His power, moves the arm of omnipotence.

Key Word: Transfiguration, v. 2. Faith, v. 20.

Strong Verse: 5. Promise: 20.

Christ Seen: The transfiguration is the answer to v. 28 of the preceding chapter. In it, we see in miniature, the elements of the coming earthly Kingdom of Christ. Jesus in His glory (v. 2); Moses standing for believers who have passed on through death (v. 3); Elijah representing those who will be translated (v. 3. Cf. 1 Thess. 4:14-17); Three disciples representing Israel in the flesh at His coming; Gentiles at foot of mountain for the living nations. It was given just following the announcement which disappointed the disciples, His rejection and death, and was for their encouragement.

CHAPTER EIGHTEEN

Contents: Sermon on the child text. Discipline in the church. Unity in prayer. Law of forgiveness.

Conclusion: Those are truly great who are truly humble and good, and God is pleased with those who multiply their pardons of others, even as they have many times been pardoned by Him.

Key Word: Greatness, v. 1. Forgiveness, v. 21.

Strong Verses: 3, 4, 11, 21, 22. Promises: 19, 20.
Christ Seen: v. 20. Where His saints are, there is the sanctuary of Christ. While as to His person He is in heaven, His Spirit is with our spirits, and He is the central figure in every gathering for prayer in His name. Not a multitude, but faith and sincere devotion on the part of worshippers, even though there be but two or three, invites His presence and the manifestation of His power among them.

CHAPTER NINETEEN

Contents: Christ and the divorce question. Little children blessed. The rich young ruler. Apostles' future place in the Kingdom.
Conclusion: God Himself instituted the relationship between husband and wife, and those joined together by the ordinance of God are not to be put asunder by an ordinance of man, except for fornication. Nothing less than the almighty grace of God can enable a man taken up with the riches of this world to get into heaven. Riches, if they are under our feet, are stepping stones, but if upon our backs, are a curse.
Key Word: Divorce, v. 7. Riches, v. 24.
Strong Verses: 6. 9, 14, 24, 26 (b). Promise: 29.
Christ Seen: vv. 16, 17. It is not implied that Jesus was not good (John 8:46; 14:30), but that He would not be called "good" by one who did not accept His deity, but looked upon Him merely as a man (Master—"teacher") and put himself on the same level (v. 20). As God (v. 17) He is the expression of all good.

CHAPTER TWENTY

Contents: Parables of laborers in the vineyard. Jesus' death and resurrection again foretold. Ambitious requests of James and John. Healing of the two blind men.
Conclusion: One hour's service in the spirit of humble trust will be as abundantly rewarded as 12 hours of legal service where reward is sought as a matter of debt. The way to true greatness is to be humble and serviceable with an eye continually to the great pattern servant, Jesus, Who came into the world not to be waited upon but to wait upon others and give His life a ransom.
Key Word: Service, vv. 1, 27.
Strong Verses: 16, 26, 27.
Christ Seen: vv. 18, 19. The death of Jesus Christ was not, as some say, the result of His being the victim of circumstances too strong for Him, but was the result of His own program. He came (v. 28) to give His life a ransom. He did not die as a martyr, but as a Victor. He never foretold His death without adding that He would be resurrected.

CHAPTER TWENTY-ONE

Contents: The triumphant entry. Jesus' second purification of the temple. Barren fig tree cursed. Jesus' authority questioned. Parable of. the two sons in the vineyard. Parable of the house-holder demanding fruit from his vineyard.
Conclusion: Jesus the King-Savior was officially offered to Israel first. He was acclaimed by an unthinking multitude who thought He would then set up His earth kingdom, but He was soon rejected by official representatives of the nation. Nevertheless His rejection by His own people turned to the riches of the Gentiles. The unbelief of sinners is their ruin.
Key Word: Triumphal entry, vv. 9, 10. Jesus' authority, v. 23.
Strong Verse: 13. Promises: 21, 22.
Christ Seen: v. 2. A colt is a symbol of peace. In Jesus' coming to take His throne He will come upon a war horse (Rev. 19). Cf. v. 44. The flippant attitude of the people toward Jesus in His first presentation was due to their conception of Him as expressed in v. 11. When He comes in power, there will be no room for doubt of the fact that He is both King and Judge.

CHAPTER TWENTY-TWO

Contents: Parable of the marriage feast. Jesus' answer to the Herodians. Sadducees and Pharisees.

Conclusion: The gospel call bids all to the great marriage feast. Some wickedly reject Christ's invitations. Some think to intrude in the rags of their hypocrisy (See Rom. 3:22) but the humble gladly accept and are satisfied. It is not wit and reason that makes one acceptable to God, but humble acceptance of His call and partaking of the feast He has provided.

Key Word: Unworthy guests, vv. 8, 12, 18.

Strong Verses: 9, 21, 37, 38, 39.

Christ Seen: The invitation to the marriage feast first extended to Israel (v. 7), was greeted with violence and the King fulfilled the latter part of the verse in A. D. 70. The world-wide call then went forth (Matt. 28:16-20; v. 9) to "as many as would receive" (John 1:12). The man without a wedding garment pictures those who think to be accepted in their own righteousness rather than the righteousness of Jesus Christ. Rom. 10:1-3; Isa. 64:6; Phil. 3:9.

CHAPTER TWENTY-THREE

Contents: Jesus denounces woes upon the Pharisees for their hypocrisy. His lament over Jerusalem.

Conclusion: Nothing is more displeasing to our Lord Jesus Christ than hypocrisy, dissimulation, stage-playing in religion. Woe be to all such for their religion is vain and their ruin will be terrible. It is wholly owing to the wicked will of sinners that they are not gathered by His love under His protecting wing—they "will not come to Him that they might have life."

Key Word: Hypocrites, v. 13.

Strong Verses: 8, 11, 37, 39. Promise: 12.

Christ Seen: v. 39. The Jews by their rejection of the Savior brought upon themselves what all must suffer who do likewise—utter desolation. There are three "untils" to be accomplished before Israel can have full blessing. 1. v. 39. 2. Luke 21:24. Gentile world power must run its course—Dan. 2:34-35. 3. Rom. 11:25-27. The elect of the Gentiles must be brought in.

CHAPTER TWENTY-FOUR

Contents: Destruction of the temple foretold. The course of the present age outlined; its culmination in the great tribulation and followed by the return of Christ in power and glory. Parable of the fig tree and exhortation to watchfulness.

Conclusion: The course of the present age is to be marked by wars, famines, pestilences, persecutions, false Christs, and religious systems, increasing in intensity as the age nears its end, and culminating in tribulation such as the world has never seen, nor ever shall see again. Jesus Christ shall suddenly, unexpectedly and gloriously appear, coming in the clouds of heaven with His hosts. Blessed are they who cherish the "blessed hope" (Tit. 2:13) and live in hourly expectation of His coming.

Key Word: End of Age, v. 3.

Strong Verses: 7, 21, 27, 35, 37, 44.

Christ Seen: The signs of the near return of Jesus are national (v. 6), religious (v. 11), missionary (v. 14), and Jewish (v. 32). (Fig tree a type of Israel).

CHAPTER TWENTY-FIVE

Contents: Parables of the wise and foolish virgins. Testing of the servants in the Lord's absence. Future testing of the Gentile nations at the Lord's return.

Conclusion: The hour of our Lord's second coming is very uncertain which is good reason why we should live not only in a state of habitual preparation but actual diligence in present service for Him, and engaged in works of charity for men. Those who have so lived will in that day receive the grandest degree in the universe, the "well-done" of Jesus Christ.

Key Word: Christ's return, vv. 6, 19, 31.

Strong Verses: 13, 29, 31, 32, 34, 40.

Christ Seen: vv. 1-13. In this parable the Church is not viewed so much in her position as the Bride of Christ, but as Virgins waiting for His return (Lk. 12:36) teaching that our attitude toward His return should be expected and longing (Tit. 2:13).

CHAPTER TWENTY-SIX

Contents: Authorities plot Christ's death. Jesus annointed by Mary of Bethany. Judas sells Jesus. The last Passover. Lord's supper instituted. Gethsemane experience. Jesus before Caiaphas and Sanhedrin. Peter's denial.

Conclusion: Having finished His work as a Prophet, Christ entered upon His work as Priest to make the great sacrifice for the remission of sin. Although wicked hearts laid the plot and put it into execution, they were but fulfilling the Scriptures and unknowingly carrying out the program for which Christ came into the world. The spotless Passover Lamb who ALONE must settle the sin question was prepared for the slaughter, not as a martyr, but as a ransom for all.

Key Word: Jesus' last night, vv. 1, 18.

Strong Verses: 28, 39, 41.

Christ Seen: v. 26. This verse marks the full end of the Mosaic dispensation. The true Paschal Lamb was Christ, and He was now ready for the sacrifice. Yet at the very hour He was offered unbelieving Jews were sacrificing useless blood in the temple. The Lord's supper which takes the place of the O. T. ceremonies is a memorial of Christ as a gift and sacrifice, a parable of the true nature of Christianity—Christ becoming a part of us, and a prophecy of His future coming and glory.

CHAPTER TWENTY-SEVEN

Contents: Jesus delivered to Pilate. Judas' remorse. Barabbas released in Jesus' place. The crucifixion of Christ. The entombment and sealing of the tomb.

Conclusion: See Isa. 53:3-6, 9, 10. (It is utter ruin of language to try to draw a human conclusion to the chapter. Rather let the Scriptures themselves interpret it.)

Key Word: Crucifixion, vv. 1, 35.

Strong Verses: 22, 35, 54 (b).

Christ Seen: Calvary's cross was the main point in the coming of Jesus into the world. His death was the object of His incarnation. He was the "Lamb of God Who beareth away the sin of the world." No man took His life from Him (John 10:17-18). He whose blood was more precious than all human blood together (v. 54-b) gave His life (Matt. 28:26). The glory of heaven is not Jesus as a great ethical teacher, but Jesus, the "slain Lamb." (Rev. 5:6-12; 7:10; 21:23.)

CHAPTER TWENTY-EIGHT

Contents: Resurrection of Jesus. Jesus in Galilee and the great commission.

Conclusion: Jesus Christ is declared to be the Son of God with power, by His resurrection from the dead (v. 18; Rom. 1:4) and the acceptance by the Father of His atoning work on the cross is thereby assured for all who will receive it. Those who would be kept in the consciousness of His presence (v. 20) must attend to that which He has appointed—the carrying of the message of salvation to all men.

Key Word: Resurrection, v. 6.

Strong Verses: 6, 18, 19. Promise: 20.

Christ Seen: The resurrection is the centre of all miraculous narratives—the sun which keeps them in their orbit. It is the waterloo of infidelity. If He did not literally rise from the grave, not only is His veracity at stake, but (1 Cor. 15) preaching is vain (v. 14); faith is vain (vv. 14, 17); the witness of the disciples is false (v. 15); we are yet in our sins (v. 17); the dead are perished (v. 18), and our state is most miserable (v. 19)—BUT—"HE IS RISEN."

MARK

Key Thought:	Number of Chapters:	Key Verse:	Christ seen as:
Servant of Man	16	10:45	Servant of Jehovah

Writer of the Book:	Date:	Conclusion of the Book:
Mark (called John)	A. D. 57-63	Jesus is the Mighty Worker, Who came, not to be ministered unto, but to minister.

SUMMARY

CHAPTER ONE

Contents: Ministry of John the Baptist. Baptism and temptation of Jesus and His first Galilean ministry. Demons cast out, sickness healed, leprosy cured.

Conclusion: The deity of Jesus Christ is fully attested by the seal of the Father from heaven, His victory over Satan, His authority to call men, and His power over evil spirits and all manner of diseases.

Key Word: First ministry, vv. 1, 14, 21, 32.

Strong Verse: 11. Promise: 17.

Christ Seen: v. 35. There is no conflict between the fact of the deity of Christ and His dependence upon the Father in prayer. His prayer life on earth was the manifestation of His perfect communion with the Father before He came into the world. The fact that Jesus never asked anyone to pray FOR Him, is a further proof of His deity. He was superior to all human intercession.

CHAPTER TWO

Contents: Healing of the palsied man. Call of Matthew. Parable of the cloth and bottles. Jesus, Lord of the Sabbath.

Conclusion: Jesus Christ was sent to a sinful world for the healing and saving of such as will acknowledge their need of salvation and put their trust in Him. He has authority to forgive sin, which strikes at the root of diseases and either cures or alters their property. True faith in Him will overcome all obstacles and bring deliverance.

Key Word: Power of Christ, vv. 10, 28.

Strong Verses: 10 (a), 17, 27, 28.

Christ Seen: v. 7. (Cf. John 10:33). Jesus was logically either a blasphemer or "God manifest in the flesh." The miracle He performed immediately proved that it was not He who was the blasphemer, but His accusers.

CHAPTER THREE

Contents: Jesus heals a withered hand on the Sabbath. Multitudes healed. The twelve chosen. The unpardonable sin.

Conclusion: Those who are bound by disease and evil spirits are the special object of Jesus' compassion and may find complete deliverance in Him, do they but stretch out the hand of faith toward Him. Those are obstinate indeed in their unbelief, who set themselves against being convinced of the power of Christ by trying to explain it away, or attributing it to the devil. All such are sinning against their last remedy.

Key Word: Healing (vv. 2, 10), Calling (v. 13).

Strong Verses: 28, 29, 35.

Christ Seen: Blaspheming the Holy Ghost is attributing to the devil the work which Christ did by the power of the Holy Ghost. Many of those who reviled Christ on the cross found mercy and Christ Himself prayed for them, but to blaspheme the Holy Ghost is unpardonable.

CHAPTER FOUR

Contents: Parable of the sower. Parable of the candle. Parable of the mustard seed. Jesus stills the storm.

Conclusion: The present age is a time for missions and testimony to the salvation offered in the Word of God. The message will be variously received because of Satanic opposition, but many will prove good soil for the Divine seed and will bring forth fruit by the power of God.

Key Word: Kingdom parables, vv. 2, 11, 26, 30.

Strong Verses: 24, 25.

Christ Seen: vv. 38, 39. He Who slept the sleep of human exhaustion arises and rebukes the elements. What manner of man is this? It is the God-man—truly man, but God manifest in the flesh.

CHAPTER FIVE

Contents: The maniac of Gadara. Woman with issue of blood healed. Daughter of Jairus raised from the dead.

Conclusion: The power of Christ over evil spirits, over incurable physical ailments, and over death itself, demonstrates to a conclusion His deity and puts honor upon the simple faith that comes to Him. Those who by faith are healed of Him, may go in peace and should go to witness of His power and grace.

Key Word: Powerful Christ, vv. 19, 29, 42.

Strong Verses: 19, 34, 36 (b).

Christ Seen: v. 7. Even devils believe in the deity of Christ and tremble before Him. Demons know that by His Word they will ultimately be sent to chains of eternal darkness.

CHAPTER SIX

Contents: The twelve sent out to preach. Murder of John the Baptist. The 5000 fed. Jesus walks on the sea. Jesus heals many at Gennesaret.

Conclusion: The divine authority of Christ is ratified by the divine wisdom which He displayed in all His teaching and the divine power which He manifested in imparting power to others for service, in overcoming all laws of nature for the relief of men and in dispelling by His mere Word or touch all manner of diseases.

Key Word: Mighty works, v. 2.

Strong Verses: 50 (b).

Christ Seen: vv. 3, 7, 41, 48. Jesus the carpenter was the Controller of the universe. Jesus the son of Mary was Jesus the Son of God.

CHAPTER SEVEN

Contents: Jesus rebukes Pharisees. Healing of daughter of Syrophenician woman and a deaf and dumb man.

Conclusion: It is worshipping God in vain to rest in the outside of religious exercises when the heart is not right with God. Our first care should be the washing of the heart from wickedness which makes us odious to God, rather than ceremonial washing. Christ never puts any away from Him who fall at His feet in humble faith, and give themselves up to be ruled by Him.

Key Word: Traditionalism (v. 3), Healing (26, 27).

Strong Verses: 37 (b).

Christ Seen: v. 37. This verse shows what the whole world will say when Christ's mediation is completed and He comes to receive His own.

CHAPTER EIGHT

Contents: 4000 fed. Meaning of leaven explained. Blind man outside Bethsaida healed. Peter's confession of faith. The value of a soul.

Conclusion: The bounty of Christ is inexhaustible and He will supply the needs of the body if with it we glorify Him. It is provoking to Him when we are overwhelmed with present distrust, because we so soon forget what we have seen of His goodness in supplying our needs in days past.

Key Word: Our Provider, vv. 8, 17, 18.

Strong Verses: 29, 34, 36, 38. Promise: 35.

Christ Seen: v. 31. The death of Jesus was clearly not one of defeat, but of victory. He was not a martyr but a divinely appointed sacrifice. "Christ Who died" would make no gospel if we could not add "And is risen again." His resurrection proves that He was "the Christ" (v. 29) and that His atoning work is accepted of God and sufficient for all who believe.

CHAPTER NINE

Contents: The transfiguration. The powerless disciples and the mighty Christ casting out a demon. The dispute over who should be greatest. Jesus' rebuke of sectarianism. Solemn warning of hell.

Conclusion: Since God has from the open heavens owned Jesus Christ as His beloved Son, we should give ourselves to be ruled by His Word, to be yielded to the mighty working of His power in us and through us and to resemble Him in the spirit of humble service to men.

Key Word: Transfiguration (v. 2), Mighty Christ (v. 19).

Strong Verses: 7, 35 (b), 42, 43, 50. Promises: 23, 41.

Christ Seen: The transfiguration fulfills the promise of Jesus to reveal Himself in His coming kingdom (v. 1); teaches us that He was exalted far above Moses (law) and Elijah (prophets) (v. 4); was intended to raise the hopes of the disciples in view of His coming death (v. 30), and warns us against seeking to any other than the Son of God (v. 7).

CHAPTER TEN

Contents: Jesus' law of divorce. The blessing of little children. The rich young ruler. The desire of James and John to be first. Bartimaeus receives his sight.

Conclusion: Marriage is a divine institution and therefore to be religiously observed. The bond which God has tied is not to be lightly untied.

The kingdom of God can be received into the heart only with humble resignation, like that of a little child, to Jesus. Those who put their affections in the wealth of the world cannot put a right value on Christ and His grace and will therefore come short of His kingdom. Those who having received Christ, would be greatly honored hereafter and honorable now, are those who are the most useful to men.

Key Word: Divorce (v. 2), Riches (v. 24), Greatness (v. 44).

Strong Verses: 9, 14 (b), 15, 25, 31, 44, 45. Promises: 29, 30.

Christ Seen: v. 18. Jesus' object was not to infer that He was not good, for the Scriptures plainly teach His goodness, above all men, but to raise the man's view of His person. The ruler had called Him "Master" (teacher) and looked upon Him merely as a great man, on the same plane with himself (v. 20). Jesus was God, but until His divinity was acknowledged He could not accept the title "good."

CHAPTER- ELEVEN

Contents: Official presentation of Jesus as King. The barren fig tree. Purifying of the temple. The prayer of faith. Jesus' authority questioned.

Conclusion: The Lord Jesus, in accordance with the Scriptures, presented Himself as King-Savior at Jerusalem where He displayed His Kingly authority by cleansing the temple. He came seeking fruit of Israel, and gave the sign of their doom knowing His coming rejection by them.

Key Word: Triumphal entry, v. 9.

Strong Verses: 22, 25. Promises: 23, 24.

CHAPTER TWELVE

Contents: Parable of householder demanding fruit from his vineyards. The tribute question. Jesus answers the Sadducees. The great commandments. The widow's mite.

Conclusion: Because Christ, God's only Son, made His demands with more authority than any prophet had done, men were enraged against Him and determined by some method to entangle Him and put Him to death. To the last He confounded the wise of the world with His wisdom and set the seal of His favor upon the humble, trusting worshipper.

Key Word: Rejected Lord, vv. 6, 10, 13.

Strong Verses: 10, 17, 30, 31.

Christ Seen: Jesus knew there could be no obstruction to His exaltation. He is the foundation stone of the Church, will be the smiting stone destroying the Gentile world powers at His coming and will yet be set as heaven's King—the headstone of the corner.

CHAPTER THIRTEEN

Contents: The course of the present age—its culmination in the great tribulation and the Second coming of Christ. Parable of the fig tree.
Conclusion: The end of the age will be marked by religious apostasy (v. 6), wars and rumors of wars (v. 7), upheavals among kingdoms (v. 8), earthquakes, famines, and trouble (v. 8), the publishing of the gospel in all nations (v. 10), disregard of law (v. 12); and manifestations of hatred toward the preachers of the gospel (v. 13). The age will culminate in a time of trouble such as the world has never known (v. 19), and will end in the glorious appearing of the Christ in the clouds (v. 26). Let it be our care that whenever He will come He may find us at our duty, ready to meet Him.
Key Word: Signs of the times, vv. 4, 29.
Strong Verses: 26, 27, 31, 33, 35, 36. Promise: 13.
Christ Seen: vv. 28-30. The fig tree is a type of Israel. When Israel again starts to bud as a nation, after hundreds of years in dispersion, we may be sure Christ's coming is near. The word "generation" in v. 30 is literally "race." The nation of Israel has a promise here that it will be preserved until these things are fulfilled. Israel is even now budding—His coming is therefore "even at the doors."

CHAPTER FOURTEEN

Contents: The plot against Jesus. Jesus annointed by Mary. The last Passover. The Lord's supper instituted. The Gethsemane experience. Peter's denial. Jesus delivered to the authorities.
Conclusion: Our Lord Jesus, betrayed into the hands of the violent by His own familiar friend and led away by wicked hands to His death, consecrated Himself to that purpose, for which He came into the world—the redemption of mankind by the blood of the cross. A great part of the load of sorrow He bore was that occasioned by His betrayal and denial by those close to Him.
Key Word: Jesus' last night.
Strong Verses: 24, 36, 38.
Christ Seen: vv. 32-35. What "hour" and "cup" was He seeking to be delivered from? Does He pray for deliverance from the cross—the very purpose for which He had come into the world? (John 12:27). Heb. 5:7 states that His prayer was heard and answered. Luke 22:44. Mark 14:34 shows that Satan was attempting to kill Him before He could accomplish His purpose and Luke 22:43 gives the answer. He was saved from death in Gethsemane. When the hour of the cross comes, He wants no angels or defenders and rebukes Peter for trying to defeat God's plan. Matt. 26:52, 53, 56.

CHAPTER FIFTEEN

Contents: Jesus before Pilate. Barabbas set free instead of Christ. The crucifixion.
Conclusion: 1 Pet. 2:24; Isa. 53:5, 9, 10. (Only God's own Word can form the conclusion of this scene.)
Key Word: Crucifixion, v. 24.
Strong Verse: 39.
Christ Seen: v. 38. Why was the veil rent from the top down? It was rent from heaven, not earth. Christ having made atonement and glorified God, the way into the holy of holies was now made manifest. Heb. 9:8, 24; 10:19-22.

CHAPTER SIXTEEN

Contents: Resurrection and ascension of Jesus.
Conclusion: Jesus Who was crucified in weakness, lives in power and appears in the midst of the praises of the heavenly host as the "Lamb that was slain" (Rev. 5:6). Let the message be declared to all persons in every land that they might be saved from the guilt and power of sin and prepared to meet Him at His coming.
Key Word: Resurrection, v. 16.

Strong Verses: 6, 15. **Promise:** 16.
Christ Seen: v. 7. "And Peter." Peter denied Jesus just before He died. Jesus owned Peter just after His resurrection: Peter's grasp of Christ relaxed. Christ's grasp of Peter was still tight. Peter lost consciousness of Jesus' love but that did not change Jesus. "Nothing shall be able to separate you from the love of God which is in Christ Jesus."

LUKE

Key Thought: Son of Man	Number of Chapters: 24	Key Verse: 19:10	Christ seen as: Perfect Son of Man

Writer of the Book: Luke	Date: A. D. 63-68	Conclusion of the Book: Jesus is the Ideal Man, the human-divine One, Who came to seek and to save that which was lost.

SUMMARY

CHAPTER ONE

Contents: Birth of John the Baptist foretold. Virgin birth of Jesus foretold. Mary's visit to Elizabeth. Mary's praise because of Jehovah's favor. Birth of John the Baptist.

Conclusion: John, the forerunner of Jesus, came to earth by divine appointment and arrangement. Jesus, the Christ was born of a virgin, conceived of the Holy Ghost, and was therefore the Son of God to Whom was promised the throne of His father, David.

Key Word: John and Jesus, vv. 31, 60.

Strong Verses: 31, 32, 35, 37, 78, 79.

Christ Seen: vv. 31-32. The name "Jesus" (Savior) links Him to humanity and suggests His career as Prophet. He is conspicuous as "Jesus" up to His resurrection. "Christ" (annointed One) links Him to Prophecy which He came to fulfill and suggests His work as Priest atoning for sin. "Lord" (the Jehovah name applied to Him) links Him with Deity and suggests His Kingship. He is coming again to rule.

CHAPTER TWO

Contents: Birth of Jesus. His adoration by the shepherds. Adoration and prophecy of Simon and Anna. Return to Nazareth. Jesus and His parents at the Passover.

Conclusion: Jesus the Christ, in the fullness of time was brought into the world according to divine counsels. Although born amid the meanest circumstances, His humiliation was attended by discoveries of His glory and His coming was announced as glad tidings to all people. From His childhood days He showed forth some of the rays of His glory in the divine wisdom which He manifested.

Key Word: Glad tidings, v. 10.

Strong Verse: 49. **Promise:** 10.

Christ Seen: v. 52. In the perfections of His divine nature there could be no increase. But as Son of Man, in His human nature, His body increased and He grew in all the endowments of a human soul. Christ accommodated Himself as Son of God, to His state of humiliation in human flesh.

CHAPTER THREE

Contents: Ministry of John the Baptist. Baptism of Jesus. Genealogy of Mary.

Conclusion: Way must be made for the reception of Christ by the removing of all obstructions that stand in the way of Him and of His grace. The seal of His divine authority has been given from the opened heavens; let us therefore prepare to bid His salvation welcome.

Key Word: Baptism, vv. 16, 21.

Strong Verses: 16.

Christ Seen: v. 23. Matthew gives Joseph's genealogy—Luke gives Mary's. Luke does not say Heli "begat" Joseph. Joseph was his son-in-law. If Jesus was the son of Joseph, as some claim, He is forever barred from the throne, being a descendant of Coniah who was cursed, that none of his line might have the throne. Jesus was accordingly conceived by the

Holy Ghost in Mary, Mary's father being a descendant of David through another line.

CHAPTER FOUR

Contents: Temptation of Jesus. Jesus in the synagogue at Nazareth. Casting of demons out of man at Capernaum. Healing of Peter's wife's mother and others.

Conclusion: Our Savior was victorious over Satan by the power of the Holy Ghost and the use of the divine Word as His sword and those are well armed who are thus equipped. The words of Christ's mouth were attended with a power which pricked the consciences of men, dispersed evil spirits and drove away disease.

Key Word: Temptation, v. 2. Fame, vv. 14, 32, 36, 37, 40.

Strong Verses: 4, 8, 12.

Christ Seen: vv. 17-19. It is interesting to notice that Jesus stopped His quotation in the middle of a passage from Isaiah. He stopped with "the acceptable year of the Lord"—which defined the purpose of His first advent. "The day of vengeance of our God" has to do with His second advent, and He therefore omitted it at the time.

CHAPTER FIVE

Contents: Miraculous draught of fishes. Healing of a leper and a paralytic. Call of Matthew. The scribes and Pharisees answered. Parables of the garment and bottles.

Conclusion: Jesus Christ has divine power to command the very fishes of the sea; to drive out incurable disease by His Word; to separate sinners from the penalty of their sins, and authority to call whom He will. Those will speed well indeed who will take Him at His word and trust to His ability and efficiency whatever their case.

Key Word: Faith in Christ, vv. 5, 12, 20, 28.

Strong Verses: 24 (a), 32.

Christ Seen: v. 21. The doctrine that Jesus Christ has power to forgive sin has been fully attested, proving that He is God. He appears to be so by what He does in this chapter alone, and human experience through the centuries witnesses to His deity. Those who charge Him with blasphemy are themselves proven to be blasphemers.

CHAPTER SIX

Contents: Jesus and the Sabbath. Healing of a withered hand. Choosing of the twelve. Sermon on the Mount. Parable of the house built on a rock.

Conclusion: Works of necessity are allowable on the Sabbath and above all it is to be spent in the servcie of and to the honor of Him Who is Lord of the Sabbath, whose good works we are to perform.

The blessings of Christ are covenanted to suffering saints who live by the precepts of His gospel, enduring hardship for His sake, in hope of the glory of heaven which will abundantly countervail all hardships. Woe to those who rest upon a false foundation, trusting in the riches of this world and holding Christ and His people in contempt.

Key Word: Lord of Sabbath, v. 5. Sermon on Mount, vv. 12, 20.

Strong Verses: 5, 27, 28, 31, 35, 37, 38, 41, 45, 46. Promises: 20, 21, 22, 23.

Christ Seen: Jesus as a human being in perfect subjection to the Father walked in constant communion with Him through prayer. In those days when His enemies were filled with madness against Him, He gave much time to prayer. If He, the Son of God, needed to pray, how much more business should we have at the throne of grace?

CHAPTER SEVEN

Contents: Centurion's servant healed. Widow's son raised. Questions from John the Baptist in prison and Jesus' testimony. Jesus annointed in the Pharisee's house. Parable of the creditor and two debtors.

Conclusion: He Who had such a commanding empire in the kingdom of nature that He could command away diseases and raise the dead, is certainly none other than the Messiah, long announced by the prophets and empowered for the forgiveness of sins.

Key Word: Healer and Forgiver, vv. 10, 48.
Strong Verses: 7, 23, 47, 50.
Christ Seen: v. 28. This is usually taken to mean that the "least" of those who preach the Gospel of the risen Lord, being employed under a more excellent dispensation, are in a more honorable office than John the Baptist, who merely announced His birth and ministry. The meanest of those who follow the Lamb, excel the greatest of those, in position, who proclaim His advent. Those living under the Gospel dispensation have therefore a greater responsibility.

CHAPTER EIGHT

Contents: Jesus preaching and healing in Galilee. Parable of the sower, the lighted candle. Stilling of the waves. Demons cast out of man of Gadara. Healing of a woman. Raising of Jairus' daughter.
Conclusion: It is the comfort of God's people that all power is given unto Jesus Christ, their Saviour. He has under His check and control, the elements of the universe, the prince of the power of the air with all his most malignant demons, all human diseases, even death itself, and exercises these powers as will best glorify God. He is rich in fact who is rich in faith in Christ, having received the good seed of His promises into their hearts.
Key Word: Preaching and showing, v. 1. (See v. 4, preaching; vv. 25, 35, 48, 55, shewing.)
Strong Verses: 11, 18, 21, 39. Promise: 17.
Christ Seen: v. 28. Demon-possessed men never have expectation to receive benefit from Jesus Christ, nor inclination to do Him service, a fact which alone proves His deity. Demons know Him to be the Son of God Who is ultimately to execute vengeance. They express only dread of Him.

CHAPTER NINE

Contents: The twelve sent forth to preach and their return. 5000 fed. Peter's confession of Christ. The transfiguration. The powerless disciples and the demon ridden boy. Jesus' rebuke of sectarianism. Tests of discipleship.
Conclusion: Jesus Christ is God's anointed, owned to be so from the opened heavens and by the lives of witnesses and shown to be so in His superiority over all forces; His ability to empower others for supernatural work; His power to supply both temporal and spiritual needs and His authority over malignant spirits. Wise are they who give up all to cleave to Him, for though they lose their lives for His sake, they shall gain life to their unspeakable advantage.
Key Word: The mighty Christ, v. 43.
Strong Verses: 23, 25, 26, 35.
Christ Seen: vv. 22, 44. When men had a fond conceit of a temporal kingdom in which Christ, the miracle worker, should reign to supply all their needs, He would have one truth "sink down into their ears"—the absolute necessity of His atonement, the one thing for which He came in His first advent. All His miracles and the interest He had gotten by them, could not prevent His sacrifice on the cross. "Without the shedding of blood there is no remission of sin"—nevertheless those who carried out the plan were "wicked men," inspired with evil motives.

CHAPTER TEN

Contents: The 70 sent out. Jesus denounces judgment on cities. Parable of the good Samaritan. Martha and Mary entertain Jesus.
Conclusion: Whom Christ sends may be sure He will go along with them and give them success. His servants should apply themselves to their work under a deep concern for precious souls, looking upon them with His compassion, and as riches which ought to be secured for Him. True service for Him comes out of communion with Him, and that service is worthless to Him which is done with motives of selfish pride.
Key Word: Service, vv. 1, 30, 38.
Strong Verses: 2, 20, 21.
Christ Seen: v. 21. Jesus rejoiced (only time recorded) to perfect strength out of weakness for His own glory. He is pleased to reveal His counsels

in those whose extraction and education have nothing in them promising until He, by the Holy Spirit, elevates their faculties and furnishes them with this knowledge. The believer need not therefore be disturbed if some of the "wise and prudent" of the world would crucify Him afresh. Vital experience of Christ in the soul over-balances all human reasonings about Christ.

CHAPTER ELEVEN

Contents: Jesus' doctrine of prayer. Jesus charged with casting out demons by Beelzebub, and His answer. Woes denounced upon the Pharisees and lawyers.

Conclusion: One great design of Christianity is to enforce upon us the duty of prayer, instruct us in it and encourage us to expect advantage by it. Prayer changes things. Our prayers are God's opportunities to do for us what He otherwise could not do. Let us therefore lay hold of God's willingness with confidence and cling to Him with persistency. Obstinate infidelity will never be at loss for something to say in its own excuse, though ever so absurd. They will yet be compelled to face Him in judgment to answer for all their absurdities and will see the emptiness of all external ceremonies.

Key Word: Prayer, v. 1. Evil generation, v. 29 (14,54).
Strong Verses: 2, 3, 4, 23, 28. Promises: 9, 13.
Christ Seen: v. 29. The sign from God for the confirmation of our faith is the resurrection of Jesus Christ. This is the greatest and most convincing proof that He was sent from·God.

CHAPTER TWELVE

Contents: Jesus warns of leaven of the Pharisees. Parable of the rich fool. Parable of the second coming. Parable of the steward and his servants. Christ, the divider of men.

Conclusion: Those who make not religion a mere cloak, but have a saving faith in Christ, can set at defiance all the opposing forces of the world, knowing that having given Him first place in their lives, they are safe in Him. They need not take anxious thought for the things of this life nor dread even the killing of the body, which can only send them to their rest and eternal joy with Christ the sooner. Let them therefore sit loose to the world, living in hourly hope of His glorious return.

Key Word: Jesus our security, vv. 7, 8, 11, 28, 31, 37.
Strong Verses: 3, 4, 5, 7, 9, 22, 24, 30, 32, 34, 40, 48. Promises: 8, 28, 31, 37.
Christ Seen: v. 40. Jesus is certainly coming back to earth in power and great glory and His people are now to live in a state of expectation, doing everything with that hope and to that end. The theology of v. 45 is characterized as the theology of unfaithful stewards who will be caught unawares to their shame.

CHAPTER THIRTEEN

Contents: Parable of barren fig tree. Woman loosed from her infirmity. Parable of mustard seed and leaven. Jesus teaching on way to Jerusalem.

Conclusion: Genuine repentance and faith toward Christ is the only avenue of escape from perishing. Nothing can be expected concerning barren and hypocritical lives except that they should be cut down and cast away. Not all who say "Lord, Lord" will find entrance to His kingdom, and to be bidden by Him that day to "depart" means hell. Those who would be saved must enter in at the strait gate, having undergone a change of heart.

Key Word: Hypocrites rejected, vv. 15, 25, 30, 35.
Strong Verses: 3, 24, 34.
Christ Seen: vv. 6-9. The fig tree symbolizes Israel in Christ's time (Psa. 80:8-16). Three years and more Jesus sought fruit of this tree and found none. Having produced all His credentials as Messiah, He made His triumphal entry with multitudes shouting "Hosanna," but He knew they would shortly shout "crucify." The next day He saw a fig tree and finding nothing but leaves, He cursed it. (Mark 11:12-14.) See v. 34. This is Israel's condition "until the times of the Gentiles be fulfilled."

CHAPTER FOURTEEN

Contents: Jesus heals on the Sabbath. Parable of the ambitious guest. Parable of the great supper. Parable of the tower, of the king going to war, and of the savorless salt.

Conclusion: Pride and hypocrisy will get shame and will at last have a fall, for the Master of the feast will marshall His guests and will not see the more honorable miss their due.

Many have been bidden to the great supper of Christ, and many there are who stay away on excuses of small concern. The ingratitude of those who slight the Gospel invitation is an abuse of His mercy, and grace despised is grace forfeited. God will however have a church in the world, though there be many who heed not the call.

Key Word: Great supper, v. 16.

Strong Verses: 26, 27, 33. Promise: 11.

Christ Seen: In the two parables of Luke 14:16-24 and Matt. 22:1-14 we see the historical development of the plan of salvation. (1) Prophetic announcement represented by the first invitation. (2) Second epoch, complete preparation followed by acts of violence. (3) Extension of the invitation to the hitherto uninvited guests, the Gentiles. The key note is Matt. 22:14.

CHAPTER FIFTEEN

Contents: Parables of the lost sheep, lost coin and lost son.

Conclusion: God has a particular care over backsliding sinners (Isr. in this case) and follows them with the calls of His Word and the strivings of the Holy Spirit until at length they are wrought upon to return. Their repentance and conversion are a matter of joy and rejoicing among the angels of heaven.

Key Word: Lost and found, vv. 4, 8, 32.

Strong Verses: 7, 10.

Christ Seen: v. 18. If one has been in the Father's house as a son, he, like the prodigal is still a son and will be constantly constrained by the Holy Spirit and the intercessory work of Christ to "arise and go to the Father," otherwise would Christ's work as our Intercessor be a failure.

CHAPTER SIXTEEN

Contents: Parable of the unjust steward. Jesus answers Pharisees. Rich man and Lazarus in the spirit world.

Conclusion: Worldlings are often more consistent with themselves and more enthusiastically pursue their ends than Christians. Though they aim low they aim better, improving their opportunities and doing that first which is most needed. Let us be thus wise in spiritual affairs.

Prosperity is not a mark of being a favorite of heaven, nor poverty a mark of God's rejection of a man. Salvation is appropriated by those only who accept the evidence of God's Word during their lifetime, and, having died outside of Christ, there is no ray of hope eternally.

Key Word: Wisdom, v. 8; opportunity lost, v. 25.

Strong Verses: 10, 13, 15.

Christ Seen: v. 23. "Hell" is lit, "hades," the prison place of departed unsaved spirits until the time of the Great White Throne judgment, when these spirits shall be resurrected for judgment and sent into the final hell forever. This is not a parable, for Jesus never names the characters in parables, with definite statements of things that took place.

CHAPTER SEVENTEEN

Contents: Instruction in forgiveness. Parable of service. Ten lepers healed. Second coming of Jesus foretold.

Conclusion: God's relation to the believer is not one of contract but of ownership, and since we never can merit His favors, we should ever let Him have the praise of His comforts, while we seek to manifest His spirit toward our fellowmen.

Our Lord Jesus is with certainty coming back to earth to reign gloriously. His coming will be with such suddenness that none can announce it in advance. The world will be moving on in its regular pursuits in disregard of the warnings of God's Word, when He appears.

Key Word: Duty, v. 10; thankfulness, v. 16; Second Coming, v. 24.
Strong Verses: 4, 24, 26, 34, 36. Promise: 6.
Christ Seen: v. 21. Jesus did not teach these wicked men that the "kingdom of the heavens was "within" them, but "among" them. It was then in their midst in the person of the Savior and His disciples. He has a kingdom which is yet to come with outward show (v. 24) and with such suddenness that men will not be able to point here and there and say "the kingdom is coming." This is exactly what men are now trying to do, thinking the earthly kingdom can be set up without the King present.

CHAPTER EIGHTEEN

Contents: Parable of the unjust judge. Parable of Pharisee and publican. Little children blessed. Rich young ruler. Death and resurrection foretold. Blind man healed near Jericho.
Conclusion: Trouble and perplexity should drive us to prayer, for it is persistent and believing prayer that drives trouble and perplexity away. There is, however, no way of approach to God on the ground of our own merits, but only on the ground of God's mercy as shown at the blood-sprinkled mercy seat ("mercy" is lit. "propitiation." The publican said, "be toward me as thou art when thou lookest upon the atoning blood").

True discipleship is conditioned upon receiving the Lord Jesus Christ with the simplicity and humility of a child, being willing to follow Him and submit to His discipline whatever it may cost us in the things of this world, being confident that whatever we have left behind for His sake will be abundantly made up to us in better things, both here and hereafter.
Key Word: Prayer, vv. 1, 10; discipleship, vv. 22, 29, 43.
Strong Verses: 1, 7, 14, 17, 27. Promises: 29, 30.
Christ Seen: vv. 31-34. Christ ever speaks of His sufferings as necessary to the fulfillment of Scripture. (1 Pet. 1:11.) His death on Calvary was absolutely essential and would have taken place in any case. He came to give His life a ransom, and therefore did not die as a martyr.

CHAPTER NINETEEN

Contents: Conversion of Zaccheus. Parable of the pounds. Triumphal entry. Jesus weeps over Jerusalem. Purification of the temple.
Conclusion: The Lord Jesus came from heaven to make possible the bringing of those that are lost to God. Having made this provision, He has gone into a far country to receive for Himself a Kingdom and return in great power. He has endued His followers in the world with advantages and capacities of serving the interests of His church until He returns to receive it, when all shall render account to Him and receive their reward accordingly.
Key Word: Coming King, vv. 12, 38.
Strong Verses: 10, 26.
Christ Seen: v. 38. The great honor paid to Christ by multitudes makes the ignominy of His death to appear the greater. He could have influenced all men as easily as those to whom the ass and colt belonged, but the Great Ambassador of heaven knew He was entering Jerusalem to be rejected and crucified according to the divine purpose. The great song of rejoicing will yet be taken up by innumerable multitudes when He returns to receive the Church and set up His Kingdom.

CHAPTER TWENTY

Contents: Jesus' authority questioned. Parable of the vineyard. Question of the tribute money. Answer to Sadducees about resurrection. Jesus questions Scribes.
Conclusion: Those who question Christ's authority, if they would but catechize themselves in the most evident principles of religion, will have their folly made manifest, for the evidence of His authority is complete and convincing. Those who are resolved not to recognize His authority, disowning Him as Lord of the Vineyard, will find themselves eventually thrown out of their lease, and stripped of all their title, for He will yet become the headstone of the corner.

Key Word: Christ's authority, vv. 2, 13, 44.
Strong Verses: 17, 25, 38.
Christ Seen: v. 44. Christ as God was David's Lord, but Christ as man was David's son.

CHAPTER TWENTY-ONE

Contents: The widow's mite. Discourse on the course of the age and return of the Lord.
Conclusion: As the time draws near when the Kingdom of God shall be fully established upon the earth, and the King shall return in glory, the days will be characterized by increasing apostasy, disturbances in the earth and in the heavens, and intense hatred of those who proclaim the Gospel. The age will culminate in a period of terrible fear upon man, and then shall Christ appear.
Key Word: Course of age, v. 7.
Strong Verses: 8, 9, 25, 26, 27, 33. Promise: 18.
Christ Seen: vv. 20-24. Two sieges of Jerusalem are in view in this chapter. These verses refer to the siege of Titus, A. D. 70, when v. 24 was fulfilled. Christ did not come then. Jerusalem has been trodden down throughout the present dispensation and will ever be disputed about until the times of the Gentiles are fulfilled and He comes Who is rightful King.

CHAPTER TWENTY-TWO

Contents: Judas covenants to betray Jesus. Last passover. Lord's supper instituted. Peter's denial predicted. Jesus' arrest. Peter's denial.
Conclusion: Jesus Christ, in fulfillment of the Scriptures, was betrayed into the hands of wicked men by His own familiar friend, and as the spotless Lamb of God was led away to the slaughter, for the purpose to which He had consecrated Himself, the shedding of His blood for the putting away of sin. He faced the issue alone, victorious over all Satanic attempts to turn Him from the divine purpose, and forsaken by His own, went forth to be slain.
Key Word: Jesus' last night, v. 1.
Strong Verses: 19, 20, 42.
Christ Seen: vv. 19-20. The Lord's supper itself is an evidence of Christ's deity, for no man could institute a memorial of himself of this character. It is a memorial of His finished work (v. 19; 1 Cor. 11:26), a symbol of the impartation of His life to us (vv. 19, 20; 1 Cor. 11:29), a vehicle of the impartation of Himself (vv. 19-20), a prophecy of His return and the marriage supper. (1 Cor. 11:26; Luke 22:16, 18.)

CHAPTER TWENTY-THREE

Contents: Jesus before Pilate and Herod. Barabbas released and Jesus condemned. The cricifixion and entombment.
Conclusion: (Only the divine Word can conclude this scene.) See Isa. 53:3-6, 10; 1 Cor. 15:3-4.
Key Word: Crucifixion.
Strong Verses: 4, 14, 33, 38, 45, 46.
Christ Seen: vv. 4, 14, 43. The holiness of Jesus is attested by adverse witnesses. Centurion, v. 47. Thief, v. 41. Pilate, vv. 4, 14. Pilate's wife, Matt. 27:19. Judas, Matt. 27:3-4.

CHAPTER TWENTY-FOUR

Contents: Resurrection of Christ. Ministry of the risen Christ. His commission to evangelization. The ascension.
Conclusion: Jesus Who suffered all things in fulfillment of the divine warrant, also came forth from the domain of death in fulfillment of the same Scriptures, thereby being shown to be the Son of God with power, whose authority may never be questioned. Those who have come to know the power of His death and resurrection must go and tell a guilty world that an act of indemnity has passed the royal assent which all that believe shall have the benefit of.
Key Word: Resurrection.
Strong Verses: 5, 6, 25, 39, 44, 46, 49.

Christ Seen: v. 49. Those who are to proclaim this supernatural Gospel need to be endued with power from on high. The church of Christ could never have been set up by any human power, neither can its message prosper without the same baptism of the Spirit. As the disciples tarried for Pentecost, so let none venture today upon their embassy until they have taken Christ at His word and received power from on high.

JOHN

Key Thought: Son of God	Number of Chapters: 21	Key Verse: 20:31	Christ seen as: Risen Son of God

Writer of the Book: John (the Apostle)	Date: A. D. 85-90	Conclusion of the Book: Jesus is the eternal Son of God, Who came into the world to reveal God in terms of human life.

SUMMARY

CHAPTER ONE

Contents: Deity of Christ. Ministry of John the Baptist. Jesus announced as the Lamb of God, and the first converts to Him.

Conclusion: The Son of God became the Son of Man that the sons of men through Him might become the sons of God. The next thing to finding Him as the Lamb of God is to find another and introduce that one to Him.

Key Word: The Word, v. 1.

Strong Verses: 12, 13, 14, 17, 29.

Christ Seen: v. 12. To teach "believing on Christ" for salvation proves His deity. If He was a created or finite being, to teach eternal salvation by believing on Him is blasphemy. Only God can bring eternal life by belief in Himself. To experience new life by believing proves that Jesus was God manifest in the flesh. (See Jer. 17:5.)

CHAPTER TWO

Contents: The marriage at Cana and the first miracle of Jesus. The passover and the purification of the temple.

Conclusion: Those who expect the favors of Christ must with an implicit obedience observe His orders. Those who follow Him shall fare with Him. The way of duty is the way to mercy.

Key Word: Obedience, vv. 5, 16.

Strong Verses: 5, 16.

Christ Seen: v. 19. The ability of Christ to drive this crowd from their posts without opposition was in itself proof of His authority, but if that does not convince, the great sign, His resurrection, will settle the question. His resurrection is the Waterloo of infidelity.

CHAPTER THREE

Contents: Nicodemus and the new birth. The last testimony of John the Baptist.

Conclusion: Since the natural man, however gifted, moral, or refined, is absolutely blind to spiritual truth and impotent to enter the kingdom, a new birth through Christ as the channel and the Holy Spirit as the power is an absolute necessity. Heaven is a prepared place for a prepared people. The only gateway to it is—Jesus.

Key Word: New birth, v. 3.

Strong Verses: 3, 6, 7, 19. Promises: 16, 18, 36.

Christ Seen: v. 14. The bitten Israelite was healed by simply looking to the brazen serpent, not by looking at his wound, although he must of course be conscious of his condition. One look healed the bite. So one look of faith to Jesus saves. It is not the way we look, but the object we look at that heals.

CHAPTER FOUR

Contents: Jesus and the Samaritan woman. The indwelling Spirit. The nobleman's son healed.

Conclusion: Jesus Christ is the gift of God, the richest token of God's love, the source and fountain of those living waters, the graces of the Holy Spirit which satisfy the thirsting soul and make a life overflowing with goodness. Those who come face to face with their own helplessness and sin and give their hearts to Him will be the recipients of these living waters.

Key Word: Living water, v. 10.
Strong Verses: 10, 23, 24. Promise: 14.
Christ Seen: v. 29. The divine knowledge of Jesus proves His omniscience. Jesus knows the thoughts, words and actions of all the children of men, and by the power of His Words is still revealing to men the secret sins of their hearts.

CHAPTER FIVE

Contents: Healing of the man at the pool of Bethesda. Jesus answers the Jews. The four-fold witness to Jesus.
Conclusion: Jesus Christ, the omnipotent Son of God, delights to help the helpless, and manifests His mercy to those who are willing to be helped. He Who thus overrules the powers of nature on behalf of trusting souls can be no other than the Son of God, in Whom the fullness of the Godhead dwells.
Key Word: Healing, v. 8.
Strong Verses: 23, 39. Promises: 24, 28, 29.
Christ Seen: v. 18. Jesus was killed because of His claims to deity, not because He desired to set up an earthly throne at that time. If He was not what He claimed to be (v. 23), He was a blasphemer, but this is out of the question, since He was raised from the dead. Therefore, those who deny His deity take their stand with His murderers.

CHAPTER SIX

Contents: Feeding the 5000. Walking on the sea. Discourse on the Bread of Life. Peter's confession of faith.
Conclusion: Jesus Christ, the true Bread, is that to the soul which bread is to the body, nourishing and supporting the spiritual life. Our bodies could live better without food than our souls without Christ. Those who have received this Bread are to be the distributors of it to other hungry souls.
Key Word: Bread, vv. 5, 33.
Strong Verses: 29, 63. Promises: 27, 35, 37, 39, 40, 44, 51.
Christ Seen: v. 27. Jesus is sealed by God the Father as the Savior of the world. By His anointing—1:32-34. By the voice from heaven—12:28-30. By His protection—7:28-30. By the character of His teaching—7:16-17. By the resurrection—20:19.

CHAPTER SEVEN

Contents: Jesus urged to go to the feast. His final departure from Galilee. Jesus at the feast of tabernacles. Prophecy concerning the Holy Spirit.
Conclusion: It is the comfort of those who embrace Christ's doctrine that it is a divine doctrine, proven so by the blessed experience of what He promises. He is the source of the refreshing fountain of the Holy Spirit, which comes to replenish the soul that thirsts for Him, and to supply a fullness of life that overflows in blessing to other lives.
Key Word: Water, vv. 37, 38.
Strong Verses: 37, 39. Promises: 17, 38.
Christ Seen: v. 12. Either Jesus was merely "a good man," a "deceiver" —or what He claimed—the divine Son of God. If He is not what He claimed, He cannot be a good man. Those who deny His deity therefore put Him on a level with the devil (Rev. 20:10).

CHAPTER EIGHT

Contents: The woman taken in adultery. Discourse after the feast on Jesus as Light of the world. Satan, the original liar and murderer, and the Satanic brotherhood.
Conclusion: Jesus was the Light of the world, the image of the invisible God. Those shall have the light of life who follow Him, being guided away from destroying error and damning sin, and having that enjoyment of God which will be to them the light of spiritual life in this world and life everlasting in the world to come. All who will have God for their Father must discover Him through the Light of the world.

Key Word: Light of the world, v. 12.
Strong Verses: 7, 42, 44, 47. Promises: 12, 32, 36.
Christ Seen: v. 18. Jesus Christ was witnessed to by the Father. He was taught by the Father—v. 28. Attended by the Father—v. 38. Sent by the Father—v. 42. Honored by the Father—v. 54. Known by the Father—v. 55. The power of Christ over the lives of men throughout the centuries demonstrates to a conclusion that He is the one sealed by the Father as the Light of the world.

CHAPTER NINE

Contents: Healing of the man born blind. The fault finding of unbelievers.
Conclusion: The Lord Jesus Christ came into the world, not only to give light, but sight to those who could not behold light. The sight that He gives to trusting souls proves Him to be the One sent of God to be the true light of the world. Experience of His saving power is a safer teaching than reason, therefore let those whose eyes have been opened be bold to witness to a world that would explain away His power.
Key Word: Light, vv. 7, 37.
Strong Verses: 4, 31.
Christ Seen: v. 39. Christ came into the world designedly to give sight to those that were spiritually blind, by His Word and Spirit to turn many from darkness to light. He came also that those who had a high conceit of their own wisdom, in contradiction to the divine revelation, might be sealed up in their infidelity. The Gospel is a savor of life unto life, or of death unto death. Blindness has happened to Israel. The Gentiles have seen a great light.

CHAPTER TEN

Contents: Discourse on the Good Shepherd. Jesus' deity asserted.
Conclusion: God, our great owner, the sheep of whose pasture we are by creation, has constituted His Son, Jesus Christ, to be our Shepherd. He has all that care of His people that a good shepherd has of his flock. In His care, the true believer is eternally secure, for the hand that was wounded and the hand of our Creator close in omnipotent, double grasp upon him.
Key Word: Shepherd, v. 11.
Strong Verses: 11, 14, 27. Promises: 9, 28, 29.
Christ Seen: v. 11. Jesus as our "Good Shepherd" died to save us. As our "Great Shepherd" He lives to guide us. Heb. 13:20. As the "Chief Shepherd" He is coming back to glorify us. 1 Peter 5:3.

CHAPTER ELEVEN

Contents: Raising of Lazarus. Enmity of the Pharisees against Jesus.
Conclusion: Jesus Christ is the resurrection and the life—the fountain of life and the head and author of the resurrection. Whoever, during life, lives by faith in Him, is born again to a heavenly life, and though the body die, yet shall it live again at His word.
Key Word: Lazarus raised, vv. 23, 44.
Promises: 25, 26, 40.
Christ Seen: vv. 5-6. Jesus' delays in answer to prayer are not necessarily denials. He may delay because He loves us, and always for His own glory. Let us not, therefore, complain because we cannot understand His dealings, but trust in Him, knowing we shall see the glory of God. (v. 40).

CHAPTER TWELVE

Contents: The supper at Bethany. The triumphal entry. Jesus' answer to Greeks.
Conclusion: The most plentiful and powerful means of conviction will not of themselves work faith in the depraved and prejudiced hearts of men. Many hear, but few heed. Their final judgment is reserved to the last day, and the Word of Christ will judge them then and make them answer for all the contempts they have put upon Him.
Key Word: Rejection, vv. 4, 11, 19, 38, 40, 48.
Strong Verses: 32, 35, 48. Promises: 25, 26, 46.

Christ Seen: v. 32. The cross of Jesus is the mightiest magnet in the universe. It is Christ that draws—and Christ crucified. The increase of the church was after His death. While He lived we read of thousands miraculously fed, but after His death we read of thousands added to the church through a single sermon. Is there a greater proof of His divine authority today?

CHAPTER THIRTEEN

Contents: Last Passover. Jesus washes disciples' feet. Betrayal foretold, also Peter's denial.

Conclusion: What was consistent with the dignity of the Lord Jesus Christ is much more consistent with ours, His servants. To sink is the way to rise. To serve in humility is the way to rule. Let us take heed lest Christ's condescensions to us and advancement of us, through our corrupt nature, cause us to think high thoughts of ourselves, or low thoughts of Him.

Key Word: Humility, vv. 5, 14, 16.

Strong Verses: 1 (b), 16, 34, 35.

Christ Seen: vv. 3, 4, 5, 12, 16. Jesus "arose" from His place in glory, laid aside the garments of divine majesty. (Phil. 2:6-7.) Took the form of a "servant" (Phil. 2:7). Provides "cleansing" (John 15:3). Applies the cleansing water (Eph. 5:26). "Took His garments" again (John 17:5), and is seated. (Heb. 10:12.)

CHAPTER FOURTEEN

Contents: Jesus foretells His second coming and promises the Holy Spirit to believers.

Conclusion: Jesus is the way—let us follow Him. Jesus is the truth—let us build with confidence upon the precious truths of His comforting promises. Jesus is the life—let us learn to abide in Him, the source of spiritual life, until He comes back to receive us to the prepared mansions above.

Key Word: Peace, vv. 1, 27.

Strong Verses: 2, 6. Promises: 3, 12, 13, 14, 21, 23, 26, 27.

Christ Seen: v. 16. The word "Comforter" means "one called alongside to help." The Holy Spirit is the indwelling representative of Christ on the earth. It is He who guides us into the truth concerning Christ, forms Christ's purposes in our hearts, and even prays through us. (Rom. 8:26.)

CHAPTER FIFTEEN

Contents: Jesus' discourse on the vine and the branches. The believer and the world.

Conclusion: Jesus is the true vine, in which the life of believers, as abiding branches, is hid. Abiding in Him, the believer is able to walk in purity of life, with Christ sharing in all the interests of his life, taking all burdens to Him, and drawing all wisdom and strength from Him. It is only the abiding life that bears fruit to the glory of the Father.

Key Word: Abiding, v. 4.

Strong Verses: 4, 13, 14, 16, 19, 20, 26. Promises: 5, 7, 10.

Christ Seen: Christ proved His love to the world by laying down His life for it (1 John 3:16) in redemption work. His love to us should ever be the standard of measure of our love to others in service for Him.

CHAPTER SIXTEEN

Contents: Warning of persecutions. The promise of the Spirit and His three-fold work. Jesus talks of His death, resurrection and second coming.

Conclusion: The sending of the Holy Spirit was the fruit of Christ's purchase on the cross and an answer to His intercession within the veil—a proof of the acceptance of His finished work with the Father. He is the companion of the true believer in every place and at all times, whereas Christ's corporal presence could be in but one place at a time. As to unbelievers, the Holy Spirit proves sin upon them because of their rejection of Christ, and warns of judgment. To the believer, He is the constant helper and the revealer of the things of Christ.

Key Word: Holy Spirit, v. 7.

Strong Verses: 7, 8, 9, 10, 27, 33.   Promises: 13, 14, 22, 23.
Christ Seen: The pope of Rome claims to be the Vicar, or representative of Christ on earth. He thus assumes to usurp the place of the Holy Spirit Who alone is Christ's Vicar on earth.

CHAPTER SEVENTEEN

Contents: Jesus' prayer of intercession.
Conclusion: If God be our Father, we have an intercessor to appear for us continually to guarantee our safe delivery to the haven above and our keeping along the way. He prays not for the world but for those who are His, that they might be preserved in their salvation, that they might have His joy, that they might be fortified against the evils of the world, that they might be purified through His Word, that they might manifest oneness with Him, that they might be edified in Him and at last behold His glory.
Key Word: Intercession, v. 9.
Strong Verses: 3, 11, 17, 18, 21, 24.
Christ Seen: This prayer, to which there is no "Amen" attached, is believed to be typical of that perfect intercession of our High Priest in heaven. (Heb. 7:25.) One who has the support of this prayer, as a true child of God, cannot be lost. Peter, when he fell, was kept by the intercession of Jesus. Judas (v. 12), when he fell, fell eternally, not being a true believer (John 6:70-71).

CHAPTER EIGHTEEN

Contents: Jesus' betrayal and arrest. Peter's denial. Jesus condemned and Barabbas released.
Conclusion: Our Lord Jesus, having put on the armor of prayer, went forth to face the great conflict with Satanic hatred and the sin of the world. Betrayed, misunderstood and denied by those of His own familiar friends, He, the perfect One, was handed over into wicked hands, to face alone the condemnation of a guilty world, that those who should believe upon Him might not be condemned.
Key Word: Betrayal and arrest, vv. 2, 3.
Strong Verses: 11, 37 (b).
Christ Seen: v. 1. In Eden's garden, the first Adam sinned. In Gethsemane's garden, the second Adam suffered and prayed. In Eden all was delightful and bright—here all was painful and dark. In Eden there was disobedience and the first Adam hid. Here there was perfect obedience, and the second Adam presented Himself as the spotless Lamb of God, ready for sacrifice.

CHAPTER NINETEEN

Contents: Pilate brings Jesus before the multitude. The rejection of the Savior and the crucifixion. His entombment.
Conclusion: Only Scripture itself can conclude this scene. Isa. 53 (whole chapter).
Key Word: Crucifixion, v. 18.
Strong Verses: 4 (b), 17, 18, 30.
Christ Seen: The death of Jesus fulfilled every sacrificial ceremony of the Old Testament. He was the "passover lamb." As the blood of the Old Testament sacrifice was sprinkled seven times (Num. .19:1-10), so there was a seven-fold sprinkling of the blood of Jesus in His crucifixion. 1. Scourged—19:1. 2. Thorns—19:2; 3-4. Each hand pierced. 5-6. Each foot pierced. 7. The spear thrust—v. 34.

CHAPTER TWENTY

Contents: Resurrection of Christ.
Conclusion: He Who gave His life as a ransom resumed His life again by the mighty power of God, proving the acceptability of His sacrifice as a satisfaction for sin, with the Father, and offering to all who should trust in Him, the peace of God that passes all understanding.
Key Word: Resurrection, v. 14.
Strong Verses: 21, 29 (b). Promise: 31.

Christ Seen: v. 31. This verse defines the purpose of God's Word—the demonstrating of the deity of Jesus Christ and the efficacy of His salvation.

CHAPTER TWENTY-ONE

Contents: The risen Christ surprises the disciples and directs their fishing. Peter given opportunity to reaffirm His allegiance to Christ.

Conclusion: In those disappointments which to us are very grievous, our Master often has designs that are very gracious. They are happy and successful in their work who know how to take hints from Him, for nothing can be lost but much gained by following His orders.

Before Christ can commit His sheep to our care, He would have us examine the love of our hearts toward Him. If we would try whether we are true disciples of His, let us ask ourselves the question, "Do we really love Jesus?"

Key Word: Service (v. 6) and love (v. 15).

Strong Verses: 15, 16, 17.

Christ Seen: v. 25. The truth about Jesus could never be exhausted. Jesus never spoke an idle word nor did an idle thing. He wrought probably thousands of miracles of which we have no record. All that is needful for our salvation is written. The ages of eternity will reveal the wonders of the life of the Son of God.

THE ACTS

Key Thought:	Number of Chapters:	Key Verse:	Christ seen as:
Witness	28	1:8	Ascended L o r d and Christ.

Writer of the Book:	Date:	Conclusion of the Book:
		The work that Jesus
Luke	A. D. 65	"began" to do was, and is, continued by Him through the Holy Spirit.

SUMMARY

CHAPTER ONE

Contents: Resurrection ministry of Christ. The apostolic commission. Promise of the Lord's second coming. Waiting for the coming of the Spirit.

Conclusion: Waiting on God for the anointing of the Spirit is the great condition of spiritual blessing and fullness of power. Those whom Jesus Christ employs as His witnesses He will qualify for it by a better spirit than their own—the Holy Spirit, His representative.

Key Word: Tarrying, vv. 4, 8, 14.

Strong Verse: 7. Promises: 8, 11.

Christ Seen: v. 11. This is one of the most definite promises of the second coming in the Scriptures. This "same Jesus"—not another (John 14: 16), is coming "in like manner" as He went up—in the clouds visibly. This could not have been fulfilled in the coming of the Spirit at Pentecost.

CHAPTER TWO

Contents: Holy Spirit's coming on day of Pentecost. The gospel given to the Jews. Peter's great sermon on the resurrected Christ, and the conviction of the people.

Conclusion: Upon Jesus Christ's return to heaven, He poured forth the Holy Spirit upon His own, proving His arrival there as the crucified Lamb of God, and distinguishing His followers as messengers from heaven. The fullness of the Holy Spirit is necessary to a true understanding of the Scriptures and to the presenting of Jesus the Christ in convicting power to unsaved men.

Key Word: Holy Ghost, v. 4. Witnessing, v. 14.

Strong Verses: 23, 24, 33, 36. Promises: 21, 38, 39.

Christ Seen: vv. 32-34. Three conclusive proofs are here given that Jesus Christ arose from the dead. 1. He was seen by the disciples. 2. The Holy Spirit has come upon men, and this promise was conditioned by Jesus upon His resurrection. 3. The prophecies declared He must not see corruption.

CHAPTER THREE

Contents: The lame man healed at the temple gate.

Conclusion: The hand of compassion, extended by Spirit-filled men, in the name of Jesus Christ, the risen Lord, is fraught with power to lift men heavenward. The cures of Christ are visible to all—let men therefore know that He Who was crucified was none other than the Prince of Life.

Key Word: Power of Christ, vv. 8, 12, 16.

Strong Verses: 15, 18, 19, 26.

Christ Seen: v. 15. They preserved a murderer, a destroyer of life, and thought to destroy the Saviour, the Author of life. But God raised Him from the dead, proving that in fighting against Jesus, they were fighting against God. The doctrine of Jesus Christ was thereby confirmed, and the reproach of His sufferings was rolled away.

CHAPTER FOUR

Contents: The first persecution. Peter's address to the Sanhedrin. Preaching in Jesus' name forbidden. Christians again filled with the Spirit. State of the Church at Jerusalem.

Conclusion: The more resolute are Christ's servants to witness of Him, the more spiteful will be the agents of Satan—therefore, let Satan's agents be ever so spiteful, Christ's witnesses must be resolute, for the Holy Spirit may be counted upon to enable them to do their part. Persecution gives wings to the truth.

Key Word: Persecution, vv. 3, 29.

Strong Verses: 11, 12, 20, 31.

Christ Seen: v. 12. Those are eternally undone who do not take shelter in the name of Jesus Christ and make it their refuge and strong tower. Only by embracing Him and Him only, receiving His doctrine, is there salvation for any.

CHAPTER FIVE

Contents: Sin and death of Ananias and Sapphira. The second persecution and answer of apostles to their persecutors. Warning of Gamaliel. Apostles beaten.

Conclusion: Beware of going to greater length in profession than the inner life will stand—being ambitious to be counted religious and liberal while secretly cherishing selfish motives—for this is lending oneself to Satan and lying, not merely to men, but to the Holy Ghost, a great affront to God.

Never does good work go on in the name of Jesus Christ but it is met with opposition, for Satan, the destroyer of men, will ever be an adversary to those who are benefactors to men. We may cheerfully trust God with our safety, so long as we keep close to the will of God and trust in Christ our leader.

Key Word: Lying (to Holy Ghost), vv. 3, 9. Persecution, vv. 18, 33, 40.

Strong Verses: 29, 31, 32, 39, 42.

Christ Seen: v. 31. God has invested Christ with the highest dignity and entrusted Him with the highest authority. It is He alone who is authorized to give repentance and remission to men. The new heart is His work, the broken spirit a sacrifice of His providing, the putting away of sin His task alone.

CHAPTER SIX

Contents: The first deacons. Third persecution. Stephen before the council.

Conclusion: Those who are called to preach the Word of God must not neglect this special ministry for church activities that should be carried on by others. Those engaged in the work of Christ's church regardless of how menial may be their task, must be free from scandal, men that can be trusted, possessed of discretion and filled with the Holy Ghost.

Key Word: Deacons, v. 3.

Strong Verse: 4.

Christ Seen: Christ can be truly represented only by those who are filled with His Spirit. How can those at the head of Christ's Church make men know what Christ is like unless they can show what Christ, by His Spirit, has made them like?

CHAPTER SEVEN

Contents: Address of Stephen before the council. Stephen martyred.

Conclusion: Those who are filled with the Holy Ghost and the Word of God cannot but speak boldly against sin, and they will be made fit for anything, either to act for Christ or to suffer for Him. As their afflictions for Christ abound, their consolation in Him may yet more abound. Let us as we witness look constantly to Christ that we may be ever set above the fear of man.

Key Word: Testimony, v. 1. Martyrdom, v. 59.

Strong Verses: 52, 55, 56.

Christ Seen: v. 56. Col. 3:1 tells us when Jesus ascended, He sat down in heaven. Stephen sees Him standing. He stood to welcome to heaven the first martyr. He will stand again when the hour of the rapture of the Church is at hand.

CHAPTER EIGHT

Contents: Saul persecuting Christians. The first missionaries. The case of Simon, the sorcerer. Philip and the Ethiopian.

Conclusion: Where Jesus Christ is preached and the gospel is embraced, Satan is forced to quit his hold of men, and those are restored to their right mind who, while they were blinded by Satan, were distracted and dissatisfied. The bringing of Christ's gospel to any place or individual is a matter of great joy to that place or person.

Key Word: Preaching Christ, vv. 4, 5, 12, 25, 35, 40.

Strong Verses: 4, 20, 37.

Christ Seen: v. 37. A short but comprehensive confession of faith. The deity of Jesus Christ is the principal doctrine of Christianity, and those who believe it with all their hearts and confess it are to be baptized— and only those.

CHAPTER NINE

Contents: Conversion of Saul of Tarsus. Paul preaches and visits Jerusalem and returns to Tarsus. Peter heals Aeneas. Tabitha raised from the dead.

Conclusion: There is no need to despair of the conversion of those who commit the worst outrages against Christianity, for the power of the Lord Jesus is able to break down the stubborn will of one who is at the same time chief of legalists and chief of sinners. God chooses the instruments He would employ in His service, and is able to fit them for His designs by the power of His Spirit.

Key Word: Saul, v. 1.

Strong Verse: 5.

Christ Seen: v. 20. One who has been filled with the Holy Ghost is sure to preach Christ, that He is the Son of God.

CHAPTER TEN

Contents: Peter opens the gospel door to the Gentiles. Cornelius sends for Peter and Peter goes to Caesarea. Peter's sermon to Gentiles in Cornelius' house. Holy Spirit comes upon Gentile believers.

Conclusion: In Jesus Christ, neither circumcision nor uncircumcision availeth anything, for by His finished work, the door of the gospel has been opened to "whosoever believeth." Whatever nation one may be of, though far remote from the seed of Abraham, though ever so despicable, that will be no prejudice to him, if he will receive God's appointed sacrifice for the remission of sins.

Key Word: Gentiles called, vv. 34-35.

Strong Verses: 15, 34, 35, 43.

Christ Seen: vv. 42-43. All men shall be accountable to Jesus Christ as Judge if they will not receive Him as Savior. He alone determines the everlasting condition of all men at the great day. Those who believe in His Name may rest assured that there will be no condemnation for them.

CHAPTER ELEVEN

Contents: Peter vindicates his ministry to the Gentiles. Name "Christians" first applied at Antioch.

Conclusion: As Christians travel the Gospel spreads, and where God's Word takes root, the hand of the Lord goes with it to give the tokens of His good will and the evidences of His work among them by the Holy Spirit.

Key Word: Antioch Christians, vv. 22, 26.

Strong Verse: 23.

Christ Seen: v. 26. The name "Christians" cannot be, as some claim, a nickname. The Holy Spirit would not draw attention to the epithets of a jeering crowd and let it pass down the centuries as their accredited name. The name was certainly divinely chosen, for it puts emphasis on "Christ" (anointed One) rather than the human name of our Lord, in which case we would have been called "Jesuits."

CHAPTER TWELVE

Contents: Persecutions of the church and arrest of Peter. Prayer for his deliverance and his miraculous release. Death of Herod.

Conclusion: Times of public distress and danger should be especially praying times for the church. However God's people are surrounded, there is always a way open heavenward, nor can the strongest bars intercept His power. God is able to do exceeding abundantly above all we ask or think.

Key Word: Delivered, v. 11.
Strong Verse: 5.
Christ Seen: The Lord Jesus Himself burst the bands of the grave and death. He is the strong and mighty One Who is able to tear down any bars that hinder the progress of His truth. Angels are at His bidding to deliver us whenever we call upon Him for release.

CHAPTER THIRTEEN

Contents: Paul and Barnabas called. Satanic opposition from a sorcerer. Paul's sermon in the synagogue at Antioch. Opposition from Jews. Paul and Barnabas turn to Gentiles.
Conclusion: Those who have been separated to Christ and the Holy Ghost will have the presence of the Holy Ghost with them to strengthen them, carry forward their work and give success to the Word preached. Those thus called may venture upon the stormy sea of persecution for Christ's sake as if it was a quiet harbor, having great joy in the sowing of the Word and confidence that He will bless it to His own glory.
Key Word: Word published, vv. 5, 44, 49.
Strong Verses: 26, 38, 39, 47.
Christ Seen: v. 33. The resurrection of Jesus Christ was the great proof of His being the Son of God with power, and was the confirmation of all that was prophesied about Him, and the ratification of His divine commissions. His resurrection is proven—v. 31.

CHAPTER FOURTEEN

Contents: Work of the Gospel at Iconium, Derbe, Lystra. An impotent man at Lystra healed. Paul stoned. Elders appointed in the churches.
Conclusion: Those who speak boldly in the Lord need not think it strange if the preaching of the Gospel occasions divisions, nor be offended by the insults heaped upon them by embittered and convicted spirits. They shall be made strong in the Lord and in the power of His might, and God shall confirm their testimony in granting wonders to be done by their hands.
Key Word: Giving testimony, v. 3.
Strong Verse: 22.
Christ Seen: v. 15. There is only one man who can, without idolatry, be worshiped—Jesus, the Christ Who was "God manifest in the flesh." "Thou shalt worship the Lord thy God and Him only."

CHAPTER FIFTEEN

Contents: The council at Jerusalem and the question of circumcision. Paul's second missionary journey. Silas chosen.
Conclusion: Those who are ever so well taught have need to stand upon their guard that they be not untaught again, and having known liberty in Christ Jesus should again be brought into bondage to law which cannot save. In a multitude of counsellors there is safety and satisfaction if the counsellors are men whom God has approved and who are instructed in His Word. When serious differences in regard to God's Word arise, let men of God come together in solemn meeting for prayer and mutual advice.
Key Word: Council, vv. 6, 25.
Strong Verses: 11, 14, 18.
Christ Seen: v. 14. This is one of the most important passages in the New Testament, stating Christ's program for the church in this dispensation. It is not the conversion of the world through the different agencies of reform, but the taking out of the world of an elect people who shall make up the Body or Bride of Christ. The Gospel everywhere calls out some, but it never, in any place, has been known to convert all, and nothing of this order is to be expected in this age. The work of the church is soul winning.

CHAPTER SIXTEEN

Contents: Paul finds Timothy. Paul's Macedonian vision. The first convert in Europe. Demons cast out of a damsel. Paul and Silas beaten. Conversion of the Philippian jailer.
Conclusion: The movements of God's servants and the dispensing of the means of grace by them are in a particular manner under a divine guidance and

direction, and those who are under the check and conduct of the Spirit, though they be called upon to suffer much for Jesus' sake, may be sure God will in some way get glory to Himself by their testimony and persecutions.

Key Word: Called (v. 10) and kept (vv. 25, 27).

Promise: 31.

Christ Seen: v. 31. Here is the sum of the whole Gospel, the covenant of grace in a nutshell. It is the only way to salvation. Admit the record that God has given in His Gospel concerning His Son, assent to it as faithful and worthy of acceptation, receive Jesus Christ as He is offered to us in the Gospel, and give up yourself to be saved and ruled by Him.

CHAPTER SEVENTEEN

Contents: Founding of church at Thessalonica and the Jewish opposition. Paul and Silas at Berea. Paul at Athens and the sermon from Mars' hill.

Conclusion: The doctrine of Christ does not fear a scrutiny, but will be borne out fully by the light of all Scripture. Those who reason from the Scriptures concerning "Christ crucified" may expect not only that God will incline some to make use of the means of grace by searching the Scriptures for themselves, but that the enmity of the restless agents of Satan will be aroused. Nevertheless, by seeking to extinguish the divine fire, enemies will but spread it the farther and faster.

Key Word: (Scriptural) Reasoning, vv. 2, 11, 22.

Strong Verses: 11, 24, 25, 26, 28, 31.

Christ Seen: v. 3. The scope of all preaching is to point to Jesus Christ as the One Who made atonement and was resurrected for the justification of all who will believe. Jesus must be the subject of all preaching, and our business is to bring people to acquaintance with Him.

CHAPTER EIGHTEEN

Contents: Paul at Corinth. The careless Gallio. Paul takes a Jewish vow. Apollos at Ephesus.

Conclusion: Let the Gospel be propagated, not by force, but by fair argument, meeting the reasonings of sinners with ready answers from the Scriptures. It is always our duty to testify with all solemnity to Christ's deity, especially where men speak reproachfully of Him, thus making ourselves clean from the blood of their souls. Those who have Christ with them need not shrink from pleading the cause of heaven with boldness.

Key Word: Testifying (v. 5) and reasoning (vv. 4, 19).

Promises: 9, 10.

Christ Seen: vv. 5, 28. Too much cannot be said of the necessity, in our preaching or witnessing, of preaching "not ourselves, but Christ Jesus, the Lord," teaching men from the Scriptures the great fundamental doctrine of His deity.

CHAPTER NINETEEN

Contents: Paul at Ephesus. Disciples of John the Baptist become Christians. Paul in the synagogue and in the school of Tyrannus. Paul's miracles. Uproar of the silversmiths.

Conclusion: Let Christ's witnesses speak undauntedly with holy resolution, as those who have not the least doubt of the things they speak of, nor the least distrust of the power of Him they speak from, nor the least dread of those they speak to. While some will oppose the Gospel because it calls many off from their sinful employments, it will lead many to true contrition for sin and confession of Christ.

Key Word: Disputing and persuading, v. 8.

Strong Verse: 18.

Christ Seen: vv. 10, 20. The Gospel is Christ's Word. To preach from the Scriptures without preaching Christ is to miss the result in v. 20, the prevailing mightily in the hearts of men. It is Christ in our preaching Who goes on conquering and to conquer.

CHAPTER TWENTY

Contents: Paul goes to Macedonia and Greece. His visits at Troas, Miletus. Paul's conference with the Ephesian elders.

Conclusion: As witnesses of the grace of God through Jesus Christ, we ought not to hold our lives of any account to ourselves in comparison with accomplishing our course and declaring the whole counsel of God.   Being ourselves made pure by the blood of the Son of Man, it behooves us to make ourselves pure from the blood of the sons of men.

Key Word: Testifying, vv. 21, 24.

Strong Verses: 20, 24, 27, 28, 32, 35.

Christ Seen: v. 28.   The priceless cost of redemption is here seen—the blood of God.   See 1 Tim. 3:16.   Christ's deity is thereby asserted.   His blood was of infinite value—being God's blood.

CHAPTER TWENTY-ONE

Contents: Holy Spirit forbids Paul to go to Jerusalem.   Paul goes to Jerusalem.   Paul takes a Jewish vow.   Seized in the temple by the Jews and bound with chains.

Conclusion: Disregard of any details of the leading of the Holy Spirit leads into a multitude of difficulties that might have been avoided.   God often protests the most devoted acts of some of His servants, even acts of self sacrifice, and would save them from bringing their greater usefulness to an abrupt end; nevertheless He is able to overrule their mistakes and bring good out of them to men and glory to Himself.

Key Word: Warnings disregarded, vv. 4, 11, 14.

Strong Verse: 13.

Christ Seen: v. 36.   As men cried "Crucify Him" and "away with Him" at Christ Himself, though they could not say what evil He had done, so they will often treat His ambassadors and desire to chase them out of the world.

CHAPTER TWENTY-TWO

Contents: Paul's defense before the multitude.   Recounts his conversion.

Conclusion: God's servants who are set upon with rage and fury because of their teachings concerning Christ cannot offer a better defense of their doctrine than to relate their own vital experience with the saving power of Jesus Christ.   Christianity is not an argument but a life.

Key Word: Experience, v. 3.

Strong Verse: 16.

Christ Seen: v. 14.   There is a three-fold preparation for the service of Christ.   1.   To know His will.   2.   To have a vision of Christ, the Just One, crucified.   3.   To hear His voice.

CHAPTER TWENTY-THREE

Contents: Paul before the Sanhedrin.   The conspiracy to kill Paul and its defeat.   Paul sent to Felix.

Conclusion: Many are the troubles of the righteous, but some way or other, the Lord delivereth them out of them all.   God is able to bring the hidden things to light and make conspirators' own tongues betray them, and above all to make the persecutions of His servants to turn to the wider spread of the Gospel.

Key Word: Dissension (v. 7) and conspiracy (v. 13).

Strong Verse: 11.

Christ Seen: It is the will of Christ that His servants should often suffer with Him, but in their trials He would have them to be "cheerful," and in the consciousness of His presence, how can one be otherwise?   If He is with us, all secular events will be ordered to give opportunity to witness for Christ.

CHAPTER TWENTY-FOUR

Contents: Paul accused before Felix, and his defense.

Conclusion: Every false cause can find men of sharp wits to plead it.   The truest Christian life is no fence against the hatred of the rejectors of Christ (John 15:18), but if God's servants can speak with the language of a clear conscience, they need have no fear.   "The angel of the Lord encampeth round about them."

Key Word: Accused, v. 2.

Strong Verse: 16.

Christ Seen: v. 14.   It is nothing new for the Scriptural and right way to worship to be called "heresy."   Jesus Christ Himself was called a heretic.

CHAPTER TWENTY-FIVE

Contents: Paul before Festus. His appeal to Caesar.

Conclusion: It is nothing for the most excellent ones of the earth to have all manner of evil said against them falsely for Christ's sake and to be represented even in courts as odious and harmful to society. Nevertheless God is able to make men's worldly policies serve His own purpose (Psa. 76:10), and when enemies think to block the gates of the Gospel, He is able to open them wider.

Key Word: Falsely accused, vv. 5, 7.

Strong Verse: 11.

Christ Seen: v. 19. What Paul affirmed concerning Jesus Christ, that He is alive, is a matter of such vast importance, that if it be not true, we are all undone. Yet many men today treat the subject slightly as did this Roman.

CHAPTER TWENTY-SIX

Contents: Paul's defense before Agrippa.

Conclusion: When God's servant is given a chance to speak for himself, it is well if he may speak for Christ instead, nor need he be ashamed of the Gospel of Christ in any company. Though they answer with scorn and contempt, it is certain that God will in some way use the testimony for His glory.

Key Word: Defense, v. 1.

Strong Verses: 8, 18, 28, 29.

Christ Seen: v. 23. Three great Gospel fundamentals to be continually emphasized. 1. That Jesus Christ was appointed to suffering and the cross. 2. That He should be the chief of the resurrection, making way for the resurrection of the saints. 3. That He arose to show a light to those in darkness, and by the power of His resurrection to give convincing proof of the truth of His doctrine.

CHAPTER TWENTY-SEVEN

Contents: Paul sent to Rome. The hurricane. God's assurance to Paul in the storm, and his safe landing.

Conclusion: Worldly men insist on being guided by human prudence, but the Christian who is in communion with Jesus, the great Pilot, may know more about sailing than any unpraying Captain could ever know. Since God has promised to be faithful to His own in the storms, let them be cheerful in the storms, knowing that while He has work for them to do, no difficulty can get in the way.

Key Word: Storm, v. 14.

Strong Verses: 23, 25.

Christ Seen: What Paul was in the ship, Christians should be in the world. If Christ is the senior member of our firm, we shall be able in the midst of the storms of earth to take upon ourselves great responsibilities, and by the power of prayer to save many a situation to the glory of God.

CHAPTER TWENTY-EIGHT

Contents: The landing at Melita. Miracle of the viper's bite. Healing of Publius' father. Paul's arrival at Rome and his ministry there to the Jews. Paul turns to the Gentiles.

Conclusion: Wherever in the providence of God the Christian is put, he is placed there to do a work for God and to represent Jesus Christ. Blessing may come to thousands out of seeming calamity that befalls God's true servants. God's ways are past finding out, but let His servant be confident always in His promises and ready to do every good work wherever the waves of events may land him.

Key Word: Healing (v. 9) and teaching (v. 31).

Strong Verses: 25, 26, 27, 28.

Christ Seen: v. 31. Paul stuck to his text "Jesus Christ" to the end. Let those who are tempted to diverge from that which is their main business— to "preach not ourselves but Christ"—ask themselves of what concern it is to Jesus Christ and His kingdom, to preach anything but **HIM.**

ROMANS

Key Thought:	Number of Chapters:	Key Verse:	Christ seen as:
Justification	16	1:17	Lord of Righteousness

Writer of the Book:	Date:	Conclusion of the Book:
Paul	About A. D. 60	Justification is by faith without works, and is the righteousness of Christ imputed to the believer, wherein he is made eternally safe.

SUMMARY

CHAPTER ONE

Contents: Words of comfort to the church at Rome. The universe a revelation of the power and deity of God. The deplorable condition of a lost world.

Conclusion: God has made Himself known to all men by the things of His creation. Though men know He exists and might infer that it was their duty to worship Him only, they glorify Him not as God, but ascribe deity to the most contemptible of creatures and give themselves over to vile affections. Those who thus dishonor Him, will be given up eventually to dishonor themselves.

Key Word: Carnality, v. 24.

Strong Verses: 4, 16, 19, 20, 21.

Christ Seen: v. 4. The demonstration of the deity of Jesus Christ is His resurrection from the dead. The sign of the prophet Jonah (Matt. 12:39) was intended for the last conviction. Those who will not be convinced by that will not be convinced by anything.

CHAPTER TWO

Contents: The equal standing of Jew and Gentile before the justice of God. Morality apart from Christ useless as means of salvation. Jews knowing the law condemned by the law.

Conclusion: All men, Jew or Gentile, good or bad, are under doom for breaking the righteous law of God—the heathen who are sinners and know it—(1:18-32)—the self-righteous who think they need no salvation (2:1-11), and the religionist who makes a mere profession (2:17-29) all stand on the same level before the justice of God and all in need of the salvation God has provided.

Key Word: No partiality (No respect of persons) v. 11.

Strong Verses: 4, 8, 11, 12. Promises: 6, 7.

Christ Seen: v. 4. The riches of His goodness are described in Eph. 1:7—"redemption through the blood of Christ and forgiveness of sins according to the riches of His grace." However moral or religious a man be, if he has despised this divine plan he is lost.

CHAPTER THREE

Contents: The common guilt of both Jew and Gentile. Justification by faith, not by the law.

Conclusion: The sum of all sin is coming short of the glory of God for which we were created—therefore all the world stands guilty before God, unable by any works to gain acceptance with God. Justification before God is resolved thereby purely into the free grace of God through Jesus Christ to all who will receive it as a free gift.

Key Word: All under sin, v. 9.

Strong Verses: 4, 10, 11, 12, 20, 22, 23, 24, 25, 26.

Christ Seen: v. 22. The gospel excludes none that do not exclude themselves by refusing to appropriate the finished work of Jesus Christ. The best brand of self-righteousness will not stand before God. We must wear the righteousness which God has ordained and which is brought in by

His Son. All men alike are welcome to God through Jesus Christ. He has but one plan of salvation.

CHAPTER FOUR

Contents: Abraham justified by faith, not works. Justifying faith defined.

Conclusion: No man can pretend to merit eternal life, nor show any worth in his work which may answer such a reward. Disclaiming any pretension he must cast himself wholly upon the free grace of God by faith in the redemptive work of Jesus Christ. To such a one faith is counted for righteousness.

Key Word: Justifying faith, v. 5.

Strong Verses: 5, 7, 8, 16, 25.

Christ Seen: vv. 24-25. Christ's death and resurrection are the two main hinges on which the door of salvation turns. He was delivered as our sacrifice for sin. He was raised for the perfecting and completing of our justification.

CHAPTER FIVE

Contents: The results of justification. Life and righteousness through Jesus Christ.

Conclusion: Justification through faith in Jesus Christ takes away guilt and so makes way for peace, and gives access into the wondrous grace of God. Through Jesus Christ alone the believer comes into fullness of joy, being saved from wrath, solaced in His love, not only going to heaven, but going triumphantly.

Key Word: Justification, v. 1.

Strong Verses: 1, 5, 6, 8, 10, 19.

Christ Seen: v. 10. The dying Jesus laid the foundation, satisfying for sin, but it is the living Jesus that perfects the work—He lives to make intercession. By His death He saves from penalty—by His life from the power of sin.

CHAPTER SIX

Contents: Deliverance from the power of indwelling sin by counting the old life dead, and yielding to the new life.

Conclusion: It is an abuse of the grace of God in Christ for the believer to think he can sin because he is justified by faith. We must cease from the acts of sin, denying the fleshly life the scepter over us, and surrender the soul to the conduct and command of the righteous law of God that our members may be instruments of righteousness unto God.

Key Word: Dead to sin, v. 2.

Strong Verses: 3, 4, 6, 11, 12, 13, 16, 22. Promise: 23.

Christ Seen: vv. 3-6. The manner of Christ's baptism is a figure of the believer's spiritual burial and resurrection. Immersion symbolizes the entrance by the gateway of Christ's death into the domain of His righteousness and resurrection life, and is the expression of the baptized one's faith that God has taken him from among the dead and given him newness of life.

CHAPTER SEVEN

Contents: The conflict of the flesh with the spiritual nature. Impossibility of victory through the law.

Conclusion: The function of the law is to detect and condemn sin, not to deliver from it. In the life of the believer there will ever be conflict between grace and corruption in the heart, between the law of God and the law of sin. Who shall deliver us? Jesus Christ is the all-sufficient Saviour and Friend, Who has not only purchased our deliverance, but is our advocate in Heaven, through Whom we may be made victorious.

Key Word: Sold under sin, v. 14.

Strong Verses: 4, 12, 13, 23, 24, 25.

Christ Seen: The believer upon acceptance of Christ receives a spiritual nature which begins at once strife with the Adamic nature, which is not eradicated until we stand in Christ's presence. The strife is effectually taken up on the believer's behalf by the Holy Spirit, and if the believer will but yield to Him in the hour of conflict, He will take the victory (8:2; Gal. 5:16-17).

CHAPTER EIGHT

Contents: The new law of the Holy Spirit in the believer, giving deliverance from sinful nature. The full result of the Gospel in the believer and his security.

Conclusion: It is the unspeakable comfort of all those who are in Christ Jesus that no condemnation remains to them, and that the indwelling Spirit does in the believer what the law never could do. He gives deliverance from the power of sin, quickens for service, imparts assurance, and inspires prayer.

Key Word: Made free, v. 2.

Strong Verses: 1, 2, 14, 16, 26, 28, 31, 34, 35. Promises: 18, 32, 38, 39.

Christ Seen: vv. 26, 34. The security of the believer as to the penalty of sin rests upon the one foundation of Christ's finished work (v. 32) and His intercession in heaven for the believer. The believer's security against the power of sin is the present work of the Holy Spirit within him and His intercession for us. Notice the two intercessors.

CHAPTER NINE

Contents: Covenants of Israel not set aside by Gospel. The seven-fold privilege of Israel. The blinding of Israel and God's mercy to the Gentiles.

Conclusion: God is absolute sovereign in disposing of the children of men with reference to their eternal state. He dispenses His gifts to whom He will without giving us His reasons, but we may rest assured He is a competent judge. Gentiles are permitted by Him, by the short cut of believing in Christ, to attain to that for which the Jews had long been "beating about the bush," but lost because of sin and unbelief.

Key Word: Election, v. 11.

Strong Verses: 20, 21, 33.

Christ Seen: v. 33. It is sad that the foundation stone should be to any a stone of stumbling, and the rock of salvation a rock of offense, but so He was to the Jews, and is still to multitudes. Those who do believe, however, shall not be ashamed, for their expectations in Him shall never be disappointed.

CHAPTER TEN

Contents: Israel's failure explained by unbelief. The plan of salvation.

Conclusion: Sincerity is not a ground of safety; self-righteousness is not a ground of salvation. The design of the law was to lead people to Christ, Who is the end of it, and the only ground for salvation is to become interested by humble faith in Christ's satisfaction of the law, and so be "justified through the redemption that is in Christ Jesus."

Key Word: Salvation, v. 1.

Strong Verses: 3, 4, 10, 11, 17. Promises: 9, 12, 13.

Christ Seen: v. 4. The law is not destroyed by the Gospel, but full satisfaction being made to the law by Jesus Christ (no one else could), for our breach of the law, the end is attained, and we are put in another way of justification, even faith in His finished work.

CHAPTER ELEVEN

Contents: A spiritual Israel finding salvation. National Israel blinded. Warning to Gentiles. Israel yet to be saved nationally.

Conclusion: The Jews, at present cast off because of unbelief, will in due time as a people be taken into God's favor again, when the fullness of the Gentiles be come in and when the Deliverer (Christ) shall have appeared again. As a people they are for this age judicially blinded, although there is a remnant according to faith in Christ. The Gentiles grafted into the Church must not trample upon the Jews as a reprobate people, but remember that the law of faith excludes all boasting, either of ourselves or against others.

Key Word: Israel, v. 1.

Strong Verses: 12, 18, 21, 22, 25, 32, 33, 36. Promise: 26.

Christ Seen: vv. 25-26. The Church is a people taken from the Gentiles (Acts 15:14) and is a "full destined number" (Rev. 7:9). When the "fullness of the Gentiles" (not world conversion) is brought in, Christ is coming again, and will be soon manifested as Israel's long looked-for Deliverer.

CHAPTER TWELVE

Contents: Christian life and service. Consecration to Christ.

Conclusion: Since we have been justified through grace, by faith in Christ, it is our first duty to surrender ourselves to God a living sacrifice, that there may be a saving change wrought in us and that we might be made serviceable in every way to our fellow men. We stand in relation not only to Christ, but to one another in Christ, and we are engaged to do all the good we can one to another and to act in conjunction for the common benefit.

Key Word: Consecration (present bodies), v. 1.

Strong Verses: 1, 2, 4, 5, 10, 12, 13, 19, 21.

Christ Seen: v. 1. The reference to "sacrifice" no doubt connects Lev. 1:6-9. The burnt offering typifies Christ offering Himself to God in perfect devotion to the Father's will. The offerer or the Priest got nothing of it—it was all devoted to God. So the believer is to live a life completely dedicated to Him—in which He has absolute right of way.

CHAPTER THIRTEEN

Contents: Believer's attitude toward civil government. Law of love toward neighbors.

Conclusion: Obedience to civil magistrates is one of the laws of Christ whose religion makes people good subjects. Love to our fellow-men is a debt that must always be in the paying, yet always owing, for love is inclusive of all duties and is the image of Christ upon the soul.

Key Word: Subjection, v. 1, and love, v. 8.

Strong Verses: 1, 7, 8, 10, 14.

Christ Seen: v. 14. Victory over the flesh may be always ours through personal dealings with Christ. To "put on Christ" is not imitation of Christ, but appropriation of Him. "Christ liveth in me"—is the victory—and if He has the right of way in us, we will make no provisions for satisfying the flesh.

CHAPTER FOURTEEN

Contents: Law of love concerning doubtful things.

Conclusion: To do what conscience allows is not always right and to do what it questions is always wrong. The strong Christian should not be contemptuous toward the opinion of a weaker brother on a doubtful question, neither should the weaker man be censorious toward the stronger because of what conscience allows him. Both have a right to opinion and both are responsible to God for it.

Key Word: Judging, vv. 4, 10.

Strong Verses: 4, 5, 7, 8, 10, 12, 17.

Christ Seen: vv. 8-9. To the Lord Jesus Christ, to Whom all judgment is committed, we are to do everything. To this end, He both died and arose, that He might be Lord of those who are living to rule them, and Lord of the dead to raise them up. We are therefore, answerable to Him in everything. Let us not intrench upon His right by arraigning our brothers at our own bar.

CHAPTER FIFTEEN

Contents: Jewish and Gentile believers under one salvation. Paul speaks of His ministry and coming journey.

Conclusion: The self-denial of our Lord Jesus Christ is the best argument against the selfishness of Christians. Let us not consult our own credit, ease, safety or pleasure, but give ourselves as He did, to bearing the infirmities of the weak, whether they be Jew or Gentile, agreeable or disagreeable, and striving to be likeminded in the Gospel to the glory of God.

Key Word: Gospel unity, v. 5.

Strong Verses: 1, 4, 13.

Christ Seen: v. 5. "According to Christ Jesus." Let Jesus Christ be the center of your unity. If in tune with Him, we will surely be in tune with each other, and we shall agree in truth rather than in error.

CHAPTER SIXTEEN

Contents: The outflow of Christian love. Closing salutations and benediction.

Conclusion: Courtesy and Christianity go together. Acknowledgment of favors

and greetings of love are returns we should make to our fellow laborers in
the Gospel for their joy and encouragement.

Key Word: Greetings, v. 3, etc.

Strong Verses: 17, 18, 20.

Christ Seen: vv. 17-18. Mark the believers attitude toward men who bring
in doctrines contrary to Jesus Christ. We are to MARK them (See Isa.
8:20). We are to AVOID them (2 Tim. 3:5; 2 John 10). We are not to
go to listen to them, nor admit them into the house to argue with them.
This is the Scriptural plan for resisting the teachings of those whose doctrines do not center around the person and all-sufficient work of Jesus.

I CORINTHIANS

Key Thought: God's Power	Number of Chapters: 16	Key Verse: 1:2	Christ seen as: First fruits of the dead.

Writer of the Book:	Date:	Conclusion of the Book: Jesus Christ our risen Lord is Head of the
Paul	A. D. 59	Body working through His people by the Holy Spirit.

SUMMARY

CHAPTER ONE

Contents: Christians' position in grace. The unspiritual condition of the Corinthian saints. Danger of following human leaders and exulting in human wisdom.

Conclusion: The consideration of being agreed in the great fundamentals of the faith should have extinguished all feuds and divisions about unessential points. Though there is not unity of sentiment, let there ever be unity of affection in the Church.

It is just with God to leave those to themselves who pour proud contempt on divine wisdom and grace. The way to divine light is to put out your own candle.

Key Word: Human wisdom, vv. 17, 18. Contentions, v. 11.

Strong Verses: 9, 18, 21, 27, 28, 30.

Christ Seen: v. 23. The plain preaching of a crucified Jesus is more powerful than all the oratory and philosophy of an unbelieving world. All the boasted science of the world cannot do for souls what "Christ crucified" does. All one needs, or can desire, they may have in Him (vv. 30-31). He is made wisdom to the foolish, righteousness to the guilty, sanctification to the corrupt, and redemption to those who are in bonds.

CHAPTER TWO

Contents: Christian revelation not indebted to human wisdom. Spiritual verities not discoverable to human wisdom.

Conclusion: The Christian on his knees can see farther than the philosopher on his tiptoes, for spiritual truth can be perceived only by the spiritually prepared mind. The truths of God are foolishness and trifling to a carnal mind. The only way to understand spiritual truth is to yield to the Author of it, the Holy Spirit.

Key Word: Spiritual wisdom, v. 10.

Strong Verses: 2, 10, 11, 14. Promise: 9.

Christ Seen: v. 2. "Christ and Him crucified" is the sum and substance of the Gospel. To display the banner of the cross and invite people under it should be the principal business of the ministers.

CHAPTER THREE

Contents: Hindrance of a carnal state to spiritual growth. Christian service and its reward.

Conclusion: Our salvation rests solely upon the completed work of Jesus Christ, but rewards are to be earned by spiritual service for God, and will be according to the quality of our works. True service done in the power of the indwelling Spirit, is of eternal standing, but fleshly service is perishable and will bring the Christian loss of reward at the final day.

Key Word: Labor, reward, v. 8.

Strong Verses: 9, 11, 13, 16, 19, 23. Promise: 14.

Christ Seen: v. 11. The doctrine of Jesus Christ and His mediation is the principal doctrine of Christianity. Those who build hopes of heaven on any other foundation build upon sinking sands. v. 23. Those who would be safe for time and happy for eternity, must be Christ's.

CHAPTER FOUR

Contents: Judgment of Christ's servants not committed to man.   Apostolic example of patience and humility.

Conclusion: God's steward awaits no judgment of man, but stands or falls by his Master's judgment—his standard being fidelity to God, not popularity with men.

Key Word: Judging, v. 3.

Strong Verses: 2, 5, 20.

Christ Seen: v. 5.   The Lord Jesus Who knows the counsels of our hearts is coming soon to reward us, not necessarily according to what we have brought to pass, but what our hearts have actually longed to do.   Many counsels formed by the heart, we have been unable to execute.

CHAPTER FIVE

Contents: Immorality rebuked and discipline enjoined.

Conclusion: The heinous sins of professed Christians are quickly noted and noised abroad to the injury of Christ's cause.   Let the believer walk circumspectly, for many eyes are upon him, and if he will not do so let the Church have no fellowship with him.

Key Word: Fornication, v. 1.

Strong Verses: 7, 8.

Christ Seen: vv. 7-8.   Christ was the fulfillment of the Jewish Passover. After the lamb was killed they kept the feast of unleavened bread.   So must we, not only seven days, but all our days.   The world life of the Christian must be one of "unleavened bread"—sincerity and truth.

CHAPTER SIX

Contents: Saints forbidden to go to law with each other.   Sanctity of the body.   The body the Lord's temple.

Conclusion: Contention of Christians before the law is much to the reproach of Christianity.   It is a forgetting of their real dignity as Christians to carry little matters about the things of life before heathen magistrates.

The question of a life of victory over sin that will glorify God will be settled by the believer recognizing to Whom he belongs and yielding to the Divine Guest Who resides within him.   Consecration is letting Christ and the Holy Spirit have what belongs to them.

Key Word: Going to law, v. 1.   The Body, v. 15.

Strong Verses: 2, 11, 12, 15, 17, 19, 20.

Christ Seen: v. 20.   Christ has purchased the believer, body, soul and spirit, by His own blood.   Let us, therefore, be careful what we do with another's property.   Let our bodies be kept as His whose they are and fit for His use and residence.

CHAPTER SEVEN

Contents: Sanctity of marriage.   Regulation of marriage among Gentile believers.

Conclusion: Marriage is by divine wisdom prescribed for the preventing of fornication.   Man and wife cannot separate at pleasure, nor for any other cause than what Christ allows, for it is a divine institution and is a compact for life by God's appointment.   Even though a Christian has been united to an unbeliever, before having accepted Christ, they are one flesh, they are to abide together and the believing one is to be sanctified for the sake of the unbelieving one.

Key Word: Marriage, v. 9.

Strong Verses: 20, 21, 22, 23, 24, 39.

Christ Seen: v. 23.   Christ, by the sacrifice of Calvary, has bought the believer, therefore the very tools of daily work should become sacred by partnership with Him.

CHAPTER EIGHT

Contents: Meats offered to idols, and the limitations of Christians' liberty.

Conclusion: There is nothing in the distinction of food that will make any distinction between men in God's account, and the Christian is free to eat that which the conscience allows.   Nevertheless he must be careful how he uses this liberty, lest it be the occasion of stumbling or hazzard the ruin of one younger or weaker in the faith.

Key Word: Christian liberty, v. 9.
Strong Verses: 2, 3, 6, 9, 13.
Christ Seen: v. 12. Injuries done to Christians are injuries done to Christ —especially to babes in Christ—weak Christians.

CHAPTER NINE

Contents: Paul vindicates his apostleship. The method and reward of true ministry and the support of the ministry.
Conclusion: It is no new thing for ministers of Christ to meet with the worst treatment where they might expect the best. Those who enjoy benefits by the ministry of the Word should not grudge the maintenance of those who are employed in this work. It is to the praise of a minister, nevertheless, to prefer the success of his ministry and the salvation of souls, to his own interest and to deny himself that he may serve Christ.
Key Word: Ministry, v. 2.
Strong Verses: 14, 19, 22. Promise: 24.
Christ Seen: v. 27. The word "castaway" is literally "disapproved," and so translated in other places. He is not expressing fear that he may fail of salvation (for his life was hid with Christ in God, Col. 3:1-3), but is speaking of service, and the possibility through unfaithfulness, of being laid on the shelf.

CHAPTER TEN

Contents: Israel in the wilderness, a warning example. Fellowship of the Lord's table demands separation. Law of love in relation to eating and drinking.
Conclusion: We should take warning from those who have gone before us, that carnal desires are the source and root of much sin and if not checked we know not whither they will carry us.
  To partake of the Lord's table is to profess to be in friendship and fellowship with Him, and communion with Christ and communion with Satan can never be had at once. Therefore let us aim in eating, drinking and in all we do, to glorify God.
Key Word: Temptation, v. 13. Communion, vv. 16, 21.
Strong Verses: 11, 12, 16, 20, 23, 31, 33. Promise: 13.
Christ Seen: v. 16. The ceremony of the Lord's supper is a token whereby we professedly hold communion with Him whose body was broken and blood shed to procure remission of our sins and the favor of God. vv. 3, 4. He is that Bread which came down from heaven. He is the Rock out of which refreshing streams come to the believer. It is impossible to be in alliance with Him without being devoted to Him.

CHAPTER ELEVEN

Contents: Christian order and the Lord's supper. Meaning of the Lord's table.
Conclusion: The Lord's supper is a memorial of His finished atonement, a parable of His present fellowship with His own and a prophecy of His second coming. The ordinances of Christ are very solemn and if they do not do our souls good, will do us harm. Let it not be eaten carelessly or with an insincere heart for it will turn to no account, but to increase guilt and ـring condemnation.
Key Word: Covered heads, v. 4. Lord's supper, v. 20.
Strong Verses: 3, 19, 23-27, 31, 32.
Christ Seen: v. 25. New covenant. These outward signs express the new covenant in Christ—His body broken, His blood shed, the benefits which flow from His death and sacrifice. His blood is the seal and sanction of all the privileges of the new covenant.

CHAPTER TWELVE

Contents: Spiritual gifts in the Body of Christ, for ministry and worship.
Conclusion: The Body of Christ in the world is for the service for, and manifestation of Christ, and the Body is to serve the Head, whose Body we are. The gifts and graces of the members of the Body greatly differ, but are freely given of God through the Holy Spirit. Since all powers in the members proceed from the Holy Ghost, no member may boast against

another, and no member, however insignificant, may consider himself un-
essential, but is equally obligated to be yielded to the Spirit.
Key Word: Gifts, vv. 1, 30.
Strong Verses: 3, 7, 13, 20, 21, 22, 26, 27.
Christ Seen: v. 13. The baptism with the Spirit forms the Body by unit-
ing believers to Christ, the risen and glorified Head, and to each other.
Regeneration is a participation in the baptism of Pentecost when the
Body of Christ was first organized.

CHAPTER THIRTEEN

Contents: Love, the supreme gift of the Spirit, and its governing power over
other gifts.
Conclusion: Love alone can give value to any service rendered in Christ's
name, and it is therefore the supreme gift of the Spirit, to be coveted and
prayed for above all others. Faith trusts and appropriates, hope expects,
but love expresses Christ and blesses men.
Key Word: Love, v. 1 (charity).
Strong Verses: 1-3, 13. Promise: 12.
Christ Seen: Jesus Christ was the supreme expression of the love of God
and His divine love and compassion is the gift of the Spirit to believers
who will be yielded to Him. Thinking of Jesus as "love" (for God is
love) substitute the name Jesus in place of "charity" and notice the force
of the text. Can you say "Christ liveth in me?"

CHAPTER FOURTEEN

Contents: Prophecy and speaking in tongues. The order of the ministry of
this gift in the church.
Conclusion: That is the best and most eligible gift which best answers the
purposes of charity and edifies the church. That which cannot be understood cannot edify, and such confusion is to be avoided in the church. No
gift of the Spirit is to be despised, and if the gift of tongues is bestowed,
it will be with interpretation among two or three brethren, and will result
in their blessing.
Key Word: Gift of tongues, v. 2.
Strong Verses: 2, 8, 9, 12, 19, 33.
Christ Seen: All believers have the Holy Spirit—1 Cor. 6:19-20, not all
were to have tongues—12:28-30. All public display of the gift, if it is
given by the Spirit, is for edification, 14:5-28, always accompanied by
interpretation, 14:13, 23-26, 28, always under control, 14:27. If accompanied by confusion, it is not of the Spirit, 14:33-40. It is the work of the
Holy Spirit to magnify Jesus Christ (Jn. 16:13), not to call attention to
Himself, hence we may judge of the source of certain manifestations, for
if more attention is drawn to manifestations than to the person of Christ,
it is not of God.

CHAPTER FIFTEEN

Contents: The resurrection of Christ and the resurrection of believers resulting from it.
Conclusion: The resurrection of Christ, together with His atoning work is
the cornerstone of all Christian doctrine. It is the evidence that sin has
been effectually put away, the ground for saving faith and the promise
that all united to the Body of Christ shall be raised at His coming to receive a glorious body like unto His own, and to bear forever the image of
the heavenly.
Key Word: Resurrection, v. 12.
Strong Verses: 3, 14, 17, 20, 42, 43, 44, 47, 58. Promises: 22, 23, 49, 51.
Christ Seen: If Christ's body lies in some nameless grave, there is no hope
for the believer, and the Gospel is nothing but emptiness. How do we
know His sacrifice for sin was accepted? How can we hope for our own
resurrection and immortality? "In Christ shall **all** be made alive" (v. 22),
but notice that the word "all" is defined—"they that are Christ's" (v. 23).

CHAPTER SIXTEEN

Contents: Closing instructions and greetings of Paul.

Conclusion: The Christian should lay by money in store for good uses, having a treasury for this purpose—a stock for others as well as for themselves. They should be ready to every good work as opportunity offers, whether it be in giving or in assisting in some other way the servants of Christ.

Key Word: Instruction.

Strong Verses: 2, 13.

Christ Seen: v. 22. Anathema Maran—atha—lit. "Accursed, our Lord cometh." Christ is here seen as the One Who is coming to execute the judgment denounced upon those who spurn His grace. Mt. 25:41, 46.

II CORINTHIANS

| Key Thought:
Our sufficiency | Number of Chapters:
13 | Key Verse:
7:6; 12:9 | Christ seen as:
Our sufficiency. |

| Writer of the Book:
Paul | Date:
A. D. 60 | Conclusion of the Book:
The Christian is God's ambassador, with a spiritual and glorious ministry, finding in Christ consolation in all his sufferings and sufficiency for every testing. |

SUMMARY

CHAPTER ONE

Contents: Paul's interest in the Corinthian Christians and his encouragement to them in Christ.

Conclusion: Man's extremity is God's opportunity. Affliction to the people of God is but a pruning knife to the vine to prepare them for greater usefulness to others. One of the greatest evidences of God's love to His own is to send them afflictions with grace to bear them.

Key Word: Consolation, v. 6.

Strong Verses: 3, 4, 5, 12.

Christ Seen: v. 5. When we truly share the sufferings of Christ, we have in Him peace in the midst of it all, and grace to bear it. The sufferings of the Christian are the sufferings of Christ. He sympathizes with His members when they suffer for His sake.

CHAPTER TWO

Contents: Forgiving those who have fallen into sin. The ministry of the Christian.

Conclusion: When a brother is truly penitent for his sin we should not be too rigid or severe with him, lest it give Satan an advantage by driving him to despair, but we should confirm our love to him by forgiving him and showing that our reproofs proceeded from love to his person rather than design to ruin him.

Key Word: Forgiveness, v. 10.

Strong Verses: 14, 15, 16.

Christ Seen: vv. 15-16. Unto some Christ becomes a savour of death unto death. Because they are willfully obstinate, they are finally blinded and Gospel hardened. They have rejected it to eternal spiritual death. To the humble and gracious, His Gospel becomes the savour of life unto life, quickening them who were "dead in trespasses and sins."

CHAPTER THREE

Contents: The ministry of Christ accredited. Its spiritual and glorious character.

Conclusion: True ministers are Christ's instruments, for He is the Author of all good that is in them and His love and His likeness are revealed in them by the Holy Spirit. They are ministers, not merely of the letter to read the written Word or to preach the letter of the Gospel only, but ministers of the Spirit also. The Spirit accompanies their ministrations and reveals Christ through their lives.

Key Word: Ministry, v. 6.

Strong Verses: 2, 3, 5, 18.

Christ Seen: v. 18. Those who yield to the working of the Holy Spirit may be made more and more into the image of Christ (Rom. 8:29). The Holy Spirit longs to bring us into conformity to the "family likeness" even before the hour when we shall see Him face to face and be made like Him.

CHAPTER FOUR

Contents: Truth taught, commended by the life. The preaching of the Lord-ship of Christ. The suffering of true ministers with Christ.

Conclusion: A steadfast adherence to the truths of the Gospel, backed by constancy and sincerity, will commend the servant of God to the opinion of wise men. They should not be of proud spirit, but realize that they themselves are but vessels of little worth and in their perplexities for Christ's sake let them know that God is able to support them and in Him they should ever trust and hope.

Key Word: Ministry, v. 1.

Strong Verses: 2, 5, 6, 7, 11, 16, 17, 18.

Christ Seen: vv. 13-14. A great sustaining power for the persecuted servant of Christ is the hope of resurrection through Him. This hope will save us from sinking. We know that Christ was raised and His resurrection is an earnest and assurance of ours. What reason has a Christian to fear death who dies in hope of being raised by the Lord Jesus?

CHAPTER FIVE

Contents: Why death has no terrors for the Lord's servant. The motive and object of ministry for Christ.

Conclusion: The servant of God who has the earnest of the Spirit to give everlasting grace and comfort, with a promise of a glorious resurrection body and the eternal fellowship of the Lord Jesus Himself, cannot but despise the brief sufferings and persecutions of this life, and be constrained by the love of Christ, manifested in the great instance of His dying for us, to persevere in testifying as ambassadors of heaven, to lost men.

Key Word: Servant's hope, v. 1, and Motive, v. 14.

Strong Verses: 7, 8, 9, 14, 15, 17, 19, 20, 21. Promises: 1, 10.

Christ Seen: v. 21. Christ was "made sin"—not a sinner, but sin—a sin-offering or sacrifice. As He Who knew no sin was made sin for us, so we who have no righteousness of our own are made the righteousness of God in Him.

CHAPTER SIX

Contents: Paul's ministry to the Corinthians. Appeal to separation and cleansing.

Conclusion: The ministers of the Gospel should look upon themselves as God's servants and act in everything suitably to that character. As they are themselves so let them seek to make the followers of Christ under their charge, not only by profession, but in reality, the temples of the Holy Ghost, dedicated to and employed for the service of God and separated from all uncleanness.

Key Word: Separation, v. 17.

Strong Verses: 2, 14, 16. Promise: 17.

Christ Seen: v. 15. Unity with Christ demands separation from the world for we cannot lead Him—He must lead us. Christ's blessing can not be with those who are in compromise or complicity with evil.

CHAPTER SEVEN

Contents: Paul opens his heart to the Corinthians concerning purpose of his former letter.

Conclusion: The true servant of God cannot but be grieved that he must rebuke Christians for sin, nor can he shun to make those sorry for a season whom he would rather make glad. If the offenders will but let their sorrow work true repentance, God's minister may rejoice in the nature of their sorrow when it is turned again to joy that is durable.

Key Word: Sorrow to repentance, v. 9.

Strong Verse: 10.

CHAPTER EIGHT

Contents: Collection for the poor. Exhortation concerning the grace of giving.

Conclusion: Those who truly love the Lord Jesus Who became poor for our sakes, making us rich in eternal things, cannot but dedicate their temporal riches to His disposal for the relief of brethren in Christ who are in need. His rewards for Christian liberality will be based on the will to do, rather

than the ability to do, and He takes notice, not of what we give, but what
we have left.

Key Word: Liberality, v. 2.

Strong Verses: 7, 9, 12, 21.

Christ Seen: v. 9.   Our Lord Jesus, equal in power and glory with the
Father, rich in all the glory and blessedness of the upper world, yet for
our sakes became, literally, "a beggar." We are thereby made rich in the
blessings and promises of the new covenant and the hopes of eternal life.
Shall we hold on to our dollars when they are needed for His cause? The
best arguments for Christian duties are those taken from the love Christ
has manifested to us.

CHAPTER NINE

Contents: Offering for the Jerusalem saints.   Encouragement for givers.

Conclusion: Our return in blessings will be proportionate to what we sow. Let
our works of charity be therefore done with thought and prayer, rather
than by accident, giving cheerfully, not grudgingly, being glad we have
ability and opportunity to be charitable. God loveth a cheerful giver,
therefore no man can be the loser by doing that with which God is pleased
for He is able to make His grace the more abundant toward us.

Key Word: Giving, v. 7.

Strong Verses: 7, 15.   Promises: 6, 8.

Christ Seen: v. 15.   The one Gift, Christ, outshines all others and draws
all other divine gifts after it (Rom. 8:32). How can one who is in possession of the "unspeakable gift" grudge money for His service?

CHAPTER TEN

Contents: Vindication of Paul's apostleship, and his appeal to Corinthians as
brethren in Christ.

Conclusion: The servants of Christ should be sensible of their own infirmities,
thinking humbly of themselves, keeping within their own province and
careful to give glory to God in all their work. At the same time let them
not betray their authority in Christ. Believers should render humble
obedience to them as men set over them by God, not comparing their personal appearance or ways with other popular leaders.

Key Word: Boasting in the Lord, vv. 8, 17.

Strong Verses: 3, 4, 5, 17, 18.

Christ Seen: v. 5.   We are here shown how to meet the difficulty of controlling
the thought life. If we contemplate the Lord Jesus as ever by our side,
as well as in us, ever watching over, aiding and sustaining us, then will we
have no cause to fear and shall be victorious.

CHAPTER ELEVEN

Contents: Paul's godly jealousy for Christ's cause.   Warning against false
teachers.   Paul's enforced boasting.

Conclusion: It is no pleasure to a good man to speak well of himself, yet in
some cases it is lawful, namely when it is for the advantage of others or
for the vindication of the cause of Christ. Those who boast in the Lord
can never boast of what they have done, though they may glory in what
they have suffered for His sake. Thus are false teachers distinguished
from true, for they boast of their works and shun sufferings.

Key Word: Paul's glorying, vv. 10, 30.

Strong Verses: 3, 14, 15, 30.

Christ Seen: v. 2.   The Church is the Bride of Christ, Eph. 5:25-32; Rev.
19:6-8; affianced, yet not married, yet as a Body. The espoused Bride is
often found flirting with old lovers of the world, a source of grief to the
true Bridegroom.

CHAPTER TWELVE

Contents: God's dealing with Paul.

Conclusion: The exalted experiences of the Spirit-filled Christian overbalance
all he is called upon to bear for Christ's sake. Whom God loves, He will
keep from being exalted above measure, and spiritual burdens will be
ordered, with grace to bear them, for the keeping down of spiritual pride.
As we communicate our experiences let us remember to take notice of
what God has done to humble us, as well as to advance us.

Key Word: Glorying (in Christ), v. 5.
Strong Verse: 10. Promise: 9.
Christ Seen: vv. 7, 9. The thorns Christ wore for us and with which He was crowned, sanctify and make easy all the thorns in the flesh we may ever be afflicted with. His grace is sufficient—and what is health if His grace is not possessed?

CHAPTER THIRTEEN

Contents: Closing exhortations of Paul to the Corinthians.
Conclusion: The great burden of God's faithful representatives is that the Gospel they preach may be honored, however their persons may be vilified. Their heavenly commission is verified through the lives of those in whom Christ is living with power, having believed in Christ through their ministry. Let us examine ourselves whether we be in the faith.
Key Word: Examine yourselves, v. 5.
Strong Verses: 4, 5, 8. 11, 14.
Christ Seen: v. 4. As Christ was crucified in weakness, or appeared to be weak to men, but lives by the power of God, so His representatives, however contemptible they may seem to some, yet are instruments manifesting the power of God, as proven by the souls regenerated, and will yet be vindicated before all men, by their resurrection unto life eternal in Christ.

GALATIANS

Key Thought: Liberty	Number of Chapters: 6	Key Verse: 3:2	Christ seen as: Our freedom

Writer of the Book: Paul	Date: A. D. 60	Conclusion of the Book: Christ is the Deliverer from the law and mere externalism and leads into glorious liberty.

SUMMARY

CHAPTER ONE

Contents: The Gospel Paul preached, a revelation not tradition.

Conclusion: The Gospel declared by the apostles was by revelation of Jesus Christ. It is a Gospel of pure grace, and any message that excludes grace or mingles legalism with grace as a means of salvation in under the curse of God and is to be shunned.

Key Word: Paul's gospel, v. 7.

Strong Verses: 4, 8.

Christ Seen: v. 4. The cross of the Lord Jesus was designed not only to separate us from the penalty of our sins, but to separate us from the power of them. Shall we who have been saved by His grace deny Him by plunging again into that from which His cross has forever delivered us?

CHAPTER TWO

Contents: Paul's journey to Jerusalem and His contest for the truth. Justification by faith in Christ without works.

Conclusion: The gospel of grace is one of justification by faith in Christ's finished work apart from deeds of the law. We do not get saved by our works, but we get saved and work. Those who put themselves under the law after seeking justification through Christ take the place of unjustified sinners seeking to be made righteous by law and works, whereas justification is wholly by faith and sanctification wholly Christ living out through our lives.

Key Word: Gospel of uncircumcision, v. 7.

Strong Verses: 16, 19, 20, 21.

Christ Seen: v. 20. The present aspect of our salvation is Christ living in us by His Holy Spirit. God does not ask us to live the Christian life, but wants us, by yieldedness to Him to let Christ live it in us.

CHAPTER THREE

Contents: Gift of Spirit by faith apart from law-works. Man under law-works is under the law curse. Christ bears the law curse that we might have the faith blessing. The true intent of the law.

Conclusion: The purpose of the law was to give to sin the character of transgression and prove man helpless to save himself—not to save man. Man is therefore shut up to faith in the work of Christ our Mediator, as the only avenue of escape from the penalty of a broken law, for Christ has borne the curse of the law for us and we become the children of God through Him, not by any works of our own.

Key Word: Works and faith, v. 5.

Strong Verses: 3, 10, 11, 13, 21, 22, 24, 26.

Christ Seen: v. 13. What Christ suffered FROM men (the cross) was nothing to what He suffered FOR men. The CURSE of the law was more than the CROSS of human suffering. He bore that curse to the full as the divine Son of God, redeeming the believer, both from the curse and the dominion of the law. Law therefore can neither justify a sinner nor sanctify a believer.

CHAPTER FOUR

Contents: Believers full redemption from the law. Sonship through the

Spirit. Dangers of lapsing into legality. Impossibility of mixing law and grace.

Conclusion: Law and grace are an impossible mixture, for salvation is wholly by faith in Christ and our sonship is immediately testified to in the heart by the incoming of the Holy Spirit, upon the basis of Christ's finished work as the full satisfaction of the law. Let us not, therefore, fall again in bondage to the legality of the law, which is merely an element of salvation to reveal to us the inveterate sinfulness of our nature and the impossibility of saving ourselves.

Key Word: Bondage and grace, vv. 3, 5.

Strong Verses: 4, 5, 6.

Christ Seen: v. 4. Jesus, Who was truly God, for our sakes became man. He Who was Lord of all took upon Himself the state of subjection and the form of a servant. The one end of all this was to redeem those under the law. He, the perfect One, took what we deserve, that we, the sinners, might get what He deserved.

CHAPTER FIVE

Contents: Liberty of the believer in Christ, apart from the law. Conflict of flesh and the Spirit. Christian character the result of the Spirit's work not self-effort.

Conclusion: Since we are justified only by faith in Christ Jesus, not by the righteousness of the law, let us not again stand in fear of, and bondage to, legal ordinances. While our salvation is settled by the work of Christ, the conflict of sin which still wars in the believer's members, may be settled by yieldedness to the Holy Spirit, Who is present in the believer to subdue the fleshly nature and to bear heavenly fruit through our lives.

Key Word: Liberty, vv. 1, 13. Flesh and Spirit, v. 16.

Strong Verses: 1, 6, 14, 16, 17, 18, 22, 23, 24.

Christ Seen: v. 4. To "fall from grace" is to fall back on legal ordinances and mix law and grace. One who is fallen from grace is not a believer who has lost his position in Christ by failure to do good works (the popular Methodist explanation), but one who is doing good works and trusting in them as a means of salvation and sanctification. Salvation is of Christ alone.

CHAPTER SIX

Contents: The regenerated life as a brotherhood of believers.

Conclusion: The new life in Christ Jesus is not simply one of being good, but of doing good. It manifests itself, not by taking a "more holy than thou" attitude, but by bearing the burdens of others and seizing every opportunity to help saints and save sinners.

Key Word: Well doing, v. 9.

Strong Verses: 1, 2, 7, 10, 14. Promises: 8, 9.

Christ Seen: v. 14. The cross which connects us with God separates us from the world. Having died with Christ we should therefore be done with the world. Having risen with Christ, we are connected with God in a new life. We cannot glory in the benefits Christ's cross secures if we refuse the rejection which His cross involves.

EPHESIANS

Key Thought:	Number of Chapters:	Key Verse:	Christ seen as:
"In Christ"	6	1:3	Head of the Church

Writer of the Book:	Date:	Conclusion of the Book:
Paul	A. D. 64	The Church is The Body of Christ. Each believer has an exalted position through grace and is to have a walk in accordance with that position.

SUMMARY

CHAPTER ONE

Contents: Believer's position in grace. The prayer for knowledge and power.
Conclusion: The believer is vitally united to Jesus Christ by the indwelling Spirit, through the redemptive work of the cross, and has in Him all spiritual blessings, including the assurance of an eternal inheritance and the working of His mighty power in and through him.
Key Word: Spiritual blessings, v. 3.
Strong Verses: 3, 4, 7, 13, 14, 22, 23.
Christ Seen: vv. 22-23. Jesus is Head of the Church which is His Body and His Bride. As Eve was of Adam's body, yet was his bride, so the Church born out of His opened side, is both the Body and the Bride. This gives Him complete disposal of all the affairs of the true Church to the designs of His grace.

CHAPTER TWO

Contents: Method of Gentile salvation. Jew and Gentile made one body in Christ, a habitation of God through the Spirit.
Conclusion: A state of sin apart from Christ, is a state of spiritual death and bondage to Satan. A great and happy change is possible on the basis of Christ's finished redemption whereby men are quickened to eternal life by faith apart from their own merits. God, the Father, is the Author of the plan, Christ, the Son, laid the foundation, and the Holy Spirit raises the superstructure.
Key Word: Reconciliation, v. 16.
Strong Verses: 4, 5, 6, 7, 8, 9, 10, 13, 14, 18, 21, 22.
Christ Seen: v. 7. One great purpose of Christ's salvation is to reveal in ages to come the exceeding riches of God's grace. If all men were saved, it could never be made to appear that we did really deserve to die. In spite of the cross, we, angels, and universe would doubt it. The loss of some men through rejection of Christ sets that doubt at rest and proves to all eternity that those who are saved were by nature the children of wrath, even as others.

CHAPTER THREE

Contents: Church, a mystery hidden in past ages. Prayer for inner fullness and knowledge.
Conclusion: The divine purpose to make of both Jew and Gentile a wholly new thing, the Church, the Body of Christ, was a mystery unrevealed in Old Testament times, the revelation of which was committed to Paul. Nothing is too hard for divine grace to do; what a mighty treasury of mercy, grace, and love is laid up in Christ Jesus, both for Jew and Gentile who will receive Him as their Lord.
Key Word: Revelation, v. 3.
Strong Verses: 8, 9, 10, 16, 17, 18, 19, 20.
Christ Seen: vv. 9, 10. The marvelous redemption of men by grace through faith, on the ground of Christ's atonement is to be a lesson eternally to Satan and his hosts, of the power of God. Angels are made to see how His glory can be displayed in His dealings with sin.

CHAPTER FOUR

Contents: Walk and service of the believer in Christ. Ministry of gifts of Christ to His Body.

Conclusion: Considering to what state and condition God has called us in Christ Jesus, let us approve ourselves good Christians, living up to our profession and calling. As members of His Body, the Holy Spirit will endue us with spiritual gifts for His service that we might confirm and build up others in the faith and that we might dispense the saving doctrines of His grace to the unsaved.

Key Word: Walk, v. 1.

Strong Verses: 1, 17, 22, 23, 24, 30, 32.

Christ Seen: v. 8. When Christ's body was laid in the grave, His spirit descended into Hades (the abode of departed spirits), and proclaimed the victory of the cross. At His ascension to the Father after three days He delivered from Hades the spirits of the justified and took them to Paradise above, leaving the unsaved spirits in Hades. The spirit of the Christian at death now goes to be with Him above. Phil. 1:23; 2 Cor. 5:9,

CHAPTER FIVE

Contents: Walk of the believer as God's child. The believer's warfare as filled with the Spirit.

Conclusion: As members of the family of God, it is our duty to put on the family likeness by walking as obedient children, and in full yieldedness to the Holy Spirit. Only as we are flexible in His hands may we be victorious in our walk, sincere in our worship or successful in our work.

Key Word: Worship, vv. 19, 20. Walk, v. 2.

Strong Verses: 9, 18, 19, 20, 25, 30.

Christ Seen: v. 32. Concerning life, the Church is the Body of Christ (1: 22, 23). Concerning love, the Church is His Bride. Notice it is the "man" who is said to leave his home to be joined unto a wife. Christ left the glory and His Father, and later parted with His earthly mother (Luke 2:35; John 19:26-27) for the redemptive work whereby He could take out from the world a spiritual Bride, of which all true believers are members.

CHAPTER SIX

Contents: Domestic life of Spirit-filled believers. Warfare of the believer.

Conclusion: The Christian life is a warfare, a struggle not only with common calamities and inner desires, but with opposing forces of the powers of darkness which seek to destroy the testimony of the believer. It is therefore requisite that the Christian soldier be stout-hearted and well armed with spiritual weapons which God supplies. The sword of the Spirit and the access of prayer are weapons against which Satan is powerless.

Key Word: Warfare, vv. 11-12.

Strong Verses: 10, 11, 12, 13, 17, 18. Promise: 8.

Christ Seen: v. 10. The Lord Jesus has met Satan at every point and defeated him. It is therefore dangerous for us to be strong except in Him Who is the Victor. Our natural courage is perfect cowardice; our natural strength is perfect weakness, but our sufficiency is always in Him.

PHILIPPIANS

Key Thought:	Number of Chapters:	Key Verse:	Christ seen as:
Gain through Christ	4	3:7, 14, 4:4	Ascended Lord

Writer of the Book:	Date:	Conclusion of the Book:
Paul	About A. D. 64	Christ is the believer's life, pattern, object, and strength.

SUMMARY

CHAPTER ONE

Contents: Triumph of the believer over suffering and persecution.

Conclusion: Those who desire that Christ may be magnified in their bodies have a holy indifference whether it be by life or death and may rejoice in all their tribulations as Christ's witnesses, knowing that the Word of God cannot be imprisoned and that though things do not turn to their comfort in this world, by God's grace, they will be made to turn to the salvation of others.

Key Word: Joyful tribulation, v. 20.

Strong Verses: 21, 23. Promise: 6.

Christ Seen: v. 6. It is Christ Who begins the good work in us; it is Christ Who carries it on in us—2:12-13; it is Christ Who will ultimately complete that work by transforming us into His own likeness—3:21.

CHAPTER TWO

Contents: Christ, the believer's pattern, rejoicing in lowly service. The outworking of inworked salvation. The apostolic example.

Conclusion: The believer should be lowly minded and like-minded, in conformity to the example of the Lord Jesus, the great pattern of humility and love in service to man. He humbled Himself in suffering and death for us, not only to satisfy God's justice, but to set us an example that we might follow His steps—bearing a resemblance to His life, since we have profited by His death.

Key Word: Humble service, vv. 5-9.

Strong Verses: 3, 5, 7, 8, 9, 13, 15.

Christ Seen: vv. 7-8. Jesus was absolutely divine, yet absolutely human. In coming into the world He did not empty Himself of His divine nature or attributes, but only of the outward and visible manifestation of the Godhead—the insignia of majesty, He had to empty Himself of His glory or He would have paralyzed the men He came to save. Although equal with God, He took upon Himself the form of a servant for our sakes, that He might meet, as God manifest in the flesh, the death of the cross.

CHAPTER THREE

Contents: Christ, the object of the believer's faith, desire and expectation.

Conclusion: Let those reckon themselves unspeakable losers, who by adhering to the things of the world and carnal pride, have no interest in the Lord Jesus. He is the object of the believer's faith for a righteousness that is untarnishable, the object of the believer's desire for a fellowship that is incomparable and the object of the believer's expectation for a resurrection body that is immortal.

Key Word: Christ, our sufficiency, vv. 7, 10, 20.

Strong Verses: 3, 7, 8, 9, 10, 13, 14, 20. Promise: 21.

Christ Seen: v. 10. Christ's resurrection is the evidence of our justification (Rom. 4:24-25); the assurance of our resurrection (1 Cor. 15:14-18); the source of our spiritual power for He was thus constituted the giver of the Holy Spirit (John 7:39; 20:22). Knowing Him, therefore, involves not only justification through His death but sanctification through His life, feeling the transforming efficacy and virtue of His life, through the Holy Spirit.

CHAPTER FOUR

Contents: Christ the believer's strength and source of joy and peace. Giver of victory over anxiety.

Conclusion: The believer's hope and prospect through our Lord Jesus Christ, should engage him to be steady, even and constant in his Christian course, rejoicing always in Him through Whom he has the peace of God, the very presence of the God of peace, and promises that should remove all anxious care. He will give strength for all things, whether to do or bear. He will supply every need of the trusting soul.

Key Word: Joy, v. 4.

Strong Verses: 4, 6, 8. Promises: 7, 13, 19.

Christ Seen: Seven things the believer is here said to have through Jesus Christ: 1. Privilege of prayer to help us—v. 6. 2. Peace to keep us—v. 7. 3. Presence to accompany us—v. 9. 4. Pattern before us—v. 8. 5. Policy to calm us—v. 11. 6. Power to strengthen us—v. 13. 7. Promise to provide for us—v. 19.

COLOSSIANS

Key Thought: Fullness in Christ	Number of Chapters: 4	Key Verse: 2:10	Christ seen as: Fullness of Godhead

Writer of the Book: Paul	Date: About A. D. 64	Conclusion of the Book: The Godhead was incarnate in Jesus Christ, in Whom the believer is complete.

SUMMARY

CHAPTER ONE

Contents: Apostolic greeting and prayer. The superiority of Christ. His reconciling work. The mystery of His indwelling.

Conclusion: He Who has reconciled us to God by His blood and made us meet to partake of eternal happiness is none other than the Creator and Lord of all, manifested in human form. As Lord of glorious power, He is able to furnish us for every good work and to fortify us by His grace against every evil. The ground of our hope is Christ in the Word, but the evidence of our hope is Christ in the heart working mightily by His Holy Spirit.

Key Word: Mighty Christ, vv. 11, 15.

Strong Verses: 10, 11, 12, 13, 16, 17, 18, 20.

Christ Seen: vv. 15-17. Jesus was the visible representation of the visible God, born before anything was created. Creation was bound up with Him as its secret, and by Him, all things earthly, angelic, celestial and infernal were created and do exist. It pleased the Father that all divine perfections should be summed up in Him. Such a One redeemed us and is Head of the Body, the Church.

CHAPTER TWO

Contents: Godhead incarnate in Christ. Danger of those who would entice away from Christ. Philosophy and legality, mysticism and asceticism.

Conclusion: Believers who understand the perfections of Christ and have a well settled judgment of the great truths of the Gospel, will be preserved from all the ensnaring insinuations of those who would corrupt the Gospel principles. All true Christians have a salvation complete in Him and need not pin their faith on the opinions of philosophers nor bear the yoke of ceremonial law. Christ alone is the hope of glory and in Him we are complete.

Key Word: Complete in Him, v. 10.

Strong Verses: 3, 6, 7, 8, 9, 10.

Christ Seen: vv. 3, 9. Christ is the wisdom of God, and is of God made wisdom to the humble. The treasures of wisdom are not hidden from us in Christ, but for us. Supposed supplies of spiritual wisdom from any other source are a delusion. The fullness of the Godhead dwells in Christ, not figuratively, but literally, for He is both God and man, the manifestation of the Father to us.

CHAPTER THREE

Contents: Believer's union with Christ here and hereafter, and the fruit of such union.

Conclusion: The true believer is united with Christ in a union which can never be broken and by virtue of that union he is justified, sanctified and yet to be glorified. Since, as to his standing, his true life is hid with Christ in God, it is his business to mind the concerns of that world to which Christ has ascended, making heaven his scope and aim, and manifesting to those about him, his title and qualifications for heaven, by a consistent Christian life.

Key Word: Union with Christ, v. 3.

Strong Verses: 1, 2, 3, 14, 15, 16, 17. Promises: 4, 23, 24.
Christ Seen: vv. 1, 3. The believer's eternal standing is in Christ. If by regeneration, we were united to Him, we are reckoned as having died when He died, having risen when He ascended, having been seated in heaven when He was seated, and as yet to appear with Him when He comes forth in glory. Our true life is therefore hid with Him. It is our part to make our state conform as nearly as possible with our standing.

CHAPTER FOUR

Contents: Consistent Christian living and fellowship of believers.
Conclusion: The friendship and fellowship together of fellow servants in the Lord, is a great refreshment under the sufferings and difficulties in the way. It adds much to the beauty and strength of the Gospel ministry when Christ's servants are loving and condescending towards one another. Let the people of God pray particularly for those over them in the Lord, that God may enable them to speak as they ought to speak and that doors of utterance may be opened.
Key Word: Fellowship, vv. 7, 10, 11, 14.
Strong Verses: 2, 5, 6.

I THESSALONIANS

Key Thought: Comfort	Number of Chapters: 5	Key Verse: 1:10	Christ seen as: Coming Lord

Writer of the Book:	Date:	Conclusion of the Book: The coming of the Lord
Paul	A. D. 54	Jesus is imminent. The hope of His return is the great hope and inspiration and comfort of the true Christian.

SUMMARY

CHAPTER ONE

Contents: The model church. Three tenses of the Christian life.

Conclusion: Those who have embraced the full Gospel, as proclaimed by the apostles will manifest it by separation from worldly idols, present service to men in the power of the living God, and expectation of the return of the Lord Jesus. Where true faith is, it will work by love and in the patience of the blessed hope.

Key Word: Our Gospel, v. 5.

Strong Verses: 9, 10.

Christ Seen: vv. 9-10. Past, present and future salvation in Christ is seen here. Note that the hope of Christ's return is made an integral part of the Gospel and Christian faith. If conscious of a lack of steadiness in the life or power in the testimony, make sure you possess these three aspects of salvation.

CHAPTER TWO

Contents: The model servant and his reward.

Conclusion: It is the great comfort of the servants of Christ to have their own conscience and the consciences of others witness for them that they set out with sincere designs and right principles, preached the Word in its fullness and that their witnessing was not in vain in the Lord. Let not the ambassadors of Christ be daunted that they must often meet opposition and persecution at the preaching of Christ, but continue faithfully knowing that they shall meet the fruit of their labors at the coming of Christ.

Key Word: Apostolic ministry, v. 1.

Strong Verses: 4, 19.

Christ Seen: vv. 19-20. At the second coming of Christ, there will be gathered all those won by the preaching of the Gospel. It is the soul-winner's joy that he will, at that time, meet all those he has won to Christ.

CHAPTER THREE

Contents: The model Christian brotherhood. The sanctification of the believer.

Conclusion: It is easy for the servant of Christ to bear afflictions or persecutions, when he finds the good success of his ministry which is the sure result of sowing in love, and the constancy of those who have accepted Christ under their ministry. Let there be the same mutual love between all Christians that, with their teachers in the Lord, they may be established unblameable at the coming of Christ.

Key Word: Brotherly love, v. 12.

Strong Verses: 12, 13.

Christ Seen: Each chapter ends with reference to Christ's second coming. Chap. 1: linked with salvation (v. 10); Chap. 2: linked with service (19-20); Chap. 3: linked with sanctification (13); Chap. 4: linked with solace (13-18); Chap. 5: linked with separation (23).

CHAPTER FOUR

Contents: The model walk of the believer. The hope of Christ's return.

Conclusion: The design of the Gospel is to teach men not only what they should believe, but also how they should live. It is God's will that all His should be holy in heart and pure in body for "He that calleth us is holy."

The Christian should not be in ignorance of the blessed hope, the return of Christ to resurrect the dead in Him and translate living believers, for this is designed to be the greatest comfort of believers.

Key Word: Sanctification, v. 3.   Comfort, vv. 13, 18.

Strong Verses: 3, 4, 7.   Promises: 14-18.

Christ Seen: v. 16.   The Lord Jesus HIMSELF, not the Holy Spirit, not the destruction of Jerusalem, not the diffusion of Christianity, not the death of the believer—this is the blessed hope.   He is coming bringing with Him the spirits of those who have died in Him.   Their bodies shall be raised and united then with their spirits.   At the same time, living believers will be instantly changed and caught up in clouds to be with Him.

CHAPTER FIVE

Contents: The model walk for the believer.   The day of Jehovah.   Exhortations to believers.

Conclusion: Let Christians live like men who are awake, living in constant expectation of Christ's return, and having all natural desires under Christ's control.   Christ's coming will be sudden, overtaking many who are in the midst of their carnal security and jollity, and bringing them destruction from which there will be no escape.

Key Word: Times and seasons, v. 1.

Strong Verses: 3, 8, 9, 10, 16-21.

Christ Seen: v. 2.   As the thief usually comes in the dead of the night, so the coming of Christ will surprise the ungodly.   It is the happy condition, however, of those who believe God's Word, that they live in momentary expectation of His return, and whether times be troublesome or peaceful, they cannot be surprised if He should come.

II THESSALONIANS

Key Thought: Waiting for Christ	Number of Chapters: 3	Key Verse: 3:5	Christ seen as: Coming Lord

Writer of the Book:	Date:	Conclusion of the Book: The Christian is to wait, watch and work for the coming of the Lord Jesus, when He will be glorified in His saints and His saints shall be eternally satisfied in Him.
Paul	A. D. 54	

SUMMARY

CHAPTER ONE

Contents: Believer's comfort in persecution.

Conclusion: The patient suffering of believers for Christ's sake, is a manifest token that they are worthy to be accounted Christians, since they can suffer for Christianity. God will recompense their trouble with rest of heart now, and with abundant reward at Christ's coming, when also He will recompense trouble to those who have troubled His people.

Key Word: Comfort, v. 7.

Promises: 7, 8, 9, 10.

Christ Seen: v. 10. As the coming of Christ will reveal His wrath and power upon His enemies, so His grace and power will be magnified in the complete salvation of His saints. This is an evidence that the Church will not pass through the Great Tribulation, the time of God's wrath.

CHAPTER TWO

Contents: Day of the Lord and the man of sin. Exhortation and instruction.

Conclusion: The blessed hope of Christ's coming is a doctrine with which believers are to be deeply affected that they might not be moved about with the conflicting and Satanic heresies of the last days, when there will be general religious apostasy and denial of the program of God's Word. Let us not be deceived by the doctrine of any man or by the trend of events, to let loose of the hope of His imminent return.

Key Word: Day of Christ, v. 2.

Strong Verses: 3, 4, 8.

Christ Seen: vv. 7, 8. The word "letteth" is lit. "restraineth" or "hindereth." The Holy Spirit is the restraining influence now in the world. He will hinder the progress of Satan's gospel until the coming of Christ when He, whose present mission is the formation of the Body of Christ will be taken out of the way with the Body. This will leave Satan unrestrained and will precipitate the Great Tribulation period.

CHAPTER THREE

Contents: Paul's encouragements and exhortations to the Thessalonians.

Conclusion: It is required of those who have professed Christianity, that they live according to the precepts of the Gospel, that they be not accounted disorderly persons devoid of the divine love and hope which they profess. If Christ is allowed to direct our love upon Himself, it will rectify all our affections toward men and keep us in the attitude of expectation of His momentary coming.

Key Word: Apostolic commands, v. 6.

Strong Verses: 5, 6, 13. Promise: 3.

Christ Seen: v. 5. Patient waiting for Christ is to be joined with the love of God. The hope of His return is the great incentive to a busy life and a life of loving deeds to others.

I TIMOTHY

Key Thought: Church order	Number of Chapters: 6	Key Verse: 3:9	Christ seen as: Only Potentate

Writer of the Book:	Date:	Conclusion of the Book: God would have the Minister and the Christian know "how they should behave in the house of God" and how "to hold the mystery of the faith in a pure conscience."
Paul	About A. D. 63	

SUMMARY

CHAPTER ONE

Contents: Legalism and unsound teaching rebuked.

Conclusion: Witnesses of Christ must not only be charged to preach the true Gospel doctrine but charged to preach no other doctrine, for it needs no improvement, and to add the letter of the law to the doctrines of grace is an impossible mixture, leading to unprofitable jangling. Those answer the end of the law who have a good conscience toward Christ and faith unfeigned.

Key Word: Vain jangling, v. 6.

Strong Verses: 5, 15.

Christ Seen: v. 15. The errand of Jesus Christ in the world was not to be a great teacher and reformer, but to die as a ransom for sinners of whom there are two classes—the sinner who thinks himself righteous (as did Paul before converted) and the sinner who feels himself a sinner.

CHAPTER TWO

Contents: Exhortation to prayer. Divine order for the sexes.

Conclusion: Christians are to be men much given to prayer, and in their prayers having a generous concern for others as well as for themselves. They are to especially desire for those in civil authority that God will turn their hearts and direct them, making use of them for the accomplishing of His purposes.

Christian women are to be modest, sober, silent and submissive as becomes their place. Woman was created in subordination to man and was never intended to usurp authority, but to be a helpmeet.

Key Word: Prayer, v. 1. Women, v. 10.

Strong Verses: 1, 2, 3, 4, 5, 8.

Christ Seen: vv. 5-6. A Mediator supposes a controversy. Sin had made a quarrel between God and man. Jesus Christ, a Mediator, undertook to make peace. He gave Himself a ransom voluntarily so that all mankind might partake of the common salvation.

CHAPTER THREE

Contents: Qualifications of elders and deacons.

Conclusion: Those having places of authority in the church must be blameless, not lying under any scandal, watchful against Satan, moderate in all their actions, proving their ability to care for God's people by keeping a Godly and well-governed household, holding the truths of the faith in a pure conscience.

Key Word: Elders, deacons, vv. 2, 8.

Strong Verses: 5, 16.

Christ Seen: v. 16. The mystery of Godliness is Christ. He was God manifest in the flesh (John 1:14). Being reproached as a sinner, He was raised by the Spirit and so justified. He was attended by and worshipped by angels. He is offered to the Gentiles as Savior and Redeemer. He is believed on by millions. He is exalted in glory.

CHAPTER FOUR

Contents: Walk of a good minister of Christ.

Conclusion: Those are good ministers of Jesus Christ who are diligent to instil into the minds of their hearers the fundamental truths of God's Word, which will prevent their being seduced by false teachers and drawn away into the apostasy of the last days. Let them not study to advance new notions, but ever be faithful in proclaiming those saving truths which they have received of the apostles and Jesus Christ.

Key Word: Good minister, v. 6.

Strong Verses: 1, 8, 12.

Christ Seen: vv. 1-3. Satan is a theologian and makes use of demons in the last days to lead many away into apostasy. Spiritualism clearly presented here. Two prominent points of its doctrine are seen in v. 3. Abstinence from meat is considered a condition of mediumistic power. Spiritual affinities are taught as against marriage. Christ alone is to be the Christian's guide and to attempt to consult with spirits is a great affront to Him Who is all-sufficient for our every need.

CHAPTER FIVE

Contents: Work of a good minister of Christ.

Conclusion: Ministers of Jesus Christ are reprovers by office, for they are not alone to preach the Word, but correct those who are inconsistent. A difference is to be made in the reproofs according to the age and circumstances of the persons rebuked. Let them know that they are accountable to God and the Lord Jesús Christ how they have observed the duties of their office, and woe to them if they have been partial in their ministrations.

Key Word: Ministerial exhortations, v. 21.

Strong Verses: 6, 8, 22.

CHAPTER SIX

Contents: Work of the minister continued.

Conclusion: The minister of Christ is to preach not only the general duties of all, but the duties of particular relations, that believers may live lives that will truly witness for Christ wherever they are. He is to endeavor after Godliness at all times himself, not making his ministry merely a trade, but a calling wherein he is content with what God allots him, fighting the fight of faith and looking for the coming of Christ, when he shall be abundantly rewarded.

Key Word: Man of God, v. 11.

Strong Verses: 6, 7, 10, 12, 20.

Christ Seen: v. 16. Jesus Christ only as yet has triumphed over death. Immortality has to do with the body, not the soul. The believer will be given immortality at His coming, being given a body like unto His glorious body.

II TIMOTHY

Key Thought:	Number of Chapters:	Key Verse:	Christ seen as:
Doctrine	4	1:13	Only Potentate

Writer of the Book:	Date:	Conclusion of the Book:
Paul	About A. D. 64	The Christian must be loyal to Christ and to the truth, enduring as a good soldier against all persecution, and in the midst of growing apostasies.

SUMMARY

CHAPTER ONE

Contents: Apostolic greetings and exhortations to Timothy.

Conclusion: The best of Christ's servants need remembrancers, and what they know, it is well to be reminded of by Godly men that their faith may be strengthened. Let them not be afraid of suffering for Christ's sake, or of owning others who are sufferers for His cause, for they are called with a holy calling, as witnesses of God's eternal purposes in Christ, and by adherence to Him in all circumstances, may be assured that He honors His testimony in and through them.

Key Word: Exhortations, v. 6.

Strong Verses: 7, 8, 9, 10, 12.

Christ Seen: v. 10. The threefold purpose of Christ's coming is here stated. 1. To abolish death which is the result of sin. 2. To bring to light salvation through His finished work. 3. To illumine the subject of immortality, which believers are to have through Him at His return. If Jesus had not arisen in a glorified body, immortality would not have been brought to light.

CHAPTER TWO

Contents: Walk of a good soldier of Christ in times of apostasy.

Conclusion: Those who have work to do for Christ must stir themselves up as soldiers to do it, and strengthen themselves for it in His power. They must count upon suffering, even unto death, and therefore must carefully train up others in the faith to succeed them who will approve themselves good soldiers.

Key Word: Good soldier, v. 3.

Strong Verses: 3, 15, 19, 21, 22, 24, 25. Promises: 11, 12, 13.

Christ Seen: v. 8. "Remember Jesus Christ"—raised from the dead. This is the great proof of the Christian mission, and confirmation of the truth of the Gospel. Let suffering saints remember this. His incarnation and resurrection, heartily believed, will support the Christian under all testings of the present life.

CHAPTER THREE

Contents: Apostasy predicted. The believer's resource, the Scriptures.

Conclusion: The last days of the Gospel dispensation will be perilous times, both on account of persecutions without, and corruptions within. These will be times when it will be difficult to keep a good conscience, and the believers recourse, will be the inspired Word of God, which is demonstrated to be the power of God unto salvation, able to furnish him unto all good works.

Key Word: Apostasy, vv. 1, 5, 13.

Strong Verses: 1-5, 12, 13, 16, 17.

Christ Seen: v. 5. The Gospel of Christ is the power of godliness (Rom. 1:16). The tendency of the apostasy of the last times will be to accept the ethical teachings of Christ, rejecting the doctrine of regeneration by the Spirit of Christ. It is no marvel that those who cling to Christ, instead of form, will in those days, be the object of bitter persecution. (v. 12).

CHAPTER FOUR

Contents: Christ's faithful servant and the faithfulness of Christ to His own.

Conclusion: It concerns the witnesses of Christ seriously to consider the account they must give the Lord Jesus Christ of the trust reposed upon them as His representatives.   Against the last days when there shall be widespread rejection of the doctrines of Christ, men grown weary of the plain Gospel and hankering for philosophies, let us faithfully preach the pure Word of God, apart from any merely human fancies, making full proof of our ministry and loving the truth of His return for His own.

Key Word: Charge, v. 1.

Strong Verses: 2, 3, 4.   Promises: 8, 18.

Christ Seen: v. 8.   "Crown" is a symbol of reward in N. T.   Here is a special reward promised to those who love the truth of Christ's second coming and work and long for it.   It is a crown the "post-millennarian" will not receive, for He hopes to set up the millennium without the presence of the King.

TITUS

Key Thought: Ministry	Number of Chapters: 3	Key Verse: 3:8, 9	Christ seen as: God our Savior

Writer of the Book:	Date:	Conclusion of the Book:
Paul	About A. D. 63	Christ's ministers should follow the divine order as revealed in the Epistles, for the conduct of the Church.

SUMMARY

CHAPTER ONE

Contents: Divine order for local churches.

Conclusion: Divine faith rests not on fallible reasonings and opinions of men, but on the infallible Word of God, the truth itself which purifies the heart of the believer. By this mark, judge of new and strange doctrines, and stop the mouths of those who handle the Word of God deceitfully.

Key Word: Deceivers, v. 10.

Strong Verses: 15.

CHAPTER TWO

Contents: Pastoral work of a true minister.

Conclusion: The ministers of Christ should discharge their duties with faithfulness, being careful to teach only such truths as are emphasized by God's Word, and dividing to each person, according to their age, and condition in life, those special portions of the truth designed for their particular spiritual needs. Let all considerations of the Gospel be ever linked to those foundation truths, the grace of God in our Lord Jesus Christ, the sanctified life through Him and the blessed hope of His return.

Key Word: Sound doctrine, vv. 1, 15.

Strong Verses: 7, 11, 12, 13, 14.

Christ Seen: vv. 11-13. We have in vv. 12, 13, the A B C's of the school of grace. The Gospel of grace teaches us (1) to **leave** the old life (2) to **live** the new life (3) to **look** for that blessed hope, the glorious appearing of Christ.

CHAPTER THREE

Contents: Further instructions concerning pastoral work of a true minister.

Conclusion: The ministers of Christ are the peoples' remembrancers of their duty as children of God. They should urge upon Christians the duty of subjection to the government, the truth of the unmerited favor of God in Christ, and the necessity of maintaining good works for His glory.

Key Word: Remembrancers, v. 1.

Strong Verses: 5, 8.

Christ Seen: vv. 5, 8. We cannot serve to get saved. Our salvation is based alone on Christ's finished work which cancels guilt, and the regenerating work of the Spirit which washes the fallen nature. (v. 5) While we are not saved by service, we are saved to serve (vv. 8, 14) which is the manifestation of the salvation wrought in us by the Spirit.

PHILEMON

Key Thought:	Number of Chapters:	Key Verse:	Christ seen as:
Brotherhood	1	v. 17	Payer of our debt

Writer of the Book:	Date:	Conclusion of the Book:
Paul	A. D. 64	See conclusion below.

SUMMARY

CHAPTER ONE

Contents: Greeting to Philemon.   Intercession for Onesimus.

Conclusion: Wise and good ministers of Jesus Christ will have great and tender care of young converts to encourage and hearten them, and get them received into the fellowship of the saints.   There is a spiritual brotherhood between all true believers, however distinguished as to their station of life, and we should therefore seek to strengthen and help those who have been newly united to the Christian family.

Key Word: Reception (of Christians), v. 17.

Christ Seen: vv. 17, 18.   These verses furnish a perfect illustration of the doctrine of "imputation" whereby guilty sinners believing on Christ are received by the Father as identified with the Son, and the sins of the believing one are reckoned to the account of Christ Who paid the price on Calvary.

HEBREWS

Key Thought: New Covenant	Number of Chapters: 13	Key Verse: 11:40	Christ seen as: Great High Priest

Writer of the Book:	Date:	Conclusion of the Book: The cure for faint- heartedness toward the Gospel is a right con- ception of the glory and work of our Great High Priest Who has passed into the heavens.
Probably Paul	About A. D. 65	

SUMMARY

CHAPTER ONE

Contents: The great salvation provided through Jesus Christ Who is above prophets and better than angels.

Conclusion: Jesus Christ as God was equal with the Father, but as God-man revealed the Father to men and became the Mediator between God and men. He is appointed heir of all things, sovereign Lord, absolute disposer and director both of all persons and all things. He is above every other messenger ever sent into the world and has a name preeminent above all heavenly beings.

Key Word: Christ's deity, vv. 3, 8.

Strong Verses: 3, 8.

Christ Seen: v. 3. The person of the Son was the true image and character of the Person of the Father. He is not said to be the "likeness" of God (implying resemblance) but "image," which means that He reveals God. In beholding His power, wisdom and goodness, men were beholding the Father, for He was God manifest in the flesh, having all the perfections of God in Him.

CHAPTER TWO

Contents: Warning against neglecting so great a salvation. Earth to be put under Christ. Jesus temporarily lower than angels to work out salvation for man.

Conclusion: The salvation provided by Jesus Christ is so great a salvation that none can express nor conceive how great it is. It discovers a great Savior Who has manifested God to be reconciled to our natures and reconcilable to our persons. He was made, for a time, lower than angels, that He might humble Himself unto death for our sakes. The fullness of the Godhead dwelling in Him, His suffering could make satisfaction for sin and make salvation possible to all. To reject so great a salvation is thereby made the worst of crimes against God.

Key Word: Great salvation, v. 3.

Strong Verses: 3, 9, 10, 14, 17, 18.

Christ Seen: vv. 17, 18. Christ became man that He might die, for as God He could not die, therefore He assumed another nature and state. To be a perfect Savior of mankind, He must in every way take man's place being proven perfect under all conditions, and then, as the perfect One, bear our sins. Because of His sufferings as a man, He is made a merciful High Priest, in every way qualified to succor His people.

CHAPTER THREE

Contents: Christ the Son better than Moses the servant. Warning against unbelief.

Conclusion: We owe to Jesus Christ as the principal messenger sent of God to man, the prime minister of the Gospel church, immediate and careful consideration, lest by delay our hearts be hardened and we should be eternally rejected because of unbelief. Turning a deaf ear to His calls and councils is the spring of all other sins, and the cause of final separation from God.

Key Word: Warning, v. 12.

Strong Verses: 1, 12, 13.

Christ Seen: v. 1. Jesus Christ as Apostle, spoke from God to men: as High Priest of our profession, He is the Head of the Church, upon whose satisfaction and intercession we profess to depend for acceptance with God. It was necessary to remind the Jews who held Moses in such esteem and were bent on mixing law with grace, that Christ as Son of God was above Moses, therefore His Word was final and His sacrifice sufficient.

CHAPTER FOUR

Contents: The better rest for the believer. The perfect work of redemption.

Conclusion: The privileges by Christ under the Gospel are far greater than those enjoyed under the Mosaic law. The seventh day rest commemorating a finished creation, was but a type of heart-rest which is to be had by covenant relation with Jesus Christ, and which is offered to those who will renounce their own works as a means of salvation and put their entire trust in the finished work of the Great High Priest Who has passed into the heavens.

Key Word: Rest, v. 1.

Strong Verses: 9, 10, 12, 13, 14, 15.

Christ Seen: vv. 14-16. The believer should encourage himself, by the excellency and finished work of his Great High Priest, to come boldly to the throne of grace which has taken the place of the throne of inexorable justice. Through Christ's sacrifice, a way is instituted by which God may with honor meet poor sinners and treat with them, no earthly priest being necessary.

CHAPTER FIVE

Contents: Christ, our Great High Priest after the order of Melchisedec.

Conclusion: God was pleased to take One from among men, His only begotten Son, Who above all others, was qualified to be a High Priest dealing between God and sinful men. By Him, we have approach to God in hope and God may receive us with honor. Let us therefore not attempt to go to God but through Christ, nor expect any favor from God except upon His merits.

Key Word: High Priest, vv. 1, 10.

Strong Verses: 8, 9.

Christ Seen: v. 10. Melchisedec was a type of Christ as High Priest, being both a King and a Priest (Gen. 14:18, Zech. 6:12, 13). Melchisedec has no recorded beginning nor end of life, and the very absence of these facts makes him a type of Him Who was from eternity. Christ is the only One in Whom universal Kingship and Priesthood may center.

CHAPTER SIX

Contents: Warning against mixture of law and grace. Danger of tasting the Spirit's work in grace and then going back to ceremonies.

Conclusion: Those who have advanced to the very threshold of Christ's salvation, even being clearly convicted by the Holy Spirit and fully enlightened in the Word of God as to the way of life, again turning to dead works and ceremonies, put Christ to an open shame and will not be renewed again to repentance by the Holy Spirit. The true believer takes refuge wholly in Christ's finished work, in which he finds a hope sure and steadfast leading him heavenward.

Key Word: Dead works, v. 1.

Strong Verses: 10, 18, 19.

Christ Seen: vv. 4-6. These verses do not apply to backsliders, for it states that there is no restoration possible after having once fallen away. The reference is to Hebrews fully enlightened in the prophecies about Christ, and having seen Him and having been carried along by the evident work of the Holy Spirit following His resurrection, yet rejecting all this light. For such there was no further conviction. v. 9 shows that this cannot occur to a true believer, who has "received" not merely "tasted" and is "sealed by the Spirit," not merely a "partaker".in His illuminating work—and whose real life is "hid with Christ in God."

CHAPTER SEVEN

Contents: Melchisedec as a type of Christ. Comparison of Melchisedec and Aaronic priesthoods.

Conclusion: Jesus Christ, the true King-Priest, the anti-type of Melchisedec is greater than all the priests of the order of Aaron, and is the mediator of all blessings to the children of men. Whereas the Levitical priesthood could bring nothing to perfection, nor justify men from guilt, Christ's priesthood brings with it a better hope—a foundation of salvation and perfect security in Him as Intercessor in heaven.

Key Word: Better priesthood, vv. 17, 22.

Strong Verses: 19, 24, 26, 27. Promise: 25.

Christ Seen: v. 26. No priest could be suitable or sufficient for our reconciliation to God, but One who could meet the conditions here laid down, and our Lord Jesus alone could meet them. He was free from all habits or principles of sin, never did the least wrong to God or man, was absolutely undefiled in His own life, and was never accessory to other man's sins. Those who come to God by Him are saved, not only FROM the uttermost, but TO the uttermost. (v. 25).

CHAPTER EIGHT

Contents: Aaronic priests a shadow of Christ Who mediates a better covenant.

Conclusion: We have in our Lord Jesus Christ such a High Priest as no other people ever had, all others being but types and shadows of Him. He is the Author of a new covenant, better than the old, which was not efficacious; established on better promises; obedience to it springing from a willing heart and mind rather than from fear; securing the personal revelation of the Lord to every believer and guaranteeing the complete oblivion of sins through His finished work.

Key Word: Better covenant, vv. 6, 13.

Promise: 12.

Christ Seen: v. 4. There are no earthly successors to the priestly tribe of Aaron, for the reason that it is now a heavenly office centered in Jesus Christ. The earthly priesthood is out of commission, for with the atoning death of Christ the vail was rent.

CHAPTER NINE

Contents: Ordinances and sanctuary of the old covenant as types of the new. The realities of the new covenant which is sealed by the blood of Christ.

Conclusion: Christ is a more excellent High Priest than any under the law, who but prefigured the work He came to do. He has entered once for all within the Holiest place. Having undertaken to be our High Priest He could not have been admitted into heaven without shedding His blood for us, having no errors of His own to offer for, and neither can any of us enter God's glorious presence except by a saving trust in the atoning sacrifice of Jesus, without which remission for sins is impossible.

Key Word: Atonement, v. 22.

Strong Verses: 11, 12, 15, 22, 24, 25, 26, 27, 28.

Christ Seen: vv. 24-28. We have here three great aspects of the work of Christ. v. 26—atonement—the past tense of His work for our salvation. v. 24—advocacy—the present tense of His work for us. v. 28.—advent—when He will return to complete our salvation from the very presence of sin.

CHAPTER TEN

Contents: Law only a shadow of things to come. Through Christ a way made into the Holiest for all believers. Warning to the Hebrews who were wavering between Jewish sacrifices and Christ's finished work.

Conclusion: The legal sacrifices under the law, which were but shadows of Christ's atonement, could never make the comers perfect nor satisfy justice. Now, under the Gospel, Christ's atonement is perfect and not to be repeated, and the sinner once pardoned, is ever pardoned as to his standing, and only needs to walk in communion with God, on the basis of Christ's blood, to have a continuous sense of God's pardon and favor.

Key Word: Better sacrifice, v. 12.

Strong Verses: 4, 10, 12, 14, 16, 19-25, 29, 31. Promises: 17, 37.

Christ Seen: vv. 26-29. In v. 26, "more sacrifice" should be "other sacrifice." If this "judgment and fiery indignation" were the penalty of every
sin, what Christian could escape for there is none who has not since conversion given way to sin by consent of the will. These verses must be taken
with the context, which contrasts the inefficacious and oft-repeated sacrifices of the law with the one sacrifice of Christ. There were many Hebrews
perfectly enlightened, having witnessed the works of Christ and the Holy
Spirit, but who deliberately put themselves under the law, trusting to
"other sacrifices," thereby treading under foot the blood of Christ.

CHAPTER ELEVEN

Contents: Superiority of the way of faith. Instances of faith.
Conclusion: Faith is the firm persuasion that God will perform all that He has
promised to us in Christ, and brings the soul a present fruition and fore-
taste of eternal things, which sets a seal that God is true. The way of
faith is the way of victory, peace, assurance, and endurance.
Key Word: Faith, v. 1.
Strong Verses: 1, 6.
Christ Seen: vv. 2, 39. The effect of faith with God is "good reputation."
Is it any wonder that God cannot be pleased when men are devoid of that
trust in His Word and in Jesus Christ Whom He has sent, which receives
Him as Savior and Lord and impels to obedience and good works?

CHAPTER TWELVE

Contents: The Father's chastening of believers and its purpose. The difference between living under law and under grace.
Conclusion: Christians have a race to run, of service and sufferings, a course
of active and passive obedience, in all of which they need to keep their
eyes fixed upon the Lord Jesus. The best of God's children may need
chastisement, but afflictions rightly endured, though they be the fruits of
God's displeasure are yet proofs of His paternal love and designed to fit
us better for His service and. to bring us closer into His fellowship.
Key Word: Chastening, v. 5.
Strong Verses: 1, 2, 5, 6, 14, 25.
Christ Seen: vv. 1, 2. Christ is not only the object, but the Author of our
faith. He is the purchaser of the Spirit of faith and the publisher of the
rule of faith and the cause of the grace of faith. He is also the finisher of
our faith—the fulfilling of all Scripture promises and prophecies, the finisher of grace, the rewarder of faith and will eventually bring faith to an
end by bringing us to Himself.

CHAPTER THIRTEEN

Contents: Exhortations to the Christian. Separation and worship. Apostolic
benediction.
Conclusion: Our Lord Jesus purchased us with His blood that He might set
us apart a peculiar people zealous of good works. Let us therefore seek
to excel in those duties becoming to Christians, such as brotherly love,
generosity, contentment, obedience to those over us, fixedness in the faith,
patient suffering with Him and continual praise.
Key Word: Instructions.
Strong Verses: 1, 5, 8, 9, 14, 15, 16.
Christ Seen: vv. 12, 13. Our Lord Jesus was the perfect anti-type of the
sin offering, being offered "without the gate," a striking illustration of
His humiliation as a sin bearer. The believer is therefore exhorted to go
forth from the ceremonial law, from sin, from the world, and identify himself with Christ, being willing to bear His reproach in gratitude for the
salvation He has provided.

JAMES

| Key Thought:
Works | Number of Chapters:
5 | Key Verse:
2:26 | Christ seen as:
Lord drawing nigh |

| Writer of the Book:
James | Date:
A. D. 60 | Conclusion of the Book:
The evidence of faith is
good works. |

SUMMARY

CHAPTER ONE

Contents: Testing of faith. Solicitation to evil not of God. Obedience as a test of true faith.

Conclusion: Such as have a true title in Jesus Christ through faith may expect to be called upon to endure many tests of faith, but the genuineness of their calling will be manifest by their stability in trial, their fidelity to God and the principles of Christianity, their activity in good works and the control of the carnal nature at all times. God is the source of wisdom and power continually.

Key Word: Tests of faith, vv. 3, 8, 12, 22, 26.

Strong Verses: 2, 3, 6, 17, 22, 25, 27. Promises: 5, 12.

CHAPTER TWO

Contents: The tests of brotherly love and good words. Justification before men by our works.

Conclusion: Those who are possessors of Christ's salvation, which the poorest Christian may partake of equally with the rich, and to which all earthly glory is but vanity, should not make men's outward advantages the measure of their respect, but should love all, rich or poor, as themselves.

The certain evidence of faith is good works. While it is faith that justifies, the faith that justifies can never be alone.

Key Word: Brotherly love, v. 8. Works, v. 14.

Strong Verses: 5, 8, 10, 14, 20.

Striking Facts: There is perfect harmony between James and Paul on justification. Paul is considering man in relation to God, in which he is "justified by faith apart from works." James is considering man in relation to his fellowman, in which case works are the visible evidence of faith. We have a right to believe that a profession of faith which bears no fruit, is an empty profession.

CHAPTER THREE

Contents: Control of the tongue.

Conclusion: The Christian who is not affected by the sins of the tongue but takes care to avoid them, has an undoubted sign of true grace. The wisdom and grace of God which enables one to control the tongue, will enable him also to control all other actions.

Key Word: Tongue, v. 5.

Strong Verses: 5, 6, 10, 17.

CHAPTER FOUR

Contents: Rebuke of worldliness and exhortation to humility before God.

Conclusion: Worldly and fleshly lusts are the distemper which will not allow contentment or satisfaction in the mind, and rise up to the exclusion of prayer and the working of our affections toward God. Let the Christian be free from the friendship of the world, and be submitted to God, thus shutting and bolting the door against the devil.

Key Word: Lusts, v. 1.

Strong Verses: 2, 3, 4, 7, 8, 13, 14, 15, 17. Promise: 10.

CHAPTER FIVE

Contents: Warning to the rich. Exhortations in view of Christ's second coming.

Conclusion: Great amassing of wealth will be a sign of the last days, but woe
to those who then heap together treasure for themselves, for when Christ
comes that in which they have placed their hopes will bring them eternal
misery.   Regardless of the prosperity of the wicked, or the affliction of
the righteous, the blessed hope of Christ's return will keep the believer
steady and patient.   Let this therefore incite him to all the duties of the
Gospel, and especially to patience and prayer.

Key Word: Last days, v. 3.

Strong Verses: 7, 8, 10, 16.   Promise: 20.

Christ Seen: vv. 7, 8.   Here we see Christ's waiting for the precious fruit
of the earth, the gathering in of the elect.   In 2 Thess. 3:5 we have the
saint's waiting for Him.   The hope of His coming is the only solution of
the complicated problems that will arise in the last days between capital
and labor.   (vv. 1-6.)

I PETER

| Key Thought:
Christian's hope | Number of Chapters:
5 | Key Verse:
2:7 | Christ seen as:
Suffering Lamb |

| Writer of the Book:

Peter | Date:

A. D. 60 | Conclusion of the Book:
Those who are walking
with Christ will be en-
abled to suffer patiently,
joyously and to the glory
of God. |

SUMMARY

CHAPTER ONE

Contents: Christian's conduct under suffering in the light of full salvation.
Conclusion: The true Christian's hope of eternal life and a glorious inherit-
ance through the precious sacrifice and resurrection of Christ, is a hope
that quickens him to service, supports him in every trial of faith and con-
ducts him in a way of holiness to heaven.
Key Word: Living hope, vv. 3, 5, 7, 13, 25.
Strong Verses: 3, 7, 8, 13, 15, 18, 19, 23, 24, 25. Promises: 4, 5.
Christ Seen: vv. 18, 19. The blood of Christ is precious because it redeems
(v. 19). Brings us nigh to God (Eph. 2:13). Blots out our sins (Rev. 1:5).
Brings peace (Col. 1:20). Justifies (Rom. 5:9). Cleanses (1 John 1:7).

CHAPTER TWO

Contents: Exhortation to holiness and growth in view of Christ's great sacrifice. Christ's vicarious sufferings.
Conclusion: The Word of God is the proper and necessary food for the soul,
which, if rightly used, does not leave a man as it finds him, but improves
him, causing him to realize his spiritual position in the world, the duty
of patient and Christlike submission, and the necessity of purging out
those things from the life which are contrary to Christ.
Key Word: Growth, vv. 2, 21.
Strong Verses: 2, 5, 9, 11, 15, 19, 20, 21, 24.
Christ Seen: v. 8. Christ crucified is the Rock. To the church He is the
foundation and chief corner stone (Eph. 2:20). To the Jews, at His
first advent, a stumbling stone (Rom. 9:32, 33; 1 Cor. 1:23). To Israel
at His second advent He will be made headstone of the corner (Zech. 6:7).
To the Gentile world powers at His second coming, He will become the
smiting stone (Dan. 2:34).

CHAPTER THREE

Contents: Duties of husbands and wives toward one another. Exhortations
to Christian consistency. Christ's vicarious sacrifice.
Conclusion: Worldly men are strict observers of the manner of life of the
professors of religion. A chaste conversation with Christian respect in
the home life and careful Christian conduct toward all, following the
Lord Jesus especially in His example of suffering for righteousness sake,
is an excellent means to win men to the faith of the Gospel.
Key Word: Good conversation, v. 16.
Strong Verses: 1, 7, 10, 12, 13, 15, 16, 17, 18.
Christ Seen: vv. 18-20. The word "preached" is lit. "Heralded." Christ's
spirit at His death heralded the triumph of the cross in the spirit world.
There is no indication of any chance for repentance either of angel or man.
The saved spirits who awaited Him in Paradise, upon the announcement
of the finished work of the cross went with Him above, whence He then
removed Paradise, and they will appear with Him at His second advent to
receive their glorified bodies.

CHAPTER FOUR

Contents: Exhortations to mortification of sin and living unto God. Suffering with Christ.

Conclusion: Christ having suffered so much for us, should cause us to fortify ourselves with His mind, courage and resolution, living no longer to the flesh but being conformed to the holy will of God, as those who must give account any day at His appearing. We should rejoice to suffer with Christ for righteousness' sake, knowing that if we are in His hands our suffering will promote the Gospel and prepare us for glory.

Key Word: Godly living, vv. 2, 7, 19.

Strong Verses: 7, 10, 14, 16, 18, 19. Promises: 12, 13.

Christ Seen: v. 1. Some of the strongest arguments against sin are taken from the suffering of Christ. He died to destroy sin, and having submitted to such sufferings on account of sin, why should we grieve Him by continuing in sin? All sympathy with Christ is lost if we do not put away sin.

CHAPTER FIVE

Contents: Christian service in view of Christ's soon coming.

Conclusion: Humility is a great preserver of peace and order in the church, giving to Christ's ministers a proper attitude toward the flock and to His people a proper submission to their leaders in the Lord. There is mutual opposition between God and the proud, but he who is humble before God will find grace for every trial and power to meet every assault of the devil.

Key Word: Humility, v. 5, vigilance, v. 8.

Strong Verses: 6, 7, 8, 10. Promise: 4.

Christ Seen: v. 6. The best definition of humility is found in John 13:4, 5. Our Lord Jesus was the perfect embodiment of humility.

II PETER

Key Thought:	Number of Chapters:	Key Verse:	Christ seen as:
Last days	3	1 Pet. 2:7	Lord of Glory

Writer of the Book:	Date:	Conclusion of the Book:
Peter	A. D. 66	The believer must be pure and loyal in the days of corruption and apostasy, and hastening the coming of Christ by every means.

SUMMARY

CHAPTER ONE

Contents: The great Christian virtues. God's Word exalted.

Conclusion: The Christian should be diligent to add one Christian grace to another that he may bring glory to God by abounding in much fruit among men and that his own calling and election may be thereby thoroughly tested out. He should the more seek to obey God's Word because it is God-inspired, of undoubted truth, and therefore of vast concern.

Key Word: Fruitful life, v. 8.

Strong Verses: 4, 5, 6, 7, 10, 19, 21.

Christ Seen: v. 16. The plan of salvation by Jesus Christ is eminently the council of the infinitely wise Jehovah, for certainly man could not have invented it. He is the Messiah promised by the prophecies and publicly owned by the Father from the opened heavens.

CHAPTER TWO

Contents: Warnings concerning apostate teachers.

Conclusion: Where God sends His true messengers with His Word, the devil always sends some to seduce and deceive, and especially to deny Christ's redemptive work. Such men bring swift destruction upon themselves, even though they prosper for a while.

Key Word: False teachers, v. 1.

Strong Verses: 1, 9.

Christ Seen: v. 1. Smooth-tongued false teachers seldom deny Jesus Christ "Who TAUGHT" but they do deny Jesus "Who BOUGHT." The devil hates the doctrine of the CROSS of Christ, and hence all the conflicting theories as to His death.

CHAPTER THREE

Contents: Return of the Lord and the Day of Jehovah. Christ's return to be generally denied.

Conclusion: The general denial that will be made in the last days of the possibility of Christ's return, should not unsettle the believer, but quicken and excite him to a serious minded and firm adhering to what God has revealed in His Word. Those who now scoff will find the day of Christ's coming a day of terrible vengeance.

Key Word: Day of the Lord, v. 10.

Strong Verses: 3, 4, 8, 9, 10, 13, 14, 15, 18.

Christ Seen: v. 3. Men may talk about the stability of natural laws and the foolishness of the doctrine of Christ's second coming, but the Christian faith signifies little without it. It is the finishing stroke which must complete all the great doctrines of the Gospel and is therefore a day for which the Christian is to look (v. 12) and strive to hasten, by the bringing in of souls for the completion of the church.

I JOHN

Key Thought:	Number of Chapters:	Key Verse:	Christ seen as:
Assurance	5	5:13	Coming Son of God

Writer of the Book:	Date:	Conclusion of the Book:
		Salvation through o u r Lord Jesus Christ brings
Apostle John	A. D. 90	a life of fellowship with God, joyfulness, victory, safety and certainty.

SUMMARY

CHAPTER ONE

Contents: Fellowship with God made poss'ble through the incarnation. Conditions of perpetual fellowship—walking in the light and confessing sins.

Conclusion: Fellowship with the Father, which has been made possible through the incarnation of Christ, the eternal Word, can be maintained only by walking in the light, which signifies the recognizing of our sins with frank confession of them and forsaking of them as they are revealed to us, and belief in Christ crucified as the remedy for sin.

Key Word: Fellowship, v. 6.

Strong Verses: 6, 8, 10. Promises: 7, 9.

Christ Seen: v. 9. Our sins were judicially dealt with at the cross (1 Pet. 2:24) which results in eternal life, but unconfessed and unforsaken sin in the believer brings the loss of fellowship with God and chastisement. (1 Cor. 11:31-33) Confession of sin would not bring fellowship with God, unless the sinner had accepted the finished work of Christ on the cross.

CHAPTER TWO

Contents: Christ's advocacy for the believer. Tests of fellowship, obedience and love. Warning against worldliness and apostates.

Conclusion: To know God and the power of His love is impossible without practical observance of His Word, which means that we must seek to walk as Christ walked, in love toward our fellowmen and in separation from the things of the world. To profess to know God and yet deny Jesus as the Christ is to brand oneself as given up to the delusions of the devil.

Key Word: Knowing Him, v. 3.

Strong Verses: 1, 2, 6, 15, 22, 23. Promise: 17.

Christ Seen: v. 1. Even the most advanced believers have their sins, but there is a distinction between them and the sinners of the world, for the former have an Advocate in heaven. As they have had Christ's blood applied to them upon their acceptance of Him, so they have an Advocate to procure their continued forgiveness as they confess their sins.

CHAPTER THREE

Contents: God's love magnified and the believer exhorted to holiness. Brotherly love urged. How our hearts may be assured before God.

Conclusion: It is a wonderful and condescending love of the Father that we, who by nature are heirs of sin, guilt and the curse, should be called the sons of God and given such hopes in Christ. It is a contradiction to such love and hope to live in sin and impurity. Purity, love and a clear conscience toward God are marks of our transition into this state of life.

Key Word: Purity, v. 3. Love, v. 14.

Strong Verses: 1, 3, 5, 6, 14, 16, 17, 18, 23, 24. Promises: 2, 22.

Christ Seen: vv. 2-3. The time of the revelation of the sons of God in their proper state and in bodies like unto His glorious body, awaits the second coming of Christ. This is the purifying hope of the church which engages all believers to the prosecution of holy living that they might be in readiness to meet Him unashamed at His coming.

CHAPTER FOUR

Contents: Christians warned of false doctrines concerning Christ's person and work. Tests of the true.

Conclusion: God's people must be ever cautious concerning false teachers that may arise to deny the incarnation, deity and atonement of the Lord Jesus, and must accept none of their claims without testing them by God's Truth in the light of the Holy Spirit's teaching. The spirit of truth is known not only by doctrine but by love which is the natural fruit of the Spirit. The manifestation of divine love through the life argues a true and just apprehension of the divine nature, and such love can never deny the Lord Jesus.

Key Word: Truth and error, v. 6. Love, v. 7.

Strong Verses: 1, 4, 7, 8, 9, 10, 11, 15, 19, 20.

Christ Seen: Seven tests of true doctrine are given here. Does it confess Christ's true humanity? vv. 9, 15. His vicarious atonement? vv. 10, 14. Does it tend to worldliness? vv. 4, 5. Do spiritually minded people agree with it? v. 6. Does it witness to the spirit of divine love? vv. 7, 8. Does it accord with the teaching of the Holy Spirit? v. 13.

CHAPTER FIVE

Contents: Faith the overcoming principle. The advantages of faith in salvation, prayer, preservation from sin.

Conclusion: He who has been born again through Jesus Christ will manifest the effect of regeneration, which is a spiritual conquest of the world. Faith is the means, the instrument and spiritual armor and artillery by which the believer may overcome the world, Satan and sin, and ask and receive of God all that is needful in this life.

Key Word: Overcoming faith, v. 4.

Strong Verses: 1, 4, 5, 10, 11, 12, 13. Promises: 14, 15.

Christ Seen: v. 6. Jesus in His death had a double purpose, not only to save us from hell but to cleanse us. We are defiled inwardly by the pollution of sin. Through Him we have "the washing of regeneration." We are defiled outwardly by the guilt of sin, and by His blood we are separated from sin's condemnation. (Heb. 9:22. See Jn. 19:34-35.)

II JOHN

Key Thought:	Number of Chapters:	Key Verse:	Christ seen as:
See below	1	See below	Son of God and Son of man

Writer of the Book:	Date:	Conclusion of the Book:
John	A. D. 90	See below.

SUMMARY

CHAPTER ONE

Contents: Truth and love inseparable in the Christian life. Doctrine the test of reality.

Conclusion: The test of our love to God is universal obedience to Him, and we have need to maintain this love, for there are many destroyers of it in the world—those who subvert the faith, denying the person or the work of Jesus Christ. Let such men not be entertained as ministers of Christ, nor given support in any way.

Key Word: Truth and love, v. 3.

Strong Verses: 6, 9, 10.

Christ Seen: v. 9. The most important doctrine in the Word is the doctrine concerning the person and work of Jesus Christ. If one is unsound in this, they are bound to be wrong everywhere. All turns on "what think ye of Christ?" He that denieth the Son hath not the Father.

III JOHN

Key Thought: See below	Number of Chapters: 1	Key Verse: See below	Christ seen as: True Helper to the Truth, v. 8

Writer of the Book: John	Date: A. D. 90	Conclusion of the Book: See below.

SUMMARY

CHAPTER ONE

Contents: Exhortation concerning ministering brethren. The domineering Diotrephes and the good Demetrius.

Conclusion: Ministers of Christ should abound in, and joy in hospitality toward fellow helpers in the Lord, and should beware of the peril of a domineering leadership which stands in the way of blessing to the people of God.

Key Word: Fellow helpers, v. 8.

Strong Verses: 4, 11.

Christ Seen: v. 4. (Lit. "THE truth"). To walk "in the truth" in the New Testament sense is to walk in fellowship with Jesus Christ, knowing Him as Redeemer and Lord. See Jno. 14:6.

JUDE

Key Thought:	Number of Chapters:	Key Verse:	Christ seen as:
Kept and contending	1	See below	Coming Judge

Writer of the Book:	Date:	Conclusion of the Book:
Jude	A. D. 66	See below.

SUMMARY

CHAPTER ONE

Contents: The apostasy and apostate teachers described. Assurance and comfort for true believers.

Conclusion: Believers must be on their guard lest they be robbed of any essential article of Christian faith by the cunning craftiness or plausible pretenses of ungodly men who pose as teachers and lie in wait to deceive. Our duty in the presence of the apostasy is to earnestly contend for the faith, trusting to be kept from stumbling by walking in the perpetual consciousness of God's love through Christ, looking toward the day when we shall be presented before Him with exceeding joy.

Key Word: Apostasy, vv. 4, 18.

Strong Verses: 3(b), 21, 24, 25.

Christ Seen: v. 21. We can be kept in the perpetual consciousness of God's love only as we depend upon the mercy of the Lord Jesus—that is—His mercy, not our merit, being our constant plea. He has merited for us what we could never, otherwise, lay claim to. The only way to stand before Him flawless is to rest in His merits and walk in His love.

REVELATION

Key Thought:	Number of Chapters:	Key Verse:	Christ seen as:
Overcome	22	1:1	Sitter upon the throne.

Writer of the Book:	Date:	Conclusion of the Book:
		The Lord Jesus Christ is the gloriously exalted One, the A l p h a and
Apostle John	A. D. 9 6	Omega. He is the High Priest of His people; the B r i d e g r o o m of the Church; the King-Judge of all mankind.

SUMMARY

CHAPTER ONE

Contents: The Patmos vision of John and the command to write.

Conclusion: Jesus Christ, the Alpha and the Omega, speaks to believers through the Apostle John concerning things past, the things which are and the things which shall be hereafter. Blessed are they who make this Book their meditation and regard those things which are written therein, for they shall shortly come to pass.

Key Word: Revelation, v. 1.

Strong Verses: 5, 6, 7, 18. Promise: 3.

Christ Seen: This book is the only book having the Lord Jesus Himself as Author (v. 1). It is a "revelation," which means "an unveiling" or "disclosure," not a mystery, and the Lord Jesus has attached His benediction to it to encourage us to read, hear and keep (v. 3). Notice in v. 5 that He Who speaks from heaven is He Who "washed us from our sins in His own blood." Heaven's anthem magnifies the blood of Christ above everything else.

CHAPTER TWO

Contents: Message to Ephesus concerning things "which are." Their first love left. Message to Pergamos concerning false doctrines. Message to Smyrna concerning persecutions. Message to Thyatira concerning Balaamism and Nicolaitanism.

Conclusion: He that hath an ear, let him hear what the Holy Spirit would say to the Church, and let him beware lest by turning a deaf ear to the voice of the Spirit he lose his faculty of spiritual hearing and thus grow cold toward Christ, be without victory in tribulations or find himself an apostate carried away by every wind of doctrine. Those are bound to be overcomers under every test whose faith keeps them in vital touch with Jesus Christ, the Head of the Church (1 Jno. 4:4).

Key Word: Messages to Churches (Overcoming), vv. 7, 11, 17, 26.

Strong Verse: 4. Promises: 7, 10, 11.

Christ Seen: The letters to the Churches are Epistles of Christ dictated before the throne (v. 1) and with holy awe we should therefore read, then obey them. While these letters deal with Churches existing in John's time, it is believed that they are also symbolical of seven stages of the Church during the present Church age, because Jesus speaks of the "mystery" connected with them; because of the number "seven" connected with them, and always symbolical in this book; because the promises and warnings are continuous and because the prophetic view corresponds exactly with events thus far in the history of the Church.

CHAPTER THREE

Contents: Message to Sardis concerning their hypocrisy. Message to Philadelphia on hollow profession. Message to Laodicea on apostasy. Christ's attitude to the Church in its final stage in the world.

Conclusion: Let the believer keep his spiritual ears open continually, for the voice of the Holy Spirit, lest he be found merely professing the name of Christian, and not having the power thereof, or lest he grow lukewarm toward Christ, and so be taken unawares, or even found to be a counterfeit at the sudden appearing of Christ in glory.

Key Word: Message to Church (overcoming), vv. 5, 12, 21.

Strong Verses: 3, 11, 18. Promises: 5, 10, 12, 20, 21.

Christ Seen: v. 20. Supper is the evening meal, the last taken before the morning breaks and the day dawns. This verse is a picture of Christ seeking entrance to the Church of the final state, and calling for individuals out of it who will sup with Him. "The night is far spent; the day is at hand." To sup with Him before the morning breaks is the foretaste of coming glory.

CHAPTER FOUR

Contents: Things which shall be. Vision of the throne in heaven, the enthroned elders, the four living creatures and their worship with the elders because of creation.

Conclusion: The day is approaching when there shall be a shifting of scenes in heaven and God shall prepare to execute all His purposes toward the earth. Thundering black clouds shall gather for His last judgment upon the earth, but even in the darkness of that day a bow in the cloud will be seen reflecting the glory of God in the storm and reminding that God has not forgotten His covenants. In that day the saints in heaven will contrast the perfect rest of heaven with the troubled waters of earth and will give great glory to Him.

Key Word: Things coming to pass, v. 1.

Strong Verse: 11.

Christ Seen: Christ is not seen here upon the throne, but as having risen for the execution of other purposes which effect the establishment of His Messianic Kingdom. Heaven is preparing to execute judgment prior to Christ's coming with His saints to reign. The elders are seen identified with Him in the judgment about to be executed. May they not be the united royal priesthood, redeemed and glorified? The answer as to how they got there is not given here, but will be found answered as we proceed.

CHAPTER FIVE

Contents: Vision of the seven sealed books. Christ seen in His Kingly character. Angels, elders and living creatures exalt the Lamb Who is King.

Conclusion: It will be none other than the Lord Jesus Christ, Who as the Lamb of God was slain and rejected of men, Who will yet be manifested as the Lion of the tribe of Judah breaking the seals of God's wrath against sinners upon the earth. He Who alone was worthy to redeem mankind with His precious blood, is worthy to take man's judgment in hand. Happy are they who shall in that day be with the ransomed ones in heaven joining in the new song, associating with Him in judgment and preparing to reign with Him.

Key Word: Sealed book, v. 1.

Strong Verses: 9, 10, 12.

Christ Seen: The Lion and the Lamb are One (v. 5). The sacrifice of the Lamb made Him the Saviour of the redeemed, but He is yet to assume power as the Lion, for the execution of judgment when His purpose in the Church is perfected. Notice in v. 9 that it is the blood that the saints are still singing about.

CHAPTER SIX

Contents: The opening of the seals.

Conclusion: Woe to those who dwell upon the earth in the days of the great Tribulation, when the wrath of God is poured forth for the final cleansing of the earth. "Except those days should be shortened no flesh should endure." There will be terrible wars, famines, pestilence, earthquakes, disturbances in the heavens, and fear among men. (See Mt. 24:1-31.)

Key Word: Day of wrath, v. 17.

Strong Verses: 15-17.

Christ Seen: vv. 16-17. This will be the last great prayer meeting of earth, when men that have rejected Christ shall discover that the Lamb Whom they have slaughtered and insulted is the Judge of all.

CHAPTER SEVEN

Contents: A parenthetical chapter on the saved of the tribulation period. The remnant of Israel sealed.

Conclusion: In the great time of unexampled trouble which is to fall upon the earth after the translation of the saints, there shall be a vast company of repentant Israelites sealed for preservation, and a multitude of the Gentiles, moved to repentance toward Christ, shall find salvation through His shed blood, but at the cost of martyrdom (v. 14. See 6:9-11).

Key Word: Remnant sealed, vv. 3, 13, 14.

Strong Verses: 9, 10, 14, 17.

Christ Seen: vv. 10, 14. The cry of these who come up out of the Great Tribulation is not the same as the cry of redemption (5:9). It is the cry of salvation from judgment. While it is the blood of Christ which has purchased them this release, yet they are not members of the Body of Christ, the Church which is to be completed by the Holy Spirit before the Tribulation begins. They are a separate company.

CHAPTER EIGHT

Contents: Opening of the seventh seal from which seven trumpets come. Four of the trumpet judgments announced.

Conclusion: Woe to those who, by their rejection of the Lord Jesus, will find themselves left upon the earth to taste the sufferings of the Great Tribulation. Satanic forces will be allowed abroad without restraint, bringing fear upon all men by reason of conditions in the earth and in the heavens above.

Key Word: Trumpet judgments, v. 6.

Strong Verse: 4.

CHAPTER NINE

Contents: Judgments of the fifth and sixth trumpets.

Conclusion: So fearful and unbearable will conditions be in the Great Tribulation days when Satanic powers are unrestrained, that men shall long for death and even try to commit suicide, but will find the power of self-destruction taken away from them. Happy are they who shall escape all these things, that shall come to pass, through true faith in the Lord Jesus Christ.

Key Word: Trumpet woes, v. 12.

Strong Verse: 6.

CHAPTER TEN

Contents: Parenthetical explanation (to 11:14). The angel and the little book. The book eaten.

Conclusion: The day is approaching when all those mysterious judgment pictures of God's Word shall be made real in action (v. 7). Apocalyptic studies are understood by those who walk in close fellowship with God and while they have their charm, to the true man of God, they have also their bitterness when really appropriated, by reason of the startling and terrible prospective they reveal (v. 9).

Key Word: Little book, v. 2.

Strong Verse: 9.

CHAPTER ELEVEN

Contents: Times of the Gentiles to end in a period of forty-two months. Two heavenly witnesses will prophecy on the earth. The seventh trumpet judgment.

Conclusion: The Tribulation days which close the times of the Gentiles shall culminate in a period of intense troubles lasting 42 months (3½ years). When these days shall come, God will send two messengers to earth to give warning. They will be despitefully treated and killed as was our Lord and the prophets before Him. Woe to those who shall see these days, but happy those who through Jesus Christ are safe with Him and engaged eternally in His praises.

Key Word: Tribulation, witnesses, v. 3.

Strong Verses: 15, 18.

Christ Seen: vv. 3, 15. As the days of Christ's reign approach there will be increased announcement of the apocalyptic truths which will be scoffed at by the majority. (2 Pet. 3:3-4) The final announcement will be made in the midst of the great Tribulation by heaven-prepared witnesses, as His first advent was announced by John the Baptist. With this testimony rejected and the witnesses killed, men will be abandoned to the terrible days of the last half of the Tribulation, after which Christ will come to reign forever.

CHAPTER TWELVE

Contents: The woman clothed with the sun (Israel). Satan drawing the stars. The man-child (Christ) caught up to the throne. The arch-angel and his angels fighting Satan. Satan and Israel in the great Tribulation.

Conclusion: Israel out of which came the Messiah Who was rejected, will in the midst of the great Tribulation suffer terrible anguish because of Him, and will be subjected to terrors of Satan himself, who will then be unrestrained and knowing that he has but a short time. However, those whom God shall seal of Israel will be brought through those terrible days, though many will suffer martyrdom, but they will then die willingly for Him, acknowledging Him their King, their sacrifice and their Lord.

Key Word: Satan's wrath, v. 12.

Strong Verses: 9, 10, 11.

Christ Seen: vv. 9-10. In the midst of the great Tribulation, Satan will be cast out of the heavenlies and will be free in the earth. This will be a happy time for those who are in heaven by the blood of the Lamb, but a time of terrible trial for Israel and eternal woe for the Gentiles who submit to the mark of the beast. The only salvation in those days will be bold confession of faith in the blood of the Lamb, which will mean martyrdom to all except those sealed for physical preservation.

CHAPTER THIRTEEN

Contents: The beast out of the sea and the beast out of the earth.

Conclusion: In the midst of the Tribulation period there shall rise up two great world leaders, one a political leader inspired by Satan himself, the other a religious leader to deceive the people with strong delusions and either lead them or force them to worship the anti-christ as the long expected world-ruler. These two Satanic deceivers shall prevail upon all except those who risk all to boldly acknowledge their belief in the Lamb of God slain from the foundation of the world.

Key Word: Two beasts, vv. 1, 11.

Strong Verses: 18.

Christ Seen: v. 8. Salvation in the great Tribulation is still based on the blood of Jesus Christ. Those who are then saved, however, must boldly confess their faith before a world of hostile witnesses, which will mean nothing short of martyrdom, except to those few sealed in Israel. May God help every reader of these words to make sure their calling and election while the days of grace are still lasting!

CHAPTER FOURTEEN

Contents: Vision of the Lamb and the 144,000 sealed Israelites. The angel with the everlasting gospel. Fall of Babylon. The doom of the beast worshippers. Blessedness of the holy dead. Vision of Armageddon.

Conclusion: There shall be preserved during the great Tribulation period a great company out of Israel, who will follow the Lamb and give glory to Him at whatever cost. There will be also a multitude of Gentiles redeemed by their acceptance of the everlasting Gospel, but at the cost of martyrdom. Woe to those who worship the beast and receive his mark, for they shall be tormented in hell forever.

Key Word: Tribulation saints and sinners, vv. 1, 9.

Strong Verses: 1, 2, 3, 9, 10, 11, 13.

Christ Seen: vv. 14-15. He who bears the golden crown is none other than the Lord Jesus, Who will a short time after this be found wearing the crown of universal sovereignty (Rev. 19:12). At the close of the great Tribulation He will thrust in the sickle to cut down the earth's harvest of evil (this will be at Armageddon) which will then have come to its culmination (see Mk. 4:29).

CHAPTER FIFTEEN

Contents: Vision of the angels of the seven last plagues and the bowls of the wrath of God.

Conclusion: In the hours when the unexampled wrath of God is being poured out upon the earth there will be a faithful redeemed company, who in spite of all their sufferings for Christ's sake, will be enabled to join in the great chorus exalting Jehovah their Deliverer and the Lamb, their Saviour.

Key Word: Wrath of God, vv. 1, 7.

Strong Verses: 3, 4.

Christ Seen: v. 3. "King of saints" is literally "King of ages, or nations." Jesus is never represented as King of the saints, or the Church, but as their Lord. The relationship of the Church saints in the present age is a nearer relationship than that of subjects of a King. He is the Bridegroom. These Tribulation saints, however, will be related to Him as subjects and they exalt Him as "King of Nations."

CHAPTER SIXTEEN

Contents: Vials of God's wrath poured out.

Conclusion: There shall, in the great Tribulation period, be poured out such manifestations of the wrath of God against Satan and sinners as man has never conceived. The terrors of those days will surpass anything known in the earth before those days, and shall never be known thereafter. Woe to those who choose, by their rejection of Christ in the Gospel day, to be left to that time.

Key Word: Vials of wrath, v. 1.

Strong Verses: 5, 6, 15.

Christ Seen: v. 15. Even in the great Tribulation there is an advent hope held out to keep the remnant looking up. Before Christ's first advent believers in the promises were inspired and kept by the expectation of His coming. Until the rapture of the Church, His second coming is held out as the "blessed hope." In the great Tribulation, the one and only hope of relief will be His return in glory with the saints to cleanse the earth and to reign.

CHAPTER SEVENTEEN

Contents: The doom of Babylon, the last great ecclesiastical order.

Conclusion: There will be in the Tribulation period a great apostate ecclesiastical system headed up under a powerful religious leader, drawing after it thousands of deluded worshippers, who in reality are worshipping the devil and the beast. This enormous world-system will be brought to a fearful end and all those connected with it will share its fate.

Key Word: Mystery Babylon, v. 5.

Strong Verse: 14.

Christ Seen: Many Bible students believe that we have here the Roman Catholic system headed up in a fearfully apostate state. A woman is symbolical of "church" (2 Cor. 11:12). This woman (v. 5) stands in contrast to the Church of Christ, which is a "chaste virgin." The true Church is "espoused to one husband;" this one is given up to the kings of the earth. The Church is the "mystery of godliness;" this one is "mystery Babylon." The Church offers "the cup of Salvation;" this one offers "cup full of abominations." Mystery Babylon is rich, and it has its seat on seven hills (Rome). Christ is seen here as the One Who shall overcome all false systems, establishing Himself as Lord of Lords and King of Kings.

CHAPTER EIGHTEEN

Contents: Last form of apostate Christendom and the warning to God's people. The human and the angelic views of Babylon.

Conclusion: As there is to be an ecclesiastical Babylon ("confusion") heading up in the great Tribulation period, so there is also a great political Babylon, the pride of the great men of the earth, which shall likewise come to a terrible and an everlasting end, when Christ shall return in glory. This great system, back of which is anti-christ, will bitterly hate any who would glorify any god but materialism and the beast and will be guilty of the blood of many prophets and saints who have stood true to the everlasting Gospel.

Key Word: Babylon's fall, vv. 2, 21.

CHAPTER NINETEEN

Contents: Parenthetical chapter on what is taking place in heaven while the Tribulation rages. The alleluias, marriage of the Lamb, second coming in glory, Armageddon, doom of the beast, False Prophet, and kings.

Conclusion: During those days when the wrath of God is poured out upon the earth, the Bride of Christ will in heaven celebrate the long looked for marriage festivities, and arrayed in her cleansed garments shall be eternally united with Him Who is to be recognized in all the universe, and for all time, as King of King and Lord of Lords. When He comes forth to make an end of all evil, His Bride shall come with Him, associated in judgment, and later to rule with Him.

Key Word: Marriage supper, v. 9. Armageddon, v. 15.

Strong Verses: 5, 7, 8, 9.

Christ Seen: vv. 11-16. We have here a vision of the departure from heaven of Christ with His saints (previously caught up to be with Him—1 Thes. 4:13-18) and with His angels preparatory to the catastrophe in which all world powers shall be smitten (Dan. 2:34-35). On Christ's head here we see many crowns ("diadems") (cf. 14:14) for the hour is now at hand when He is to be exalted and enthroned in His Kingdom, to "sit upon the throne of His father David."

CHAPTER TWENTY

Contents: Satan bound for the Kingdom age. The first resurrection. Satan loosed at the end of the millenium, and his final doom. Judgment of the great White Throne.

Conclusion: When the Tribulation days shall have run their course, Christ shall come with His saints, and having cast down all opposing powers, will fling Satan into the bottomless pit for a thousand years, during which time He, with the saints, shall rule over the earth. At the end of the millenium Satan will be temporarily released, but he and his quickly gathered followers will be cast into the final hell forever. At that time also the unsaved dead of all the ages will be resurrected and after being judged according to their works will be given their portion in perdition.

Key Word: Judgment, vv. 2, 11.

Strong Verses: 4, 12. Promise: 6.

Christ Seen: vv. 4, 6. Christ is seen in this chapter as the Judge and then as the millenial King. Those who are associated with Him in this Kingdom are the Church and the Tribulation saints. Those who are now being called unto Christ are therefore appointed, not to be subjects of the Kingdom, but co-rulers, priests of God and of Christ, and will have their specific work in connection with the work of His universal empire.

CHAPTER TWENTY-ONE

Contents: The seven new things of the Kingdom age—earth, peoples, Jerusalem, temple, light, Paradise (Chap. 22).

Conclusion: It will be the perfect happiness of the saints, when Christ returns to reign, to have God's immediate presence with them, His love fully manifested to them and His glory fully put upon them. No remembrance of former sorrows shall remain and all causes for future sorrow shall be removed. Whatever is excellent and valuable in this world will be there enjoyed to a far greater degree, and Christ will be the everlasting fountain of knowledge and joy to His people.

Key Word: Heaven, v. 1.

Strong Verses: 2, 23, 24, 25. Promises: 4, 6, 7.

Christ Seen: vv. 9, 23. The peculiar glory of the Lord Jesus to all eternity is as the "Lamb" which will ever remind of His sacrificial act upon the cross. This title is applied to Him 27 times in Revelation. In the presence of "the Lamb," there will be no need of sun nor moon, any more than here we need to light candles at noon-day, for "the Lamb is the light thereof."

CHAPTER TWENTY-TWO

Contents: The New Paradise and its river of the water of life. The last exhortation of Christ—to be ready for His second coming.

Conclusion: The Paradise lost by the first Adam shall be restored by the Second Adam, and in this Paradise there shall be multitudes saved through the Lamb, to behold its beauties and to taste its pleasures forever.   Let all men labor to understand the prophecies of these things shortly coming to pass that they might be prepared to meet the Lord Jesus, having embraced His salvation, yea, and earnestly longing and praying for the hour of His appearance.   "Even so, come, Lord Jesus."

Key Word: Imminent return, vv. 7, 12, 20.

Strong Verses: 3, 7, 17, 18, 19, 20, 21.   Promises: 4, 5, 12, 14.

Christ Seen: The Bible closes with emphasis on the fidelity of the Scriptures (v. 6) on salvation by grace the free gift of the Lord Jesus (v. 17) and on the doctrine of the pre-millennial return of Christ (**vv. 7, 12, 20**). The great "peace prayer" of the Bible, and the last prayer of the Bible, is "Come, Lord Jesus," and Jesus' last recorded words are, "Surely, I come quickly.   Amen."   This is the thought He would leave with us.   May God open the eyes of every reader to the "blessed hope, the glorious appearing of the Great God and our Saviour, the Lord Jesus Christ."— Tit. 2:13.

GENESIS TO REVELATION

Genesis begins with creation. Revelation ends with the New Creation.

In Genesis we have the first Sabbath. Revelation closes with the holy rest in the new creation.

Genesis gives us the first Adam, head of the old humanity. Revelation leaves us with the second Adam, head of the new humanity.

Genesis gives us Eve, the wife of the first Adam, sinning, condemned and sorrowing. Revelation leaves us with the second Eve, the Bride of Christ, exalted, holy and glorious.

In Genesis we have exclusion from the tree of life. Revelation leaves us with access to it and authority over it.

In Genesis we have an earth cursed. In Revelation we have the earth fully delivered from the curse.

Genesis gives us Satan tempting and bruising. In Revelation we leave him bruised and in the lake of fire forever.

In Genesis we have the first sob and tear. In Revelation all tears and sighing are forever gone.

Index of Bible Events

Elijah, Fed at Cherith and Zarephath—1 Kgs. 17:1-16.
Elijah Raises Widow's Son—1 Kgs. 17:17-24.
Elijah, Translation of—2 Kgs. 2.
Elijah under Juniper Tree in Discouragement—1 Kgs. 19.
Elisha and Lost Axe—2 Kgs. 6.
Elisha and Noxious Pottage—2 Kgs. 4:38-41.
Elisha and Widow's Cruse of Oil and Raising Son of Shunammite—2 Kgs. 4.
Elisha, Call of—1 Kgs. 19:19-21.
Elisha, Call of—2 Kgs. 2.
Elisha Feeds One Hundred Men—2 Kgs. 4:42-44.
Elisha, Illness and Death of—2 Kgs. 13:14-25.
Elisha Leads the Blinded Syrians to Samaria—2 Kgs. 6:18-23.
Elisha's Promise of Water—2 Kgs. 3.
Ephesian Elders, Paul and—Acts 20.
Esau, Birth of—Gen. 25:24-26.
Esau, Sale of Birthright—Gen. 25:27-34.
Esther Made Queen, and Her Courage—Esther 2-5.
Eunuch, Philip and the—Acts 8.
Exaltation Chapter—Heb. 1.
Excuses—Lk. 14.
Ezra, His Expedition from Babylon—Ezra 7-8.

Faith Chapter—Heb. 11.
Faithless Shepherds—Ezek. 34.
Fall of Man and Woman Through Sin—Gen. 3.
False Prophets, Test of—Deut. 13.
False Teachers, Test of—Mt. 7:15-20.
Feasts of Jehovah—Lev. 23. Passover, Unleavened Bread, First Fruits, Wave Loaves, Trumpets, Day of Atonement, Tabernacles.
Felix, Paul before—Acts 23-24.
Festus, Paul before—Acts 25.
Figs, Sign of the—Jer. 24.
Fig Tree, Parable of—Mt. 24:32-36; Mk. 13; Lk. 21.
Five Thousand Fed—Mt. 14:15-21; Mk. 6; Lk. 9; John 6.
Flesh Pots of Egypt—Num. 11:12-13.
Flood—Gen. 6-8.
Food for Israel; Dietary Laws—Deut. 14.
Food, Prescribed for Israelites—Lev. 11.
Four Thousand Fed—Mt. 15:32-39; Mk. 8:1-9.
Foxes and Firebrands, Samson's—Judges 15.
Furnace, the Harmless—Dan. 3.

Gallio and Paul—Acts 18.
Gamaliel, Warning of—Acts 5:34-39.
Garment and Bottles, Parable of—Mt. 9:16, 17; Mk. 5:22-43; Lk. 8:41-56.
Gedaliah, Governor over Palestine—2 Kgs. 25:22-30.
Genealogy, of Adam—Gen. 5.
Genealogy of Jesus—Mt. 1; Lk. 1.
Genealogy, of Noah, Shem, Ham and Japheth—Gen. 10.
Genealogy, Shem—Gen. 11:10-32.
Gethsemane, Jesus in—Mt. 26:36-46; Mk. 14; Lk. 22.
Gideon, Call of—Judges 6. His Victory—Judges 7.
Gifts, Spiritual—1 Cor. 12.
Glory, Daniel's Vision of—Dan. 10.
Glory, Vision of—Ezek. 1.
God, as El Elyon (Most High God)—Gen. 14:17-24.
God, as El Shad-dai (Almighty God)—Gen. 17:1.
Goliath Defies Israel—1 Sam. 17.
Good Shepherd—Jn. 10.
Great Commission—Mt. 28:16-20; Mk. 16:15-18.
Great Eagle, Parable of—Ezek. 17.

Haman, Conspiracy of—Esther 3.
Handwriting on the Wall—Dan. 5.
Heaven—Rev. 21.
Herodians, Jesus' Answer to—Mt. 22:15-22; Mk. 12; Lk. 20.
Hezekiah, Reign over Judah—2 Kgs. 16:19, 20.

Hezekiah's Illness and Recovery—2 Kgs. 20.
Hezekiah's Prayer and the Answer—2 Kgs. 19.
Hid Treasure, Parable of—Mt. 13:44.
Hidden Stones, Sign of—Jer. 43.
Holy Spirit—Jn. 16.
Hoshea, Reign over Israel—2 Kgs. 17:1, 2.
Householder, Parable of—Mt. 21:33-46; Mk. 12; Lk. 20.

Idolatry, Penalty of—Deut. 17:2-7; 18:9-14.
Image of Nebuchadnezzar's Dream—Dan. 2.
Importunate Friend, Parable of—Lk. 11:5-10.
Impotent Man of Lystra—Acts 14.
Intemperance—Prov. 23.
Intercessory Prayer of Jesus—Jn. 17.
Isaac, a Bride for—Gen. 24.
Isaac, Birth of—Gen. 21.
Isaac, Death of—Gen. 35:27-29.
Isaac, Offering of—Gen. 22.
Isaac, Promise of—Gen. 17:15-19.
Isaiah's Transforming Vision—Is. 6.
Ishmael, Birth of—Gen. 16.
Israel, Assyrian Captivity of—2 Kgs. 17.
Israel Chapter—Rom. 11.
Israel Demands a King—1 Sam. 8.
Israel, Egyptian Bondage—Ex. 1, etc.
Israel, the Adulterous Wife—Hosea 2.
Israel, Wandering—Num. 15-20; Deut. 2-3.

Jacob and Esau Reconciled—Gen. 33.
Jacob and Esau, Stolen Blessing—Gen. 27.
Jacob at Haran—Gen. 29.
Jacob, Birth of—Gen. 25:24-26.
Jacob's Dying Blessing—Gen. 49.
Jacob's Vision—Gen. 28.
Jacob Wrestling with Angel—Gen. 32:24-32.
Jairus' Daughter Raised—Mt. 9; Mk. 5; Lk. 8.
James and John, Ambitions of—Mt. 20:20-28; Mk. 10:35-45.
Jehoahaz, Reign over Israel—2 Kgs. 13.
Jehoash, Accession over Israel—2 Kgs. 13.
Jehoiachin, Reign over Judah—2 Kgs. 24:6-9.
Jehoiakim, Reign over Judah—2 Kgs. 23:34-37.
Jehoram, Accession of over Israel—2 Kgs. 1:17, 18.
Jehoshaphat, Accession of over Judah—1 Kgs. 22:41-49.
Jehu, Anointed King of Israel—2 Kgs. 9.
Jephtha's Vow—Judges 11.
Jericho, Conquest of—Josh. 6.
Jeroboam, Disobedience and Death of—1 Kgs. 14.
Jeroboam II, Reign over Israel—2 Kgs. 14:23-27.
Jeroboam, The Rise of—1 Kgs. 11:26-40.
Jesus, Baptism of—Mt. 3:13-16; Lk. 3:21, 22; Jn. 1:31-34.
Jesus, Birth of—Mt. 1:18-25; Lk. 1:26-35; 2:1-7.
Jezebel, Slaying of—2 Kgs. 9:30-37.
Joab, Flight and Death of—1 Kgs. 2:28-34.
Joash, Accession of over Judah—2 Kgs. 11.
Job's Humility before God—Job 42.
Job's Opinion of Himself—Job 30.
John the Baptist, Ministry of—Mt. 3; Lk. 3; Jn. 1.
John the Baptist, Murder of—Mt. 14; Mk. 6; Lk. 9.
Jonah and the Great Fish—Jonah 1-4.
Jonathan and David, Their Love Covenant—1 Sam. 18.
Jonathan's Protection of David—1 Sam. 20.
Jonathan's Victory over Philistines—1 Sam. 14.
Joseph, Story of—Gen. 37, 39, 40, 41, 42, 43, 44, 45, 46, 47.
Joshua, Appointment of—Num. 27:15-23.
Joshua, His Call—Josh. 1.
Joshua, Last Counsels of—Josh. 23.
Josiah, Reign over Judah—2 Kgs. 21:23-26; ch. 22.
Jotham, Reign over Judah—2 Kgs. 15:32-38.
Judas Sells Christ—Mt. 26:14-16; Mk. 14; Lk. 22.
Judges, Selected to Solve Problems of Israelites—Ex. 18.

Index of Precious Promises of the Bible

(Note: In appropriating these promises, let it be noted that to practically all of them, there are conditions attached).

Blessing — Spiritual: Ex. 19:5-6; Mt. 5:6; Jn. 6:35, 5; 10:9; Prov. 19:23. Temporal: Ex. 23:25; Deut. 6:33; 7:9; Ps. 84:11; Prov. 19: 17; Eccl. 11:1; Phil. 4:19; Rev. 3: 20; Ps. 23:1; 34:10; 37:3, 4; Prov. 8:35; 11:25; Isa. 33:15-16; Jer. 7:23; Mal. 3:10-11; Ro. 8: 32; Ps. 36:8; 92:12-13; 1:3; Jn. 12:26.

Comfort: Isa. 51:12-13; Mt. 5:4. (See under Presence of God).

Deliverance—From Danger: Ps. 34: 7; Trouble: Ps. 41:1; 50:15; Pestilence: Ps. 91:3; Enemies: Ps. 94:23; Jer. 15:21; 39:17-18. (See under Refuge, Difficulties Overcome).

Difficulties Overcome: Ps. 37:5; Jer. 32:27; Mt. 17:20; 21:21-22; Mk. 11:23; Lk. 17:6; Mk. 9:23. (See under Strength, Refuge).

Eternal Bliss—For the Saved: Isa. 25:8; 29:18-19; Jn. 14:3; Ro. 2: 6-7; 8:18; 1 Jn. 2:17; 3:2; Rev. 21:4-7; 22:4-5. (See under Salvation).

Exaltation of the Humble: Mt. 5:5, 7; Lk. 14:11; Jas. 4:10.

Forgiveness of the Penitent: Isa. 43:25; 55:7; Hos. 14:14; Mt. 6: 14; Heb. 8:12; 10:17; Jas. 5:20; 1 Jn. 1:7-9. (See under Grace and Mercy).

Freedom—Spiritual: Jn. 8:32, 36.

Fruitfulness in Service: Psa. 1:3; Jn. 15:5; 2 Cor. 9:8. (See under Power, Strength).

Grace and Mercy: Ex. 34:6-7; For confession: Prov. 26:13; For rendering mercy: Mt. 5:7; Grace for needs: 2 Cor. 12:9; Grace and glory: Ps. 84:11. (See under Forgiveness).

Guidance: Ps. 25:14; 32:8; 48:14; Prov. 3:6; Isa. 58:11. (See under Illumination).

Holy Spirit: (See under Power).

Illumination — Spiritual: Ps. 36:9; Mt. 5:8; Jn. 7:17; 8:12; 14:26; Jn. 16:13-14. (See under Guidance).

Israel: Blessing on those who aid: Gen. 12:3; Shall bless earth: Gen. 22:18; God's presence with: Ex. 29:45-46; Reign over nations: Deut. 15:6; Not forgotten: 1 Sam. 12:22; Restoration to land: Isa. 27:6; Regathering: Isa. 56:7; Ezek. 34:12, 15; Hos. 3:5; National conversion: Jer. 31:33-34; Ezek. 11:19-20; 36:26-27; 37:5-6, 28; Hos. 2:18-20; Zeph. 3:9, 17; Zech. 12:10; 13:1; Ro. 11:26; Preservation of: Jer. 46:28; Hos. 1:10; Forgiveness for: Hos. 14:14.

Keeping—In the Way: Ex. 23:20; 1 Sam. 2:9; Ps. 91:11; Ps. 121:7-8; Mt. 4:6. (See under Preservation, Safety, Security).

Needs Supplied: (See under Blessing, temporal).

Peace of Heart: Ps. 29:11; 119: 165; Isa. 26:3, 12; 32:17-18; Jn. 14:27; Phil. 4:7. (See under Rest, Presence of God).

Poor—Rest For: Ps. 109:31; Isa. 41:17; Lk. 6:20.

Power in Service: Deut. 31:6, 8; Josh. 1:9; Jn. 14:12; Acts 1:8; Jn. 7:38; 4:14. (See under Fruitfulness, Strength).

Prayer—Answers to: Ps. 2:8; 34: 15; 37:4; 102:17; 145:18-19; Isa. 65:24; Jer. 29:12-13; 3:3; Mt. 6: 6; 7:7-8; 18:19-20; Mk. 11:24; Jn. 14:13-14; 15:7; 16:23; 1 Jn. 3:22; 5:14-15.

Presence of God: Ex. 33:14; Ps. 23: 4; 94:4; Isa. 43:2; Mt. 28:20; Jn. 14:21, 23. (See under Peace, Rest).

Preservation from Persecutors: Mk. 13:13; Isa. 50:7; From evil: Lk. 21:18; 2 Thes. 3:3; To the end: 2 Tim. 4:18; 1 Pet. 1:5. (See under Safety, Security).

Prosperity: (See under Blessing, temporal).

Protection for the Fearful: Gen. 15: 1; Ps. 27:5; 91:1, 4, 7; Against enemies: Isa. 54:17. (See under Refuge, Presence of God, Keeping, Preservation).

Refuge for Fearful: Deut. 33:27; Prov. 18:10; Ps. 27:3, 5; For oppressed: Ps. 9:9-10; 46:1; 55:22; 94:22; From enemies: Ps. 31:20. (See under Preservation, Safety, Difficulties Overcome).

Recognition of loved ones in Heaven: 1 Cor. 13:12.

Restoration — Of the earth under Christ: Isa. 4:2; 35:1; Of all things; Isa. 11:4, 5, 9; 35:4-6, 10; 40:5; 61:11; 65:17; Mic. 4:1-5; Of universal righteousness: Isa. 16::; Of universal peace: Hos. 2: 18; Hag. 2:7, 9; Zech. 2:10-11.

Rest, Heart: Ex. 33:14; Jer. 6: 16, Mt. 11:28-29. (See under Peace, Presence of God).

Reward for Service: 2 Chron. 15:7; Mt. 10:42; Mk. 9:41; 1 Cor. 3: 14; 2 Cor. 9:6; Gal. 6:8-9; Col. 3:23-24; 1 Pet. 1:4; Rev. 22:12; For soul winning: Ps. 126:5-6; For obedience: Prov. 13:13; For charity: Prov. 25:21-22; For righteousness: Prov. 3:10; For enduring persecution: Mt. 5:10-12; 19:29; Mk. 10:29-30; Lk. 18:29-30; 6:22-23; For suffering for Christ: Mk. 8:35; 2 Tim. 2:11-12; For loving His appearing: 2 Tim. 4:8; For enduring temptation: Jas. 1:12; For enduring trials: 1 Pet. 4:12-13.

Resurrection: Ps. 49:15; Hos. 13: 14; Jn. 5:28, 29; 6:39; 44; 11:25-26; 1 Cor. 15:22-23, 49, 51; 2 Cor. 5:1; Phil. 3:21.

Security in Salvation: Ex. 12:13; Ps. 37:23-24; Jn. 6:39; 10:28-29; Ro. 8:38-39; Phil. 1:6; Heb. 7:25; Rev. 3:5, 12. (See under Safety, Preservation, Keeping).

Safety — In disquieting circumstances: Prov. 1:33; 2:21; 12:21; 29:25. (See under Keeping, Presence of God).

Salvation through Faith: Isa. 1:18 Heb. 2:14; Mk. 16:16; Jn. 3:16, 18, 36; 5:24; 6:37; 20:31; Acts 2:21; 16:31; Ro. 6:23; 10:9-10, 12-13.

Soul Winning—Gift of: Mk. 1:17. ˋ

Second Coming of Christ: Acts 1: 11; Jn. 14:3; Heb. 10:37; Rev. 3:21; 20:6.

Strength—For witnessing: Ex. 3: 12, 14; 4:12; Daily: Deut. 33:25; For the faint: Ps. 27:14; 31:24; Isa. 57:15; For service: Isa. 26: 4; 40:31; 41:10, 13; To endure: Phil. 4:13. (See under Power, Difficulties Overcome).

Temptation—Way of escape: 1. Cor. 10:13.

Victory—In Conflict: Ex. 23:22; 14: 13-14; Lev. 26:8-9; Deut. 3:22; 20:4; 23:14; 33:27; Josh. 23:10.

Vindication: Ps. 57:3; Prov. 20:22; Isa. 33:22; 54:4.

Wisdom: Jas. 1:5.

Word of God: Shall endure: Isa. 40: 8; Shall accomplish its purpose: Isa. 55:11.